D1825766

Ashley
Williams

To

Phil

Best wishes

A. Williams

Ashley Williams

my **Premier League** diary

with David Brayley

*To my wife Vanessa
and my son Raphael*

First impression: 2012

© Copyright Ashley Williams, David Brayley and Y Lolfa Cyf., 2012

Swansea City photographs courtesy of Dimitris Legakis /
Athena Photography & www.swanseacity.net;
Wales photographs courtesy of propaganda-photo.com

The contents of this book are subject to copyright, and may
not be reproduced by any means, mechanical or electronic,
without the prior, written consent of the publishers.

The publishers wish to acknowledge the support of
Cyngor Llyfrau Cymru

Cover design: Y Lolfa
Cover photographs: Emyr Young

ISBN: 978 184771 517 3

FSC
Published and printed in Wales
on paper from well maintained forests by
Y Lolfa Cyf., Talybont, Ceredigion SY24 5HE
website www.ylolfa.com
e-mail ylolfa@ylolfa.com
tel 01970 832 304
fax 832 782

Contents

by Rio Ferdinand

It is with great pleasure that I write this foreword for Ashley Williams' excellent book, which gives a unique view into what it takes to be a successful footballer at the highest level. I've known Ashley for some time now, and really got to know him well when he was introduced to me by the head of my management team, Jamie Moralee of New Era Global Sports, who had just taken Ash on as a client. Prior to that, I'd been aware of Ash and his journey through the leagues with Stockport County, and then following his move to Swansea, when he finally made it to the Premier League.

Prior to Swansea's promotion, it would have been natural for any player to possibly wonder how they would cope playing in the Premier League, having never played there before. I have no idea if Ash had any of those concerns, but if he did, he never showed them. The fact that he performed so well in his debut season didn't surprise me in the slightest either. For any footballer to play professionally, they have to have ability, that goes without saying, but to succeed at the highest stage of the Premier League – especially as a centre half – you have to have something extra. When I started to get to know Ash, I could see that he possessed this something extra which is strength of character, determination and most importantly, the desire to succeed. All of those strengths were displayed regularly and consistently by Ash over the season. I remember before Swansea got promoted, I told our advisor Jamie, that Ash had everything required to go on and prosper at the very top of the game. Having watched him throughout 2011–12 season, I haven't seen one thing to change my mind on that.

Every season, I have a look at the fixture list and see when some of the key games are, such as the Manchester derby games and, of course, historical opponents like Liverpool. But for the 2011–12 season, the 6th of May 2012 was an extra game I pencilled in as a match I was looking forward to playing in. That was when Swansea City would visit Old Trafford. Even though I treat every game that I play in the same, I must admit that I was really looking forward to welcoming Ash to my home pitch, which would be a big occasion for us both. What I didn't realise though, was that towards the end of a tough game for us both, he'd try to crock me! As with everything with Ash though, it was an honest, committed challenge with no malice... but I think we both bore the bruises for a few weeks after!

What I like most about Ash is that he is his own man, and he's not afraid to stand up and speak his mind. This shines through in this diary, which is as honest and detailed an account of a footballer's season as you could ever read. He leaves the reader in no doubt exactly what it takes to be a successful player in the Premier League.

I wish Ash every success with this book, which is an excellent record of his and Swansea's first season in the top flight and also his time internationally with Wales. I'm now already looking forward to the 12th of May 2013, which is when Ash and Swansea next visit Old Trafford. Just try not to kick me next time mate!

All the best.

Rio Ferdinand
Manchester
November 2012

Introduction

As the final whistle blew at Wembley on the 30th of May 2011, I dropped to the ground in the happiest, proudest moment of my football career. For 21 years I had worked towards my dream of playing in the Premier League. I had imagined how I would celebrate if this moment ever came, but when it did, all I could do was drop to the ground in disbelief with tears in my eyes. I was finally going to be playing in the best league in the world!

When we came back for the start of pre-season I was focused from the first minute. The main reason for this was because I'd heard all the so-called 'experts' write my team off and, on top of that, I had to prove to myself that I was good enough to thrive in this league. From the first minute we, as a team, never looked or spoke about relegation, instead we just focused on how many points we could attain and how high we could finish in the league. The Gaffer constantly reminded us to enjoy the ride as we'd all worked hard enough in our careers to get here.

I had already started to keep a diary from pre-season when writer David Brayley, who I had worked with before, had the same idea and contacted me asking if I would like to work with him again on a book about my first season in the Premier League. We then decided to try and give the reader a unique detailed view of what it was like for me in my first season in the Premier League. Every game I played in is here, seen through my eyes, and based on what happened and how I saw events unfold in front of me. I mention on-field bust-ups, moments of triumph and disaster, training sessions, meetings that followed crisis games and events that happened to me. I wanted the reader to see what it is like to live this life and realise it's not all parties, WAGS, cars and champagne. Most of us are just normal guys who have worked hard to get where we are, and are privileged to be doing this amazing job for a living. We can get down or nervous or insecure just like the next guy, we aren't untouchable and we do mundane things most days like change an unimaginable amount of nappies, walk the dogs, go food shopping – just normal everyday things that we all do. Hopefully, by reading this book, you will realise this.

I have 38 caps for Wales and 2011/12 was also a landmark season: from turning around our fortunes and climbing the world rankings through to losing one of football's greatest men and my international manager, Gary Speed, in such tragic circumstances. All my thoughts on my bittersweet international journey of the past season are recorded here too.

I would like to thank my co-writer Dave for helping me put this book together and basically stalking me for 90 minutes in each game I played, home and away, making sure I didn't forget anything that happened. So if you were sitting next to a guy with a notepad doing more writing than watching... yes, that was Dave. Thanks for trying to see if you could block up my e-mail account mate – you gave it a good go! Thanks also to Lefi Gruffudd at Y Lolfa for sharing in our vision for the book and agreeing to publish it. I'd also like to thank Jonathan Wilsher of Swansea City FC for his support in providing photographs, Dave Rawcliffe of Propaganda Photos for the Wales ones, Emyr Young for the cover photo of the book, and Rio Ferdinand for his kind foreword.

Finally, I would like to thank my wife Vanessa for always supporting me and working hard on this book also. She is my best friend. We have come a long way since she watched me in a snowstorm at Accrington Stanley on the concrete steps. She never misses a game home or away and is constantly doing a lot of miles up and down the motorway to support me. I would also like to thank my mom and dad who have supported me from my first ever football game when I was six years old and are still watching my games now, 21 years later. Also, my son Raphael, who is the reason I get up every morning and go to do my best at training and is my inspiration when times get hard on the football pitch. It's to them I dedicate this book for always believing in me.

Thank you.

Ashley Williams
November 2012

CHAPTER ONE

July 2011

Sunday 10th July

First day back tomorrow.

I'm back in Swansea and I can't believe six weeks have passed since the Reading game at Wembley. It only seems like yesterday that we were on the Wembley pitch, celebrating the greatest achievement in all of our careers. At that moment out there you forget about everything else and just celebrate with the team mates that you've been to war with every day for the last ten months. My feelings then were that the team would go down in history and the members of that year's squad will never be forgotten. Because that's exactly what we did that day, made history.

By the time we made it back from the chaotic on-pitch celebrations and into the dressing room, there, in the centre of the floor, somebody at the Football League had laid out a large canvas banner with 'Play-Off Winners' on it with champagne bottles all around its edges.

I was one of the first ones back in there once we'd finally made our way off the pitch and as the lads filtered in, most of them made a beeline for the champagne. But before we could start popping the bottles, Sky told us we had to wait for them to give us the nod before the champagne explosion could begin. As soon as Sky told us to go, we fired the corks, sprayed champagne everywhere and just started jumping around and singing. It was one of the happiest moments of my life.

Days of success like the play-off final simply don't come around very often for a professional footballer, so when we went up to the players' lounge, still in our kit, to spend time celebrating with our families, it was really special. One person who was missing though, was my room-mate, Nath (Nathan Dyer).

When the presentation of the cup and medals and the on-pitch celebrations were done, Nath received the dreaded call from the drugs tester. No one realised that he was gone until we started celebrating, and then everyone was thinking, 'Thank God they didn't pick me!'

When you're chosen for the test at a normal game you're allowed out of the toilet as long as the drugs test man goes with you. So if you want a shower you can do that, but the man will come in with you and just stand in the corner watching you shower. And if you need to take a shit, he's just stood there in front of you, watching the whole time. At Wembley you are kept in complete isolation until the test is done.

When in the test room, the official gives you a plastic specimen bottle and you have to pee a certain amount into it for it to be a legal test. There's a little line on the tube that you must pass before it can be accepted as a valid test. But that's not as easy as it sounds. During training sessions and games, all players get really dehydrated, you just have to try and get as many fluids into you as possible and hope your bladder springs into life quickly.

There is one golden rule though. When you get the feeling that you finally want to go, you have to be *absolutely* certain that you're going to do enough to pass that little line on the bottle. If you have any doubts at all, you simply keep everything in and keep hanging on. You know that you only get one chance to get enough out of your bladder to make sure you satisfy the demands of the drugs guy and to make the test count.

It seems however, that Nath made the schoolboy error of emptying his little bladder at its first sign of life and, of course, he then didn't pass enough to reach the limit. Absolute nightmare! Imagine Nath, stuck in a toilet with a middle aged FA official, and we're embarking on the celebration party of our careers. I took a bottle of champagne down to the room which they let Nath consume, I'm always looking after him.

But talk about taking the piss!

If you ever look at any DVDs or pictures taken of the celebrations once we are back in the dressing room, you'll see that Nath doesn't appear in a single one. He was just whisked away as soon as we came in off the pitch and he missed every memorable second. It's completely understandable why we have to be drugs tested, but Nath will never have those moments back, and that's a real shame. I can't understand how some way can't be found to allow the tester and the tested into the room and even just sit in the corner, so at least the person concerned could experience some part of the rewards for all their hard work over a long ten-month season.

By the time we thought we should get into the showers, the celebrations were starting to wind down and we were just chatting between ourselves about the game and stuff. All of a sudden the door burst open and in came Nath, shouting and jumping around. We all just burst out laughing. He took it well though, and it's moments like that that make our group of players one of the tightest bunches I've ever been lucky enough to play with throughout my whole career.

Once Nathan and his now empty bladder had got showered and changed, we jumped on the coach, left Wembley, and it was back to Swansea where we had a party in Morgans with our wives and girlfriends. It was funny because there we were, newly promoted into the biggest and richest football league in the world, and what did we do on the way back to Swansea? Stop off in a petrol garage to fill up with alcohol for the bus trip home. Classy.

That play-off final remains one of the greatest days of my life. But I'd be lying if I didn't say that I honestly believe that in this first season in the Premier League, there could be even more memorable and potentially unforgettable occasions ahead.

My whole life to this point has been aimed at this moment – becoming a Premier League player. There have been so many times – the bulk of my career to be honest – when that dream has looked as if it would never come true, yet it appears it has, and I am so grateful for that. But in truth, as I sit here and write this diary of my first ever season in the top flight, I still realise that

I'm not quite there yet. First of all I've got to get through pre-season and all that that entails. It's not the training or hard work that worries me, as gone are the days when players returned to clubs overweight, after a summer of pigging out, to be tortured by long runs in the summer sun. No, the physical rigours of pre-season are something that I actually enjoy and embrace. The only thing that can stop me finally walking out on a Premier League pitch, and which is a little niggle in the back of my mind, is injury. All of us who play the game professionally know it can happen at any time, either the result of a bad tackle from someone, or a freak hamstring or something as stupid as just injuring yourself doing something mundane in your everyday life. Injury is the sportsman's curse, and one I'm praying to avoid. I've played every game for the past three seasons and am aware that at some point my luck's going to run out. Some people think it's not an issue when you're injured because you're still getting paid, but for a footballer the whole week revolves around Saturday.

Tomorrow is also the start of my fourth full season at Swansea, and for the first time, I'll return to work as a Premier League player!

Monday 11th July

It felt good walking in and seeing all my mates again, and even though the main target is that first game at Man City, when I can really say I've played in the Premier League, I have to say that the buzz about the place, the mickey taking, the new faces and the excitement all meant that I felt different today. I actually felt like a Premier League footballer. That may be a strange thing to admit, but it feels really good to say.

All of the lads have their own stories of how they got to this point. You've got the youngsters like Joe Allen who've come up right through the club and probably can't believe they are going to play in the Premier League at such a young age. Then you've got the likes of Tatey (Alan Tate), Britts (Leon Britton) and Monks (Garry Monk) who have come to Swansea from elsewhere but have been around the club for a lifetime, playing in every division.

Me? Well, I'm really proud of the fact that I've come through non-league and made it all the way through the divisions to be on the brink of playing in the best league in the world. It's been bloody hard at times, especially after getting released by West Brom as a 16-year-old and then spending time out of the professional game while attempting to make my way back in to the pro ranks at Hednesford Town. When I was at Hednesford, I was five whole leagues below the Premier League and any hope of playing there was extremely distant. Even when I finally got my break back into professional football with Stockport in League One, we were relegated to League Two in my second season. As bad as it was for the club, that second season was really positive for me in that I had managed to play every single minute of every game, but to experience relegation was another massive step backwards in my career. It was during that following season in League Two that I thought that the Premier League was never really going to happen for me.

I'm proud of my journey. It's got me where I am today, and now I can't imagine any of it happening differently.

The Gaffer called me in today and said he wants me to sign a new and improved contract with the club. It was fantastic to hear that from him so soon, especially as lots of the other boys have signed new deals recently. I told him straight away that I would love to, but it's not as simple as yes or no, so it's all now been handed over to my agent to sort out. I really hope it can be all sorted out reasonably quickly though so that I can just concentrate on playing football.

Wednesday 13th July

I've put my body through a lot playing football, especially from my battles in the lower leagues, so every season it is important that I do my own work to keep in top shape. Weights are important to keep my strength, as well as aerobic training on the bike and treadmill to maintain my fitness and burn fat. The older you get the harder you have to work to keep flexible. At other clubs I know they do yoga. Maybe I'll give it a go when I get as old as Garry Monk.

Thursday 14th July

It's amazing the detail the club is going to now that we are in the Premier League. Obviously, ever since I was at West Brom as a kid, I've always had lots of different medical tests, but today we went to a whole new level as I was told to get my teeth checked at Swansea's Eastside Dental Practice. Apparently, bad teeth can have all sorts of impact on your athletic performance and general health and can even affect nerves in your back and legs. I had no idea! After that was done, I was told to move on and get my eyes tested for the first time in my life. Needless to say, I don't need it explained why good eyesight is important for a footballer, and after the test the optician told me I have perfect 20/20 vision. Good teeth and good eyes. What more can anyone ask?

Friday 15th July

We are playing two different squads tomorrow as we have two games, so for the first time this season the squad lists were put up on the clipboard. I'm playing in the game against Neath.

Saturday 16th July

We got beaten by Neath 1–0 today in my first pre-season game, which on the face of it is not a great result. But bearing in mind that we'd only really trained properly on Thursday/Friday this week, the game was very much a practice match for us, which is how we treated it. I was captain for the first half and Neath very kindly gave us a guard of honour when we walked out in recognition of our promotion which was a nice touch.

I played alongside Caulks (Steven Caulker) our new loan signing from Spurs for the first time. During half-time the Gaffer changed everyone for the second half, to give the whole squad a run out. It's never nice to lose, but am not too worried about it to be honest. It's just another step on our road to pre-season fitness.

In the other game, Ferrie Bodde made his comeback. The Gaffer didn't run him for long, but I really hope he can get back to where he used to be. He's a fantastic player who deserves a bit of luck for a change because he's been to hell and back with his injuries and, when fit, is quite simply one of the best footballers I've seen. I hope this season sees him back out there for the first team. He's a genuine Premier League player.

Sunday 17th July

The Gaffer gave us a day off today, so I travelled back to Birmingham last night after the game because it was my godson's birthday party this afternoon. A nice day chilling with family and friends.

Wednesday 20th July

I travelled back from Birmingham late on Sunday night so that I was back in time for a tough session on Monday, and that was followed up yesterday with a lighter session starting at 10 a.m.

After training today, travel itineraries were given out for our pre-season tour to Austria. They give us all the info we need and inform us of daily training session times and any free time we have. A night out is included and it's always nice when we can get a night out, especially with the new lads joining us. It's great for team bonding.

Thursday 21st July

I was in early today, which I like to do most days so that I can do extra work in the gym. Today it was stretching and some physical work – press-ups and sit-ups.

Friday 22nd July

The Gaffer worked us on shape and formation for the game tomorrow, but because it's only a friendly he didn't go into as much detail as he usually would before a League or Cup game.

Saturday 23rd July

Played my second pre-season game today against Afan Lido. The Gaffer swapped it around again during the game, so I played the second half after we were already 2–0 up. Nothing much to report about the game. It was another good run out and probably just what we needed before going away to Austria. Whoever you play, it's always nice to get a win.

I played alongside Caulks again for the second half. Impressed again. I think the Gaffer's managed to find a good one there.

Sunday 24th July

We leave for Austria in the morning for our week-long pre-season camp. Early start. Bag already packed.

Monday 25th July

An early start this morning to what became the longest day in history. We met at the training ground at around 7 a.m. and as expected, most of the lads were still knackered so it was a quiet journey for a while. As usual, there's always somebody who doesn't set their alarm clock and misses the bus and this time it was Kemy Agustien. The Gaffer still had sleep in his eyes and was still in a bit of a mood due to the early morning, so we just got off. After a short while, one of the lads' phones started ringing and it was Kemy asking where we were. We helpfully told him that we were on the bus, so after a couple of expletives, he said that he'd follow us and catch us up. The next hour or so was amusing as we continued getting phone calls from Kemy, as we moved up the M4, asking exactly where the bus was so that he could track us down. It was funny because almost every time we passed a junction, he'd ring and say that he'd just passed one and where were we? We'd be laughing as he'd say he just passed Junction 30 and we were already at 27! This went on for a while until we approached Junction 23 and he said he was behind us, flashing his lights. He stayed behind the bus all the way into Heathrow and caught up with us in the baggage hall.

At Heathrow we boarded a Lufthansa flight to Munich,

Germany – even though we were staying in Austria. Strange. Must've been a cheaper flight for the chairman! That meant that we piled onto another coach for the final leg of our journey, a 200km, three-hour plus drive to a small village called Obertraun, a holiday destination in the winter but outdoor pursuit centre in the summer. We weren't the happiest of travellers a couple of hours into the bus trip – it was never-ending.

We finally arrived in the evening at about 8 p.m. after stopping at the petrol station to buy our dinner, which consisted of foreign chocolate and crisps. You never really know what you're buying! Obertraun is designed for sports and the complex we're staying at is not a hotel as such. The rooms are like dormitories, sleeping either two or three to each room. I'm with Nath and Luke (Moore), and Nath doesn't even have a bed. It's some sort of futon contraption and he had to go down to reception to collect the cushions for it. Seriously feels like we're back in school.

Today has been, without doubt, the longest travelling day I've ever experienced as a footballer. I can't for the life of me understand how we've ended up flying into a country different to the one we are staying in! Tatey has just said that he's always flown to a different country to where we are staying since he's been with the team. Just want to get my head down, try and get a good sleep for a fresh start tomorrow.

Tuesday 26th July

Looking ahead, we've been told that we have games against Inter Baku of Azerbaijan on Wednesday and the United Arab Emirates under-23 Olympic team on Sunday. I'm really looking forward to getting down to the training this week and seeing how the games go. It's going to be hard. It's where we will do the bulk of our fitness work, so it certainly isn't going to be a picnic in the Alps. But I've never been one who hates pre-season – unlike Gows (Mark Gower) and his nappies for example – so am ready to give it a blast.

Oh, nearly forgot. We all met our new keeper today, Gerhard Tremmel. He's a big German who's been playing for Salzburg and he made an instant impression on all of us, which turned to hilarious laughter before we'd even said hello to him! He must have wondered what the hell he'd let himself in for, the way we were all just cracking up and pointing at him, but he got the joke straight away when we pointed across to Monks – they looked like identical twins separated at birth! The likeness is uncanny. I don't think he'll ever forget his first meeting with his new team mates.

We aren't the only team out here using the facilities. There's also a Cypriot first division side called Enosis Neon Paralimni FC. They have a former Celtic and Scotland international playing for them called Mark Burchill, who Dobbs (Stephen Dobbie) knows, so he stopped to chat to him. The person who has organised all this for the club is Kenny Moyes, brother of Everton manager David, and the week before we were here, Everton were out here themselves. Just been told that the Cypriot team have all the rooms in the new part of the building because apparently someone in the office at the Liberty forgot to book the trip in time. It might seem really petty but when you're away from home details like this really annoy you.

We're now having two training sessions a day. Today was really high intensity, top-notch stuff. The Gaffer doesn't believe in miles of running, or rather if he does it's always with a ball. When I've been at previous clubs for pre-season training, running has been so much to the fore that it hasn't been uncommon to not even set eyes on a ball for the first couple of weeks. The Gaffer doesn't believe in that, and whatever he wants us to do in terms of running, he sets up drills with the ball to deliver it. There's lots of quick sharp stuff in small spaces, lots of contact with the other players and just getting you ready for what you'd expect in a match situation. This afternoon we went onto a larger pitch, but again kept up the intensity. It was really hard work today, but I really enjoyed it.

After lunch, I was knackered and just went and got my head down and tried to sleep till the afternoon session which began at about half four and lasted till about half six. After that was done, it was straight into the shower, got myself changed and went straight to dinner. There's nothing to do here in the evening, so Joe, Jazz (Richards) and Tayls (Neil Taylor) came to our room and we just hung out chatting until it was time to turn in.

That's going to be the pattern for this pre-season trip: train very hard in the morning, food, kip and then train hard again in the afternoon before doing nothing and then starting over the next day. Apart from the boredom I welcome it all, because I know all the pain and hard work we get through here is all going to pay off further on down the line when we get deep into the season. It's the only way you can look at it really.

Wednesday 27th July

Swansea City 3 (Sinclair 47, Dyer 54, Moore 73) **Inter Baku 1** (Shahriyar 70)

We were on the bus for about an hour before the game tonight which wasn't ideal because we didn't really want to travel at all, but it was good to get a run out all the same. I should have scored from Joe's corner about quarter of an hour in, but I headed just wide which was disappointing.

The Gaffer made his usual changes on the hour, but kept me on because we were are a bit short of centre halves. Tatey went off on the hour, being subbed by Tayls, but then Tatey came back on and subbed me with about fifteen minutes to go and then he played till the end. I hope we don't have problems like that when the season starts properly. It's crucial you have plenty of cover in the squad, especially at centre half. It only takes one stupid injury and then we can quickly be under pressure.

Thursday 28th July

Went cycling today for the first time in about ten years and really enjoyed it. Because of their injuries Monks and Ferrie have been doing quite a bit of cycling since they've been out here, so they'd made up a sort of course which was up the side of a river, over a bridge at the top and then back down and around. We did a couple of laps that took about thirty minutes and the physios came too. You can't just let us all go off alone without staff in case we get injured. I honestly can't remember when I last rode a bike, I'm sure I was still about sixteen. It was really weird jumping back on one after so long.

Some of the lads had some stick about their bikes though which was fun. They were those ones with the skinny tyres and baskets on the front like an old woman might use to go to the shops, so needless to say the rest of us took the mickey. The only thing missing was the beret and the string of onions.

Friday 29th July

It's my wife's birthday today and I'm missing it for the fourth year in a row. It doesn't matter what presents I get her, nothing makes up for me not actually being there to celebrate with her! I'll Skype her later so at least we get to see each other.

Saturday 30th July

Another first. I went up an Alp today. Despite it being pre-season, thankfully we weren't asked to run up it, but went up in a cable car instead. Mind you, once the cable car started to move, I would have given anything to get out and run up instead.

I've never been good with heights, and when we all got in and could see just how steep it was going to be, I knew I was going to struggle. The car was really big, so not only were the squad in it, there were some holidaymakers too. I wasn't the only one who was terrified, Jazz and Andrea Orlandi were petrified too. Jazz and I actually refused to do it at the start, but when everyone else decided to go and we were left in the reception on our own, we decided to grow a set and get involved.

It started off really steep which was bad enough, but then we came to the first pylon and we just clattered into it, and the car jerked about making a noise, and it was just about the worst feeling in the world. It was terrible. I was so scared I was absolutely screaming and swearing at the top of my voice. Honestly, I didn't care who heard me.

As we went higher up the mountain, we got to the next station for some people to get in and out, and then had to carry on from there right to the very top. As I looked up to the top, I could see that the mist and fog had started to come in which made it more frightening. There were lots of the lads keeping brave faces, but as we clattered into the next pylon, I just looked up at the Gaffer's face and he looked as terrified as me. Normally I would have laughed at that, but I was too scared to care.

When we got to the top, there was a café-type place up there so we all had some apple strudel and juice to calm ourselves down after that awful ride up and then we did some initiation ceremonies. Most clubs have some sort of initiation routine and we're no different. Ours is based on singing. So there we were at the top of this Alp, and Curt (Alan Curtis) and our new media guy, Chris Barney, had to do a song while everyone listened. They did really well and all the boys joined in – much better than a cable car ride.

It's one of my best friend's surprise 30th birthday party tonight which I'm disappointed to be missing.

Sunday 31st July

I'm supposed to be best man today at my friend's wedding. I've known him since I was 11 and am upset to be missing this. Gutted.

Swansea City 0 UAE Olympic Team 1 (Abdulrahman)

Last game of our trip today and, disappointingly, it wasn't the best. The day didn't start well because the Gaffer had to fly home this morning because his dad isn't too well, so that was obviously very hard for him. I know he's close to his dad and we all know he's been seriously ill for a while, so we are just hoping for the best for the Gaffer to be honest. I'm really close to my dad too, so I can understand how hard this must be for the Gaffer. He never shows us though, which is no surprise really and is a measure of the man. I hope he gets some hopeful news.

The game itself was one of those odd ones. It came at the end of a very hard week and it looked a little like we'd left our legs out on the training pitch. Occasionally, you get a game where you know from the very first touch of the ball that it's not going to go well. This was one of those. I can't explain it, it was just one of those days. I only played the first half, but that's when we conceded the goal after a bit of a mix up, so I'm not too happy about that.

The feeling at the end was that we were just glad to get the game out of the way. It was a nothing game really. They weren't the best and we should've done better. It would have been nice to have at least kept a clean sheet, I'm annoyed about that.

Still, we've got our work in this week, which is more important than the result and, in terms of fitness, what we came to Austria for, we've achieved. After the game, the Gaffer had left instructions that we were allowed our first night out since we began pre-season, so we all went straight back to the hotel in Salzburg after the match, arranged to meet down in the foyer after half an hour, had a drink there and went out. Kenny Moyes had given us the names of the best bars to call in and we had a good night. It was a Sunday so we weren't out too late, but it was good to get out and relax, especially as it was the first time we'd had a chance to socialize with the new lads like Caulks and Danny.

All in all, it's been a pretty successful pre-season trip and it's just over a week now until the serious stuff begins against Manchester City.

I can't wait.

CHAPTER TWO

August 2011

Monday 1st August

"The more you sweat in practice, the less you bleed in war."

Tuesday 2nd August

Wayne Routledge signed today for £2m from Newcastle on a three-year deal. It's a great signing by the club because Wayne's going to provide another genuine, experienced attacking option for us. The bonus is that he's a quality player with experience of the division and will be able to share that knowledge with the rest of us. I understand that there was nearly a last minute hiccup with the deal because apparently Wayne wasn't 100 per cent certain that the infrastructure at the club was as strong as some of the other Premier League clubs he's been at. Knowing the fantastic facilities that he's leaving at Newcastle for ours at the side of the M4, and changing rooms that we share with members of the public, that's completely understandable. It's not ideal having a training set-up like ours for obvious reasons. As much as I love the fans, it can be a bit off-putting when you're having a shower at the end of a tough session and when you rinse the soap out of your eyes, there's a middle-aged man standing next to you, naked, smiling and asking how you think you're gonna cope with Andy Carroll on Saturday. I'm not sure Jamie Carragher gets that at Melwood.

Wednesday 3rd August

Swansea City 2 (Rangel 64, Dobbie 85) Celtic 0

Even though today's game against Celtic was our fifth pre-season game, it was definitely the first one that felt like a genuine match. We are right up to speed with our fitness now after all we did in Austria, and today's game had that 'proper' feel to it that had been missing from all the other warm-up games so far.

Obviously, playing at home and with the challenge being offered by a club as big as Celtic resembling the type we'll be facing from here on in, it meant that we were all a bit more switched on today than we've been in our previous games. It was the first of the pre-season games where the Gaffer gave us our specific jobs to do in a game, just like he'll do when we face Man City a week Monday. There was a definite feeling against Celtic that we were much more into the swing of things and I thought it was a pretty good performance and a great result.

I also found out that Leroy Lita completed his deal and signed for us today from Middlesbrough on a three-year contract for a fee of £1.75m, having agreed personal terms a couple of days ago, and he played today. My thoughts on his signing are much the same as with Wayne's on Monday, namely, a really good acquisition by the club for a player with plenty of experience at the top level. I've marked Leroy many times over the years and have had plenty of battles with him and I can tell you from first-hand experience how tough a player he is to mark. He's strong, quick, great in the air and a proven finisher. I've always found him a bit of a handful in the past and it's nice to know that he's our handful now and somebody else's problem.

Thursday 4th August

Big day for me today – I signed a new contract with the club for three years, replacing the contract I was on, which had two years to run. The new deal potentially keeps me at Swansea until 2014 and I am absolutely delighted at that prospect, and chuffed to sign the contract that guarantees that I'll take part in the biggest season in the club's history.

In terms of the contract talks, I basically let the club and my agent get on with it really. When the Gaffer mentioned it first and said what was on offer, he told me to contact my agent to tell them what was on the table and then we both just let the process take over from there. When it comes down to the detail of negotiating the terms of the contract, me and the Gaffer just step away from it all and leave the club and my agent thrash it out until everybody agrees. It's far better that it's done like that as it takes all the emotion out of it. I know agents get a bit of a bad press these days, but they are a necessity for a player now, and with them handling all the details rather than the player, the outcome is a far better one for all concerned.

The way the contract dealings have been reported in the press you'd think that we've been talking in detail about it after every training session as some big issue, but it hasn't been like that at all. In fact, the Gaffer's only mentioned it a couple of times since he first told me he wanted me to sign last month, right up until everything was sorted today and I signed it. Really glad I can move on now.

Friday 5th August

Received some bad news today about a close friend. Pissed off about it all, ruined my whole day.

Saturday 6th August

Swansea City 1 (Graham 61) Real Betis 0

Before the game today there was a decent buzz around the ground and it felt like a proper game, building on Celtic last Saturday. During the warm-up we always wear bibs, which are usually yellow for defenders and either one midfielder or striker, and orange for the rest of the midfield and attackers. Pasc (Colin Pascoe) always gives the bibs out before the game and the tradition in the club is that whoever is captain on the day, gets given their bib in the dressing room first. Once we've done our stretches the players split according to their bib colour, and then take part in the keep ball sessions we do on the pitch before the match. After the stretches, the keep ball stuff and the sprints that follow at the end to finish, we're usually right where we need to be to start the game. It was a good warm-up today, and it's become a massively important part of our match day routine.

Sunday 7th August

Travelled to Cardiff and met up with the Wales squad today for the first time since I played in the disappointing defeat against England at the Millennium Stadium last March. The lads have played two games since then in the Nations Cup against Scotland and Northern Ireland, but I wasn't a part of them because they took place in the middle of the play-offs, so it was good to catch up with everyone again. I have a room to myself with Wales which is good, not everyone does.

It's funny to think that after the intensity of pre-season at Swansea, and with the whole town buzzing about the first ever season in the Premier League, I've been removed from all that now and instead have a few days to focus on a completely different objective, that of preparing for our next game in our Euro 2012 qualifiers against Montenegro in September. Australia may seem odd opponents to have as a warm-up, but it'll all be about bonding this week and working on the things that Speedo (Gary Speed) and Raymond (Verheijen) feel are holding us back from being successful consistently at international level. All that will start tomorrow, but today it was just nice to catch up with good mates again like Bellars (Craig Bellamy), Gabbs (Danny Gabbidon), Gunts (Chris Gunter) and Owain (Tudur-Jones). We're lucky with Wales at the moment in that the whole squad is full of good lads, and as with Swansea there are no bad eggs, which is such a bonus. Added to this, the way that Speedo treats us, basically like adults, means that there's a real collective feeling about Wales now that everyone involved is singing from the same hymn sheet and all pulling in the same direction. It's my experience that when that's the background in team sport, there's every chance of success being the ultimate outcome.

We were given our itineraries today for the days ahead, where we need to be in the hotel and at what time for the evening meetings, for example, and what time we need to be down for breakfast and on the coach for training and stuff. I must admit I like all that, knowing what's expected of us, as I can be a little disorganised at times to say the least. There are subtle changes in the routine with Wales compared to Swansea. For example, little things like breakfast. At Swansea it's optional and my roomie, Nath, hardly ever makes it down for breakfast, and that's fine. But with Wales, everyone has to be down at 9 a.m. to eat together, no exceptions. We have a floor to ourselves at the hotel this week, and all around it are TVs with the daily itinerary constantly showing on them, so wherever we are we can see exactly where we should be. For someone with a memory like mine that's never a bad thing.

Monday 8th August

Light training for me at the Vale of Glamorgan Hotel this morning because I played a full game on Saturday. The lads who didn't play on the weekend had a full session. While they were being put through their hard work, I was just doing some ball work, stretches and jogging. I know it sounds a bit lazy, but these days recovery is hugely important, so it was a gentle day.

After getting back to the hotel and doing some swimming and exercises in the pool, it was free time later in the afternoon, then dinner followed by the first of our video meetings where Speedo and Raymond looked back at the England game and pinpointed exactly what went on and what we should do about it. Speedo stood up first, explained what he was looking to achieve from the meeting, and said that throughout the week we'd be focusing on the same thing to ensure that it doesn't happen again against Australia. He told us that we'd be starting with unit meetings, i.e. one for defence, one for midfield and one for attack, and then meet up at the end for an overall discussion with the whole of the squad.

When we split up, Raymond took control of the DVD and started to dissect what had happened defensively against England. What I like about the way Speedo and Raymond approach things is that they see our improvement and development as a journey.

Yes, there are lots of things wrong with Wales at the moment, that's clear if you look at our results, but in the limited time that Speedo and Raymond have with us, they can't fix everything at once. Raymond explained that as the season develops we will meet and put things right, but it will be very much a stepped process. In this camp he told us that we would be focusing on the main glaring problem from the England game, namely the way the defence interacted with midfield.

It became crystal clear when Raymond pointed out a couple of things in the first few minutes of the DVD. In our eagerness to pass around England and retain possession at all costs, we defenders made the mistake of playing too deep, and the midfielders made the mistake of joining us and not allowing us to have any depth in our play. The two outcomes to this were that our striker Steve Morison was just too isolated when we eventually played the ball up to him, resulting in England winning it back too quickly. Secondly, when we had possession England still had all the territory, without ever having to actually work to gain it.

Raymond is very talented at this side of the game. He is much more of a theorist than Speedo which is why they have gelled so well together. Speedo gets into us with all the traditional football stuff about working hard, having commitment, responsibility and understanding the privilege of representing our country and everything that comes with that, and of course he also knows his football inside out. Raymond's strength however is very much in the understanding of the game, the tactics and the science behind it. And he proved that again tonight when he dissected the game against England, identified the problem and explained what we would have to do to put it right. It was an intense meeting, but I have to say – as I've been from the start really – I was very impressed with Raymond's knowledge.

Tuesday 9th August

Good training session today where I had full involvement, and it was good to get a decent sweat on. Speedo was very vocal throughout it, but he also kept it light and interesting. He's a good coach like that and because he's been so recent a player, he knows what a player wants and needs from a training session the day before a game.

Tonight, there was another detailed meeting about what we spoke about yesterday. Raymond went into things a little deeper and reinforced what we had to do to prevent our midfield falling too deep with us, to realise that we must commit to our passing game and so they always have to be available. Raymond's great at getting his point across and all the lads left the meeting in no doubt about what we had to make happen tomorrow to prevent the negatives of the England game happening again.

Wednesday 10th August

Wales 1 (Blake 82) **Australia 2** (Cahill 42, Kruse 60)

I spent the bulk of the morning in the café having a coffee with Bellars today, just talking about the game. We mostly chat about football. He has good opinions on it and is completely professional about everything to do with his career. He's got funny stories from his experiences in football and I always take the time at Wales camps to sit and pick his brain.

After lunch, the day dragged a little because we'd done all our prep in the detailed meetings we'd had this week, putting the shortcomings of our defence and midfield link right. It felt like an age until the pre-match meal at 4 p.m., after which it was up for a shower, into my suit then back downstairs for our final talk from Speedo and Raymond. There was also a briefing from Osian (Roberts, our assistant coach) to remind us about the set plays he'd already been through with us. We've not talked about Australia at all this week because, quite simply, none of this is about them, it's all about us developing as a team and dealing with our own issues. Speedo has made it clear that this game is about us, not our opponents.

Before the game, Speedo kept it short and direct and reminded us about the message that Raymond had been giving us all week. Speedo's already come under a bit of pressure because results haven't been great since he came in, but because he's all about the bigger picture, he wanted us to put the wrong things right rather than worry too much about the scoreline. I was impressed with that. It was a brave message to give us.

Even though it was never going to be about the result tonight, we really could have won this game if we'd have approached it differently at the start. Almost from the kick-off, we had the ball for the first twenty minutes, hardly allowing them a kick. But in all honesty we hardly did a thing with it. I couldn't put my finger on it at the time, and will probably need to see the video of it to really find out why that was, but it just felt like we had to keep hold of the ball for the sake of it.

Personally, I felt I did OK today which is always pleasing, but despite Speedo emphasising the importance of the performance, it's still a loss and at the very least I'd have much preferred a draw. People may not realise that for us players there's a lot of pressure playing for Wales, even in friendlies like tonight where the crowd wasn't the biggest. With all the media interest and the constant speculation that first Tosh and even now Speedo has come under – which sometimes borders on certain people wanting to see them fail – we as players realise that the chances of the manager having a positive press that will give him the time to put his ideas for improvement into practice, largely depend on us.

It's always an awkward date for an international friendly fixture, a couple of days before the start of the season. Personally I'll always turn up and give 100 per cent and just concentrate on this game, but you can understand why club managers get frustrated when they've planned all through pre-season with a starting XI and a player comes back injured.

Thursday 11th August

The Gaffer signed a goalie today called Michel Vorm. I have to admit that I've never heard of him before, but from what some of the lads tell me, he's meant to be good.

Friday 12th August

The club released the news to the press today about me signing my new contract. Even though I signed it last week, the club just wait until a quiet news day, like today, and then put out a press release.

Saturday 13th August

Trained this morning and then came home to watch *Gillette Soccer Saturday* and kept an eye on all the results. It felt weird watching knowing that all these teams are now my competition.

Sunday 14th August

Leets (Leroy Lita) and Wayne had their singing initiation tonight and both of their performances were two of the maddest ones I've seen while at the club. We had a private room in the hotel and none of the lads would let them get away without singing. As soon as everyone finished eating, all the lads were tapping their forks on the glasses, the usual signal for 'we want a song!'

Leets grabbed an empty water bottle as his microphone, went over to the chair in the middle of the room – you're not allowed to be on your own chair – and started singing some sort of British grime rap song with his eyes closed, doing all the hand actions and gestures as if he was on stage in front of 30,000. He was pulling his top up to show his stomach and really got into it, getting more aggressive as he went and even ended up chucking the water bottle away as part of his act!

Normally, half way through we all join in and help out whoever it is, because they are usually dying of embarrassment. Not tonight. We just sat there in hysterics, none of us had ever seen anything like it. He really went into the zone and took it so seriously that it was absolutely hysterical to watch.

After Leets had sat down I looked across to Wayne who was sat next to him and his face sort of fell as if to say, 'How the hell do I follow that?' Anyway, as we were still laughing and getting over Leets' effort, Wayne just got up, got himself ready and then basically outrapped Leets! We were stunned. If anything, he picked a rap that was louder, a quicker tempo and even more aggressive than Leets', and actually topped his effort. It was unreal. Normally players are quite timid and nervous about doing their song, so it was a bit of shock to see the way they both went into it so hard. They were without doubt the best initiations that I've seen.

After dinner we had our usual 9 o'clock meeting where the Gaffer gave us the team for tomorrow and I think there'll be a couple of surprises for the fans when they get to see it. Tatey plays and will captain, not a surprise as such, but he is in because Tayls is still suspended from last season's play-off game against Forest. Kemy will start in place of Joe, which was a surprise to me given how well Joe did last season. I think the Gaffer thinks maybe we need something a bit more physical, especially as it's our first game and away. Dobbs also gets his chance and we are all happy for him as he gave us a different edge in the play-offs and towards the end of the season. He deserves his opportunity.

Monday 15th August

Manchester City 4 (Džeko 57, Agüero 68, 90 + 1, Silva 71) **Swansea City 0**

Bollocks.

At the risk of stating the obvious, that was not the result that we were after.

Before the game I couldn't care too much about the result, to be honest. My focus was just on enjoying it. I knew my wife and baby would be there, along with my parents, my father-in-law and my nephew Jacob. I was happy at the thought of them going to such a magnificent stadium to see me running out to play on such a big occasion. All of them have shared in my dream of getting this far in my career, and I sometimes doubted that I'd ever get here. I never actually doubted myself, but sometimes it looked like it was too far to reach.

When I spoke to my wife earlier, I told her to make sure she enjoys the whole occasion because it is as much a reward for her as it is for me. She was the one who would be standing in the snow at places like Accrington Stanley, Bury and Rochdale when the Premier League was an unachievable dream to both of us. I've also had lots of requests for tickets for this game, but anyone who hadn't watched me in the lower leagues didn't stand a chance of getting one.

In the dressing room Tatey surpassed himself again. For those who don't know him, he's a great lad who also happens to be the rawest northern guy ever, who doesn't care about all the stuff that's going on around him. It's just another game of football to him. He was captain tonight and as we were getting ready in this state of the art dressing room, about to go and play against the richest club in the world, Tatey delved into his kitbag to get out his boots to take on the likes of Džeko and Agüero. Now it's the first game of the season, and that means everything is brand new and gleaming. We all had new boots of all brands and colours, but then Tatey drags out his old, battered, muddy Adidas Predators, about three or four versions old, with the elastic around the lace covers all snapped off and in a shocking state. Unbelievable. Honestly, he still manages to treat a debut match in the Premier League exactly as he would a Sunday League game on a park pitch – you've got to respect the guy for that.

After the huddle today I was thinking that I didn't care if I only played one minute of the game. It would be enough to say to myself that I did it, that after such a long journey, I got to the top, and all the hard work was worth it. It was a special feeling.

I've decided to do a direct account of my very first premiership game, how I saw the game in my own head, as it was happening. Hopefully this one game will give you an idea of exactly what it feels to be on the pitch for 90 minutes. No other match in the diary is going to be reported in this frenzied and chaotic manner, but it was such a special game for me, I wanted everyone to know exactly how excited I felt during the match and what was flying through my head and how I talked myself through it.

I look at the players facing me in sky blue on the opposite side of the pitch and think OK Ash let's see what you've got, you always claimed you were good enough at this level, now prove it.

Kick-off – early touch and a pass to my new centre half partner Caulks. Well at least I've touched the ball in the Prem. First minute;

ball rolls back to my new goalkeeper who I've never played with before and only met three days ago, he kicks left foot straight off the pitch and into touch. Hmm, OK. 'Anyone can make a mistake' I shout to him and tell him not to worry about it; he looks at me like I'm crazy and says 'Yeah I know.' Well this one looks a cool character!

Four mins later; I read the play well and sweep up a through ball, take a touch to steady myself and go to clear down the line left footed but Džeko is onto me like a flash and charges it down! Our throw. OK, so you really don't have as much time in the Prem Ash.

Ten minutes in; we are dominating the game like we did in the Championship. I can't believe this, we are playing Man City and are in total control. I feel that they have made a change and instead of leaving Džeko up front on his own they push Touré further forwards to close me and Caulks down and I instantly feel a bit of a shift in the rhythm of the game.

Twenty mins in; I make my first block of the season on a Johnson shot and it goes over. OK Ash, that was a good block now defend this corner, what a team of giants they have and we are marking zonally for the first time since the Gaffer arrived! Great, what a day to start trying new things! We clear it, pressure's off for a minute!

Minute later; good play by them down our right and the ball comes in low, Džeko takes a touch and I slide and make another block as the ball flies up and hits my hand! No penalty! As he turns to shoot I think, quick move your feet, he is rolling left. As he pulls his left foot back, I slide down instantly, slide, slide, slide, I feel pain in my right ankle straightaway and the ball comes up and slams into my hand. Džeko's foot landed studs first onto my ankle and all his weight went onto it. As I get up I can just feel pain in my ankle, I didn't really care that everyone was appealing for a penalty! No chance anyway, I couldn't have moved my hand if I tried, it happened that quick! Run it off Ash, get the blood going again, it's just a knock, no biggie! Yeah, but it's sore though! As I look down I see blood coming through my sock.

We are still trying to control the game but our flow has been disrupted somewhat by them playing higher up the field. After I play a couple of one-twos with Michel, he then kicks it straight out of play again! AGAIN? OK, maybe he is not used to playing this way. I turn to look at him and his face hasn't changed one bit as if nothing happened! Wow, this guy is ice cold!

Silva hits our bar in what seems like slow-motion. All of a sudden we seemed to be doing more and more defending!

I read the play brilliantly again and beat Džeko to the ball and try to carry it out instead of just clearing it, he nicks it and is on my byline getting a cross in! As I beat him to the ball I think, well done Ash, now stay calm and composed and carry it, then pass it out, woah where did he come from?! Oh shit, if this goes in I look like a right prick on national TV! Phew nothing came of it! OK Ash, that's your last one, you can't take time on the ball in this game like you're used to.

Barry shoots, I block and end up on the floor, I look up to see where the ball is and it's gonna SMASH straight into my face! Good block Ash, get up quick, whack, OK so that was the ball hitting you in the face! Take a minute, feel a bit dazed. Michel is on my shoulder saying 'f***ing great block' and is buzzing with me, all I can think is what the hell just happened?!

As I get up and walk back to my station, Mike Dean, the ref says 'It's a lot quicker up here in the Prem isn't it Willo?' Nobody calls me Willo! Don't talk to me mate, I still haven't forgotten that pen at Ninian Park! I was thinking, whilst flashing a false smile!

By then, David Silva's impact on the game was starting to grow. He was unplayable tonight, one of the best players I have ever come up against. No matter what we did against him, he just seemed to ghost into a position to get the ball and make space for himself. He was very impressive. He nearly scored from a corner about five minutes before half-time and I had to have a real go at Scott and Nath because of it. Before a game, the Gaffer puts these pages up on the dressing room wall which shows everyone exactly where they need to stand for every scenario involving a corner or set piece, both defending and attacking. They show where we must stand for throw ins, deep free kicks, edge of box free kicks, inswinging corners, outswinging corners – everything you can think of. Silva's shot came from a short corner and I went nuts at Scott and Nath *because they were not where they were meant to be, so weren't in position to stop it going short to Silva. We can't afford to switch off even for a minute I feel in the Prem.*

Another guy who impressed me tonight was Yaya (the train) Touré. What a beast this guy is when he starts running with the ball, it's almost impossible to stop him. We make it to half-time with Barry rattling our crossbar also, but we survive.

OK, great half couldn't have asked for anymore. I feel good, I feel strong, we look strong. Rode our luck at times but that's going to happen. Collect your thoughts get some fluid on board, get dry and listen to the Gaffer.

The Gaffer is happy with us and we are happy too. We had forced them into an early change in the way they were playing by us completely controlling the game with our possession, as we did in the Championship, 0–0 was the critical score, the longer we keep a clean sheet the better, as the pressure will mount on them and they will get frustrated! Hopefully!

Change my shirt for a dry one and get up on my feet so I don't go stiff.

Back out into this amazing arena. Can we do it again and hold on?

Johnson gets on to the ball and runs at Tatey. 'Cover Tatey Ash' I shout 'send him inside', we are stronger here with more bodies. Keep your hands down Ash, you're inside the box. I put them behind my back as I don't want to give any silly pens away. It comes to nothing.

Already this half feels different, we are stretched more and the pitch somehow feels way bigger. I beat Džeko to the ball and do a nice bit of skill past him. Well done Ash, great turn, keep calm don't get too excited, Britts is offering an angle as usual, one-two, here we go, we are out, I'm going to carry the ball up the pitch and get us out of our half. Play a one-two with Britts and then overrun it and lose out to De Jong – WHACK where the hell did he come from?! Now I'm blowing and need to get back into my position! Thought you learnt your lesson first half Ash!

Johnson is on another drive and I go to help Tatey again as he advances to our box. He somehow sneaks a shot between the both of us which Michel saves and Džeko taps in, one down. That goal happened so quick, but what a shit goal to give away, he must be offside? I turned to look at the lino but he is giving nothing. I turn straight back to Àngel and Caulks, 'If he isn't off how did we let him in to score?'

We really needed to hold out for longer than this, ten mins into the second half and we are one down. I start to shout and try to encourage the boys not to drop their heads and keep it to one and see what happens, we might nick one at the other end.

Agüero's on now, there's been a lot of hype about him but I've never seen him play. Great, this is the last thing I need, starting to tire and they bring on a sub striker on his debut who is bound to be double lively.

We come together for the first time, he rides my challenge and gets a cross in that goes over the box. He is small, give him some shoulder! OK, so that didn't work he is pretty strong, just get there first! Now slide, bastard! He wriggled out of it, phew, the cross goes behind. I get up and look at him, I think this guy is very sharp, quick and strong! Great!

Three mins later and we finally get an attacking set piece. No better time to score than now Ash, who's marking me? Lescott, he is a unit but then so are most of the team. Let's try to lose him and get free as I'm not going to be able to jump over him. Here we go it's coming, go, go, go, argh, that wasn't a bad chance Ash, move your feet quicker! I win the header at the back stick but can't direct it and it goes over.

Tatey and Scott both go with the same man and Richards plays a great ball across the goal and Agüero taps it in at the same far post as Džeko did. Now we really are up against it, only 67 mins gone and we are two down, tired and they are bringing subs like Agüero on. I turn and look into the crowd and they are all doing the Poznań dance, I can't help thinking that it looks impressive, but my main concern now is that we will get run over and concede a few goals. I try to get the message out to the team, to just sit in our shape, don't go and chase a goal, if it comes then great but let's not concede any more.

Wow, we are looking tired, I feel knackered, Britts looks it too.

Let's just stay tight, don't do anything stupid now Ash because you're tired, keep concentrating even if your legs feel like concrete.

A couple of minutes later it was Poznań time again as Silva scored. It shouldn't have stood because the ball that Agüero hooked back had clearly gone behind, but them's the breaks I guess. My overwhelming thought then was that I knew the world would be watching this on Sky, and I didn't want us to be embarrassed by allowing them to run away with five or six. There's nothing else to do at times like that but dig deep. Come on boys stay strong! No more goals! Let's keep it respectable now 3–0. OK these guys are favourites to win the league and I can see why.

Credit to us though, we never buckled and we had a decent last twenty, where we still retained possession well and managed to keep them out until right at the end, which when it came was a wonder strike from Agüero that flew over the top of my head and dipped beyond Michel. I don't think we deserved to concede four goals, but there wasn't much any of us could do about it really. As Michel picked the last one out of the net, I just thought, welcome to the Prem Ash, I'm so tired now the ref needs to just blow the whistle! I'm enjoying myself out here even though we are four down, strange feeling, I'm just glad I'm on the big stage!

Final whistle, I swap shirts with Joleon Lescott, who I know from Birmingham. I wave to my family in the stand and make my way off the pitch feeling proud for a couple of reasons. First, because I thought we played well and didn't let ourselves down. Second, I am officially a Premier League footballer.

I can't wait to play more games against teams who aren't as good as this lot. Wigan next week and I'm more than confident we can beat them.

Played 1 Won 0 Drawn 0 Lost 1 Points 0 League Position – Bottom*
(40 more points needed for 40) NB: * League Position at the end of the game.

Tuesday 16th August

We didn't get back until the early hours this morning, so we didn't have to come in for our recovery session until 12.30 p.m.

Wednesday 17th August

Usual training session. The Gaffer was very positive about how we're going to perform against Wigan.

Thursday 18th August

Good training session today, the boys were buzzing, a massage was definitely essential afterwards. Lunch at a restaurant with the squad and staff.

Friday 19th August

Before training this morning we had a meeting to discuss Wigan. We watched some of our positive play from the Man City game, with the Gaffer highlighting where we had succeeded in what he wanted us to do, and we followed that by watching some footage of Wigan, focusing on their set pieces and general play.

Saturday 20th August
Swansea City 0 Wigan Athletic 0

The Gaffer brought Tayls back in for Tatey. Because of that, he needed a new skipper and chose me. To be fair, I don't normally make a big deal about the captaincy because I try to be a leader on the pitch with or without the armband, but today I can't describe how proud I felt being captain for our first home game in the Prem, such an historic day for the club.

If only we could have won.

When you are captain there are a few duties you have to carry out off the field that don't normally concern you when you're back in the ranks. One is a meeting that's always called before a game by the referee, in his room, between both managers and captains. It's held so that you can hand over the team-sheets, but the refs also use it to give you some warnings about what they are looking to clamp down on in the game, perhaps two-footed tackles or imaginary card waving. Even though it's supposed to be a meeting for managers, generally it's the assistants who go in, so today it was me and Pasc and, for Wigan, Roberto's assistant Bonner (Graeme Jones) was there who was his assistant manager here, so I knew him well. He's a top bloke who I've always got on well with, so it was nice to see him again, and have a quick catch up.

Back in the dressing room, even though Monks wasn't playing, he was desperate for us to win. It hurt him when we lost to Wigan in the Cup a couple of years ago and he wanted to put that right. He was very vocal and aggressive, and showed once again what a fantastic leader he is for this club. I know the club has had some great captains over the years, but I honestly can't imagine there's been a better one than Monks, whose passion for the club is simply unbelievable. As he went about the dressing room, encouraging and winding everyone up, I simply wanted to win it today, just for him.

As I stood in the tunnel, waiting to go out, I could sense that the atmosphere from outside was going to be special. I wasn't disappointed. When I led the team out, our fans were the loudest I've heard in my four years at the club. It was incredible. As I walked over to line up for the handshakes, I thought, 'Is this just for today, or is it going to be like this every week?' I can't tell you how different it was compared to last season's home games.

Wigan hardly had a kick in the first ten minutes, giving the crowd the start they deserved. We began with a great move that led to a very early chance for Danny from a cross by Àngel and, despite a good contact, he put it straight at the goalie. Either side of him and we'd have gone one up.

It didn't seem to matter that he didn't though, because we settled right into our flow from the off and it began to feel like a normal Swans home game, where we were taking control with our usual rhythm, using the ball well and our transitions were also great. It was important that the game got normal, because it would have been easy to have become overawed by it all, which would have helped Wigan.

Wigan only played Di Santo up front, and I felt confident about that. He's a talented lad who began chasing down me and Caulks when we had the ball. But if I'm being honest it was clear from his attitude that he wasn't going to be arsed to keep that up for long – and he didn't. Leets told me recently how much opposing strikers hate playing us at home, because of the way we keep the ball, and even if they do keep chasing, they don't have much energy left for a chance which may eventually come their way late in the game.

But it wasn't a striker who annoyed me today. Instead it was a former team mate. Midway through the half, over in the left back position, Jordi Gómez went straight down after the slightest of brushes by Scott. It was never a foul and was typical Jordi. It made me really angry and I shouted across to him, but I suppose I have to own up to double standards here, because when he used to do stuff like that for us I used to turn a blind eye. That's the way of the world I suppose in professional sport, it's all about the 'W' and when he used that side of his game to our advantage, I never used to worry about it too much.

There was worse to come from him, but we had to defend the cheap free kick first which, after Caulks had missed a tackle, led to my best contribution as a Premier League defender so far when I made a sliding tackle on the edge of the box to clear it. It was a nice confidence booster, and as nice as it is to see plenty of the ball by passing it round, I'm paid to defend and that little tackle made me feel really good. From it, Nath dribbled out of defence well and won us a free kick on the halfway line. That piece of play demonstrates what the Gaffer wants us to do. I've played for lots of teams who would have been under orders to 'clear the lines' and knock it long from my tackle, thereby losing possession. But the Gaffer encourages our wingers to carry the ball in situations like that because they do it so well, meaning we not only get out of danger but also keep possession. It's key to the way we play and also gives the rest of the team a breather and gets us up the pitch.

The one thing missing from our first-half performance was a goal, and it nearly arrived from the most unlikely of sources, Britts. With about a quarter of an hour to go to half-time, from a corner the ball dropped to Britts outside the box and, as we all held our breath, surprise, surprise, he smashed it over.

As I ran back past him he laughed when he saw me looking at him, because he knew what was coming. 'Just don't bother shooting, Leon' I laughed. We always banter about his goal-scoring record, or rather lack of it. Having said that, after the goal he scored against Forest last year in the play-offs, he does now have a comeback in his locker. But I'm still gonna give him stick if he shoots like he did today!

As good as our first home half in the Premier League was, there were still a couple of defensive lapses that annoyed me. Similar to the City game, our wingers know exactly what their defensive responsibilities are from corners and they let them slip twice, which could have proved costly. The first was when they didn't switch on at all, allowing their winger to get a cross in that I had to head behind for a corner. Michel was particularly angry about that, which I was really pleased about. I've only played two games with him now, and it's great to see that he's a keeper who's vocal, and not worried about handing out defensive rollickings. I'm getting more impressed by him with every passing minute.

The second lapse came right on half-time from another corner on our right that they played short again, this time into the feet of Moses, eight yards inside our box. If I was being generous I could maybe excuse the first lapse, but not this one. Something like that can't happen – ever. The whole defensive unit, and pleasingly Michel again, were fuming with Scott and Nath because we all knew what their jobs were, and by not doing them it could have resulted in a goal just before half-time. That would have been a real insult to all the hard work everyone else had put in up to that point. In all fairness to them, when you're an attacking player it's hard to switch your mentality to a defensive one in a split second, but in this division you have to do it.

At the break, apart from having words about our short corner defending generally, we were all pretty happy with our first home half in the top division. The Gaffer was pleased and said we had played really well and was most pleased that we were winning the ball back quickly and then keeping it for long periods. He did emphasize though, that we needed to convert our possession into chances, as the longer it stayed 0–0, the bigger the risk that they'd feel they could get something out of it that they didn't deserve. We needed to get ahead to prevent that happening.

Personally I'd been pretty tired up to about thirty minutes which had been a bit of a concern, but around then I got my second wind, and then felt heaps better. It's easy to panic and forget that this is only game two of a very long season and from experience I know it'll take about three or four games until I get right up to speed and feel fully fit.

There was a pretty even start to the second half and I still felt we were the more dangerous thanks to Nath and Scotty. But apart from an Àngel shot and goal line scramble, along with a second chance that Danny had that he was unlucky not to tuck away, we hadn't really done what the Gaffer had asked us to, and that was create more chances. About fifteen minutes in I also felt that we had lost some intensity in our defending, which meant they were getting on the ball more, as the Gaffer had warned us they might. When I recognised this, I just got more vocal, trying to drive us on and making sure we were keeping our standards high.

Soon after, we produced probably the move of the match. It was really top-notch. It began with Michel, went all the way down the right from Àngel, with great movement from Nath, onto Wayne who finally just pulled his shot wide. If Wayne had scored, they would have been talking about it on TV for days. Our development as a team as we go forward has to be creating more moves like that with all the possession we're getting, because eventually, it will lead to just one thing – goals.

For the rest of the game as far as I was concerned, it could best be summed up in two words. Jordi Gómez.

The first part was his good side. He's a player of top quality and he showed that when he picked the ball up outside the area and hit a sort of lob-cum-shot that flew past Michel onto the post. It was a fantastic piece of football, real quality, which I'd seen many times in training when he was here. I was really relieved when it hit the post though, because I really didn't want him to score today, and the reason for that is for the type of behaviour he has in his locker that he displayed straight after.

They started a decent move that left us exposed, because we

were pushing on and trying to score, which ended with Moses who smashed his shot against the bar. I thought it was going in initially so stopped, but then it came back out straight towards me. It took me a split second to stick out my foot for the ball, but that was enough for Gómez to make sure his foot made contact with mine, then scream and chuck himself down on the floor as if I'd cut him in half. That was followed by Phil Dowd's whistle, and I was horrified to see him pointing to the spot. I went straight over to Gómez and called him a pussy, but with an appropriate swear word in front of it. I was furious. He just looked back at me and said, 'It was a foul. Watch it back on TV.' That was almost enough for me to burst with rage, so I responded with, 'I will give you something to roll on the floor about by the end of this game you little cheating p***k.'

Now I know all that might sound a bit harsh and unnecessary but in my head I was certain that they were going to score the penalty and, with it being so late in the game, take all three points too. For it to be a foul there had to be some intent from me, and my foot hadn't moved towards Gómez at all. Actually, he had found my foot with his. Also I definitely touched the ball because it went to my left after coming off my shin and in the split second that followed, our feet collided – and the key word is collide – because my foot was dangling there the same as his. The only difference between us was that I didn't do a pathetic fall to the floor.

What also really wound me up was Watson and their fans virtually celebrating as if he'd already scored. Watson struck his pen well, hard and low to Michel's right, but Michel was on the ground in a flash and stuck out a strong right hand to save. I don't think I could have been happier if I'd have scored a goal myself. I was so pumped, I had to refrain from celebrating in front of their fans, but instead turned to Jordi straight away and said, 'That's justice. Don't come near me again today.'

We settled down after the penalty but despite finishing well we couldn't get the goal to give us the victory I felt our all-round play and possession deserved. At the end, Jordi came up to me to shake hands. I pointed to the penalty spot and said, 'That was justice and stop being a f****** cheat.' I wasn't happy with him at all.

On reflection I definitely think we should have won today. Di Santo didn't really cause me and Caulks any problems and, talking to Caulks about him afterwards, we both agreed that it looked like he just lost interest as the game went on. But, after the pen, I have to be honest and say that I was happy to walk off with a draw.

In terms of quality, Wigan weren't a patch on Man City. Listening to everyone in the dressing room afterwards it was clear that we've gained heaps of confidence knowing we outplayed them, but there was a tinge of disappointment that we didn't get the win. However we were all agreed on one thing; we now know we can get wins in this league. The performance today showed us all that, and that was the exact message from the Gaffer.

The last thing he said was, 'After that, I'm certain we'll get enough wins in this league to never have to worry about staying in it.'

I agree.

Played 2 Won 0 Drawn 1 Lost 1 Points 1 League Position – 16th
(39 more points needed for 40)

Monday 22nd August

Footballers are a very superstitious bunch and, like many, I've got a few superstitions that I wouldn't want to change just in case it brings me a little bad luck. For example, since my Hednesford days I have always worn a white strapping on my left wrist. I can't actually remember why I first put it on, but we won, and because of that I wore it the next game, which we also won, and I've worn it ever since. I also make sure I've got the same shin pads for every game, which I've had since Stockport. You probably think they're flashy ones, but I bought them from JJB Sports and they cost me four quid.

Tuesday 23rd August

Shrewsbury Town 3 (Morgan 19, Wright 67, Wroe 90 + 1)

Swansea City 1 (Cansdell-Sherriff og 10)

Happy birthday to me. But it's not one I'm going to remember with any fondness.

I'm really annoyed writing this and don't really want to say what I feel because I may upset a few people. The reality was we just weren't up for it today, and that's just not acceptable.

There was a definite feel that Shrewsbury saw us as a big scalp to take, and we've just got to accept that now and understand that we have to work just as hard against a team with that as their motivation and earn the right to play our football as we would if we were playing Manchester United. We simply didn't do that tonight, and despite taking the lead we were scruffy with what we did, and just didn't play with the same intensity we had against Wigan. I don't absolve myself from any of the blame either. I had a senior role to play for the team tonight so I take lots of the responsibility for the defeat. I don't think any of us walked out onto the pitch thinking, 'This isn't a Premier League game, so we can't be bothered'. But maybe subconsciously we carried an attitude where we thought things were going to happen for us, rather than make things happen. To concede three goals absolutely kills me, because with no disrespect to Shrewsbury we shouldn't be conceding one to them, but at the other end of the field we were pretty wasteful too. It's all a bit raw still for me at the moment and I'm feeling angry and embarrassed as I write this. The Gaffer was furious too and he gave us a real rollicking afterwards. He told us to remember how we felt playing against Manchester City, and playing well against Wigan, but also to remember to tell our grandchildren about the night Shrewsbury knocked us out of the Cup. Point taken.

I've never been one of these who believes it's better to concentrate on the league, because I'm in the camp that thinks that winning breeds confidence, whatever the competition. And, as we stand, the fact is we haven't won a game yet this season. All of which means we have to look for Sunderland now to get that monkey off our back.

While I don't think our confidence will necessarily be harmed by tonight's defeat, I do think it would have been improved by a good win and performance. Still, the last word goes to the Gaffer. Before we left the dressing room to come home, having calmed down from his initial fury he said, 'Put this behind you all now and look forward to Saturday. You've had a bad day. It's how you get over it that counts.'

I couldn't agree more.

Friday 26th August

Popped round to see Titus (Bramble) tonight at his hotel for a quick chat before tomorrow's game. It was funny really, we've been mates for years and now we get the chance to play against each other in the Premier League. It was a little bit awkward because of that and we actually steered clear of discussing the match. I got the feeling that he was worried that he might not get a game because they've just signed John O'Shea from Man United. I hope not, because I'd love him to play, then lose me at a corner and watch me rifle home the winner – ha-ha!

Saturday 27th August
Swansea City 0 Sunderland 0

The focus of the Gaffer before the game was simple: today was the day we needed to deliver our first Premier League win. As usual, he went into the detail of players, like their attackers – Gyan and Sessègnon – and how they are a pair of livewires that we'd have to keep an eye on, but he made it clear that while the solidness of our play has been excellent so far, we have to step up now and deliver goals to give us our first win. Points at home are what will keep us in the division, and the Gaffer said that taking three off a team like Sunderland would prove crucial as the season unfolded.

We nearly got off to the worst possible start in pursuit of that win though, when O'Shea – who did start in front of Titus – got free in the box after a couple of minutes, and hit the bar from a corner. We mark zonally, with Caulks, Danny and me as a line of three and, while the tactic has its critics, it works well enough for us as we all know exactly what we have to do. The one problem with zonal defending though, is in the tiny area between the zones. Effectively, each one of us is marking an imaginary box that we stand in the middle of and deal with the ball when it comes into it. For 99 per cent of the time there's no problem. But on occasion a ball will fall at say the very front of my zone and the very back of Danny's, and if the opponent player times his run to be there at the exact moment that the ball arrives, that's when there's a problem and that's what happened with O'Shea today.

A couple of minutes later I had my own chance from a corner, when I managed to get a flick and the rebound didn't quite fall for me. Anton Ferdinand was marking me, and I hate it when a mate is marking as I always prefer it to be someone I don't know so that I can take some liberties! One thing the Gaffer has put into my game since he's been coaching me is aggression. He's told me that every challenge I make, defensively, or in attack like this one was, I should put everything into it and let whoever is marking me know that I'm about. I never have a problem with this, as to be honest I'm not in the Premier League to make mates. So if any of my opponents don't like it then, frankly, tough. But when it's a mate, like Anton is, it just doesn't seem right to take a liberty with them. I still do, of course. I just don't feel too happy about it!

Before the game had started, I remember looking across at Gyan having a stretch and saying quietly to myself, 'I can't wait to get stuck into you.' It's a little bit of self motivation I use to force me to almost dislike him, so that I get my mind in the right place to be aggressive with an opponent. It makes me realise how crucial it is to not allow him to have a minute's peace today when he comes near me. It helps me to focus on the task ahead, and I was determined not to let him score. As I was in my little world looking at him I said to myself, 'Ash, you have played two Prem games now and you have done OK, but it's time to step it up and start stamping your authority on games.' It might sound a bit daft to you reading that, but success at this level has got nothing to do with ability really. Everyone who plays in the Premier League has got ability, but it all comes down to attitude and mentality. I'm forever setting myself personal mental challenges like this, and I made my battle with Gyan personal, even though I'd never met the bloke before.

Once the game had started to settle down there were a couple of moments which highlighted that while Caulks is an exceptional young talent, with a fantastic future ahead of him, it's going to take a few matches yet before we are really solid as a pairing. It isn't something that just clicks overnight. First there was a moment when my mate Gyan got in behind me with a run from deep that I couldn't see, but Caulks could. Caulks stopped as I stepped up, which meant Gyan had oceans of space to run into. Caulks should have run with him into my channel, knowing that I wasn't aware Gyan had gone. That's what I would have done if the roles had been reversed. Michel was furious with Caulks because it could have proved expensive. Then, about five minutes later, Caulks played a back pass that was short and intercepted by Gyan, but fortunately Michel rushed out with a well-timed tackle. As I could see what Caulks was thinking but could also see Gyan anticipating it, I was shouting my head off, 'No backpass!' but he said later he hadn't heard me. As stressful as they are when they occur, these are the things that have to happen to a new partnership, so that we can iron them out and prevent them from happening again.

We then came into the game offensively a bit more, with both Scotty and Danny coming close. Scotty's would have been a goal of the season contender if it had gone in, after he cut inside and hit the bar with a great strike from about 30 yards, while Danny's chance was blocked by Wes Brown. It would have been great for both of them if they'd scored; Scott for his confidence, because like many who play in his position, he sometimes lacks self belief, while for Danny it would have been great for him to get off the mark to settle any doubts he may have had about needing to get the goals for us. Apart from another fantastic chance for Danny from six yards out with a header from a corner that I know he'd score nine times out of ten, the only other point of interest was a crazy minute where things kicked off following a clash between Kemy and Cattermole which saw Cattermole down, holding his face. It had all started with Larsson, when he had a lash at Tayls and missed, then Gardner tried to leave a bit on him and also missed, with the ball finally going to Kemy who used his body well against Cattermole. Now I'm not sure if Kemy caught him or not, but playing with Kemy everyday I see him use his body well all the time. It's a real strength of his. Gardner took offence to his challenge and cleaned Kemy out. In all fairness to Kemy, he got straight up and went to see if Cattermole was OK, but then Larsson came in and kicked it all off by getting right in the middle, stirring it all up and trying to get Kemy in trouble. I'm not sure why he had to get involved at all but, just watching him, he seemed like a very busy and annoying type of man. I grabbed Kem straight away in case he reacted, to make sure that he didn't get a silly yellow. It's part of the captain's job and, being quite hot-headed myself, it's something I've had to work on. I just tried to stay as calm as possible and make sure we all kept a lid on it. And that's harder than it sounds when there's people like Larsson around trying to wind us all up.

At half-time, the basic message from the Gaffer was just more of the same and that we should get that crucial first goal. He wasn't concerned about them at all really, but just warned us that the second half would be physically demanding as it was a boiling hot day and we needed to get the fluids on board. He warned us at the back that their front two were pure runners, so we'd have to stay with them at all times. He said that concentration was going to be the key and that if we kept a clean sheet he was certain we'd win the game. He wanted to get Scott on the ball a little more, and told him that when he had it, he needed to go direct at O'Shea to see if he'd get any joy there. He also wanted us to get Wayne on the ball more and told him to get facing their goal more to create problems. It was a very positive break for us and I felt it was simply going to be down to our attackers to bring home the win for us.

Our first chance came to Danny ten minutes in after a fantastic cross by Tayls, following a good team move. I thought straight away it was a goal, but Danny's point blank header at the far post went straight at Mignolet. Still he waits.

On the hour, Kemy had a bang on the head so the ref stopped the play. When he came to restart, Cattermole and I got in a discussion about who should return the ball to who. Shock, as we were talking about it, Larsson came and got involved when it was nothing to do with him. This really annoyed me and put a little edge on things that needn't have been there. Catts asked, 'Do you want to give it back to us?' and I laughed and asked back, 'Do you want to give it back to us, more like, because we had the ball!' We couldn't agree, so referee Mark Halsey said, 'Fine, I'm going to drop it then.' It was something and nothing really, but again I was wound up with Larsson's involvement. Players like him irritate me so much, seemingly intent on making life difficult at any opportunity.

I don't know whether the hot conditions had got to both sides but as the half carried on the intensity of the play seemed to drop off, even though it was clear to me that we had the upper hand and were comfortably the better side. With about a quarter of an hour to go, Gyan got the hook from Steve Bruce, right after possibly my best tackle of the match. The ball was played in behind Tayls tight to the touchline for Gyan, and I had chance to line him up for a well-timed challenge. I went in as hard as I could, and with as much intensity as I could find, but completely, 100 per cent, fairly. It's important that as a defender you remain in complete control of tackles like that otherwise you can end up giving the ref a decision to make. But believe me, as a defender, if you ever have a chance like that to drop a heavy – fair – tackle on a top striker, you will.

After that, apart from a run from Wickham, I don't think we had any more threats from them, but more importantly we didn't really open them up either. To be honest, I think a draw was a fair result as despite the chances that fell to Danny, and Scott's great shot, they did have some chances too. Back in the dressing room I felt for Dan as he looked a little down about not taking one of his chances and most of the boys gave him a mention to say keep your head up it will come soon enough. He's experienced enough to know this anyway, but having said that, he wouldn't be human if he wasn't disappointed.

In terms of where we are in the season, I know the doom merchants will be pointing to the fact that we haven't scored, but I'm happy about where we are. I would like to have won at least one of the last two games, but clean sheets are what I'm all about. People shouldn't underestimate the achievement of a newly-promoted team keeping two clean sheets, especially after what Man City did to us in the last half hour at the Etihad. I think the thing which is maybe even more important than the points is the belief we have got from our first three Premier League games, even the City defeat. We have outplayed Sunderland and Wigan, two established Prem teams, and this has given every single one of us the belief that we have the right to be here, and can actually perform at this level. That understanding will be crucial to us as we go forward. The Gaffer gave me a special mention in the dressing room about the way I controlled Gyan and said my performance underlined the progress every single one of us has made. I'd been up for this game from the warm-up, so to shut out Gyan and then hear the Gaffer's words was very pleasing to say the least.

Played 3 Won 0 Drawn 2 Lost 1 Points 2 League Position – 15th
(38 more points needed for 40)

Sunday 28th August

With the Wales squad today preparing for the Montenegro game on Friday which is a massive one, but I can't believe the news I've had from Swansea City about Tatey. I was having a massage off the masseur when the doctor told me that Tatey had broken his leg following an accident with a golf buggy. I didn't believe it at first and just didn't know what to make of it, but the doc said it was definitely true and that his leg was broken. I texted him saying that I hope he's alright, and he replied saying he was OK, that he was in the hospital and just waiting to find out the full damage. I just hope that it's not going to be too serious and he won't be out for long. It's heartbreaking.

When we went down for dinner tonight, Gary Speed mentioned the incident to us all, and warned us to be careful, especially as a few of the lads are playing golf during the week in their free time. There were plenty of giggles when Speedo mentioned it, and to be fair, they weren't laughing at Tatey, just the circumstances behind it which are bizarre to say the least. I mean, a golf buggy! A broken leg is an occupational hazard for a footballer but to do it in a golf buggy, well, that's classic Tatey.

As sympathetic as I am for him getting injured, I can't wait to get back to the lads at Swansea and find out the story behind it.

Monday 29th August

We had our first detailed meeting with Raymond tonight about the Australia game and analysed how we carried out his pre-match instructions not to sit so deep in defence and to make sure the midfield gave us more room to operate in. The DVD of the game showed that we had dealt with that really well, and had shown Raymond the most important thing for him, progress. Now that we had identified one weakness and sorted it out, it was time to work on another.

Against Australia, as we had done against England, we had started slowly. Yes, he and Speedo want us to develop a passing style to our play, but it looked like we were so obsessed with it; there was no speed or intensity. There was no zip to our game. Having watched the clips back, Raymond was absolutely right and we had good discussions about it within our groups and then back as a collective at the end.

It's amazing how sensible and logical Speedo and Raymond's approach is. Building on the Australia camp in August, it was clear that both of them were systematically reviewing our style and play, discovering our shortcomings, but then putting them right almost in order of importance. I've got the feeling that under Speedo we are building and improving as a squad every time we meet up. His approach is very impressive and for the first time in a long time I have a very good feeling about our future, and the ultimate goal for everyone: qualification for a major tournament.

Tuesday 30th August

Speedo called together the defenders and our keeper, Wayne, today and spoke to us about that lack of intensity that we showed in that opening spell against Australia. He asked us what we thought about going a bit longer in the first ten minutes of the game when we have the ball and then, once we've set the tempo of the game and are on the front foot, controlling our passing a bit more. I agreed with him completely. It's different to Swansea City where we have all been playing and practising like this for twelve months under the Gaffer. At Wales, twenty-odd players are brought together from different clubs with different ways of playing, so to ask them to come in and just pass it like we do at Swansea is not easy for them.

Wednesday 31st August

Today at training at Spytty Park in Newport, Speedo got us together again as a defensive unit and worked on what we discussed yesterday. We did a long session where we worked with Wayne in goal and our midfield as opponents in front of us, passing and retaining possession while they closed us down, exactly as Speedo hoped we would do after we'd set the tone for the match after that positive ten minutes. We've done quite a lot of this sort of stuff in training this week, but today was the most we've done. It was a really good session. This type of training is essential to ensure that the repetition in these practice sessions becomes second nature out on the field. It's exactly the same principal as the golfer who practises his putting hour after hour, or the basketball player who practises his shooting. When game time comes, if you've repeated your practice enough, the body just seems to know exactly what to do when the moment arrives. Even though Speedo's worked us hard on the passing all week, every single moment of it will be positive and beneficial to us come game time. Added to all of that, it is really enjoyable training, too, because you are on your toes, working with the ball all the time.

Tonight after our meeting we just chilled and as usual, when that happens, we all tend to fall into the little groups that we have within the squad. There are no childish cliques in our squad, which sometimes can be quite negative and divisive, and generally, everyone is happy to sit next to anyone and talk to anyone without any trouble at all. I spend most time with Bellars, Joe and Tayls, and over the years I've also spent time with Sam (Ricketts), Ginge (James Collins) and Gabbs (Danny Gabbidon). The Wolves boys, Wayne, Dave Edwards and Sam (Vokes) all spend time together if they're all in, and then the Cardiff boys like Gunts, Rob Earnshaw, Joe (Ledley), Danny again and Aaron, are also close. Then there's the younger players, like Gareth (Bale), Darcy, Adam (Matthews) and Jack (Collison), and Vaughany (David Vaughan) and Crofty (Andrew Crofts), who are usually inseparable. But even though there are all these groups and alliances, there is no malice between anyone, and all the lads want to be here, which hasn't always been the case with Wales since I began.

It's an exciting time to be involved.

CHAPTER THREE

September 2011

Thursday 1st September

We trained at Cardiff City Stadium today, as we do the day before every game, just to have a session on the pitch we'll be playing on. This happens whether we play home or away, and it gives you a feel of what to expect on game night. We took the coach from the hotel already dressed in our training kit, and were only in the dressing room for a few minutes to put our boots on, before going straight out onto the pitch. These sessions are never too intense because we've done all our work by this stage, so it was just a case of doing some stretches with fitness coach Ryland Morgans and a light jog to warm up. Then we split into units, with Osian taking the defenders, and just worked the ball around, getting a light sweat on and familiarising ourselves with the pitch and conditions. We did some low intensity keep ball and a bit of shooting, before Speedo brought us together for an eleven versus eleven. Again, there was no real intensity, and he stopped it from time to time to reinforce the points he's made this week, showing us how we should deal with certain situations that arise and talking us through what we should be doing.

Once done, it was back on the coach to the hotel, into the pool for a swim and then to our rooms for a shower and change for dinner. Our final meeting of the day was taken by Raymond. Again, he emphasised not only how we should manage the start of the game in the way that Speedo had been on about all week, but also to remember our success in the Australia game when we'd sorted out the issues about falling too deep.

There's definite improvement in this squad now, I've seen it on the training field this week, and there's a real confidence among us all that we're going to finally put it all together and pull out a result tomorrow. It might surprise some people to see me as confident as this but to my mind, all the work Speedo and Raymond have done with us over the past two camps has really paid off.

Friday 2nd September

Wales 2 (Morison 29, Ramsey 50) **Montenegro 1** (Jovetić 71)

We started the game so much better than we did against Australia, and carried out Speedo's plan perfectly, by being more direct at the start and bringing Gareth and Bellars into the game earlier. The perfect start would have been to have got a goal nice and early, but scoring first, when Steve slid in after a well-worked passing move after half an hour or so, was just as good to be honest. It was the best opening to a game that we've had for Wales for a long time, and probably the best ever under Speedo. We'd brought our confidence from training on to the pitch, and that was probably more important than the result, because for all our hard work we'd suffered a high ratio of losses, and it's easy to lose the belief that you can win. That belief was there from the start today, and so was the performance. It probably also helped us that all the experts thought before the game that we would lose, but of course they had no idea of just how detailed and intense Speedo and Raymond had been with us, so they weren't expecting us to be so organised and focused on what we had to do, especially against one of the really emerging sides in Europe who'd already held England at Wembley and beaten Switzerland and Bulgaria in the group.

Mirko Vučinić is a great striker. I have played against him before and know that the Juventus man is a really clever player. He gave us some problems early on and got a couple of shots away. Darcy and I paid closer attention to him and he didn't really get any more joy after that.

Bale nearly got a second for us when he received a throw from Gunts in the right wing position, rolled inside past two of them, then fired in a rocket of a shot from about 35 yards that their goalie did well to tip over as it was moving everywhere. We started to get that good feeling you get when you are high on confidence as a team. It almost got much better a few minutes later when I nearly scored from a corner.

I had a header at the back stick, lobbed their keeper, only for a man to get back on the line and clear it. I was so gutted, as getting two goals clear in an international is really important. Personally I would have loved to have got my second goal for Wales because I know I should score more goals from set pieces than I do.

We had a few more chances before half-time and we were flying. It was easily the best I've felt in any game I've played for Wales. All the boys were on it and it felt like we were playing to the potential that we are supposed to have with the talented players that we possess. The only downside of the half was Vaughany and Bellars getting yellow cards, which means they'll miss the England game at Wembley on Tuesday. Bellars was upset at half-time and told me that he's never had the chance to play at Wembley and that had been taken away from him again tonight by a petty yellow, that I don't think he deserved. I felt gutted for him.

We scored very early on in the second half when I played a cross-field ball to Bale who did great to control it on the run, drive into the box and then cut it back for Rambo who couldn't help but score. We were 2–0 up and flying against a strong Montenegro side. It felt like everything had finally clicked for us.

As the game progressed Bale caused them absolute havoc and nearly got Bellars another goal when he was inches off a tap-in. Sometimes when you miss chances like that, you fear it will come back and haunt you, but not tonight because we were playing too well and with too much confidence to let it slip.

I got handed the armband on 64 minutes as Rambo got a rest and replaced with Crofty. I can never get enough of captaining Wales.

They gave it a go towards the end as you would expect them to, and managed to pull a goal back when Jovetić cut inside Gunts and rifled a shot past Wayne. This gave them some hope and as a result we had some defending to do. We were all involved, as it got quite intense. I was especially locked on and keeping everyone on their toes. I still felt comfortable and confident about what we were doing, and I could tell by the way we were all playing that we weren't going to let it slip. This was summed up with two great blocks by Darce and Crofty late on, with both putting their bodies on the line to get the win. I let them know straight away that those blocks were as good as a goal at the other end. It's important to recognise committed defending like that. Not long afterwards, the ref blew and we'd got the win.

What a relief and it wasn't a one-off. I could tell that we deserved it and now feel we can beat more teams.

Saturday 3rd September

Speedo is very similar to the Gaffer at Swansea in that he recognises that just because we are footballers it doesn't mean that we enjoy being cut off from our families for days at a time. So when we have extended camps, as we've had this week with a double-header which finishes at Wembley against England on Tuesday, he always tries to find a little bit of time for the families. This meant that last night they were allowed to stay over. He also reinforced that family approach today, by inviting all the players' families to a barbecue at the Celtic Manor this lunchtime, because we're not travelling up to London until tomorrow. I think it's details like this that really form a bond between players and managers, and we feel a huge respect and loyalty towards Speedo, which can only be positive towards what he wants us all to achieve in the future for Wales.

Sunday 4th September

Travelled by coach to London this afternoon. When we arrived, we went straight to the swimming pool. Did a recovery session in the pool, and then afterwards we went back to our rooms to freshen up for dinner. Just chilled this evening.

Monday 5th September

We had our first run out in training since the game on Friday night today at Watford's training ground, which is at London Colney and is only separated from Arsenal's training ground by a hedge. The facilities are superb at both grounds and they certainly leave me longing for the day that we get our own facilities at Swansea instead of having to share it with members of the sports club at which we are based. It wasn't the first time I'd been to London Colney, because we trained at Arsenal's training ground prior to the play-off final back in May, the last time I played at Wembley.

Hope that proves to be a good omen.

After training today, it was back to the hotel for another swim, then after food we had a meeting in which our training was analysed and certain things pointed out. This is another important thing that Speedo has brought in. He films training and then if there's anything that he wants to go over later to reinforce in our minds, we'll get to see it. This provides us all with another dimension with which to learn the things that Speedo wants to focus on.

The feeling the win over Montenegro has given us all is a feeling of optimism. In the past a decent win often had us feeling quite relieved more than anything else, and never made us feel that we were about to go on a run of wins as a result of it. Now I've no idea if we are going to beat England tomorrow – I really think we'll perform well there, but the result is anyone's guess to be honest – but after the Montenegro win, we all feel that we are starting out on something special. It's as if, finally, we are moving forward with a considered plan, and improving all the time as a squad. That's what Speedo and Raymond have brought to us. There has been quite a difference in our training since we played England last time. We have identified and then rectified our faults as we have gone along. Implementing this gradual change, rather than trying to change everything at once. It has given us all a belief that the Montenegro win is not another false dawn, but a very important stepping stone in a successful journey. I guess time will tell on that ultimately, but that's how Speedo has got us thinking. In sport, if you've got the belief, then you're already halfway there.

Tuesday 6th September

England 1 (Young 35) Wales 0

If someone had told me five years ago that one day I'd play football against England at Wembley and that my feelings towards playing them would be almost an irrelevance, then I'd have said you were mental. Up until I was about 22, I'd never really considered international football as an option, full stop. Any dreams that I might have had about playing international football would have been for England and nobody else, because being born and bred in the Midlands, England was always the team I supported.

Growing up like any young sports-mad lad at the time, I was England in everything. I was a product of England and when you are a teenager growing up in England, and you are making your way in football and end up getting attached to a club like I was at West Brom, then obviously one of your dreams is to play for your country – England.

The first I heard about Wales's interest in me was 2007 when I had a phone call from my assistant manager at Stockport, Peter Ward. I answered the call and he just said, 'Hi Ash, have you got any Welsh in you?' I just laughed thinking how strange that question sounded before telling him, 'Yes' and explaining about the Welsh background of my grandfather.

Peter explained that Brian Flynn from Wales had been down to Stockport a couple of times to have a look at our keeper, Wayne Hennessey, who was on loan with us at the time from Wolverhampton Wanderers, but had also apparently liked the look of me. As my surname was Williams he put two and two together and thought that I might be Welsh qualified. He was right, of course, but for completely the wrong reason. The name Williams comes from my dad's family whereas I actually qualify for Wales through my mom's father, William

Rowlands, so my surname has nothing to do with my Welsh qualification.

On the phone Peter was quite funny about it. 'You can get a cap here!' he laughed. It was as if he meant I might be lucky to get in through the back door, become a one-cap wonder and at least finish my career being able to say I'd played internationally. In fairness I was just a young footballer playing in League Two at the time so I doubt anyone would have put much money on me having a long international career for any country.

Anyway, Peter got back to the FAW and told them that I 'had some Welsh in me' and it set the wheels in motion. As usual with me, there was a bit of a snag. My grandad had passed away about 18 years previously and nobody in the family had any of his papers, especially not his crucial birth certificate. Even though I'd been up to Manchester to meet Brian Flynn, who was great and told me I had a big future with Wales if I kept progressing at Stockport, the FAW got in touch with me and told me that they hadn't been able to track down my grandfather's birth certificate. Without it my career with Wales would be a nonstarter. My wife got all the details of my grandad from my mom, started researching on the internet, and finally tracked his birth certificate down through the records office. Needless to say, if it wasn't for her hard work I may not have won a single cap for Wales, let alone the 31 I've proudly won to date.

At Wembley today it was completely different to our trip here with Swansea just four months ago. Gone was all the Swansea City art that featured me and Nath and lots of the other lads and, instead, even in our dressing room, everything was England and England colours. There was nothing at all for us whatsoever.

Bellars missed out after his booking against Montenegro and he was absolutely gutted as he'd never played here, but the bigger surprise in terms of selection was that Speedo left Ginge out of the side and stuck with Darcy. I thought that was a brave decision by Speedo because obviously Ginge has been a cornerstone for Wales in recent years, but it's clear that he sees Darcy as a better fit in terms of the way he wants us to play. It's a tough one for me because I'm mates with both and obviously it affects me directly because I play alongside them. I'd be happy playing with either to be honest, but I think that Speedo has shown in picking Darcy that he's not afraid to make tough decisions, and what it also does is remind all of us that none of us are untouchable in this side.

It was incredible walking out tonight at Wembley, but not for a moment did I reflect on any of my younger days when I'd dreamed of walking out there for England. The only thing I was concerned with was soaking up the atmosphere and then getting completely focused on the challenge ahead. It was an incredibly special sensation though, and as the crowd were cranking it up, waiting for the ref to blow his whistle to start, I remember thinking this is why I play.

I had Terry to mark on corners and had an early scare when he nodded wide of the post, but I did enough to put him off. Obviously he is one of the strongest players on attacking set pieces in the Prem, so I knew it was going to be a tough job, and I relished it. I tried to get tight and physical with him all night and he didn't complain once. I got the feeling that he respected that sort of defending!

The plan early on was to allow them to have possession in their own half but then try and close them down when they crossed the halfway line. We were all comfortable with this and I think we did it well, because apart from the odd deep cross we didn't have too much to deal with. In terms of our play tonight, we tried to set our tempo by me hitting diagonals to Bale early. It was something Speedo was insistent that I tried often.

In the first half hour our game plan seemed to be working really well because we had a few decent chances in that period. One fell to me from a corner where I beat Terry, who was now having to mark me, but put it wide. In terms of their attacking threat I felt comfortable at the back and not under any pressure. One thing that did concern me was their left side, where Cole and Young were linking up very well and combining to cause Gunts a few problems, but fortunately, it came to nothing.

Despite Speedo's game plan working well for us, we failed to get into our rhythm as well as we did on Friday against

Montenegro. Maybe we gave England a bit too much respect in that regard, but you have to understand that this was a massive game. For most of us it was the biggest game in our career, so it was to be expected. Saying that, we didn't let ourselves down.

As the half developed Steve Morison became a real handful for Terry and Cahill and became a good outlet for us. Then, around the half hour, Bale came alive and got on the ball lots more. He was unplayable at times and was getting past Cole at will. Predictably, they then started to hack him down but the ref ignored it, so I had words with him about giving Bale some protection.

Just as we were finding our feet and coming out of our shell a bit more, disaster struck, with them taking the lead through Young. Downing got played in by Smalling and because Milner was coming back from an offside position, very wide on their right, our hesitation was enough to allow Downing to get to the byline and pull it back for Young to score. From their point of view it was a good goal, but I couldn't help feeling that we could have done better in that wide area to stop it getting that far. I had a big fear as we got ready for the restart that we'd just go back to the Wales of old, and sink, and end up going down 3–0 or 4–0. That's what happens when you lose confidence in a game at the highest level, so it was vital that we all stayed positive, despite the setback.

Unsurprisingly, they came into it a bit more towards the end of the half, and as I feared, the goal had hit our confidence pretty hard. I was desperate for us to get in for half-time without conceding again. Fortunately, that's exactly what happened.

The atmosphere on the pitch had been quite strange in that first half and I felt we were very tentative and never really took the game to them as a team. Despite that, during the break, and listening to Speedo and Raymond, I still had the feeling that we could do something really special in this game if we just showed more belief. I started to get quite vocal about that after Speedo had finished and said, 'Let's not wait for this lot to do something in the second half. Let's just take it to their front door and see how they like it.' I also said that we could definitely control the game with our possession and, defensively, we'd coped with everything they'd tried and the one thing we should do is raise our pressing a little bit more. The response from the lads was positive, which was great to see. I just felt that in the first half we had played like the away team and, if we were going to get anything from the game, in the second half we needed to play as if we were at home and just take it to them. After some final words from Speedo, we left the dressing room in a far more assertive frame of mind than we'd left it at the start.

As often happens in football, in spite of how positive you are something can quickly go against you. They had the first chance of the half in the first minute when Young got free, but Wayne made a good save. We didn't let it affect us, and after some good play we began to feel our way into the game. I could just feel the confidence in us rise. We were so unlucky soon afterwards, when an unbelievable passing move that ended with Bale in a one-on-one with Hart ended with the lino flagging him offside. I could see clearly from where I was that he wasn't offside. It was so frustrating, because if we were to get anything out of a game like this, we needed all the little things to go for us. We had another chance nearly straight away after I hit a very long diagonal ball, one of my best of the night, over Cole's head and into Bale's path. He then played Rambo in, but Barry managed to get back to put him off. After a pass like that I'm on top of the world, and I could tell that our positive start meant we all were all up for it and there was a definite feeling we could score.

Despite how well we were doing offensively and how little was coming back from them, I kept reminding the boys at the back to keep concentrating. I knew from the way the game was developing, with us beginning to control it, that they would probably look to hit us on the counter. With the pace and quality they had going forward, it was an obvious option for them. I looked around and saw Rooney looking a bit frustrated about the way the half had gone, and was delighted that we'd all managed to keep him so quiet.

With about twenty minutes to go Speedo brought Earnie on for Steve. I thought Steve had a real good game, putting himself about all night and being a real handful for them. Not long afterwards the chance we had worked so hard for all night finally came. We had a free kick and the second ball dropped to Earnie, the one person on our team you would want it to drop to right in front of the goal and with their keeper Hart over on the other side of it. We all started to celebrate, but he fired over. The whole match came down to that moment. I know it's a cliché, but it was one of those slow motion moments for all of us as we realised what had happened. We were playing so well, and they were offering little. I instantly thought it must have hit a bobble, as I couldn't see how Earnie could miss that. No matter how well we had played, or how confident we were, at a moment like that you can't help but think that you'll get no more chances.

Despite not creating anything else as clear cut as Earnie's chance, we managed to carve out another couple of chances, one from Gunts that the ref called back for some unknown reason, and another for Earnie from way out which came to nothing. When the ref blew I was absolutely gutted, just as disappointed as I can ever remember feeling after a Wales game because we had been excellent on the night. We were a team ranked 117th in the world taking on England, who were fourth. After tonight the rankings make no sense to the neutral because – especially in the second half – we outplayed them to such an extent that few people would have complained if we had won. At the very least we deserved a draw.

There was a big dose of mixed feelings in the dressing room after the game because we had been beaten, which was not what we had come here for. But the disappointment was made less because of the way that we'd played, especially in the second half. Understandably, Earnie was distraught in the dressing room, just sitting on the floor with a towel over his head. I really felt for him and, like many of the other lads, had a quick word, but at times like that there's nothing you can say really.

Speedo and Raymond were very upbeat in there and once again looked at the bigger picture by focusing on the performance rather than the result. Speedo told us to be proud of our performance and said it was clear to everyone who saw the game that we deserved a draw. Especially in the second half, where we had outplayed them comfortably and dominated. He also made a point of telling us that when we had played the way that he'd been telling us, passing with pace and intent, they simply hadn't been able to get close to us. Once again, the confidence we all felt leaving a Wales game was massive. It reinforced that we are making definite progress under Speedo and that the future is brighter than it has been for a long time.

Despite the defeat, we were all upbeat on the coach on the way back to the hotel, but then Osian told us there were reports that a Welsh fan had been killed at the game. It appeared that it had involved violence of some sort and instantly the mood on the bus among the players changed. I know there's a perception that players are remote and removed from real life, but we all have families and friends who come to games to support us, and to think that a fan, just like them, had been killed was absolutely shocking to us. I'm sure the circumstances will become clear in the coming days, but nobody should go to a football match and not return home. It was an awful way to end what had been a very positive day on our journey of improvement with Wales.

Wednesday 7th September

After the game last night we went back to the hotel, apart from some of the lads who hadn't been involved, like Joe who went straight home so that they could train with their clubs this morning. For the rest of us, it was back on the coach from London to Celtic Manor this morning and then home. The Gaffer had said he didn't want to see Tayls and me back at Swansea until Thursday morning, so it's just been a case of chilling and relaxing since I've got back home today and spending some quality time with my family. Thinking about the Welsh fan who died, it puts life into perspective and has reinforced to me again something I've fortunately always known, and that's just how important family are.

Thursday 8th September

Tayls and me just did a light session at Llandarcy today. We joined in the first part with the rest of the team, and then went back in for a massage.

Friday 9th September

I started to feel ill today, and have got worse as the day's gone on. Whenever I get run down or start feeling unwell, it goes straight to my throat. It's my weak spot and whenever it happens I know I'm about to struggle. I can't believe it's had to happen now, the day before such a massive game against Arsenal. When I felt the tonsillitis coming on this morning I was gutted because I've had it so many times, and I know what to expect. I'm just hoping I get a mild dose and that I can get a decent night's kip. I've been back up the M4 again for what seems like the tenth time this week, and we're staying in a Spanish hotel, even though we're in London which is a bit weird. Everything around the hotel is written in Spanish and all the workers are Spanish, so it's a little strange to be honest, but it's a nice hotel.

Saturday 10th September

Arsenal 1 (Arshavin 40) Swansea City 0

Woke up this morning after a terrible night's sleep and my throat was awful and seemed to get worse on the coach on the way to the Emirates. I made the decision to play, so I'm not going to use this as an excuse. I knew the adrenalin would start going once we got to the ground, so I wasn't going to let the throat affect me from that point on.

If I needed any help about putting my woes into perspective I got it when we arrived at the ground. The Gaffer had to leave us at the hotel last night because his father had been taken seriously ill again, which wasn't the first time he'd been called to rush home to Northern Ireland to see his dad and, even though we all knew how ill his dad has been, we just all really hoped that there was some positive news for him. Sadly, that wasn't the case, and Pasc told us before the game that the Gaffer's dad had passed away early this morning. As you can imagine, that put a cloud over things, and I just couldn't help feeling for the Gaffer.

When he first arrived at the club, he sat with me on the training field for the best part of an hour, just talking about life in general, but mainly about our families. He was clearly very proud of his and emphasised to me the importance of keeping close to my family and how they have such an important role to play with a footballer, who obviously has so many distractions in his life that can be detrimental to his career. He told me at the time how important his dad had been to him, so it was with great sadness that I recalled that first chat before the game today. But one thing we have to do at times like this is use our mentality to blot out the Gaffer's bad news and focus on the game. It's the heartless side of football really, but it's just the way it's always been and after putting on the black armbands and having a thought for the Gaffer, you don't really think of it again until after the game. Heartless? Yes. Necessary? In top flight football, sadly, yes.

I was really confident about today for a couple of reasons. First, apart from the last thirty minutes at the Etihad, we have performed exceptionally well in all our games so far, and our style of play has been working superbly at this level. We're extremely confident at the back, and in Michel we have found a serious gem of a keeper, who I was certain was going to have another big say in things today. All in all, that meant that the dressing room before the game was extremely confident. The second reason was Arsenal's start to the season. They've had a bit of a shocker to say the least, and we lie above them in the table. They lost their last home game to Liverpool, and got smashed 8–2 at Old Trafford last time out. There was never going to be a better time to play them.

Within ten minutes we made our first positive impact on the game with a chance that fell to Danny. The move started at the back with me, then ended with a decent cross by Kemy and Danny hitting the target. It was great play by Kemy, who really has quality, and from where I was I thought it was a certain goal. I even started to put my arms in the air. This is Danny's fourth league game now, and I was desperate for him to score so that not scoring wasn't an issue for him. We picked up play from that move and started to impose ourselves on them, and that was largely due to Joey pressing so well early on. Danny, in particular, really started to put in a shift. He works so incredibly hard for the team, and his work rate, movement and touch are going to be absolutely crucial to us surviving at this level.

Caulks got a decent bang on the knee, sliding back to clear a goal-bound shot from Walcott and needed a bit of treatment. It was a great clearance and showed what awareness he has for such a young player. He didn't get any sympathy from us though, if you're going to get injured it might as well be worth it, and saving a goal certainly is.

As the half developed and we got more comfortable, I thought it was our three youngsters, Caulks, Joey and Tayls, who really started to stand out, playing with no fear, which was pretty impressive to watch. Playing Arsenal at the Emirates could easily get into a youngster's head, but not those three. They were superb throughout the whole game.

Michel had also been impressive again and just before half-time he confirmed my belief that he would have a big influence on the game – though not in the way that I'd imagined. I actually didn't see it at the time, so couldn't really work out from my scrambled brain how on earth Arsenal had managed to get the ball to score. I was moaning to Tayls, on my favourite topic about him not letting crosses come in, when I just heard something and swung round to see Arshavin scoring from a tight angle. Now he's not the most likeable of fellas, Arshavin, and like the prick he is, he celebrated right in front of our fans, basically taunting them. I felt my rage coming on pretty quick and I just thought, 'If I get a chance of a 50-50 with you, you're gonna know about it.' He really annoyed me.

As confused about the goal as I was at the time, I now know that it was a freak accident, just one of those things that can happen when we play the way the Gaffer wants us to. Michel had just swept up the ball and was just trying to keep our momentum up by quickly rolling the ball out into midfield. Unfortunately his throw just caught the back of Àngel's heel, and the ball bounced straight into the path of the annoying 'Meerkat'. As furious as I was with Arshavin's behaviour, I had no anger towards Michel at all. It really was just one of those things. I had a quick word with him to make sure he hadn't dropped his head, but as soon as I spoke to him I could tell he had enough character to not let it bother him. He quickly apologised for his error, then just got back on with his job. It takes a strong character to react like that. I was extremely impressed with his response.

Half-time came soon afterwards and I think it was only then that we really noticed the Gaffer's absence. Caulks had treatment throughout the break on his knee, but it couldn't have been too bad because he wasn't making a meal out of it. Pasc took over the Gaffer's duties and spoke well. The senior players then got a bit more vocal than usual, as if we all wanted to do our bit in the absence of the Gaffer. We have so many leaders in our team who are willing to stand up and take responsibility, it's really one of our strengths and we showed it today. Michel, despite his error, was also very vocal, which again was pretty impressive. We were all happy with our performance and felt we would definitely get more chances. The one thing I said was that we should continue to impose ourselves on them and the game a bit more, as I'd not seen anything from them that really worried me at all. Despite the disappointment of losing the goal to Michel's mistake I think we actually left that dressing room more confident than we had at the start.

Bearing in mind all the comments in recent years by Wenger about all the terrible tackles his players have had to endure, one of his committed a shocker against Tayls five minutes in, and it was the most unlikely player on the pitch – Theo Walcott. He left his foot in on Tayls as he cleared, and was rightly booked. It was clear that Walcott had been frustrated by Tayls when he'd won the ball – Tayls loves to pull a shirt – but in my view, Walcott really did him as Tayls cleared. As he was treated, you should have seen the mess Walcott's studs had left on Tayls' ankle. When I saw that, I flew over fuming at Theo because I really thought he was out of order. The referee, Mr Atwell, came straight across and said calmly, 'Yes, it was a foul. I've dealt with it, so you can leave it go now, Ashley.' I just said, 'Yeah, but that was a terrible tackle, so sort him out.' A few seasons ago, I'd have probably swung for Theo after a challenge like that because I used to be a proper hothead, but age and experience, not to mention the responsibility of the captaincy, certainly mellows you, so I walked away. I'm just grateful that it wasn't Arshavin who'd done it, because I probably would have swung for him!

Ten minutes later Robin van Persie hit the outside of the post, in what was probably the only chance that Caulks and me allowed him throughout the whole game. We both knew that if we kept him quiet, we'd probably get another nil, because frankly, the way that Arsenal had started the season, we just couldn't see where else they were going to score from. Apart from this shot, we'd snuffed him out completely, and as chuffed as I was for my role in that, I was probably even more pleased for Caulks. For a 19-year-old lad, who'd had a pretty nasty smack on his knee early on, to keep one of the world's hottest strikers so quiet was a fantastic achievement. He used his strength, pace and power every time van Persie was near him, and it was clear from RVP's demeanour and body language that the further the game went, the less happy he became. When he was hooked, I just shouted across to Caulks, 'Well done' and he smiled. It's not every day a teenager gets one of the world's greatest strikers taken off.

We finally got the chance we had worked so hard for, right at the end, when a header I got from a corner fell to Dan in the six-yard box. It was an awkward height for him, but he knows there's no excuses, and realises he should have scored. As it was, he hooked it over the bar. It's amazing how much can go through your mind in a split second like that. Your body is completely full of adrenalin, you know there's only moments left, you see the ball, win the header, see it drop to your striker and have massive expectation that he's going to score and deliver you a point. Then, in the blink of an eye, he misses, your expectation levels drop like a stone and an instant depression hits you. You feel like screaming, but then you get hit by a wave of compassion for Danny, who was distraught. Your body experiences all those emotions in about half a second. As gutted as I was, I really felt for Danny. Instead of any anger, I just went straight to him, grabbed his head and said, 'Keep going mate. Don't worry, it will come.' Understandably, he said nothing.

In the dressing room afterwards, initially there was disappointment, but then Pasc came in and said that he was really happy with us and said that we had done ourselves proud, especially as the Gaffer wasn't there, which was difficult. The boys all came around pretty quickly. There's always a bigger picture, and if we'd have come here today and stunk the place up, but hung on to lose 1–0, we would have been gutted. Yet we outplayed Arsenal for large periods today, very much at their own game, and it was only a bizarre mistake that stopped us leaving with a point. By the time we were leaving, the boys were bubbling, because once again we've proved to ourselves that we can perform in this league and, having done so at possibly one the hardest places to go and play, we have absolutely no reason to fear anyone at any venue now.

Played 4 Won 0 Drawn 2 Lost 2 Points 2 League Position – 17th
(38 more points needed for 40)

Tuesday 13th September

After a couple of days back in Birmingham, where thankfully my throat returned to normal, I travelled back down to Swansea last night, ready for training this morning. When I got in I found out that Caulks' injury is pretty serious. It's such bad timing because I thought he had an excellent game on Saturday, probably his best of the season so far, and what makes it more impressive now is knowing that he played that well with an injury for the bulk of the game.

Wednesday 14th September

The bad news on the injury front continued today when we found out that Kemy had come off on Saturday with quite a bad hamstring injury. You can never tell with hamstrings how long they are going to be, but with a bad one it's going to be a while. We are going to miss his physical presence.

Thursday 15th September

Because of his injury, we were told today that Caulks has gone back for treatment at Spurs. It is normal for a loan player to go back to a parent club to receive treatment, but because of the seriousness of it, none of us have a clue when we'll see him back here again.

The Gaffer was back in today after time off for his dad's funeral. To be honest, not much was said by him or any of us about the situation as we had all sent him texts offering our condolences since Saturday, so he just seemed to want to pick things straight back up and get on with it, which is what we all did too.

Friday 16th September

Today's training was a typical Friday morning session. We had a warm-up followed by boxes – where two people have a circle of players around them and have to chase the ball and intercept it, while the others are just trying to do quick, one-touch passes. All the boys love boxes. It's one of the best things you can do in training banterwise. It gets everyone lively and there's always lots of laughs and plenty of stick flying around. It's definitely the lads' favourite day of the week when we do them. This morning, Gows and Joe were chasing and Joe, being Joe, got quickly frustrated. Then, in the space of about a minute and a half, he was nutmegged four times. It was hysterical. The more we were laughing, the angrier he was getting and when it happened the fourth time, I think we were all going to burst from laughter and Joe was going to burst from anger. Someone even kneed the ball away from him while all this was going on and Joe then smashed into the next player, nearly taking him out. And of course, the angrier Joe was getting the louder everyone else was getting and doing even more stupid things like sitting and standing on the ball, even doing a headstand on it. There are plenty of repetitive days of training when you're a sportsman, so that's why all the lads love boxes so much. As usual, boxes lasted quite a while and then we went into a game where the starting XI for West Brom were taken through some specifics by the Gaffer. After we were done, the rest of the squad finished with some six- and seven-a-sides.

Saturday 17th September

Swansea City 3 (Sinclair Pen 14, Lita 24, Dyer 49)
West Bromwich Albion 0

Everyone in our club has been aware of the personal tragedy of the Gaffer and the loss of his father. Sometimes, you just realise that there is nothing more important than your family. Obviously it was seriously affecting the Gaffer, but before, during and after the game today, I don't think I've ever seen him more professional in the way that he has approached his job. I think he wanted to make sure that any of the solemn feelings that he must be experiencing were not going to be transferred on to us. He is such a strong character that, speaking personally, all I wanted to do today was win the game for him and his family. If that wasn't enough motivation, there was also the other story that has gripped the world this week, the awful plight of the Gleision miners. It's hard to comprehend that men who just went to work did not return to their families. I can only guess what suffering they are going through at the moment and my thoughts and sincere condolences go out to them.

The match today began with a minute's silence and, as footballers, we do get used to dealing with these from time to time. Today, with the silence being for someone so close to our football family at the club, Brendan's dad, and also so close to the larger Swansea family for the miners, I have to say that it was a very powerful minute that we experienced, and I made sure I focused my thoughts on my own family throughout it.

We started the way exactly as Monks had asked us to in the huddle. He drummed into us that we must start aggressively and, for the first ten minutes, West Brom hardly had a touch. Most of that dominance was due to the aggressive way that we approached that early period.

They played into our hands a little bit too, and it was clear from the start what Roy Hodgson had in mind – containment.

Odemwingie and Long didn't get involved in trying to close Monks and I down, meaning that when either of us had the ball, they allowed us to advance with it higher up the field, and then pick a pass into midfield. For the fan, this can often make for a more boring game, but today, because we carried the aggression that Monks had asked for, that was never the case.

When we play the way we do and a team like West Brom come to contain us, what we really need is an early goal. A problem for us is when we get all of the ball and no goal follows. We then often become anxious and they gain in confidence because their plan of frustrating us is working. It's a disaster when they score early, because they've got what they've come for and can make our lives a bit of a misery by just closing us out of the game. Thankfully, there was none of that today, largely thanks to a ridiculous challenge by Paul Scharner.

Joe was going nowhere in the box and was actually heading away from goal into their right back area but, next thing, Scharner just slid in and took him out. It was an awful penalty to give away. In truth, I couldn't have cared less because Scott dispatched the penalty and became the scorer of Swansea City's first ever Premier League goal. I couldn't have been more pleased that it was Scott. For such a confident looking lad, Scott needs a boost now and again, and this accolade is just the type of thing he'll thrive on now.

After about twenty minutes there was a great example of the organisation the Gaffer has brought to our play and also the discipline the lads in our team show in understanding their responsibilities and carrying them out. Basically, Tayls was drawn inside and, as he was, Odemwingie saw the space behind him and ran into it. I had no option but to go with him and cover his run. Because they had the ball and had a short spell with it, Tayls realised that he now had his defensive duties to take care of, but because I was in his left back position, I'd left a hole in central defence. There was no time for me and him to swap, so Tayls dropped into my space and covered until the ball eventually found its way to me and I cleared. The way the Gaffer gets us playing in training is that everybody is not only comfortable on the ball, but also comfortable playing most positions. Not all teams have players as alert and willing to work as we are. If Tayls wasn't that sort of player and had just ambled back or couldn't have been bothered to fill the hole, then I'd have had to have left Odemwingie and they'd have had a free unmarked player up front. That's when teams concede sloppy goals.

A few minutes later our solid defensive play was rewarded with our second goal, which really took the game away from them. It came from a corner and was one of those fantastic moments when a training ground move comes off. The plan was to drive the ball towards Scotty at the nearside of the area, and for him to head it goalwards towards the far post, where Leets would be waiting to nod it in. And that's exactly what happened. The move sounds and looks simple enough, but what you probably won't have noticed as a fan was Monks involvement in it, which was a key instruction from the Gaffer. Before the ball was even kicked, Monks knew that to allow Scotty the header on to Leets he had to block off Scotty's man. Every move you see on the field will have dummy runners and blockers, who do their job so subtly, that nobody apart from us knows what's going on. It's a game within a game, and some of the instructions the Gaffer gives us resemble plays in American Football.

I love a celebration but Leets is one of the few people who gets more excited than me when they score. He's been doing the same celebration for years, where he sprints at full pace and takes his top off. He gets beyond excited. He took the inevitable yellow when the ref caught up with him.

Usually I get quite annoyed when the lads pick up unnecessary yellows during a game, because in the case of midfielders or defenders it can really cause us a problem if later on a tackle is mistimed, or maybe a freak handball occurs, and we're down to ten men. But I don't get so uptight about strikers getting one because they don't tackle anyway! I've always thought being booked for celebrating is just a stupid, pointless rule.

At half-time the Gaffer told us not to get complacent but to push on and get more goals. He'd mentioned the negative goals deficit that we had before the game, and we knew we had a chance to deal with that being two up. Apart from one or two specific things about the lads in midfield screening and rotating, his message was just to do exactly what we did in the first half and we would win the game. He could see no other possible outcome. As we left the room, he reminded us that the first ten minutes of the second half were going to be crucial.

Who says we haven't got a Plan B? Early in the half, Michel hit a rare long ball, which was flicked on by Leets, who showed great athleticism in winning it, then Nath ran in on it and finished really well. He didn't dare do a Leets celebration as people would have laughed at his puny body, so instead he ran and jumped on me.

It was a great feeling as the game was restarted with us 3–0 up, because for the first time since the start of the season we felt like we were in complete control of the game. As you'd expect, they threw caution to the wind after that and put us under a little pressure from a couple of corners. Apart from an offside 'goal' from Brunt, the only real scare came from a free kick thirty yards out, which was heading for the top corner when Michel flew across to keep it out. He's pulled off 'worldies' in every game now and, for me, it makes my job easier knowing I've got someone so strong behind me.

From then on we really shut the game out and while we didn't run away with it goalwise, we were doing a really professional job on them. There was one horrible moment, which came as a direct result of the excellent commitment that we had brought to our defending. They threw a deep cross to the back post which Odemwingie was sprinting onto, but Tayls threw himself in for a great defending header only to be cleaned out by Odemwingie after the ball was gone. I was absolutely fuming when it happened because it looked like Tayls was knocked out cold, but I could tell from Odemwingie's reaction that he didn't mean it and was just going for the ball.

The header was typical of Tayls as he's one of the bravest players I've ever played with, but he certainly paid for that today. I knew he was struggling straight away and started to worry, especially when they put him on oxygen and the spine board.

It's your worst nightmare to see your mate being treated that seriously on the pitch. He had a massive gash in his head with blood spurting out and I'd never seen a head injury like it before. It was really worrying. But as with all these things, as a pro you are taught to push negatives like that out of your mind and accept that the medical people will do what they need to do. So I just used the break to get my head right and stay composed and then, along with Monks, got around the team to make sure they did the same and concentrated on the last fifteen minutes. We'd be doing Tayls no favours by letting a three-goal lead slip because we were all worrying about him. As they were getting ready to lift Tayls and take him off, there was a nice touch by Odemwingie when he came back on to apologise to Tayls and explained to me that he didn't mean it and was just going for the ball. From what I'd seen, I believed him and it was good of him to come back over and speak to Tayls.

The only compensation of Tayls leaving the field was that one of my best mates, Fede (Bessone), came on for his Premier League debut. As he took up his position next to me, I said to him, 'Come on Fed, see us through,' and right after the game I went over to him and said, 'Congrats, mate, you can now say you have played in the greatest league in the world.' Even though the circumstances were not what he would have wished for, it was still a really great moment for him and I wanted to recognise that.

The dressing room was bouncing afterwards, such was the dominance and style of our victory, and for the first time this season we were able to let down our hair and enjoy such a fantastic moment. There's no better feeling in football than a happy dressing room following a comprehensive win. It's why we all play. But I think the happiest two in there were definitely the two pensioners, Monks and Gows. They'd both come back into the team today, Monks for Caulks and Gows for Kemy. Gows was just walking round saying, 'Why is everyone surprised about the win? We were obviously gonna get it with me and Monks back in the side. It's called experience, fellas!' I was really pleased that the pair of them played such an important part in our win and it will now stop all the people who doubted them from piping up.

So today was our first win, which felt fantastic, but above anything else, as we left the dressing room to go and meet our families, the lads were thinking about the Gaffer and his family, and also the families of Charles Breslin, David Powell, Garry Jenkins and Philip Hill, the Gleision miners. I know that nothing can ever compensate the families for their tragic loss, but having spoken to the lads about it in the dressing room following the game, we were all in agreement that after such an historic moment for both us and Swansea City Football Club, our first ever win in the Premier League, we would respectfully all like to dedicate the win to them.

Played 5 Won 1 Drawn 2 Lost 2 Points 5 League Position – 12th
(35 more points needed for 40)

Sunday 18th September

Just spent the day chilling at home today. A nice relaxing one for a change and didn't really get up to much. We normally like to travel home to Birmingham to see our family but some days that seems too much and I just appreciate the rest.

Monday 19th September

Another day off, but I had an offer from Pizza Express to take ten children to their restaurant in Swansea to host a pizza party for them. We started our charity WillsWorld in December 2010 because I wanted to make a difference to some children's lives at Christmas. We decided to buy a whole bunch of toys and brought 23 children down to the Liberty Stadium where we had arranged a Santa to present them with their gifts. It was a very humbling experience to realise that the presents we gave to them might have been the only gifts they would have received that Christmas. I would like to do more with the charity, but at the moment it's just me and my wife dealing with it and I feel there are not enough hours in the day to get everything done.

Wednesday 21st September

Training session this morning, then a busy afternoon on the phone arranging all the details for the pizza party. I confirmed with AG Swansea, a local charity, that the Swansea Bay Asylum Seekers group had ten children that could come. These kids have a tough life, and could do with an afternoon of fun to remember that they are just children.

Thursday 22nd September

After training this morning, I rushed to get ready as Barclays Premier TV World were covering the pizza event and I needed to meet them straight after training. They filmed myself and my family, interviewing about me about the charity as they like to cover what footballers get up to off the field. They filmed us in the car travelling to the restaurant, and it felt like we were on a reality TV show. I had to watch what I was saying as I was miked up!

The afternoon was a great success with all the kids having lots of fun. They got to make their own pizzas from scratch, with the ingredients of their choice, and got to see behind the scenes of a working restaurant. Obviously my pizza was the best, and the chefs there were nervous about losing their jobs. All in all, a great day.

Friday 23rd September

Normal Friday morning training today, short and sharp with lots of intensity and, as usual, always a fun day for the lads as we start to get our heads ready for tomorrow. We travelled by train to London, which is a lot easier than sitting in traffic on the coach, because you can get up and walk around. It is a much more enjoyable trip for us all. There was plenty of the usual away days banter with the team, tweeting pics of anyone who dares to go to sleep, that type of thing.

Saturday 24th September

Chelsea 4 (Torres 29, Ramires 36, 76, Drogba 90 + 4)

Swansea City 1 (Williams 86)

We learnt a lesson today. It was a very important one and one that we can't afford to repeat again this season because it will cost us.

Now, in a 4–1 defeat you'd expect me to say that the lesson was about how we were outplayed and outclassed by a better team. No, that's not what I'm referring to. Chelsea were good, and clearly deserved their win, but what I'm getting at is our mentality. Despite what Monks had told us in the huddle – as usual he was aggressive and told us not to think about them and their reputations for one minute – we gave them too much respect, which made the game too easy for them.

I can't actually point to any specific players and say they were off it but we didn't start positively enough and played too deep to get a result here today. We need to make sure we start games against the top teams on the front foot, like we did against Arsenal.

Lampard and Drogba were both left out, which was great because they are such fantastic players and, as much as I rate Torres, he didn't threaten Monks and me too much, even though at times he did show that he has his pace and power when he needs it. Looking back, we had a lot of early possession but we never made it count.

Even allowing for that we still had a couple of chances to score from the set plays we had in the first half, and I really thought we should have done better with them. In the first half alone I think I must have had three decent chances, and that was largely due to the way that Ivanović was marking me. It was really strange. Whenever I was in position waiting for the ball to come in he was physical, and getting in the way of me and being the nuisance I'd expect him to be. But the split second that the ball was delivered, it was if he'd switch off. It happened every time I went up and, each time, that split second was enough for me to get ahead of him and get something on the ball. After the third of these today, which again came to nothing, I said to Monks on the way back, 'I'm gonna score today. He's letting me get a yard on him every time I get in the box.' Happily, I was proved correct but, unhappily, it wasn't to count for much.

I was also right about Torres showing his power too, although, the way he demonstrated it on Gows saw him leaving for an early bath. Whatever way you look at it, it was a pretty stupid challenge. Gows was going nowhere, near the halfway line, and Torres flew in. To be fair to him, there wasn't a hell of a lot of contact, which was the basic complaint from Torres and co. but, speaking to Gows about it, he said he was definitely caught, and he'd have told me if he hadn't been. So that was the end of Torres, but to be fair to him, he'd already notched one in Chelsea's two-goal lead, with a goal that was slightly disappointing from a defensive view. Initially, Monks had been drawn out to try and win the ball, leaving a hole. Àngel had come across to look after Torres, and had to make the decision to run with him or play him off. He decided to go with him, which is fair enough because he only had a split second to make that call, but Mata's ball into Torres was so precise it was really hard for him. What would disappoint Àngel though, was that he probably feels he could have done more to block the shot after Torres swivelled to shoot, with the ball going underneath Àngel's foot. It was really disappointing to be a goal down so early, especially as we could have defended it better.

About five minutes later it was two and, again, we could have defended a lot better. In fairness though, it was a pretty decent move by them. Cole managed to play a one-two around Àngel, and get away from him, leaving me and Tayls in a 3 v 2 situation, so we both tried to look after the nearest two players and leave the furthest, which is the basic rule if you are outnumbered. I had to go to Cole and Tayls had to go Anelka, which left Ramires free and Cole played him in. He finished well. Two-nil down in just over half an hour was not what we wanted, and if you compared how well we played in the first halves against Man City and Arsenal, then it wouldn't take a footballing genius to work out that we underperformed today in comparison.

At half-time the Gaffer made a change, sacrificing Leon. As we now had a man advantage for forty-five minutes he wanted us to be more attacking, so on came Wayne. The Gaffer told us that we'd really have to give it a go in the first ten minutes, and if we could nick an early goal, we'd be right back in the game as it was unlikely that they'd be very offensive while down to ten and with a two-goal lead. He also said that we needed to move the ball quicker and keep switching it side to side to keep them moving. He told us he knew if we did that, there would be a point where they'd get lazy and stop doing the work, and that would allow us to exploit the gaps.

We had a great start to the second half, but despite having plenty of ball, we weren't really getting the chances that we should have been getting. This is something the fans can get frustrated with. Once your opponents go down to ten men, most people think it's going to be a matter of time before that space is found and the goal will come, but it's not as easy as that if the side has been well organised. In the Nottingham Forest play-off game, when Tayls was sent off after two minutes, the Gaffer left Fabio Borini up top on his own, which meant that they still had to have two defenders and a keeper in their half looking after him. But in our half we had nine men against their eight. That night at half-time the Gaffer convinced us that we had the advantage and the fact that we kept them out for eighty-eight minutes proved him right. As we struggled to break Chelsea down today, I did cast my mind back to that Forest game and realised the half was going to be tough if Chelsea organised themselves properly as we had done. It's no surprise to report that they did.

They also hadn't given up offensively either, and on the hour Anelka really stung our bar. He picked it up deep and we didn't do a good enough job of closing him down, especially with the numbers we had around him, so he carried on with his run. As I went to meet him, quite a way out, he shaped to make the shot, and to be honest I was happy enough for him to shoot from that distance as I didn't think for a second that he could beat Michel from there. But it was such a great strike that when it smacked back out of the bar, I knew we'd been let off the hook.

About ten minutes after that, Anelka picked the ball up again in a similar area and began another run, but this time Monks wasn't going to wait to see if he'd test our crossbar again and brought him down with a good tactical foul. It may be an unpalatable truth for those who believe in the beautiful game, but good defenders are key to the fabric of football, and that's exactly what Monks is, and sometimes – like it or not – good defending involves a foul.

A minute after Monks' free kick, they scored a goal which I know I could have done better with. I had a 50-50 with Ramires and I tried to nick the ball, but he got there first. I could have just blocked him and taken a booking or just gone in with a strong tackle, and I would have won the ball. Whatever way I look at it, the fact is I was involved in a goal that I could have stopped, and that is hard to take. As was the scoreline. At 2–0 we still had enough time left to get one and then really give it a go. But at 3–0, I knew it was over.

Still, just as I thought it couldn't get any worse they brought on Drogba. I'd always wanted to play against him, but at 3–0 down, with me having just given away the last goal, it was probably not the moment I'd have chosen. One thing that did surprise me about him though, was his size. When he came over to stand by me, he was much bigger than I thought he would be, and he looked as fresh as a daisy while I was starting to blow a bit. Not a great combination.

Still, as unpredictable as football often is, within about five minutes of Drogba standing next to me after coming on, one of us scored. And it wasn't him. I got free from Ivanović again from a corner, and finished well with a header past Čech. Maybe I should explain my reaction to the goal because I've had plenty of stick on Twitter tonight for celebrating when we'd lost the game. Basically, at the very moment I scored my first ever goal in the Premier League, at Stamford Bridge, I spun round and the first people I saw were my family, jumping up and down celebrating. So when you saw me turning away, pointing, I was pointing at them. I do understand why some people would moan at my joyful reaction, but speaking from experience I can tell you that if you scored your first Prem goal at Stamford Bridge, you'd celebrate too. I'm human, and I intend to embrace every minute of my time in the Premier League, even the bad ones. But when a good moment comes along, I'm going to make the most of that too.

My wife told me later that our baby son, as usual, had fallen asleep, and when that happens, she's always ready to put her hands over his ears when we get a corner or free kick so that if someone scores, he's not frightened by the roar. Anyway, she said that even when I went up for the corner, she thought we had no chance of scoring so didn't bother to cover his ears. Not only was there a goal, and a roar, but I caused it and woke him up too! What bad parents we are!

Still, despite that personal moment of achievement, Chelsea, or more accurately Drogba, had the last word. Àngel was caught upfield, meaning Monks had to go across and cover. By now, Monks was blowing due to his lack of games, which was understandable, and I was really annoyed with Àngel because he should have dropped as soon as he could see the ball going over his head. When he didn't, I was more frustrated by the fact that he didn't help Monks when we all knew at that point that he was struggling. To top it off, Àngel then put his hands out as if to blame Monks for the goal. I lost my rag with him then and told him not to blame anyone else because he could have stopped that.

Unsurprisingly, the atmosphere was down when we got off the pitch, and we all sensed a bit of a lost opportunity, especially after Torres' moment of madness. But we learnt a lot, especially about how to manage a game. Chelsea were excellent at that, and showed that they not only kept us out, but actually prospered despite having a man less and being under pressure. The Gaffer didn't have a go at us, he just told us that we'd done well in the second half, and Drogba's late goal had flattered them. He said we hadn't done enough to win, but that we didn't deserve to lose 4–1 either. He also said that defeat at Chelsea away wouldn't define our season, but the home game against Stoke next Saturday might, so we needed to forget about today, and start to think about that game.

Played 6 Won 1 Drawn 2 Lost 3 Points 5 League Position – 16th (35 more points needed for 40)

Sunday 25th September

The Gaffer gave us the day off today, so we travelled back to Birmingham after the game yesterday. I have a lot of young children in my family so we try to get back to see them as much as possible, because if you don't see them for a couple of weeks they seem to have completely changed and you miss so much. It's hectic when we go home trying to get to see everyone as we have so many family and friends, and a lot of them don't get the opportunity to come down to Swansea that much. We also try to go shopping when we are home, because they have better stores up here, so we'll be hitting them tomorrow!

Tuesday 27th September

It's my mom's birthday today, so we spent the evening with her yesterday before we travelled home last night to be in for training this morning. Being an only child it's difficult that I don't get to see her on her birthday.

Wednesday 28th September

Another story broke in the press today about footballers being bad role models. It pisses me off that the press focuses on a handful of individuals and says we are all the same, when there are around 2,000 players in over 90 teams in the professional leagues who never do anything wrong. If someone makes a mistake, it is nothing to do with his bloody career. Idiots!

Thursday 29th September

Scott was showing off before training today, saying he had a pair of Ugg boots. Wayne, who is totally against men wearing Uggs, threatened that if he ever wore them in, he would burn them. He wouldn't actually do it, it's just part of the everyday banter we have.

Friday 30th September

Training today was the usual Thursday session. As the game is on Sunday this week everything gets pushed back a day, as we try to keep to the same routine. Afterwards it was the normal media session, then across to Vesuvios for our team lunch.

October 2011

Saturday 1st October

Well, if ever there's a game that will tell us how we're going to fare in this division it's tomorrow. Stoke City. Now I've got no problem whatsoever with how Stoke City play. They've had success in the Prem for a few seasons now, getting among people and ruffling the feathers of the likes of Arsenal over the years. If Tony Pulis signed me tomorrow and told me to play the way they do – basically, get it forward at every opportunity from the back – then I'd have absolutely no problem doing it. I actually don't like the way people point at what we are trying to do and say that we are some sort of football purists and that Stoke should be laughed at. They've found a way to play at this level and not just survive but prosper, and they should be respected for that. But having said that, their approach is a million miles away from what we are trying to achieve at Swansea and, listening to the critics this week, this is the game in which they have said we will be found out. All week I've read how we will be overpowered all around the park and how we won't be up for the challenge and buckle under it.

Wrong. That simply isn't going to happen.

Sunday 2nd October

Swansea City 2 (Sinclair Pen 9, Graham 85) Stoke City 0

Every one knows what a threat Stoke can be from set plays, so the Gaffer's plan today was simple, don't give them any. One of his main messages was to play more centrally than we usually do and keep the ball in play as much as possible. He said if we could limit the number of throws, corners and free kicks that we gave them, then that would negate most of the opportunities they would have to threaten us. Apart from that basic plan, the Gaffer's message was clear, we were just going to carry on and do our thing, and not get dragged into the battle that they would want us to. The last message the Gaffer had for us was to take personal responsibility, to show that we had balls and that we could stand up to that physical kind of game. I hadn't left a dressing room so determined this season as I did today.

We were helped by the perfect early start when we took the lead with a Scott penalty which was absolutely perfect for our game plan. We knew that they weren't going to come and try and beat us 3–0, because what they're all about is keeping it tight for as long as possible, maybe nicking a goal from a set piece, and then frustrating us. The one thing that we knew would ruin that game plan was an early goal from us, and that's exactly what we delivered. Wayne was fouled by Shawcross, drawing a similar tackle like Scharner's against West Brom, after an excellent driving run from Joe. Scott's penalty gave us something to protect for the rest of the game and build upon. That was a nice feeling to have with just ten minutes gone.

Despite our early lead, Crouch and Walters were still keeping Monks and me busy in the early stages, and to be fair that was exactly what I expected from Walters as he's someone who gives it his all and puts in a decent shift for his team, same as he did when he was at Ipswich. Regarding Crouch, what we did really well as a team today was to stop the quality balls being played into him, especially crosses. Because we managed to do that it really neutralised him as a threat.

After about quarter of an hour the ref pinged me for a free kick on the edge of the box for a foul on Shawcross. Apart from the fact that I got a toe to the ball and it clearly changed direction, it was a good decision! What didn't really help me was Shawcross going down like a striker. I couldn't believe it. I stood over him and had a few strong words for him, but he'd done his job and that was that. From then it was just a case of defending the free kick.

Nothing came of the free kick but about five minutes later

we had one of our own which showed their frustration. Gows misplaced a pass to me along the halfway line, which meant that I had to slide in to beat Walters to it, but just got the ball away to Wayne, who quickly moved it on to Joe. As he did, Whelan came in and stamped on Wayne's ankle. I was boiling with this one. It was clear that he'd left his foot in and it looked like he just did Wayne. As angry as I was, I was also strangely pleased as I knew that his tackle was purely frustration because they couldn't keep the ball, whereas we could. They were seeing so little of it, which became pretty much the story of the half.

About ten minutes before half-time I had a bit of a moment in the box that Walters got excited about. It was something or nothing really, just a messy challenge that neither of us had control of and we both went down, but he got up waving his arms looking for a penalty. It wasn't a foul either way, but I did laugh on *Match of the Day* tonight when Tony Pulis had a pop at me and said that he didn't know what game I'd been watching because I'd rugby tackled Walters. Well, Wilkinson nearly broke Nath's back with possibly the highest tackle I've ever seen when he had both his legs up around Nath's waist, yet he didn't say anything about that.

Funny that.

At half-time, the feeling among us was not to get ahead of ourselves because with their set plays, 1–0 was still a very anxious scoreline. But I told the boys that if we just defended properly, and continued to stop the ball from coming to Crouch, I couldn't see them scoring. The Gaffer was happy enough but said we needed another goal and that we should have dictated the speed of the game a bit better by keeping the ball for longer periods. But all in all, we were extremely calm about the state of things, and I don't think any of us were overly concerned that they were going to threaten us much during the second half, but we all knew that a second goal was crucial. If we got it, it was definitely game over.

Despite a stupid foul I gave away that was never a foul in a million years against Crouch, we started the second half positively and had an early corner. Shawcross was marking me and Walters was picking up Monks, when the usual pushing and shoving began before the ball was even kicked. The ref got a bit stroppy and called us all together and gave us a talking to. As he did, Monks said, 'All right, calm down!' and Walters just burst out laughing. It was one of those nice moments in the heat of battle that reminds us that we're all human, even though the stakes are incredibly high for us.

On the hour there were handbags on the edge of our box which, inexplicably, Tayls ended up getting booked for. Basically, Jerome decided to throw himself down when he made contact with me. It was never a foul. How strikers get decisions like that I'll never know. Then Whelan came from nowhere and decided to barge into me. For a split second I considered dropping to the floor as Jerome had done, but didn't want to be associated with what he'd been up to and thought better of it, so I just went back to my position. They hit the post from it, and I'd have gone nuts if they'd scored, but it showed how vulnerable any team is to a one-goal lead.

Over the next ten minutes or so they were getting right back in it. Monks though, with one piece of defending where he just stepped up to play Jerome offside, demonstrated such a fantastic piece of skill, as important as any ball played in to a striker to score. He's got such awareness and vision. A couple of minutes later I pulled off a block I will be happy with for a while, after a long ball was played in to Crouch who flicked on to Walters. Just as he was shaping up to shoot I flew in with a block that hit me in the stomach. Predictably, Walters went up for a handball – it was nowhere near – but I have to say that it was the best defensive moment of the season for me. I really love a block!

After that, it seemed like it was all us and the only question was whether we would get the second to finish them off. We did, and it was a landmark goal that all the lads were chuffed to bits about – Danny's first goal since joining. What I loved most about the goal was that it wasn't an instinctive finish, but one that he had to run in, which meant he had plenty of time to think about it. Most people have been questioning him for this reason and that, but to score with such a cool finish under such pressure showed what we all have known for a long while, Danny's going to do really well at this level and score his share.

There was one little heart-in-the-mouth moment left for me with a minute to go when, after a long throw from the left, I got a half header in that went to the edge of the box to Whitehead. I managed to get there to win the ball, but as I got a foot to it my momentum meant that I clattered him. I knew it was inside the box and I must admit for a moment I feared the worst, but when I looked up I was relieved to see the ref wave play on. I knew it was never a foul, but I've seen plenty of these 'momentum' fouls given – which really winds me up. It's as if the law makers are trying to make the game perfect. Before long, if there's any contact at all made with a player, every tackle will be a foul – whether you win the ball or not, it really makes me angry. Nobody is more against foul play and looking to 'do' someone like in the bad old days than me, but we must never lose the art of defending or tackling. If my skill as a defender sees me nip in front of you to win a ball, but my momentum knocks you off your feet, that should never be a foul. I really feel that if we carry on refereeing games like this, we will soon see football as a non-contact sport. Credit to the ref, he made the right call today, but I know of plenty of others who would have pointed to the spot.

After the final whistle, my first emotions were that it was one of the most enjoyable wins I've had in a very long time and one we deserved completely. In fairness to them, they didn't moan about anything and just shook our hands and said well done. Afterwards, we all felt like 'the passing game' won today and the victory was a complete vindication of the way the Gaffer wants us to play. We've had some great performances and some decent wins now, but what was important today was that our style worked against the 'hardest' team in the division, when many thought we'd be crushed.

It may only be seven games gone, but we've got to tenth place now. What price would we have been for that at the start of the season, and what price for us finishing here? I have no idea. But

I'll tell you something for nothing, there's nothing myself, the lads or the Gaffer fear in this division after today, so why not tenth?

Played 7 Won 2 Drawn 2 Lost 3 Points 8 League Position – 10th
(32 more points needed for 40)

Monday 3rd October

I came up to Cardiff straight after the Stoke game yesterday to hook up with Wales to start our prep for the Switzerland game at the Liberty on Friday, and following on from the recent upturn in performances, the camp has already got a confidence about it that I haven't really experienced before. There's already a feeling that we'll win on Friday, and that's not based on arrogance, but based on complete confidence in the way that Speedo, Raymond and Osian are preparing us.

Tuesday 4th October

It was the FAW awards tonight, which on the whole is a straightforward dinner, the highlight of which is collecting your cap for the year. Most people think that you get a cap every time you play, but you don't. I'm not certain about other countries but we get one for the year. It's a good night to celebrate all the people that do great work for Welsh football, but it's safe to say by the end of the night all the lads are ready to get back to the hotel, as it can sometimes be drawn out and run on a bit. Anyway, I was glad to win another cap and to win the Welsh Player of the Year which is awarded to the player of the year between the Welsh teams.

Thursday 6th October

Back to Swansea today to train at the Liberty. I love when we play here for obvious reasons and, as I'm quite a senior member of the squad now, I feel quite proud turning up at the ground with the other lads, as if I'm welcoming them to my place. We had our usual light run out with Osian, concentrating on our defensive group, but instead of going straight back up to Cardiff we had a shower at the Liberty and then Adrian Davies took us to a place he knew in Llanelli for a meal before heading back to the hotel.

An interesting character is Adrian. He's a mate of Speedo's and he was asked to get involved because Speedo basically told him, 'I've got twenty lads here and you'd be happy for your daughter to marry any one of them, and while they're as determined and committed as anyone on the pitch, off it they are all really quiet.' When Adrian told me that I did laugh but, to be fair, Speedo was spot on. None of the lads are big, loud characters, which sometimes means there isn't the energy around the place that you often need. Adrian said that Speedo had asked him to get involved for that very reason and just to inject some fun around the place during the downtime in the camps and for us all basically to chill out and have a laugh more and liven things up a bit. Adrian is perfect for the role, and what he's actually ended up doing is a type of player liaison role where he helps out with any issues or problems that the players have, but also has a good laugh and a joke with us too. Quite quickly he's become a really popular personality among the lads, always having a laugh and winding us up. He's a former Wales squash international and he's quite simply one of the funniest guys I've ever met. He always plans and puts on events with us, like fun quizzes and games and stuff, and he's also invented 'Show Off', where a player is chosen after dinner to stand on a chair and basically brag about their achievements away from football. If we like what the player concerned is telling us then we laugh and clap and their torture ends. But if it's poor, we all shut up, stare at them and let their ordeal continue. We've had some good nights doing that, and Speedo loves us doing stuff like this as he can see the way that it bonds us. Another thing that Adrian does around the place is to hammer people during meal times for loads of different reasons, but in a way that has everybody in stitches. Believe it or not, the person that he hammers most is Bellars, and he's probably the only guy I know who could get away with that.

There was one occasion when Bellars asked Adrian to sort something out with his car while we were in a late team meeting and gave him his room key. When Bellars rolled into bed later on and pulled back the sheets, on the other side of the bed was a cut out of Adrian, dressed in his squash kit from back in the day, complete with headband and skimpy shorts with 'Goodnight Craig, love Adrian' on it. Needless to say, we found that hilarious, and we all have our suspicions that Bellars kept it alongside him until morning... ha-ha! Adrian's become a big part of what Speedo's trying to achieve, which again is credit to Speedo, because it's another weakness he feels he'd found in the squad, and then discovered a way to remedy it.

Friday 7th October

Wales 2 (Ramsey Pen 60, Bale 71) **Switzerland 0**

Interesting start to the day today. It's the Michael Jackson tribute concert in the Millennium Stadium tomorrow night and the stars were all arriving at the hotel we are staying at, the St David's in Cardiff. This morning I saw some of the Jackson family, and JLS who had lots and lots of very big security guards! Jamie Foxx has been at the hotel the last two days but he's only got one security man! I'm a big fan of his films and his music, so I took the chance to have a chat and a pic with him. He was a cool guy and told me that he was going to try and make the game tonight.

I've no idea if Foxx made it to the Liberty, but if he did he would have seen one of the most complete performances by Wales in ages. Against England last month we had the performance and not the result, but tonight we delivered on both counts.

It was a great moment for Joe tonight when he had his first full game for Wales and where better to do it than the Liberty? Joe's developing into a fantastic player and already this season, playing in the Prem, I've seen massive improvements in him. I know he's going to become a really top player and if he stays clear of injuries, he's going to be a central part of this Wales team for years to come.

It was a bit of a frustrating start for us tonight to be honest, and for the first ten minutes or so we didn't see much of the ball as the Swiss maintained possession quite effectively. They had put some pressure on us using their possession well and we had to defend a few corners early on which we did comfortably enough.

After some instructions from Speedo, we then started pressing better and higher. This meant that although they were still keeping possession it was mostly in their half and more importantly further away from our goal.

A little later I hit a diagonal pass which is a big part of both my game and the team's, it was right in Bellars' path and he was through. Unfortunately his shot went wide, but we were starting to impose ourselves on the game a bit more. You could now feel the confidence growing in the lads, and it began to feel similar to the last couple of games. I felt like we were definitely going to go and win the game at that point and made sure all the back line were switched on to any counter attacks. I have played enough games at this level now to know that counter attacks is how the majority of goals are scored. When you are in control of the game and feeling comfortable, they can always hit you on the break. If we keep it tight, I know we will score with the quality we have going forward.

Speedo was pleased with us at half-time, especially with how well we had defended when they had had their spell of possession. He told us that despite them edging possession we definitely had the better of the chances, and that we had to get Bale and Bellars on the ball more as they were struggling to cope with them. There was a slight worry about Bale after he got clattered before half-time and he had treatment throughout the break, but he was OK.

We started really well after the break with our attacking players seeing plenty of the ball. About five minutes in, we nearly threw it away after Tayls was blown up for a pretty heavy challenge from their counter attack. It was a free kick about 30-odd yards out and our line was pretty good, but we didn't drop in quick enough to defend the free kick and the striker scored. However I instantly saw the lino with his flag up for offside. I took that as a warning, because if we conceded then it would have been a massive blow.

We raised our game again and should have won a pen which I think everyone in the ground could see but the ref gave a corner. It was so frustrating, especially when it was so blatant. Not long afterwards one of theirs brought down Gunts and was sent off. This gave us a boost again and I could tell we were going to go on and score. Then, unbelievably, the ref ignored a second blatant penalty on Bale.

At the back of my mind I was beginning to wonder if it was going to be one of those nights for us, because we were dominating so much, but getting frustrated because they seemed to be getting the better of the ref's decisions. That all changed on the hour though, when Gunts went down in the box for a soft pen. I don't know if the ref was evening it up after not giving the previous ones because it was less of a pen than the ones that went before it, but I wasn't complaining. Rambo took it, not the best I've seen if I'm honest, but it went in under the keeper and we fully deserved our lead.

We just grew into the game after the goal, with Rambo, Joe and Bale excellent for us. Bale was rewarded for his superb play after a great one-two with Steve Morison, which he finished clinically. I was so pleased with the goal as it was a result of doing to the Swiss what good international teams have done to us in the past. We were on top, showed no mercy and just pressed and pressed until the goal came to us. It was a really good second-half performance.

Speedo was happy afterwards and congratulated us all on our performances, especially in the second half. I can't tell you how positive it was in the dressing room tonight, every single one of the lads were buzzing and all looking forward to Bulgaria. Looking at the table, we can actually finish third now if we win and a couple of results go for us.

We are getting closer and closer to being a team that can qualify for a tournament. We have a big opportunity to make a statement in Bulgaria on Tuesday and judging by the positivity from all the players and staff tonight after the game, I see absolutely no reason why we can't go there and win.

Saturday 8th October

It felt great this morning, knowing we won a crucial game and against a top team too. We won convincingly, which was pleasing and possibly the best win since I've been playing for Wales. We really can start to see the success coming now with all the work we have put in.

The rest of today has been a chill-out day with the family in the hotel. It's been good to spend time with them and it breaks the trip up a bit. Speedo is very family orientated so he arranged a barbecue with all the players and their families this afternoon.

Sunday 9th October

It was the second day of recovery today, which consisted of some running and easy drills like passing and head tennis. I beat Chris Gunter convincingly and, as always, he wasn't happy about it! I'm used to beating him now and he is still a sore loser. And, yes, he will cheat to win.

Monday 10th October

We flew into Bulgaria this morning and were greeted by really miserable weather for training. We are staying at the Sofia Hilton and when we went for a stroll earlier into the city, it wasn't very nice. There were armed guards around the outside of the hotel, the city seemed pretty run down and you could tell that there have obviously been problems here over the years.

We trained in the stadium this afternoon, and the pitch was absolutely terrible, made worse by the pouring rain. All the talk from the media to me since I arrived in the Wales camp has been about the racist issues that apparently exist here. I've got pretty fed up about it to be honest, so when I was asked again today by somebody, I just said, 'I've got no comment to make about it until it happens. If nothing happens, then there's no issue. If something does, then I'll talk about it.'

It's a huge issue, of course, but I hate that some people just hijack it, probably just to have something different to write about. It's obviously something I'm going to be sensitive about, and of course it's something I would love to see eradicated all around the world. But I get the feeling sometimes that people in the media only focus on it when they sniff a story and a scandal, and actually have no interest in the topic as a whole. That winds me up.

We were also told today that due to some protests around the dismissal last month of their manager, Lothar Matthäus, there are going to be no Bulgaria fans at the game which is a bit odd. It was a massive old stadium, with over 40,000 capacity, all open with no roof, and to have been told that the atmosphere is going to be more or less the same as it was for training this afternoon is amazing. I'm sure some Welsh fans will have travelled though, and they always make plenty of noise. Maybe it'll feel like a home game!

Tuesday 11th October
Bulgaria 0 Wales 1 (Bale 45)

Every game I ever take the field in, I focus on one thing – a clean sheet. It doesn't happen often for obvious reasons, especially internationally and especially away from home. But tonight not only did we achieve that, we also managed to prevent them having a single shot on target throughout the whole 90 minutes. It doesn't get much better than that for defenders like me, so to say I'm pleased by our performance tonight is a bit of an understatement.

When I saw the ball that we had to play with tonight I thought where's Beadle? As the home team they get to pick the ball and it was an absolute joke. Remember those 99p beach balls you'd have as a kid? Well, it wasn't far off that. It was awful. They move everywhere and all they do is make you look stupid. FIFA really should sort out this issue and get back to using proper balls and not these beach balls.

Added to the worry about the balls, as we'd been told, the game was played in the most weird atmosphere I've ever experienced for Wales. The Bulgarian fans kept their promise and stayed away, so we walked out into this massive stadium, and all we could hear were the Welsh fans whose cheers and chants echoed around the empty ground. It was very weird.

What was also pretty weird was the team. For the first time in my career with Wales, and apparently the first time since 2003, Wales walked out with the same team as the previous game. This again is a really positive sign of the strides that Speedo and Raymond are making with their vision and, on the back of our excellent win on Friday, I knew from the off that if we performed with the authority and intensity of Friday night, and were disciplined on and off the ball, we would win. That was Speedo's basic message before we walked out. He wasn't wrong.

Bulgaria had obviously done their homework on us too. Apart from the rubbish ball their groundstaff had obviously stayed away with their fans, because it didn't look like the pitch had seen a mower for a few weeks. It was annoying to see the grass so long, but we also knew that it showed they respected our passing game. I told the lads that in the warm-up, and there was a definite feeling among the boys to show them what we could do, whatever pitch they'd given us.

It was a very quiet half for me, the only problem was an injury to Darcy that saw him leave the field, which was a blow because the pair of us have gelled well in recent games and I really enjoy playing alongside him. Fate was on our side though, because as soon as his replacement, Adam Matthews, came on he played a long ball to Bale down the right, who swept inside and smashed a shot that deflected past their keeper for what proved to be our winner. I thought at that moment that it was probably game over. I don't think Bulgaria's hearts were in it from the start tonight, and Bale scoring when he did, right on half-time, killed them.

At half-time Speedo sorted out the defence, with Gunts coming across from right back to join me in the middle, and Adam filling in for him. As good as Darcy has been for us, it's a tribute to our depth as a squad now that I honestly didn't feel we were weakened by these changes, and was happy to have Gunts alongside as he's a great lad and top player who can play that central defensive role with no problems.

Speedo's other message at half-time was basically to go and

win the game. He was completely unconcerned with them and just focused on us instead, telling us to believe in ourselves and our attacking abilities and to go and get the goals our dominance deserved. He told us that we had the attacking players to completely dominate them and all we needed was the composure in front of goal to prove it. Going out for the second half I was certain we'd win by two or three at least.

The second half flew by and I think we dominated it too, and how we didn't score in that second period I'll never know. Both Bale and Bellars hit the bar and Bellars also put one over which he probably thinks he should have scored, but unlike previous games, when we've missed chances and I've worried that we may pay for them, I didn't worry about them scoring for a minute, such was our dominance in possession and discipline when we didn't have the ball. Maybe with the grass a bit shorter, and no beach ball, we'd have scored more, but at the final whistle that didn't matter as we'd come away from home to an historically tricky eastern European nation and outclassed them. For me personally, it was the quietest game I've had for Wales, hence the lack of detail in my report. I love the cut and thrust of defending, but it was no bad thing to sit back and watch for large periods tonight, and the neutral watching would say that he'd witnessed the performance of an accomplished international team. And that's a very pleasing feeling to leave this qualifying campaign with.

The only disappointment tonight was finding out that the Swiss had beaten Montenegro, denying us third place, but that's the end of another qualifying campaign, and the sad fact is that we haven't qualified again. However, instead of the obvious disappointment that we have got used to with Wales, this time we are very satisfied with the end of this campaign, especially finishing as we have with wins over Montenegro, Switzerland and Bulgaria. And with a bit more luck, if Earnie had finished against England, we also would have drawn against one of the world's heavyweights as well. Two clean sheets on the bounce was an impressive way to finish, but perhaps more important were the performances.

Wales are going places. I'm as certain about that as I can be, and with every passing camp we are improving under Speedo and Raymond. Exciting times ahead for us all.

Wednesday 12th October

We flew back from Bulgaria this morning on the chartered plane that Wales hire, which is great because we never have to suffer delays. It's just a case of arriving at the airport, showing passports at the gate, getting on and taking off. That suits me because I'm such a rubbish flyer and I haven't got any time to worry about crashing, which I do!

On the plane all the players sit at the front, and the staff and media sit at the back. It's always been that way for as long as I remember. I don't remember who planned it like that... maybe it's for them all to keep an eye on us.

I also found out today that I'm on the cover of *Match Attax* cards. They are the little cards that kids collect and swap. We all did it when we were young, so I'm buzzing just to have my own card, never mind being on the cover of the packet! I love little things like this that make me reminisce about being a kid. It also puts into perspective how far I have come in my life. Some people may think it's not a big deal, but for me it is. I used to love collecting these cards and stickers as a kid and bothering my parents for more money to get another packet.

Thursday 13th October

Back into training today for the Norwich game. It's odd because my body needed a recovery session but I also needed to get my mind on the game on Saturday, so had to join in the session to find out if the team had been working on any specifics during my absence.

Friday 14th October

Bit of a treat for the lads today. We flew to Norwich from Cardiff instead of having to face the eight-hour coach trip we've done in the past. As much as I hate that trip, I think I hate flying more, so there were mixed emotions when I found out. Like the Wales flight, the press were also on the flight which meant that we had to behave ourselves, which was harder for Leets and Gows than the rest of us!

It was pouring down today which never bothers me, especially after the weather we had in Bulgaria. But I told Nathan that it'll probably be boiling hot tomorrow. There's something about Norwich. Things have never gone to plan here over the years. I'm not being negative saying that, it's just the way it's always been. I'm sure nothing will go wrong tomorrow. But I bet it's going to be boiling though!

Saturday 15th October

Norwich City 3 (Pilkington 1, 63, R Martin 10) **Swansea City 1** (Graham 12)

Woke up this morning and was greeted with bright sunshine when I opened the curtains. I knew it was going to be hot.

The start of our game today was also hot, but for me in the worst way imaginable. I think we'd only been going about forty-five seconds when the ball was played in-field around the edge of the box to David Fox. As I rushed to charge him down, as quickly as I always do, he caught it as sweet as a nut, which is exactly where it went – straight into mine. Plural. The pain was excruciating and I was genuinely poleaxed. It was the worst one of its kind I've ever had in my career and I was in so much pain I genuinely thought something really bad had happened to me down there.

It was a horrible moment when I realised that the ball hadn't gone out – the football that is – but had just rebounded off me to my Welsh team mate Steve Morison. That meant that I had to try to get up straight away and get back. In the time it took me to do that, Steve crossed it and Anthony Pilkington, who was with me at Stockport, lashed it home. There was nothing else I could do but fall to the ground, desperately gasping for air and hoping the pain would go away. It didn't.

The most annoying thing was that had I just let the ball go past me, it would have either been saved by Michel or flown over the bar, and if it had hit me anywhere else on the body I'd have been able to quickly get back in position. As it was, Britts saw that I was down and immediately ran past me to cover my position, and when that happens, it's my job to just get up as quickly as possible and cover the position that Britts would have been in if he wasn't covering for me. The problem was, because of the pain I was in, I just couldn't get up in time. Pilks was where Leon would have been and just fired home unmarked. Leon is such a good pro that his instinctive reaction was to work hard and get back and cover for me in the position I should have been in.

Once they'd scored though, my main concern was whether I'd have to go off. I had some treatment and got back on, but I was in proper pain for about twenty minutes. I've never known anything like it before.

Things never bloody go to plan in Norwich.

Sadly, that horribly painful incident set the scene for the rest of the match. We just went from bad to worse and by a mile it was our worst performance of the season. It was the only game so far in which we haven't performed.

If I wasn't in enough pain from my gonads, it got a hell of a lot worse when they scored a second. Àngel gave a free kick away on the right, which was down to me really as I should have dealt with the ball played into Steve Morison a lot better and should have just put it into the stand. Martin then got in between Monks and Danny to score from a free header. It was such a disappointing goal to concede and, as I'm the first to moan at people stopping danger at source, I have to hold my hand up for not doing that myself.

Fortunately we were thrown a lifeline by Danny, following a good run into the box by Scott. It was exactly what we needed and was a great finish from Danny. He really showed his class and I know he's going to go and score plenty at this level now if the quality of his finish today was anything to go by.

I nearly opened my assist account for the season a little later when I decided to go long for Danny who'd made another run into their box. I hit it as well as I can, so was chuffed to see it drop for him exactly where I wanted it to. I thought that Danny could have maybe hit it first time, but he tried to take a touch and the chance was lost. This is a ball I can play, but it's a pretty tough one to hit and because I'm generally playing on the left, it isn't really on for me that much. Still, the pleasure I had in hitting that ball took my mind off the pain I was feeling in my other ball.

After the frantic start thankfully, the game calmed down as the half went on and we had good possession but didn't make any inroads. I was trying to push on as much as possible and carry the ball and team forward, but we never settled into any rhythm and it just didn't feel right, as if something was missing with us. I got the feeling that we as a team were very lethargic – I know I was – and even though I could see the lads were trying, I had a feeling that something collectively was missing from us today. This sort of thing always seems to happen at Norwich. If I have to admit to a bogey team and ground, then it's definitely them, here, today. I can't stand playing here.

Half-time gave me chance to put more ice on the gonads, but was still worried as to why the pain didn't seem to be going away. The Gaffer wasn't pleased with us at all and he'd picked up on the lethargy bit and told us that we weren't looking sharp. There was definitely something up because I could see just chatting to the lads at half-time that something just wasn't quite right. Maybe we'd lost belief from the shocking start, or maybe everyone just had the same feeling as me about this as our bogey ground.

My negative feelings were confirmed after the break, and we really struggled to lift ourselves. Normally, we'd be looking to get back on terms early, and be positive yet patient, but today we were just getting more anxious and frustrated, and at no point did it look like we would threaten them. Then, about twenty minutes in, it was all over anyway, when Pilkington beat me to a second ball from a corner, scored, and whatever stuffing we had left was just knocked out of us. Again, it was such a sloppy goal, with so many people standing around and not anticipating anything. Simply not good enough.

Not long afterwards they took off Morison, who had had one of the best games I'd seen him play. But any thoughts of relief from the physical battle were removed when Grant Holt jogged on. It didn't take too long for us to have a clash and it seemed to stir up Paul Lambert for some reason. The ball was played out wide to Holt right in front of the Norwich bench, and he didn't shield it too well so I saw I had a decent chance of getting to it – which I did – but also bundled him over when I won the ball. No foul was given but Lambert went nuts. For some reason they all thought it was a foul and acted like Holt is an angel and that the last thing he'd do is rough me up if the roles were reversed. Yeah, right. I was pretty angry with lots of things at this point, so wasn't interested in what Lambert and Holt were saying, and instead just concentrated on keeping my head and not doing anything stupid that would see me get a yellow or red. Both were a strong possibility at that point.

Apart from a chance by Danny, the rest of the match was played out in a really weird atmosphere, both on and off the pitch, where I think the fans could see that something was just missing from us today. Then, as if to confirm that this really is our bogey ground, Dobbs suffered a bad ankle twist following a kick, and could hardly walk, but as we'd used our three subs, he just had to hobble about until the end as a passenger.

Unsurprisingly, it was a very quiet dressing room with the Gaffer obviously disappointed and as if to confirm that there was a spark missing from all of us today, there wasn't much even he could say. It wasn't like we didn't give it a go, it's just that nothing really happened for us from minute one and once the third goal went in we had nothing at all to give. The Gaffer knows when to give us a rollicking, and I think he recognised that today wasn't one of those days. It was just a bad day at the office. Whether it was my injury or the heat, I was very tired afterwards for some reason and felt completely drained. After changing I got straight out of the dressing room as soon as I could and just wanted to get out of the stadium and out of Norwich to be honest. I wanted to put it all behind me and just move onto the next one.

Played 8 Won 2 Drawn 2 Lost 4 Points 8 League Position – 11th
(32 more points needed for 40)

Sunday 16th October

I didn't travel back with the lads after the game as we have some friends in Colchester who we haven't really had the chance to see that much, living so far away, so we spent the day with them today which was nice.

Tuesday 18th October

After training today the Gaffer called a defensive meeting with all the defenders in the squad and the goalkeepers. We were shown the video and the specifics of the goals we conceded at Norwich, and the Gaffer was stopping it and showing us where we went wrong and where we should have been standing. We knew we'd been bad at Norwich and we knew what had happened, but we still needed to see it. It didn't make pretty viewing – we just played really poorly. The basic upshot was that the Gaffer felt that we weren't aggressive enough in our defending and we effectively lost the battle with Morison and Pilkington, and that's what cost us in the end.

After the video meeting we went back out on the training ground and worked on defending everything – crosses, corners, free kicks, the lot. It was really back to basics stuff and the Gaffer had us doing 1 v 1s, 2 v 2s and 3 v 3s. In these sessions it's attackers v defenders, so in today's 3 v 3 it was me, Monks and Tayls against three of the strikers at the club in rotation. It was a really hard session, but I think it was needed and, quite simply, the lessons have to be learned. We all accept and understand that. But the way that footballers are sometimes, as we were going deeper into the session another reason for the session started to spring into my mind. Punishment.

In fairness, the Gaffer's not that sort of manager and doesn't usually go down that 'naughty boy' route, so maybe it was a figment of my imagination, but if it was intended, then maybe that's needed now and again. To be honest, I think I'd do it myself if I was a manager.

One thing was clear in my mind after training finished, I don't want to repeat any of what happened today – or at Norwich – anytime soon.

Thursday 20th October

I loved today's five-a-side tournament in training. One group, four teams – Wales, England, under-21s, Rest of the World. This is where the Gaffer's clever. Up to today we'd had a pretty tough week and while it was deserved, if you're not careful, it can turn into a bit of a slog. Not today.

Our tournament was set up like a proper league table where each team played each other twice with a points system in place with three for a win, two for a draw and one for a loss. The games were great fun and we all wanted to win because there was a cracking forfeit at the end for the losing team. Whoever finished bottom at the end of the tournament had to go and line up along the goal line in between the goals, turn round and bend over. Then, the team that had come top of the group would place a line of balls down at penalty spot distance, and get the chance to smash balls at the backsides of the losers. There were two important things for me: first, not to finish bottom and, second, to win, so that I'd get a chance to be one of the players smashing a ball at someone's backside.

After a fun and competitive tournament, it was the under-21s who were the losers and they lined up along the goal line as the winners, The Rest of the World, sadly not including me, put down the balls to smash at them.

Now it was at this point that maybe the difference between a good old British mentality and that of the sophisticated continental came to the fore. There we all were, watching this shoot out (or perhaps more accurately this arse out) taking place, shouting and laughing and looking forward to the pain that would surely follow for the losers, when up stepped our foreign cousins, who didn't quite understand the opportunity that they were being presented with. Instead of completely blasting balls at the defenceless backsides, they all just started chipping, clipping and hitting the balls soft. Even worse than all that, they were missing with every single one. We couldn't believe it! The rest of us were all standing there on the side bantering and shouting, 'What are you doing? Hit it!', but they kept on hitting it soft and missing. Unbelievable! The only player of the under-21s team who was hit was Darnel Situ, and he was hit with the very last kick and it didn't even hurt. Madness!

Good laugh though. If it happens again I hope the Rest of the World lose and we win, 'cos I promise you we will absolutely smash them. And we won't miss.

Friday 21st October

After training today, we jumped on the coach and were off back to my old stomping ground, the Midlands, for our trip to Wolves.

Playing for Swansea City, you get used to the peculiar delights of coach travel. Because of the location of the city, our nearest trips are the three Midlands clubs which take about two and a half hours minimum. The London and Lancashire clubs take much longer again, so Friday afternoons cooped up on a coach becomes something of a way of life. And as with anything in life that becomes a little mundane, people have different ways of dealing with it. In our squad there are three specific types really when it comes to away trips – the poker school, the sleepers and the iPod/DVD lads. I'm a member of the iPod/DVD group. I like nothing better than getting lost in my music to help the journey pass by, and today I also brought a new DVD box set with me, so spent the bulk of the trip getting into series one of *The Wire*.

We left at 2 p.m. from Llandarcy, as we do most away trips, and I took my usual seat next to Luke and opposite Leets and Wayne. As on most trips, Luke and I have a bet on how long it takes Leets to fall asleep. Today he was gone before we'd passed Cardiff!

When we arrived at the hotel, Scott Sinclair's barber was already there, and he got down to work, sorting out the match day styles for his usual customers – Luke, Wayne, Leets and Scott himself. Those boys spend lots to keep themselves looking sharp. I'm not so vain though, after all I'm going to war the next day. I don't want to look too pretty.

At the hotel, I got sorted with my regular roomie Nathan. It's important that you room with someone you get on with as you spend so much time together and as we've roomed for the last few years, Nathan and I are pretty much the perfect fit now, we get on great, have the same interests and like the same music. The only complaint I've currently got with him is that he's right into *Big Brother*, which means it's always on the box in our room. I have no idea why anyone would want to spend time watching people doing absolutely nothing apart from sitting around in a house! It's a good job I'm the big dog of our room and boss the remote always!

Had our 9 p.m. meeting tonight where the Gaffer showed us clips of the opposition on video and then went over some tactics so that we're all completely aware of the challenge facing us and what we can expect tomorrow. It will be physical.

Saturday 22nd October

Wolverhampton Wanderers 2 (Doyle 84, O'Hara 86)

Swansea City 2 (Graham 23, Allen 35)

I hope to God we don't end up regretting that last ten minutes today. Two points thrown away and that is very, very hard to take, especially as we produced by far our best away performance of the season.

There was quite a dark atmosphere at the ground from the home fans today. I got the feeling they aren't happy with Mick McCarthy. As we walked out for the warm-up, I looked into the crowd and saw a girl of no more than five or six giving us the fingers.

Nice.

Wolves away means something to me. It's where I was born and spent my first few years. I'm not a fan of them exactly, but of all the Midlands clubs, they are the one I lean towards most in terms of hoping they win. When we played here a couple of years ago though, they slaughtered me because they knew I'm from the area and were giving me the 'Williams, Williams what's the score?'

I would have loved a win today.

We arrived with as solid a mind-set as I've noticed with the lads all season, especially in an away game, and I think that's all to do with the work we've done this week in trying to get last week's horrors out of the system. In the Gaffer's huddle in the dressing room before going out, where he brings everyone together including all players and staff, we were very determined, with a feeling that there was going to be no messing about coming here. We all knew our roles and were coming to play ball – nothing else. I really liked the attitude of the whole group before kick-off. In the huddle, Monks continued this theme by telling us there was no way that we would be letting each other down like last week and we had to make up for that today. He told us to defend a lot more aggressively, and really wound us up. I was buzzing when the huddle peeled away.

I was so up for it I was straight into it after about ten seconds when Wayne Hennessy played it long and I got up and all over Doyle to win that first header which is so vital. It was a great feeling, but about thirty seconds later Monks won his own first header, but it fell to Henry who absolutely lashed one and I was convinced it was going in until Michel got there. It was a frantic opening minute and, what with my attitude before the start, my adrenalin was absolutely flying! This was also helped by the fans who were really involved from the off and gave the game a fantastic atmosphere. I loved the start today. It's why I play.

There was a moment about twenty minutes in, just before we scored, which summed up the difference between us today and last week. There was a scramble in the six-yard box, which saw me jump in to challenge Ebanks-Blake with the ball squirting to O'Hara, whose shot Michel turned round for a corner. It was a brilliant moment because every one of us around O'Hara was throwing our bodies in to try to block his shot. To see everyone diving in and putting their bodies on the line at the first sight of danger and not willing to let that ball go towards our goal was exactly the type of defending we were lacking last week. Another lesson learned.

Our determination in defence was rewarded a couple of minutes later when Dan finished nicely after a great ball from Gows that was straight out of the Barcelona training manual.

All week the Gaffer played a video showing Xavi and the types of balls he plays into strikers and told Gows that if he could replicate them he would get the assist of the season. Gows was obviously watching because his ball into Dan was Xaviesque. This quality is something that Gows brings to the team as he has great ability with the ball and can really pick a pass and unlock the defence like this. It was important we got our noses in front.

Fair play to them, they still kept up the pressure on us and it was during this time that Michel came to the fore, but not in his usual shot stopping way. I thought I could moan, but I'm nothing compared to Michel! Today he really got amongst us and was very vocal, especially from corners and free kicks where he's always organising. As a defender, I love this because there's nothing better than having a strong presence behind you and an extra set of eyes, keeping you on your toes. Dorus was very vocal too, but his voice was so deep no one could understand what he was saying, at least we know what Michel is moaning to us about!

Ten minutes before the break, we got a second which was as a direct result of their crowd, and I've never seen anything like it before. We had kept the ball for a spell, and all of a sudden their crowd just started booing and jeering them for letting us keep it, so that in the end they lost their discipline, snapped and just started chasing the ball crazily and losing their shape. It played completely into our hands and style of play when Danny went on a great run, had a nice ball into space to him by Àngel which completely unlocked their defence and then topped off with a really calm finish by Joe. We played well to score it, but I'm convinced the goal was totally down to their crowd getting restless and booing their team. I've never seen a goal like this in a game that I have been involved before, it was amazing. The crowd then completely turned on the team, and McCarthy, and I was smiling to myself thinking, 'You all caused this yourselves!'

At half-time the Gaffer singled out a moment of defending that had happened late in the half to demonstrate how much better and aggressively we were defending this week compared to last, but when it had happened, we were all laughing. Basically, the ball fell to Henry on edge of box, he shaped to hit it right foot, then me, Monks, Tayls all flew in together to block, quickly followed by Gows, but the first three of us were so committed, we all got tangled and took each other out, allowing Henry to drag it onto his left foot with the three of us on the floor. Then, with a free shot, he dragged it wide! As we got up we just all started laughing at how we'd clattered each other. Still, as the Gaffer said, we were all showing the right attitude and that last week no one would have attempted the block.

During the second half, I've never known a crowd treat the team and manager so badly. From almost the kick-off, they just kept on slaughtering McCarthy and I could hear all the abuse they were giving everyone as clear as a bell. I couldn't believe what I was hearing and I wondered how it was going to affect them, whether they'd just collapse, or maybe it would actually spur them into something. But if I thought the crowd was bad in the early part of the half, when McCarthy made two subs they just went ballistic. I was genuinely shocked at how much abuse they were shovelling at him and the ground absolutely shook with, 'You don't know what you're doing' chants.

With about a quarter of an hour to go, the Gaffer made a change that was far more significant than the double substitution of McCarthy's, taking off Leon and bringing on Andrea. When I saw Leon's number go up I thought it was a real strange one to make because, as usual, he was controlling midfield and they weren't causing us any problems at all, so I don't know if the Gaffer thought we had it sewn up by then but I definitely thought it was a strange one. And it ended up costing us big time.

With just six minutes left and us cruising at 2–0, they scored after some real sloppy defending by us. Nobody blocked Vokes when the danger came so he had a free run at the ball, then no one reacted to the second ball which led to the shot and then Gows, who was on the line, turned his back and it went through his legs. Monks and me were absolutely fuming and let everyone know about it.

Straight away, everything changed and that's when we really missed Britts' control. The change in them – and their fans – was instant and incredible and I couldn't believe it was happening. The Gaffer sensed it too and reacted straight away by bringing on Moras for Gows and told us to go five at the back with three centre halves. I've never been a fan of that, and I'd have preferred that the Gaffer kept it the same to be honest. What made it worse was that none of us had played with Moras before, so all of a sudden nobody was sure what our jobs were. Then, almost straight away, they scored again. Moras should have done better, but I appreciate it was a tough game for him to come into for his debut, but there's no excuse for Andrea not to stick with his midfield runner, O'Hara, at that point in the game. That's just basic and was unacceptable. I guarantee that goal wouldn't have happened if Leon was still on the pitch. When it went in, I completely and utterly lost it. I was so angry I could have smashed someone's face in, my head had totally gone and Monks was even angrier than me. But then at the same time we were both telling each other to just make sure we don't lose the game now, which was a very real possibility. How the hell it got to that, I just don't know.

All hell broke loose in the dressing room. I totally lost it and threw about three bottles at anyone and everyone, and Michel and Monks were exactly the same and were going nuts at certain people. Some other lads were moaning to each other, and there were a few just sitting there quietly, almost in shock at how we'd thrown it away.

Don't ever tell me that footballers don't care. It's our livelihoods that are at stake, and the anger and frustration displayed in the dressing room today, clearly showed that!

Played 9 Won 2 Drawn 3 Lost 4 Points 9 League Position – 13th
(31 more points needed for 40)

Monday 24th October

Back down to Swansea today, and I must admit a smile has returned to my face following the massive disappointment of the last ten minutes at Wolves. I don't know whether the Gaffer does it by design, but he gave us yesterday and today off, and to relax for a couple of days after Saturday's disappointments has been absolutely spot on. I sometimes forget how fantastic it is to just spend some normal, quality time with Vanessa and Raphael. The benefits of having a rest physically are obvious, but mentally I'm in such a better frame of mind now than I was on Saturday, and I think that had the Gaffer hauled us in for 'naughty boy' training on Sunday and today, that simply wouldn't be the case.

Tuesday 25th October

I just stubbed my little toe in the kitchen – the same little toe on the right foot that David Haye reckons cost him his world title against Klitschko in the summer. I actually don't know how the hell I managed to do it. I was just walking out of the kitchen – I wasn't even rushing – the dog was in the way, and somehow I must have just walked too near the edge of the doorway. As I went to walk through the opening as I have done a thousand times, the next thing I knew I was seeing stars. My toe hit the frame with such a force, that the pain was instant and excruciating. I was astonished I'd actually managed to do it more than anything, but when the pain came, it really hurt and has been throbbing ever since.

I've played 150 consecutive games for the Swans, and I don't want that run to ever end, let alone end because I walked into a bloody doorframe.

I'm desperate to play on Saturday – please don't tell me it's broken.

Wednesday 26th October

Kate, our physio, thinks the toe is broken. Shit.

It's really painful, but I decided to go ahead with training. Kate had a good look at it, but there's nothing she can do about it anyway, so thought I may as well play. I'm not looking for a medal, I just would rather it didn't hurt so much, but am not going to miss a match because of that. No way.

Training was a bit intense about defending today, especially learning the lesson of the last ten minutes against Wolves and making sure that never happens again. The main message from the Gaffer was making sure we retain our composure if we have to see out a game like that again.

After training, we had a video meeting with the defenders and keepers and the Gaffer emphasised how well we had all defended in that first eighty minutes, despite ending up with a draw.

It still feels like a loss to me.

*

I started planning one of the most important projects we've done for WillsWorld – ensuring we raise £40,000 for an operation for little Hari Kieft to go to America to enable him to walk. I was told about Hari's situation by my mate Jonathan Thomas – aka Doey – who is involved in the AG Swansea charity and often approaches Vanessa and I about charities WillsWorld can support. He recently told us about little Hari's story. Hari's just two years old and has been diagnosed with two heart conditions along with spastic diplegic cerebral palsy which directly affects his ability to walk unaided. In a nutshell, without the operation – which is not available in the UK – Hari will never be able to walk. With some hard work and help of lots of committed and charitable people, we can all make sure that that particular outcome will be changed.

Thursday 27th October

Caulks was back at the club today after he banged his knee on the post in the Arsenal game, which saw him go under the knife. He's been back to Spurs for the operation and also to do the first part of his rehab. It was good to see him back on the field and running. He did quite a long session with our new physio Glen Driscoll, who used to be at Chelsea. He'll be a great addition back in the squad.

We've worked loads this week on how we defended in the last ten minutes against Wolves, and we did some more today. The Gaffer took the four of us who were on the field in that last part of the match – along with Michel – and set up the forwards against us to replicate what Wolves were doing. He told us to treat it exactly as we would have on a match day, and prove to him we could defend the ten minutes by keeping a clean sheet between us. He gave us our final briefing, set us up, and we all switched on because we knew how serious he was. We were all determined to keep a clean sheet for the ten minutes the Gaffer was going to time us for.

Anyway, the Gaffer whistles, throws the ball in to the strikers, and after about twenty seconds the ball is played straight to Monks. He tries to deal with it, but as it bounces, it hits a particularly wet patch of turf and just doesn't bounce up as high as he was expecting. Monks then misses the ball, Luke nips in and rifles straight past Michel for a goal. Our ten-minute shut out lasted no more than thirty seconds – and the Gaffer's face was thunder. It was so comical though, and Monks' face was a picture as he just looked down at the wet piece of turf by way of explanation. It was just one of those crazy things that happen that you can't really do anything about except laugh. Just make sure that you are out of sight of the Gaffer when you do.

Friday 28th October

The Gaffer lays out printed sheets on the dressing room wall for everyone to know who's in the wall from any given position on the pitch. All that changes is whether Michel decides if he wants 2, 3, 4 or 5 defenders in the wall. Behind the wall, we'll pick a defensive line and then just try to mark a man. One of our rules under the Gaffer is that if you're in the wall, you must always stand still and never jump as loads of goals go in under the wall. Added to that, we always have Leon or Joe charging the ball down from the inside of the wall. I had a look at these sheets today, the Gaffer puts up around twenty of them, it doesn't do any harm to familiarise yourself with them before a match day.

Saturday 29th October

Swansea City 3 (Allen 49, Sinclair Pen 57, Graham 90 + 3)

Bolton Wanderers 1 (Graham og 73)

I got up earlier than normal today as Raphael decided it was time to turn into a human alarm clock and woke us all up. I love seeing him first thing in the morning, and is so nice just to spend some time with him and watching him just changing and developing so much every day.

At the ground, I had an extra strapping – my broken little toe strapped tight to the one next to it. It was painful and was hoping nobody would tread on it. When something like this happens you can be sure that someone will step on it inside about five minutes – and it's usually one of your own players.

There was a nice surprise when I saw their team-sheet – no Kevin Davies. I don't know why he's on the bench, but I wasn't disappointed because you know with him in the side it's going to be very tough and physical for the full ninety minutes. I knew I wasn't going to get any of that from David N'Gog.

The first half seemed to pass quickly, with no real dramas and not much to report, it was comfortably the easiest half we've had defensively this season. The only concern for me was when Gary Cahill caught me across the bridge of the nose after about quarter of an hour. PAIN! I'm pretty sure it wasn't deliberate, and I think it was one of those things that happens when a ball comes in and you get in amongst it all to head it clear. It always hurts when it happens, but when you consider how often we make headed challenges during a match and over a season, it's amazing we don't get clouts and bangs more often than we do. My wife dreads me breaking my nose, and it turning fat and flat at the top.

The Gaffer was pleased at half-time. As he does most games, we didn't see him straight away because when we all filed in, he went into the medical room to let us get anything we had out of our system. I'm always the first back into the dressing room as I always run off, and even though I didn't feel I had much to say today, sometimes I feel the need to have a word with someone or sometimes a couple of players may be having words with each other – good or bad depending on the way the half has gone. After those little chats are done, it's a question of going to the toilet, loosening laces on boots, changing into a dry clean shirt for the second half and then getting some drinks on board. It's only once all this is done that we then see the Gaffer. I think he does this because he likes to take the emotion out of it, for himself as much as us probably, so that we avoid any slanging matches, and then he'll have his notebook with all the details he wants to talk about from what he's seen in the first half. Depending how much the Gaffer speaks, he might get interrupted by the buzzer which is set off by the ref in his room, which means we've got a couple of minutes to get out for the second half. If we hang around too long, the lino comes and bangs on the door to get us out, as happened today. The one thing the Gaffer said today which stuck in my mind was that they were getting tired and agitated from all the chasing they were doing and if we got an early goal, he was certain that their discipline would go.

Within just three minutes, the game swung on Ricardo Gardner's sending off after he lost his discipline go and clattered into Nath. He'd been fouling persistently from the start, in fact his first tackle when he clattered Nath was probably the worst of the lot and he was lucky to get away with a warning. The ref was lenient because it was so soon, but any other time in the match he'd have had a yellow for that too. To add to his sending off we soon scored through Joe. Ironically, our former team mate Darren Pratley of all people had his defensive run blocked off by the ref, allowing Joe space at the edge of the box before deciding to shoot and score.

It was such a relief to get the goal, and then ten minutes later, Prats' return to the Liberty turned into a bit of a nightmare for him, when he fouled Àngel in the box allowing Scott to put us two ahead from the spot. And that, pretty much, was that.

Apart from Danny's own goal, they never really troubled us and when Danny then ran in to beat Jussi Jääskeläinen to kill it off, I just turned round and hugged Michel and reflected on a good team performance where we completely outclassed a very experienced Premier League side.

After last week at Wolves, there were genuine feelings of relief and joy about the place because we proved that we can shut out a game in which we are ahead in and have dominated so much. It was important that we proved to ourselves that we could do that.

Played 10 Won 3 Drawn 3 Lost 4 Points 12 League Position – 10th
(28 more points needed for 40)

CHAPTER FIVE

November 2011

Wednesday 2nd November

The official launch was made this evening for our fundraising night for Hari Keift and the appeal to raise £40,000. I'm really excited about this. It's going to be held on 13th January at Manor Park in Clydach and Nath, football freestyler Billy Wingrove and many others will be there to help make a big dent in the £40k required. We'll be auctioning plenty of items and there'll be guest speakers too. I really hope this will be a big success and need to spread the word to everyone now to get it publicised. Thank God for Twitter!

Thursday 3rd November

A new 3G artificial pitch has been put in at Llandarcy and we trained on it this morning for the first time. It's not ideal to have to train on this type of surface, as there's no substitute for playing on grass, and for our training pitch to be so cut up this early just isn't good enough considering we are a Premier League team. It's just another one of those little things that this squad is so good at dealing with. I don't know the reasons why the training pitch has cut up so soon, but it's not the best preparation for one of the club's biggest games of the season against Liverpool on Saturday.

Sky Sports News has just confirmed that Steven Gerrard is out with an ankle infection and won't be playing. Mixed feelings about that. Liverpool are a far better side with him in it, so him missing clearly helps us, but personally I want to play against the best players every week. It's the only way that you can really test yourself and understand what level you are at in the game. I would have loved to have played against him.

We leave for Liverpool straight after training tomorrow morning, so I have just packed my bag with everything I'll be needing for the weekend. I've packed that bag for five away games so far this season and only have one point to show for it – hope we can add to that on Saturday. It's going to be a tough task though.

Friday 4th November

This morning's session was quite light because we've had a pretty tough week, and we had our usual warm-up – on the grass surprisingly – followed by some short, sharp drills along with passing and keep ball drills which are always enjoyable. After that, the Gaffer had a meeting with tomorrow's starting XI out on the pitch and then that was us done.

The Gaffer said something during the meeting though that had a pretty positive impact on me. He made a big point to us that we are all now Premiership footballers, and we should realise and understand exactly what that means. He said that when we take the field against a Gerrard, a Lampard, a Rooney, a van Persie or anyone else you can think of, we have proved now that we are there as of right and we are their equal. He told us that we should never underestimate what that means and should never, ever, be intimidated by anyone just because they have a big name in the game and that tomorrow, we can take a massive step forward as a club *and* as players by getting something at Liverpool.

After he'd spoken, I had a look at the lads and got the feeling that the Gaffer had really hit the nail on the head for us all. His words made us feel that little bit more optimistic about our future this season, and ensured that we realised that we have every right to be playing against any player that Liverpool choose to select.

Tomorrow gives us a great opportunity to prove that.

I know fans would love to believe that all their players support their club with the same feeling and passion as they do. But in reality that's not the case, and unless they are home grown, nearly all footballers support other clubs. I've supported Liverpool all my life, and today after training, Neil Taylor and I had a long chat about tomorrow's game because he's a lifelong Liverpool fan too. When I first became a fan of them, the likes of John Barnes, Ian Rush, Bruce Grobbelaar, Rob Jones and Dean Saunders were all in the team and like any kid at the time, I had their posters all over my bedroom wall and added the likes of Robbie Fowler and Michael Owen when they made their breakthroughs. Just chatting about those players made me realise what an impact the club had on me following the path as a professional footballer, and it's exciting to think that tomorrow I'm going to get that chance I dreamt about almost throughout my life of playing at Anfield.

Tayls and me discussed what we are going to do when we pass underneath the 'This is Anfield' sign when we go out onto the pitch for kick-off. We've both been inspired by that sign for years, so we agreed we'll touch it – you never know, it might bring us a bit of luck. I know that this may offend some fans, but I'd like to say that I've never, ever given anything less than 100 per cent for my team when I have taken the field, nor will I ever in the future.

At tonight's team meeting at our hotel near Albert Dock, we were given a pretty impressive stat about one of the squad. Apparently, we don't just possess the best player in the Premiership, but in the whole of Europe. Mark Gower has created more chances per game, than any other player in the top five European Leagues. Gows was real chirpy when it was announced 'What did you expect lads?' he laughed as we were all groaning and giving him stick. Still, good luck to him. I just hope he makes one tomorrow!

Saturday 5th November
Liverpool 0 Swansea City 0

It was the usual breakfast this morning before a stroll around the docks in Liverpool till about 11.30. One of the lads mentioned that Bellars was very complimentary about Swansea City on

BBC Two's *Sport Wales* last night. That didn't surprise me and is typical of him. He loves the way we play and is always flattering towards us whenever we speak. I know he's a hate figure for the bulk of Swansea City's fans because he's a Bluebird, but I hoped they would change their opinion somewhat because he's a great bloke and if they knew that and understood how much he rated us, perhaps they'd cut him a bit of slack.

At Anfield, we were brought in through the gates next to the Hillsborough Memorial and then driven into a sort of courtyard area behind the main Liverpool stand where there were hundreds of fans waiting to see us off the bus. It was a really pleasant surprise to see both sets of fans clapping us in. Everyone has always told me that there's something 'proper' about Anfield on a match day, and experiencing such a warm welcome confirmed that.

As we lined up outside the dressing room, I couldn't help but remember a day I'd had at Anfield with my mom and dad as a kid, and the 'This is Anfield' sign that had impressed me so much. That day with my dad, I'd wanted to touch the sign as I'd seen so many of my heroes do, but I couldn't reach it, so he had to lift me up to do it. All those memories were in my mind along with my conversation with Tayls yesterday. Trouble is, we both knew how it would look, not just to our team mates, but also to some of the Liverpool players. Truthfully, I really didn't care, and just hoped Tayls would still do it so we'd both get bantered together!

As the two teams walked out, I looked over and saw their captain, Pepe Reina, touch it, but the player behind him didn't. As I got underneath it, I put my hands up and touched it, but because I couldn't see behind me, I didn't know if Tayls had gone through with it, and waited for the stick to come, but he told me later that he had and nobody said a word, so that was another one of life's little milestones ticked off.

We had a minute's silence for Poppy Day before kick-off, and as usual, I always find it amazing how a stadium so full of energy can go from such noise and passion to complete silence so quickly. The crowd then sang 'You'll Never Walk Alone' and even though I'd been looking forward to it, I'd never heard or seen anything like it in my life. It was so loud and clear, I found myself singing along to it at one point and the stands were just a blaze of raised red and white scarves wherever I looked. It was another special moment.

Now it was on with the game and I had a big decision to make early on. Stewart Downing fizzed a cross in from the left that flew into the space behind me and in front of Michel. I was running back towards Michel and realised if I got anything on it, there was every chance the ball would just rifle into the net past Michel, point blank. One thing I've learnt with all the own goals I've scored in my career, is that it's best not to try to get anything on a ball like that. In the split second that I chose not to play it, I made a dummy move as if I was, and I'd like to think that was enough to put Carroll off because he just smashed the ball against the bar, missing a glorious chance to put them ahead.

As the half developed, we got into the game and everything we had talked about in the lead up went to plan. We had far more possession than them, and by the end of the half there was certainly a feeling that they – and their fans – were getting frustrated by their lack of possession.

Having a drink at half-time the Gaffer emphasised how well we'd played and was insistent that we stayed positive and carried on with our game plan of controlling the ball and keeping them frustrated. The dressing room was extremely positive and I was certain we'd continue to frustrate them in the second period, but more importantly, we wouldn't collapse as we'd done at the Etihad and Stamford Bridge.

We began the second half as we ended the first, passing and playing out of defence, but it was that bit harder today and that was down to one man, Dirk Kuyt. Kuyt is a player I really admire. He doesn't possess the silky skills of some forward players at the top clubs, but his work rate is as good as anyone I've ever played against. I didn't really give him enough credit until I played against him at international level. Our style is based on not panicking and delivering a pass to a team mate – even if it looks as though it may be a bit tight. The Gaffer's philosophy is to rely on his players to deal with the pass, but also for the players around to understand their duty to give him options so that an instant one-touch lay-off is always available. That generally works well if you keep your head, but someone like Kuyt is a player who never gives up and can force a mistake out of you and today he made some moments tighter than they should have been with his closing down. I was very impressed with him.

There was a bit of a comical moment today when Michel gave Suárez the eyes, but also succeeded in giving them to me too, and passed the ball straight past me into touch. Michel's an extra outfield player, and whenever he has the ball, our two fullbacks push straight up to the right and left wing positions on the halfway line at the same time that Monks and me split to the edge of our penalty area. What then tends to happen is that Michel will draw the striker in, before passing to either Monks or me. Michel is so good and confident at this, that on occasion he employs the skills of a striker bearing down on goal when he gives the keeper 'the eyes' – looking one way while shooting the other. That's what Michel did to Suárez, and me too unfortunately, as the ball sailed past me into touch. Still, it kept me on my toes! We both looked at each other and just laughed.

I had a couple of bangs today that gave me a bit of a worry, one accidental and one, well, maybe not so. For the first one, we had a corner at the Kop end on the hour which Andy Carroll went for. When the ball fell loose just in front of me, I volleyed it only to connect with the underneath of his boot and caught his studs across my instep.

The second happened about fifteen minutes later when my £4 shin pads let me down as Suárez left his mark on me, literally. I went to block a shot from him at the edge of the box and he caught me flush on the shin with four studs. Then, as the ball spun loose I tried another block which caught me square in the face, and then I had another block straight after which hit me in the chest somewhere. It was carnage. As I got up, all I could think of was the incredible pain in my shin from Suárez's nasty challenge and was thinking of staying down, but we had a corner to defend, so I just got on with it.

Leading up to the Suárez challenge, we could tell that the fact that we were playing so well and starving Liverpool of possession was working as it was all starting to get a bit irritable from their side of things. I ended up getting into an argument with Lucas Leiva that I didn't really need to, but he gave me the f**k off fingers so I just let him know that it was probably in his best interests not to do that again. Phil Dowd got us together and told us to apologise and it wasn't too pleasant between us, but getting involved in stuff like that is all part of the job.

A couple of minutes after the initial painful challenge by Suárez, I clashed with him again at the edge of the box and the ref gave the foul and also booked me. I was pissed with Suárez because, as he'd done from the very start, he made a real meal of it. I reacted to him and gave him a patronising rub on the head which he didn't like and it all got a bit heated between us. Bellars, who was on as a sub for Carroll, came straight across and took me away before it all had a chance to kick-off.

Suárez has that aura about him that says 'I'm untouchable' and his manner and behaviour made me want to knock him out. Having played against him for ninety minutes now, all I can say is that for such a talented player, he's very annoying. Football's a contact sport, meaning opposition players touch, grab and push you throughout, and often it happens when the ball is nowhere near. When a goal kick was being taken today, Reina was setting it up to kick long and Suárez moved across in front of me. Now anyone who has ever played centre back at any level of football knows what happens next. I just held out my hands to touch him in the small of his back, just for him to know I was there, nothing more. When I did it to Suárez, he just stopped dead, turned on me and said, 'Don't touch me.' I couldn't believe it. I must have done this thousands of times to players and occasionally you get a swinging arm to brush you off, but Suárez's reaction was one of complete contempt for me that I had dared to touch him. Obviously, then I kept touching him and grabbing him more just to piss him and his annoying face off! In fact, I'd go as far as to say that the manner in which he approached the game today, with utter contempt for us all, means that he's streets ahead of any player I've truly disliked since we've been in the Premier League. The sad thing is that he's a brilliant player and I rate him very highly, but he just possesses this temperament that I can't stand to see in a fellow footballer. The lack of respect he shows everyone means he gets no respect from me.

And then there's the diving.

Today, he dived more than any other player I've played against before – it was so bad I was genuinely shocked. Throughout the game, he just dived down and screamed at any given moment. Now, obviously, diving has crept into the game more and more in recent years and, as a defender, you have to be aware of it. But even the players you know that like a dive, at least wait until there is some sort of challenge or contact. Not Suárez. A couple of times today I'd hear the scream, see him writhing on the floor and for the life of me couldn't see where the contact could have been. He was a prick. Even Phil Dowd had enough of him and said, 'You're doing too much, Luis' at one point.

When he did the foul on me that I mentioned earlier, he overran the ball, which tempted me in for the challenge and then because I got there before him, four of his studs just raked me down the shin. Next thing I know he's screaming out loud again and rolling round on the floor, looking for the foul, after *he'd* just done *me*! I was boiling with anger. You can only judge a player from how he behaves towards you on the pitch. Well, to me, his behaviour was embarrassing.

Anyway, after we defended the free kick that I'd been booked for, we then began to have more regular glances up at the clock because our belief was growing that we would get something from the game. We nearly did when the ball dropped loose in the box, right into the path of Gows, who had a free shot from about 16 yards. I was right behind it, and could see it was a great chance but, unfortunately, under pressure from a sliding challenge, he smashed it over Reina and the bar and into the Kop. There were groans from our fans when he put it over, but that's life, it didn't matter to me. I turned to Monks and said, 'Forget that, lets still defend this point.' You've got no option but to put things like that straight out of your mind, you simply can't allow yourself to wallow in the 'what might have beens' while the game is still going on.

A couple of minutes after Gows' miss, it did look like we had paid the ultimate price for it though when Kuyt scored for Liverpool. When I saw it go in it was like a knife through the heart, but I instantly looked to Sian Massey and saw her flag go up. The relief I felt was the same as scoring a goal, it was a fantastic feeling. Liverpool still managed to carve out one last chance which fell to Glen Johnson, but Michel magnificently tipped it over the bar to round off yet another fantastic game for him. He was incredible again today.

I was still concentrating on defending our point when the final whistle went and I was hit by a wave of emotion as I realised what we'd achieved. I was relieved, proud, happy and in plenty of pain, but delighted it was all over and our job had been done. At the end as we shook hands, Joey decided it was time to tell Suárez what he thought of him and had a few choice words for him – well-deserved, I have to admit – but it was my turn to act as peacemaker now. I normally provide the calming influence for Joe as his temperament reminds me so much of my own when I was his age.

After we walked over to the fans and gave them a wave for their incredible and constant support throughout the whole game, we all turned and walked back towards the tunnel when I experienced something I had never known in the best part of 350 games of football. All the Liverpool fans in the four parts of the ground who had stayed behind, just began clapping and cheering us off. What a fantastic gesture, it was a really amazing and humbling feeling to walk off an away ground with a tribute like that ringing in your ears.

Those people who speak so highly of Anfield and the Liverpool fans were right, there's definitely something traditional about them and their ground.

It was interesting after the game to reflect on the two strikers I'd faced today in Carroll and Suárez, and how we managed to keep them out. A lot of it has to do with the mentality you adopt when marking two such different strikers, and how you deal with it when they swap constantly throughout the game. When that happens you have to change your approach, depending on which player is near you, because the challenge you face can change instantly. Because we mark zonally at Swansea, this means that if Andy Carroll stays in my zone for ten minutes and the ball is played up to him for lots of headers and, let's say, I win them all, he may well decide to move across to Monks and try his luck there. When that happens, I'd never go with him. No matter how well I might have done against him, I'd always stay in my zone. When Carroll did switch today, it meant that I had Suárez to mark. Now obviously Suárez poses a completely different set of problems to his taller partner – he's far quicker over the ground, a much more darting runner, with quicker feet and so not so much will be played up to him in the air. Sometimes that can happen for longer periods of the game, five or ten minutes, or sometimes it can be pretty instant, perhaps in the change of direction of a run either of them may make.

In times when you are under the cosh, which happened quite a bit today, then these switches can happen several times during a minute or two. That means that I have to be alert at all times to a) not be tempted to be dragged out of position by the attacker's run and b) remember to alter my approach of defending, depending who is in my zone at any given time. It really is a lot to remember at times, like whether I will stay tight to a certain striker – Suárez, or be able to allow another slightly more room – Carroll. You always have to have your wits about you when working within a defensive system, otherwise the whole thing will collapse around you. And that would mean only one thing – conceding goals.

Played 11 Won 3 Drawn 4 Lost 4 Points 13 League Position – 10th
(27 more points needed for 40)

Tuesday 8th November

Straight up to Cardiff this morning to the St David's Hotel to begin our prep for the Wales game against Norway on Saturday. I got here at midday and got shown my room – I am on my own in a big double room, which is nice – then chilled a bit for an hour until we all had lunch at one o'clock.

When I met up with Bellars today I told him about my 'This is Anfield' sign touching incident on Saturday, and how much I was hoping that he hadn't seen me as I knew that he'd have given me some stick.

I was right.

He hadn't seen me do it, but after I told him, he just burst out laughing and couldn't believe that I'd touched it and said that if he'd seen me, he'd have hammered me for it in the tunnel. He doesn't even do it himself and there's me touching it and not even playing for them!

We had dinner after light afternoon training, and then Speedo called a couple of meetings, one of which was about Team GB and the Olympics. Speedo said that neither he nor the Football Association of Wales (FAW) can publically support anyone who is selected for the team because of the stance of the FAW regarding their worry of losing the independence of Wales as a footballing nation. However, Speedo then said that despite that being the official position, he or they won't be stopping anyone either.

After that meeting, Aaron, Bellars and I had another with Speedo and some of the other staff to talk about the upcoming World Cup qualification. The meeting was basically about the planning behind the campaign, discussing things like when and where we would prefer to play the teams in our group – Croatia, Serbia, Belgium, Scotland and Macedonia. It was the first time I'd been included in this meeting and even though it's extremely complicated and detailed, I enjoyed having an input. The meeting lasted over two hours and anything and everything was discussed. The whole point was to look at all the things that may have an impact on our potential qualification, no matter how small. Speedo is intent on us controlling what we can control and he doesn't want to leave any stone unturned. His attitude to qualification is quite clear, there are to be no ifs or buts in the squad and management this time, and no excuses if we fail. We simply have to qualify. End of story.

In the meeting we considered what the average temperatures

would be in the countries that we will be going to for the optional dates. For example, will it be too hot in Croatia if we play there in June compared to October? We also had every squad list up on the wall which showed us in what European league each player plays and when their respective leagues go into shutdown. This is important because we'll then know when they are likely to be rusty and when we won't and vice versa. We need to make sure we don't agree to play someone in early September at the very start of our season if they've been back at theirs since June and will be fully match fit while we won't. We looked at where the airports are, where the hotels are located, how far away the ground will be, whether we want to stay in the city or outside, do we want to fly in two or three days before the game, do we want to fly straight out after full time, all things like that, and based our answers on our collective experiences of previous qualifying games that we've all taken part in – good and bad. Initially the staff were keen that we get the 'harder' games out of the way first but we players disagreed. Not that there are any easy games as such, but Bellars, Aaron and me wanted to try and identify those games that we felt most confident of winning, play them first, hopefully get some points on the board and get our confidence on a roll. We felt that not only would this give us the chance of a good start to the campaign, but we also know that a couple of the FAs of our opponents can be a little volatile. If we were to beat them early on and they then went on and lost to someone else, there was a history of sacking coaches and their form tailing off which could rule them out of the qualifying places. That's an important aspect we considered, especially for the return game. We also looked at the venues we'd like for our home games to give us the best possible advantage. In terms of football, all the squad all love playing at the Liberty because the surface is the best available to us. Also, what the Liberty has over other grounds is that it's a pain for foreign nations to get to, as they can't fly directly in as they can to Cardiff, nor are there any purpose-built hotels nearby for them to use as a training base. We even discussed the footballs we'd prefer to use – any little thing really that may give us that one per cent that will get us qualified. We just have to do it this time.

We all know that.

Wednesday 9th November

Up for breakfast at 9 a.m. today and then off to the Vale for training. I sat with Bellars again and he was still giving me stick about the Anfield sign. He said that he was in bed last night, just trying to get to sleep and the thought of me sneakily touching the sign hoping he wouldn't see me made him burst out laughing. I guess I'm going to struggle to live that down for a while.

Training was more intense today, but not too hard. Ryland warmed us up and we followed this with passing drills and some eight-a-side games.

Thursday 10th November

We stay in hotels a lot in this job. Most people think that it's a privileged thing, probably from their experiences of trips away and nice relaxing breaks. I can tell you that when you stay in hotels as much as we do, it's not so nice. Between international camps and Swansea away games, we change beds and pillows quite a lot. It can get tedious checking into hotels with all your bags and out again for one night, and sometimes it fees like all you do is spend time in hotels and airports.

Of course it comes with the job and we don't mind so much, but there is no place like your own bed. And if you ask any footballer they would agree that the novelty of staying in hotels wears off pretty quickly.

Friday 11th November

This afternoon we had our run out at the Cardiff City Stadium. It's always nice when this session comes around because you know that it means you are close to game time. We didn't work too hard, just mainly shooting, crossing and finishing after which we had another meeting, discussing how Norway will play and what to expect.

Saturday 12th November

Wales 4 (Bale 11, Bellamy 16, Vokes 88, 89) **Norway 1** (Huseklepp 61)

In the warm-up today, Osian took the back four to one side and took us through a fifteen-minute drill where we all lined up as we would in the game. Today it was Gunts at right back, Darcy, me and then Adam at left back. Osian played a mixture of balls into us along the ground and also in the air to head away. All this is done to try to replicate the feeling of defending as a unit as we'll be doing when the game starts. It took place on the edge of the pitch in front of the main stand, so it was a more condensed area than we'd be dealing with later, but it was a valuable exercise because we need to reinforce our habits, rules, spaces and our natural movements, so that all of us know exactly what to expect of each other.

Despite the crowd not being the best, which is understandable at the moment with money being so tight for so many people, it was fantastic to look up and see my family in the stand as we were lining up for the anthems – it's a time I always enjoy and feel incredibly proud.

Norway started the game with just the one striker up top for Darcy and me to worry about, Mohammed Abdellaoue. I'd never heard of him before, but during the week Speedo and the staff went through plenty of videos with us about Norway, so I got to see quite a bit of him – I wonder if Norway have had to sit through videos of me this week.

We had a cracking start and in the first twenty-five minutes everything went to plan, which doesn't often happen at international level. We went one up after just eleven minutes through Bale's typically powerful left foot strike to do their keeper at the near post. Then, Bellars put us two up when he bent a cracker into the top corner. Not often do Wales get 2–0 up in the first quarter of an hour so the boys really celebrated by piling on Bellars.

Norway didn't pack up after we went two goals up and, as the half started to develop, they changed their strategy and formation by starting to play a lot higher up the pitch and began to disrupt our rhythm and possession. After ten minutes of this, we changed what we were doing slightly to counteract them, which worked to a degree, before they started to come back into it more. This is quite common in international games. At half-time Speedo was really pleased that we had stayed strong and committed when they started to unsettle us.

Fifteen minutes into the second half, Speedo called me over to the touchline with new instructions to start to stretch the game more as Norway were still restricting us. He told me to use the longer ball more to Bale if the pass was on. It's a big part of our game to get him involved and make sure he sees plenty of the ball and Speedo didn't think that was happening enough.

Just as we thought we were getting hold of the game, disaster. There was a big mix up between Wayne (Hennessey) and Crofty and it resulted in a goal for them against the run of play. I didn't really see what happened until I watched it on TV tonight, but it was more an own goal by us rather than anything Norway created. But the effect on the game was stunning.

Norway smelt blood and, it was during this pretty intense period, that they made a change and their striker Abdellaoue was subbed. I immediately focussed on the new striker they sent on and started to impose myself on him.

Our third goal, scored by Sam Vokes, was a great one and, coming so late, it knocked the stuffing out of them, and if it didn't, his second a minute later certainly did. Back in the dressing room Speedo and Raymond were really pleased by both the performance and scoreline. There's no better place than a happy dressing room and with Wales in recent times that's become very much the norm. We've won four out of our last five now, and that defeat was against England at Wembley in a game we did more than enough to get a point from.

Speedo has come in after Tosh and really made it a better environment. I'll never say a bad word about Tosh because he was absolutely brilliant for me. He has been a massive influence on my career and made me his captain and I will never forget him for that. What Speedo has done now though, is brought in a more modern approach in terms of sports science and nutrition, and changed the structure in which we work to give us more of a voice, which is a little more inclusive perhaps than Tosh was. For whatever reason, I got the feeling not everyone wanted to be there back then, and that fact was sometimes backed up by some of the withdrawals. Those players would have had their reasons I guess, but pulling out of playing for Wales has never crossed my mind. One thing I will say is that Tosh was brilliant with the youngsters – and I count myself as one of those – because he showed a lot of faith in us and really believed that we could deliver success for him. That sort of faith a manager shows in you is not easily forgotten.

Tuesday 15th November

Back at Llandarcy today for training with Swansea. The Gaffer went easy on us internationals and we had a gentle warm-up followed by some passing drills and small sided games. As Tayls didn't play on Saturday, the Gaffer gave him a full session.

Wednesday 16th November

I have a top three of shirts that I've swapped in my career to date, and they are Ruud van Nistelrooy, John Terry's England shirt and Sol Campbell when he was at Portsmouth. Van Nistelrooy was just about the best striker in the world for a while and to play against him for Wales was a real test for me about where I was as a player. I don't know John Terry at all and probably like most people I'm not overly impressed as to how he's conducted himself at times, but as a player he's been one of the best British central defenders of my generation, so getting his shirt at the Millennium was special. Finally, Sol Campbell was a real hero of mine as a kid and I got his shirt when we played Portsmouth. Sol gave me such belief as a young lad growing up that I could perhaps someday follow in his footsteps, which means that I really treasure his shirt.

People might not understnad why we swap shirts, but it's a sign of respect to a player that you might think highly of, almost a job well done. I definitely get some as a reminder of any personal battles that have meant something to me.

Thursday 17th November

Had a meeting before training to highlight the many positives from the Liverpool game. It was good for those who've been away for the internationals to get switched back on to the Premier League. The Gaffer focused on a lot of the footage that showed how well Gows on the left, Joe on the right and Britts in the middle screened and rotated – in effect how they lined up when we hadn't got the ball, being clever defensively and holding their positions. The key is preventing the opposition midfielders, when they've got the ball, from being able to pick a pass easily up to their striker. In the Liverpool game Lucas would have the ball and I'd call to Gows to screen him so that he wouldn't be able to play the ball up to Suárez. Obviously Gows won't be able to see behind him to see where Suárez has run, so if he's run left, then I'll call to Gows to screen left. The Gaffer also showed us how well the lads had rotated when someone had been drawn out of position and one of the others filled in to his place with the other one eventually rotating into his. Without this it would just result in loads of gaps and pile the pressure straight on to us in defence. It was one of the key reasons why we kept a clean sheet at Anfield.

Friday 18th November

The atmosphere around the town is like nothing I've ever experienced in Swansea before, in terms of anticipating the visit of Man United. Everyone I've seen has mentioned the game and I can see what a positive effect just being in the Premier League is having on the people of Swansea. The build-up to the game has been a bit of a circus all this week with more media demands than normal, but it is vital for the players to remain focused as a group and try to stay detached from the hype. But it is difficult, because having Manchester United next up is such a massive occasion.

Usual Friday meeting this morning where we went through a video of our opponents. It was really strange going over an analysis of what we can expect certain Manchester United players to do, because we've watched them all do it before hundreds of times on Sky. We almost knew what was coming!

Only a light training session today, and had a bit of a laugh doing keep ball. Some players are better than others at this, especially Gows and Britts, and also Kemy who's got great feet as he's always been into his street football and probably has the most tricks of us all. We have great banter doing this and Caulker gets hammered all the time for giving the ball away.

I had a text chat with Rio tonight where we wished each other all the best for the game tomorrow. They flew down to Cardiff this afternoon and are staying at the Marriott. He wished me good luck and we agreed to swap shirts at the end of the game.

Saturday 19th November
Swansea City 0 Manchester United 1 (Hernández 11)

The intensity today in the tunnel was fantastic. I walked to my place in the line behind Monks and Michel, and standing in the same spot across from me was Rio. I gave him a quick glance to see if I could catch his eye, and this bloke who was texting me good luck just 24 hours earlier, just kept staring straight ahead – all business.

As soon as the game started we could see that Rooney was playing really deep with Hernández playing right on the shoulder of me and Monks. I thought we started out showing them too much respect and we were playing deeper than we would have liked as a result. Monks and I agreed to forget about Rooney when he was patrolling around in that deep area and left him for Britts to mark.

Unfortunately, Àngel made a mistake early on, giving a simple ball away, which led to Hernández's goal. It was a bad mistake by Àngel, but can happen playing the way we do, especially from the back. It was a pretty big blow because we then had to score two to win the game, which was always going to be tough against

143

the champions. I told Àngel not to worry and to continue with his game and he looked unfazed which is always good to see.

There was a big moment in the game not too much later which after good build-up play by Wayne and Danny, that led to the ball being played across the box by Wayne in front of De Gea to Scotty who found himself unmarked at the far post. Frustratingly, Scott got his timing wrong and he ended up missing an open goal from about six yards. It was bitterly disappointing as we all knew we'd probably only get one chance and we'd have to take it. Seeing the opportunity spurned was actually harder to take than conceding the goal earlier.

I don't know whether it was them and their quality, the size of the occasion or just an off day by us, but for the rest of the half we gave away far too much possession which just isn't like us and, as a result, we couldn't get into any sort of rhythm.

There was lots of frustration in the dressing room at half-time and nobody was really happy, especially the Gaffer. It felt like we never really got stuck in to them and he obviously agreed because he let us know it. He made a change at half-time, replacing Wayne with Joe. I looked across at Wayne and must admit I felt a little sorry for him. He's not really a centre midfield so playing slightly out of position against the champions was always going to be tough for him. I was pleased to see Joe coming on though as he's been in great form recently. We have a really good understanding as we play in similar areas of the pitch and link up quite a bit during the game.

We started the second half with far more energy and creativity with Joey slotting into things instantly. I had a chance from a corner when the ball fell to me about fifteen yards out. I was gutted that it fell on my left side as that isn't my strongest and my shot was easily blocked by Rio. As the half developed, we began to dominate. We got back into our usual rhythm a bit more and were playing our football much further up the pitch and began to pressurise them into mistakes and really started to create some problems for them. It was a great feeling knowing that we were starting to impose ourselves on such a good team.

Hernández got subbed, but sadly he'd already done his job.

He looks so young and is very quiet on the pitch, but he had just one chance and took it. Simple as that. That's why he's world class.

A couple of minutes later I heard the announcement giving me Man of the Match. Sometimes, I'm that involved in the game, that I don't always hear it. I was shocked to hear my name called out because I never win it. I appreciated Man of the Match, but would have preferred three points.

We took a lot of confidence from the second half today, as we stretched them and were on top for long periods. Nevertheless, the top sides punish you for your mistakes. I also hated losing our undefeated home record.

Swapped shirts with Rio. It has instantly become the best in my collection, knocking van Nistelrooy, Terry and Sol all down a rung!

In the dressing room after the game there was a definite feeling of anticlimax. It stemmed from the first half and how we gave them too much respect. It wasn't that way in the second half and we did enough to get a point. However, despite that, I have to say that United were a class act. Even when we rallied and got about them later in the game, they still managed to stay calm and composed under pressure. The Gaffer always tells us that every game in this league will be a learning curve and he told us that we should all have learned a lot from what happened, especially in terms of believing in ourselves from the very start and not being overawed by the opposition.

Played 12 Won 3 Drawn 4 Lost 5 Points 13 League Position – 13th
(27 more points needed for 40)

Sunday 20th November

Straight after the game yesterday we shot back to Birmingham with our already packed suitcases for our flight to New York. With the amount of games I play without a break, a few days off like this to get away is always appreciated. The other boys get a short break when I play international games, so when we have a chance, the Gaffer gives me time off and says get away and just forget about football for a few days. This is one of the brilliant sides of the Gaffer. His man management is second to none. This morning we flew from Heathrow to JFK and after we landed and were standing in the passport queue, we met a lady and her two daughters who were Swansea City fans. It was very strange to be in New York talking to Swansea fans!

Wednesday 23rd November

We had two and a half days in New York and got everything done that we wanted to, all of the usual tourist things, and it was so good to get a mental break from the day job.

Coming back I feel much fresher and ready to attack the next part of the season. The guy who checked us in at Newark airport recognised me as well as a few others. It's crazy to think that people who live in New York know who you are. Just shows how big the Premier League is these days.

Thursday 24th November

Back in work today. I've had a great time away with Vanessa and Raphael and feel really refreshed, so was happy to get back into it today. Things are so scientific with sport now that the staff treated me differently in training today compared to when I last trained. They instructed me to take things slightly easier because my body hasn't trained for four days and they don't want me to risk some muscles and ligaments reacting badly from my brief lay off. They got no complaints from me.

Friday 25th November

It was a nice sharp session this morning and I really enjoyed it. Did some shape work at the end with some really sharp passing drills and small sided games.

Because it's the Villa on Sunday, all the family are down from Birmingham, so I had a nice, relaxed family evening. I fancy us against Villa. They won't like it down here, running around chasing the ball. It's a big game for us and a definite three points up for grabs. In terms of survival and the race for 40 points, it doesn't take Einstein to work out that our home form is what will probably save us in the end. The squad believes we will win our home games – the result isn't really in question, just the score. Against United we know we could have won had we started better. We will start better against Villa and we will win. I have not the smallest shred of doubt about that.

Saturday 26th November

In training we often work on shape, meaning we focus on the position of the players in the shape of the team. Sometimes we have the youngsters against us, but we also do it without opposition and just pass the ball and try to replicate the shape we would have in certain situations. Dedicating part of training to it every week means you know exactly where you need to be standing, wherever the ball is. Most teams do this and it just reinforces a bit of discipline in us in terms of always being organised for any situation.

Sunday 27th November
Swansea City 0   Aston Villa 0

See below.

Played 13 Won 3 Drawn 5 Lost 5 Points 14 League Position – 13th
(26 more points needed for 40)

Wednesday 30th November

Since I started writing this diary back in July, the last few days has been the only time that I've wanted to throw it away and jack it all in. The reason for this is that on Sunday, prior to our match with Aston Villa, my manager for Wales, Gary Speed died. As I reread that last sentence, I still can't believe what those words mean. I feel just numb thinking about it. It's as if my mind still won't allow me to accept that it is true.

Throughout this diary I have given you an insight into every match that I've taken part in this season, but there'll be no match report about Sunday's game with Villa, I'm afraid, because to me it's as if it didn't happen. I didn't care about it when I was playing in it, and I don't care about it now. That's the first time I've ever said that about any match I've played in since I've become a footballer.

I prepared for the game as I usually do, breakfast, walk with the dogs, spot of lunch and then drove to the Liberty. Nothing that happened in my pre-match routine suggested that I was about to receive the news that has shocked me more than any other news that I have received in my life to this point.

I was in the dressing room before getting changed, when I had a message saying that James Collins, my Wales team mate and Villa centre half, wanted to have a word with me in the tunnel. When I went out to see him, I could tell by the look on his face that something was up, and then he just quietly broke the news to me.

The life of a professional footballer is one of wind-ups, dodgy humour and merciless stick, so, when you get told something serious you nearly always assume that it's some sort of stitch-up that is going to make you look a fool. As I tried to take in what Ginge was saying, part of my brain was just telling me, 'This is a wind-up, don't fall for it, he's having you on'. I know you might think that's a stupid reaction to have, but of nearly everyone I know, Speedo was absolutely the last person who I would have believed could have died. As I was trying to digest what Ginge had said, just looking into his eyes and the ashen colour of his face told me that, sadly, this was no joke and no wind-up. It was real. Horribly real.

Ginge told me that he'd found out on the Villa coach on the way to the Liberty from their hotel as Alan Shearer – who was a great mate of Speedo – had rung Villa keeper Shay Given and told him. All three of them, Shay, Shearer and Gary, were very close when they were at Newcastle, and had all remained the best of friends along with their wives and children. Ginge said that he himself had been physically sick on hearing the news and that Shay was in absolute bits in the dressing room. I just simply couldn't believe what I was hearing. I can't really remember what I said to Ginge when I turned and went back into the dressing room as everything seemed to go into slow motion. I was in a world of my own as if detached from it all. I just felt numb, unable to take the awful news in.

I walked into the dressing room and it seemed everyone, by then, knew. Someone had been looking at the net on their phone and it came in as a newsflash. Someone started to speak to me about it, but even though I'd just had Ginge telling me not thirty seconds before, I still refused to believe it. I just said that it all must be some sort of horrible mistake and walked to my place and started to change.

After the decision was made to go ahead with the game as usual we went out for our warm-up at twenty past two. Normally when we come out of the tunnel for the first time, there's a decent buzz from the fans who have taken their seats early and give us a round of applause and some cheers. On Sunday, there was nothing as we set foot out there, no cheers, no clapping, nothing We could tell from the fans' faces that they had either just been told the news or were in the process of being told. It was if the stadium itself had gone into shock.

One of the things about being a professional footballer is that you have to have a very strong mind. We are trained from a very young age to ignore the off-field issues when we go out to play, and anytime we experience adversity we are taught to deal with it in a positive way, almost thrive on it. Once the decision was made to play, that part of my psyche kicked in, or more accurately, it tried to kick in. The reality about the situation was much different though, I simply didn't care about the match at all. I don't think I was alone either. By now, most people have seen the pictures of Shay Given at the minute's silence. He was just heartbroken. He had a different relationship to Speedo than I did, they'd been team mates who'd become best friends, so I can only guess at how awful he was feeling. Players like me, Joe Allen, Tayls and Britts had a different relationship with Speedo as we knew him as our manager or coach. However, even though we couldn't call ourselves close mates in the way that Shay could, Speedo was such a fantastic bloke that even as a manager we all still felt incredibly close to him on a personal level. He was such a decent, honest and good man who included you in so much. Every player in our side was badly affected by the news, and from a Villa point of view, I think the players were so shocked at how upset Shay was with the situation, that they also played the game in shock. That's certainly how it felt for me, and is shown by the 0–0 scoreline.

I'll never forget that minute's silence for as long as I live. Unfortunately we've had a few this year, with Brendan's dad and the miners at the West Brom game, and then for Poppy Day up at Anfield. As respectful as all those other occasions were, Speedo's on Sunday was completely different. The crowd actually went totally silent as Monks was doing the toss with the ref and still having photos taken with the mascots. Then, even before Kevin Johns started speaking to announce everything, he began against a background of complete silence. I'd never experienced that before. After saying some kind words about Speedo, Kevin called for the minute's silence and everybody stood up. The silence that had fallen over the ground was then broken by the sound of the seats clacking back into place all around as people stood. It was unbelievably eerie. A few seconds into the silence, one set of hands started clapping on their own from within the Villa fans and it took a few seconds before more joined in, but then in an instant, the silence had been replaced by this respectful round of applause which then erupted into 'There's only one Gary Speed'. It was the first time, but not the last, that the tears came for me. In the last couple of days we've all seen the pictures of that moment, and the images of Shay that were so touching and emotional. To then turn around and try and start a game of football after that was one of the hardest, and somehow most pointless things I've ever had to do in my life.

The match was a nothing game after that and even if I wanted to talk about it, frankly, there's not much I remember. Like the rest of the players I just kind of drifted through it on autopilot and the next thing I knew I was in the tunnel swapping shirts with Ginge. It seemed fitting somehow that him and I did that, given our Welsh connections with Speedo and that he'd been the one to break the awful news to me.

My family had a box for the game and my next duty was to go up and see them. When I walked in, the room was really quiet and I think, like me, everyone was in genuine shock. Naturally, everyone was worried about me and how I'd taken the news so we discussed it briefly, but I think everyone realised that I didn't really want to talk about it, and Vanessa and I left soon after.

When I got home, the only thing I could think of doing was to scour the internet for any news that I could find, maybe just something that I didn't already know that would somehow help me to make sense of the whole thing. I couldn't find anything and then spoke to Titus who was also struggling to come to terms with the news. Like me and everyone else I'd spoken to, Titus was asking the same question – why?

Even though Vanessa didn't know Speedo on a personal level, she was really struggling to deal with the news and was very upset, not just because she knew how much Speedo meant to me, but like all the other many thousands of football fans around the country, she just knew a good guy when she saw one and Speedo was certainly one of those.

As I write this now and try to put my feelings down, the best way I can describe things is to say that I simply feel honoured and privileged to have known Gary Speed on a personal level. He was a really special man, and it's clear that many people whose paths crossed with his in the football world feel exactly the same way.

A few days have passed now since Sunday, but I still don't feel comfortable talking about the circumstances of his death, as nobody knows anything for sure yet apart from how it happened. For the last three days, all I've been able to do is keep asking myself why? Why did this great footballing man choose to end his life when he had so much going for him and the love and respect of so many people? On Monday morning, I woke up with a headache after not sleeping well and having weird dreams all linked to the same issue – 'Why?' Then I spoke with my former Swansea City team mate Owain Tudur Jones on the phone, and the basis of our conversation was the same – why?

The rest of the day was spent in this almost surreal state

of watching everything I could about Speedo on the TV, still struggling to believe what I was seeing and I couldn't help myself but trawl the net, again looking for answers. I didn't find any.

Yesterday, sporadic memories were coming into my mind about him. Like the time when Tosh made me captain of Wales for the first time when we played Scotland. My phone went off, and it was a 'well done' text to me from Gary Speed. Gary Speed! The text was congratulating me on becoming Wales captain and wishing me all the best for the game. I was genuinely gobsmacked as I'd never even met him at the time, I'd just known him as a great player I'd watched loads on TV when I was growing up. For him to take the time out to do that kindness to someone he'd never met was nice enough, but when I realised that it would have meant him finding someone who knew me, contacting them, getting my number and then sending the text, well, for him to go to so much trouble for me was, I thought, very humbling.

Mind you, as much as his kind actions shocked me then, I know it won't shock those that knew him well.

I've also been recalling all the chats we had on the phone and in person about Wales and where he wanted us to go. I remember a call I had from Speedo just a couple of days after he'd been officially announced as manager. When I knew that Tosh was gone and that a new manager would come in, I questioned if I would still be involved and in what capacity. I didn't know Speedo really, apart from his excellent reputation within footballing circles, so there was no way that I was going to assume that he rated me as a player or that I would feature as a regular under him, just because that had been the case under Tosh. All this was going through my mind when I answered the phone and heard 'Hi Ashley, it's Gary Speed here'. He went on to introduce himself to me but then quickly put me at ease by telling me that he thought of me very highly as a player and that he wanted me to be one of the senior members of his group and one whose opinion he wanted to value. He then quickly told me of his vision and what he expected from himself and what he expected from us. It was quite simple, direct and straightforward, 'I want us to qualify for the next World Cup. That's all, and I want myself as a manager and you as players to be judged on that and nothing else.' It was so refreshing and to hear that target laid out so bare in front of me. Sometimes, players need that simplistic approach; one goal, one outcome that nobody misunderstands or can confuse with anything else. He asked me about the general feeling and morale within the camp and asked me some detail about certain players and what sort of characters they were. He thanked me for my openness and honesty, arranged to come down to Swansea City to meet me for a coffee and a further chat and wished me all the best. It was typical of Speedo, thoughtful, organised, well planned, but with a steely determination behind it that left you in no doubt about where he was heading. He also left me in no doubt that he saw me in a certain way which meant that I would play a reasonably big part with Wales under him, and that was fantastic to hear.

Not long afterwards, we met up for Wales for the first time under him and he made me his vice captain. He called me into his room at the hotel and explained that he was going with Aaron Ramsey as his Welsh captain. He had worked out that I'd probably had an eye on it myself – which I did – and wanted to explain his reasons for going with Aaron, to tell me how close I had been to getting the job myself and to announce officially that I was going to be his vice captain. He told me that he hadn't wanted to embarrass me in front of the rest of the lads, letting me find out in such a public way in case I'd be disappointed; instead, he wanted to tell me personally to get my head around it before going public with it. That's the type of guy he was, always thinking of others and always concerned with how certain news – good or bad – would potentially affect someone. With all that has happened now, I am so hugely proud that he treated me that way and trusted me enough to pick me as his vice captain. In an odd way, that means even more now than it did at the time. The way he did that again showed what a compassionate side he had to his nature which, as I can vouch for, isn't always a trait that appears within a professional football manager.

I've got another headache coming on as I write this, and they've been pretty much constant since Sunday and I never normally suffer with them. I think it's because I'm constantly walking round and continuously asking myself that same horrible question, 'why?' all the time, and racking my brain to try to remember if there is something that I saw and should have picked up on to explain all this. Since Sunday, and this is unlike me, I have gone to do things in and around the house or at training and have just been doing everything half-heartedly and asking myself, 'What's the point?' I've been thinking about his kids a lot, who I've met, and simply can't imagine what they are going through right now. I've also been thinking of Speedo's strong vision for Wales which was basically achieving success – with no excuses if we fail – but achieving it in the right way, by playing 'proper' football, and I've been wondering what the future holds for that in particular and for us all involved in the Wales set-up in general. There were very definite similarities in the way that Speedo wanted Wales to play and the way that the Gaffer has got us playing at Swansea City. He'd obviously seen Swansea play plenty of times and he'd often chat to me to clarify certain little bits about what we did in certain circumstances with Swansea and I think he was really succeeding in bringing Wales along by playing in a similar passing and possession style. Ultimately, he wanted to play attractive football and win with it. And that's exactly what he had started to achieve on a regular basis. We were doing so well under Speedo's leadership in playing that way after admittedly an uncertain start, that it would be a sporting tragedy if Speedo's fantastic work isn't built upon in the same manner that he was progressing things forward.

I'm not surprised to see the outpouring of grief, love and affection for this true Welsh great from all across the footballing world.

CHAPTER SIX

December 2011

Friday 2nd December

Training was short and sharp this morning, just what we needed really and the Gaffer announced the team which was the same XI as recent weeks, meaning Jazz keeps his place at right back.

By the time we arrived at the hotel, which we've used before, we were straight in for dinner because it was so late. After food the Gaffer called our usual Friday evening team meeting and Junior Hoilett was highlighted as their danger man and we were told that Chris Samba is back in the squad but don't know if he'll play. If he does, he'll be a headache at set pieces and corners – he's a big old unit.

Saturday 3rd December

Blackburn Rovers 4 (Yakubu 20, 45, 57, 82)

Swansea City 2 (Lita 35, Moore 66)

Breakfast is optional on away trips, but as usual I go down and as usual Nath stays kipping. Got back up to my room around tenish, grabbed a shower, relaxed, chatted with Nath and then went down to meet for our walk around 11.45. The walk was cancelled though because of the rain – too heavy. It was the first of many things that went wrong today.

Before kick-off, we lined up for a minute's applause again for Speedo, and once more the emotion of it all got to me, and made me think how futile a game of football appears to be in the grand scheme of things compared to Speedo's tragic death.

From kick-off, everything seemed to be going perfectly. We settled into our normal passing rhythm straight away, managed to get into a good flow of possession but just failed to turn that possession into any real clear-cut chances. Then out of nothing, Blackburn scored through Yakubu, which for us was a very sloppy goal as we had a few chances to win the ball back, but paid the price for not doing so. I was fuming we had lost another clean sheet.

Blackburn were so poor though, I was convinced we'd get back in the game quickly and, thankfully, my optimism was rewarded with an excellent team goal. It started with Michel at the back, was orchestrated by Leon as usual, set up by Gows and finished brilliantly in the air by Leets. I said to Monks that I'd happily take 1–1 going in at half-time. We then gave away a needless corner on the right, that was played long to the edge of the box on the left, where I thought, 'No danger from that', until Formica just smashed a ridiculous volley from nowhere back across the box that would have probably gone out for a throw on another day. Instead, it found Yakubu who had just wandered off his marker, and guided it past Michel with his head.

Anyone who follows football knows how significant it is to concede so close to the break because it changes momentum in an instant. We had been on top since we had scored, and were looking to capitalise on our possession in the second half.

We had a few choice words from the Gaffer in the dressing room, which was fair enough, but he also emphasised that we were much better than them, that we would definitely score again and that we had to keep going exactly as we had done in the first forty-five minutes, and commit 100 per cent to our game plan. By the time he'd finished speaking and giving us our instructions, such was his positivity that we were convinced that at the very least we'd go out and win the second half.

I don't know if the weather can be an indicator as to how things are likely to go, but just as the second half got underway, the weather broke and it started absolutely lashing down. That just proved to dampen an already crap atmosphere at the ground, which was largely to do with the Blackburn fans. In all my years, I have never heard a manager being booed when his team are in front in the match.

We started the half well, sticking to our principles and started to turn the game around. They didn't really offer anything, but then their keeper Paul Robinson just punted one the complete length of the field which skipped off the wet turf and meant Michel had no option but to tip it over for an unwanted corner. They played another deep one beyond the back post to Samba, who's an absolute beast. He headed it back across to Yakubu, and he completed his hat-trick from about a yard. I just couldn't believe it. We were two behind and they'd hardly had a kick.

The Gaffer reacted immediately by bringing on Luke for Gows, playing him just off Leets, to join Wayne in attack who had replaced Nath at half-time. The change worked as Luke really got into the game quickly and made a really positive impact which meant we were starting to put them under some decent pressure, but I realised that getting two goals back just to get even was going to be pretty tough. Still, we didn't give up and we got our reward for the pressure after some great work by Wayne down the right with a cross shot which Robinson couldn't hold, and it fell to Luke who lashed it home. 3–2. We were right back in it then and the only outcome I could see was another goal by us – at the very least. But it wasn't to be. About a quarter of an hour after Luke's goal, Joey got a very unlucky second yellow card as he was chasing back behind Hoilett and he was gone. Ten men, a goal down, away from home in awful conditions, that's about as bad as it gets.

Almost straight after Joey's red, Vukčević made a run into the box, Tayls mistimed his challenge and gave away a penalty. Yakubu stepped up with a chance for his fourth goal, took it, scored, and that was the game. It felt like he'd had four touches and scored four goals, I was absolutely stunned.

It was a very quiet and disappointed dressing room as we all understood the significance of the defeat. None of us think we are in a relegation battle as such, but we all know that to avoid that ever becoming a reality we have to take points off those teams that clearly are, to ensure that we manage to put as much daylight as possible between us and them. With all the off-field goings-on at Blackburn and the shocking start that they've had, we really had the team to take points off them. We gifted Yakubu three goals and that's not good enough.

We had 68 per cent possession today and if we add that to the two goals we managed away from home, then you can understand why I'm so frustrated and annoyed that we lost. Stats like that, especially away from home, should be enough for you to win any game.

Played 14 Won 3 Drawn 5 Lost 6 Points 14 League Position – 14th (26 more points needed for 40)

Sunday 4th December

Our Christmas party up in Newcastle. It was a great laugh and a good idea to be in a town where nobody knows who you are so you can have a bit of fun, without feeling that everyone is scrutinising your every move.

We got a coach up to Newcastle after the Blackburn game which took a couple of hours and it wasn't the best of starts to a night out to be honest because of the result and the mood on the bus was sombre to say the least. We had a couple of drinks to try to make the time pass easier, but not Gows, who had a bit of travel sickness so ended up sitting down the front by the driver while we were all up the back. A pretty crap trip if I'm honest.

Today was better and we had some fun with the choice of outfits we had to wear. All the boys had drawn a name out of the hat last week, and then had to go out and buy the person a really crap jumper – like some of those minging Christmas ones with reindeer on – give it to the player concerned on the afternoon of the do, and obviously, they'd have to wear the jumper they'd been given for the rest of the day. As usual, something that sounds so simple often gets complicated. Not content with just buying an awful jumper, some of the lads decided to customise them with glitter and create various shapes on the front that had best remain not described here. I drew Lee Lucas from the hat, and because my memory is so rubbish, after I'd pulled his name and made my plan as to what jumper I was going to buy him – I went to bed that night and then completely forgot all about it. When I finally remembered it was too late to buy one, so I brought one of Vanessa's with me to Blackburn and then in the hotel on Saturday night, Nath and I redesigned it and cut bits out of it until it was fit for Lee to wear! It was a shambles really. We got the little milk cartons from the hotel room and stuck them on it, I got random items from the medical kit and stuck them on it, cut circles out on the front – I'll leave you work out where. It was a shocker.

Luke did mine and went easy on me with a typical Christmas woolly effort. I've worn worse!

Monday 5th December

It was good to let our hair down yesterday, just what we needed after the Blackburn game.

We flew back this morning and I'm a bit shattered now, but it turned out we had a pretty decent time. I'm so glad we did it, despite feeling so crap initially after the result.

Tuesday 6th December

It was back to training today, the first session of the week after the disappointments of Blackburn, so it wasn't too hard. Back on the AstroTurf again as the field is too bad and we need to let it breathe.

The Gaffer told me today that we might be having a bit of a mid season break in the New Year, probably after the Norwich game in February. Apparently Dubai is on the cards, which sounds pretty good. We'll have to wait and see on that one, because we've heard things like this in the past at Swansea City and nothing's come of it so I'm not getting my hopes up just yet, but it's nice to know that we've potentially got a trip to look forward to. One thing I've learnt in my career to date is that once half the season is done, it's quite easy to get a bit fatigued, so a trip to relax a bit and train with the sun on our backs will be welcomed by everyone.

Wednesday 7th December

Training was a little bit tougher today with the emphasis on flexibility and agility. The boys were still laughing over the stories from the Christmas party, but we all still have a pretty bad taste in our mouths about the Blackburn game. We had a chat among ourselves about Fulham and how vital that game is. I don't think for a minute that Fulham are relegation candidates, they are too good a side, but at the moment they are around us, so we must take three points off them just in case we become rivals as the season develops.

After training I had a meeting with a guy called Nigel from A Touch Far Vetched who has raised over £500 for Hari Keift, thanks to a comedy and crisps night. He also donated some prizes for our night at the Manor Park in January and I also spoke to him about another fundraising event for Hari in February. I love the involvement of doing stuff for charity and for Hari in particular. But I'm fully aware that without people like Nigel coming up with ideas and running the events so well, we'd only achieve limited success.

Thursday 8th December

Training this morning paid specific detail to the goals conceded at Blackburn which is normal for the Gaffer after a defeat like that. What's different this season compared to last year in the Championship is that we've all seen the goals about a hundred times since Saturday because everything is highlighted so much more on Sky, now that we're in the Prem. I must admit it's great to see all the replays when we've done well, but having to watch Yakubu score his four repeatedly, really pisses me off.

Friday 9th December

We had a video meeting before training today where the Gaffer ran us through some of the things to expect against Fulham, including a look at Bobby Zamora. He's been in and out under Martin Jol with loads of rumours doing the rounds that they've fallen out and that he's going to be on his way. The Gaffer showed us how he takes the ball into feet and rolls defenders so that he opens up his left side for shooting opportunities whenever he can, so we'll all have to be aware of that. We also saw how effective Hangeland is at set pieces, both in defence and attack. In defence he doesn't actually mark anyone, he just waits in the middle of the box for the ball to come and just tries to head it clear – succeeding most of the time because he's just so tall. It's annoying because what you'd normally do is get your own big guy – Caulker for us – to go and stand on him, then as the ball comes in, Caulker would make a run away, taking the big defender with him. Hangeland doesn't do this, though. He lets all the runners go and just concentrates on heading the ball away, wherever it is played in to.

I like Martin Jol and I think that Fulham are a great team with quality players who are all technically very good. They play narrower than us, and their league position is probably a bit false at the moment. I'm pretty confident that they'll end up in the top half of the table come the end of the season. So with that in mind if we want to cement ourselves in this league, then teams like Fulham, especially when we play them at home, are the type of teams we really must beat.

It was Gary Speed's funeral today and it brought a lot of feelings back to that awful Sunday morning when I first found out the news. We are still no wiser as to why he took his own life. He obviously had his reasons, and maybe we'll never know. I found myself looking on the internet again today to see if I could find any answers at all, but I couldn't. It's a very sad day because as weird as it sounds, now that he has been buried it's so real, and confirms that he is never coming back. Until today, I've carried this strange feeling that one day it's going to come out that it was all a big mistake and he is still with us. Today has finally ended that imaginary hope.

Saturday 10th December

Swansea City 2 (Sinclair 56, Graham 90 + 1) **Fulham 0**

Changes today, with Nath being left out after being hooked by the Gaffer at half-time last week, and Monks left out as Caulks is fit. That was a bit of a tough one for me because Monks has done fantastic for us since Caulks' injury at Arsenal, but in fairness, before his injury, Caulks was on fire. Instead of leading one of the two lines in the warm-up behind the goal as he does when skipper, Monks moved to the back today to allow the rest of us to concentrate on the warm-up. As it's not so important for him, he's happy to take a back seat.

As skipper, I went for the toss with Hangeland, who didn't say a single word. I won it and chose to attack the away fans first. We always do this if we win it, and you'd be amazed how much it gets in your mind if the opposition win it and turn you around, which is what I always try to do if I win the toss away from home. I was very aggressive in the huddle, and as I hadn't spoken in it for a while, probably went over the top with my swearing. It's important I set the tone.

I was pleased that Jazz kept his place today after a promising game at Blackburn last week. It's hugely important for Jazz's development that he gets some game time and keeps his place as a reward for doing well. He's also a great lad, one of my best mates at the club, so I had an extra word with him at the start to make sure he was OK with everything and hopefully give him some confidence before kick-off. I'm certain he's going to develop into a top player and will also play for Wales if he keeps developing as he has.

My benchmark for a good start happened again today when I played a raking crossfield ball to Wayne, a couple of minutes after I was first going to do one but pulled out of it because I didn't think it was on.

Midway through the half, Luke had a great shot which fizzed onto the bar and I made a point of shouting well done to him. He's a quiet lad who cares about the game, but because he doesn't wear that on his sleeve, I get the feeling the fans misunderstand him. He is a great talent and I would love to see what he could do with a run in the team, but as the Gaffer's system only caters for one striker and it's clear that his number one is Danny, it's difficult for Luke. But I hoped the shot would lead to good things for him today.

We definitely edged the half, and had a couple of decent shouts against Riise for a penalty, but there was nothing. From a defensive point of view the game was as quiet as the Bolton game and, while Dempsey was busy enough, he didn't cause Caulks and I many problems and I have to say Ruiz was quiet.

The Gaffer sent us out for the second half with instructions to be more creative in the final third and to put their keeper under more pressure, and Leets took this literally when he chased a long ball down after five minutes. In fairness to Leets, he followed the ball perfectly, never taking his eye off it, and I could see that he had no idea where Schwarzer was. But as he went up for it, Schwarzer tried to get over and in front of Leets to claim it, but Leets' momentum flipped the keeper over and he landed on his neck. It was a really horrible moment, and the shocked gasp from the crowd down at that end of the ground told me all I needed to know. Schwarzer landed so awkwardly on his neck that the ref stopped it straight away, and I have to admit I feared the worst. He had treatment for the best part of ten minutes and it was a relief to see him up and about and able to carry on.

Whether Schwarzer was feeling groggy, I don't know, but about five minutes later we went ahead after his punch from a corner fell to Wayne, whose scruffy shot fell to Scotty and, as he helped it on, Dempsey swung a leg and deflected it in. We were laughing after telling Scott it was an O.G., but he kept saying, 'No way, that's mine'. Most people think that strikers claim everything because they're always thinking of their goals record, and of course it's got nothing to do with the bonus they get for scoring. Scotty's hair costs him a lot to keep that perfect so needs to claim as many as he can!

Fair play to Fulham, after the goal they had a decent ten minutes where Michel kept our lead with a couple of great saves and Riise also hit a post. I never really felt worried that we were going to be overrun by them, and still felt we'd get another, but 1–0 is never a comfortable lead. We nearly doubled our lead when Kemy had a great low strike after a pass from Scott that beat the keeper but hit a post. Kemy has great feet and possesses the ability to score goals from outside of the box and we really could have done with that one going in at that stage.

Five minutes from the end it looked like our failure to get a second was going to cost us when Jazz gave away a penalty. He was a bit naïve as he was being honest and tried to win the ball from Frei, but I could see it was going to be a pen a mile off because of the way Frei had put his body in between Jazz and the ball and was clearly looking for the challenge. Normally I'd have been distraught at that point, as I was when Wigan won that late one in our first home game, but I didn't really know Michel back then. By now, I've had almost four months of seeing how agile and brilliant he is in training, and I felt confident he was going to save it. It helped that Dempsey had had a quiet game and his body language wasn't good, but it was still a brilliant feeling to see Michel go the right way and save it and then switch back on straight away to defend the corner.

Danny's goal, when it came, was such a relief because we'd shut up shop to protect the goal lead by then and weren't really being that offensive, just concentrating on staying organised. Scoring so late was really the icing on the cake. At the final whistle, I went straight to Michel and just said to him, 'You won us that game!' He just laughed and said thanks, but he showed again how vital he's already become to us. We've got 17 points now, but I dread to think what we'd have if it wasn't for him. He's easily the best keeper I've ever played with and at the moment I'm struggling to think of many better in the Prem.

Played 15 Won 4 Drawn 5 Lost 6 Points 17 League Position – 11th (23 more points needed for 40)

Sunday 11th December

Some days in this job, it's tough to get out of bed physically. If you've had a particularly tough game the night before, the next morning can be pretty rough. I think from when pre-season starts in July until when the season ends in May, there isn't a single day in which you don't have aches and pains all over your body. These might be small cuts, grazes, dead legs to tight muscles.

Most players have stiff backs, ankles, knees and hips throughout the course of the season. On certain days, especially match days, it wouldn't be unusual for footballers to take up to 18 tablets from morning to night. These will be a variety of vitamins, a number of different painkillers and tablets to help you recover straight after the game. On top of these, a lot of players struggle to sleep after games and will take a sleeping tablet as well before bed. Most players will do whatever it takes to get out onto the pitch, so some have painkilling injections on top of the tablets if they have an injury, but still want to play. Sometimes I try to get out of the car or up off the sofa and I feel about 70 years old – which is about how old Monks actually is. Me and Monks often joke about the way we abuse our bodies, and the fact that when we are older, we probably won't be able to walk, but all that matters at this point is the game at the end of the week, and playing in it.

Monday 12th December

I attended the BBC Wales Sports Personality of the Year awards at the Liberty tonight, and really enjoyed it, especially as we were awarded the Team of the Year prize. I must admit I was a little surprised as I assumed that the Wales rugby team would walk it after getting to the semis of the World Cup, so it was pleasing to hear our name called out. Most of the lads were there and went up on the stage with the Gaffer who was asked a few questions along with Monks. It was a good night and a great reward for everyone associated with the club, but especially the Gaffer who deserved it for the way that he's turned us into a very good Premier League team.

Tuesday 13th December

This evening, Vanessa, Raphael and I went round to Hari Kieft's house to meet him and his parents, Cerianne and Richard, and Hari's sister, Olivia, for the first time. Hari is a great little kid and I'm so pleased we are able to help him in his dream to walk. Personally, I haven't done too much in terms of the fundraising but I'm aware that these days most sports people and footballers in general have an ability to connect with the public, hopefully in a positive way. That was the whole idea behind WillsWorld really, that I would use my 'name' in order to boost causes for people less fortunate. Cerianne and Richard were kind enough to say how well that approach has worked for Hari and how the profile of his fight and their efforts for fundraising have been boosted by some of the interviews I've done about WillsWorld that have highlighted Hari's cause. It was great to hear that from them and I am delighted that everything seems to be moving in the right direction.

Wednesday 14th December

Training is generally good fun. There are the bad days, of course, but on the whole we all enjoy what we do. This morning there was a really good feel about everything we did. Swansea City is quite unique in terms of football clubs because we have no big egos in the squad and everyone really gets on well. A lot of that is due to the way the Gaffer treats us of course, but it's great to be a part of and I think all of us have a feeling that we are involved in something special and unique in our careers. It helps, too, that we had the win on Saturday. Training seems so much better when we focus on positive things rather than having to work on stuff to put right after a defeat. All in all a good morning today, no pressure for a few days and it really felt like the world was a better place again. Amazing what a positive effect a win has on the mind. Be great if we could finally break our away duck on Tyneside on the weekend.

Thursday 15th December

It was back on the AstroTurf today, which is getting tough on the knees, back and ankles, before a lunchtime jaunt to Vesuvio's, our regular Thursday eaterie, with the whole squad. After that it was over to the Liberty where kids from the local hospital came to see us all for a party where we had photos with them and gave loads of autographs and gifts. As fantastic a thing it is for the kids, I have to admit as a new dad I find it quite difficult to see young kids ill and in pain. The one present we'd all like to give them is their health, but tragically life isn't fair for everybody, so as painful as it is for us to see the kids so poorly, the lads in the squad are genuinely pleased to help out in a small way like this, and hopefully bring some happiness to these children who are facing such a tough time in their lives. None of the lads complain about doing it, and as long as we've had some positive impact on these lovely kids then, hopefully, it's all worthwhile for them.

Friday 16th December

Training started earlier this morning at 9.30 a.m. because we flew up to Newcastle from Cardiff at 1 p.m. There was plenty of banter flying around about the flight and the weather conditions; it was freezing and VERY windy. The poor flyers like me and Gows got plenty of stick from Kemy and Tayls who didn't seem to care if we all crashed and died!

Nathan's headphones broke on the way to the airport which predictably led to him getting plenty of stick. Stephen Dobbie, the caring team mate that he is, bought him a new pair at the airport. Pink ones.

Now Nath was faced with a dilemma. He loves his music but his only way of hearing it was putting these pink beauties on his head. On the plane, I was sitting next to Nath as always, and it was funny watching him as he fretted over what he was going to do – silence or pink headphones. In the end he made his choice, and slipped these big pink things on over his head and as he did, me, Danny and Wayne papped him and shared the image with the wonderful world of Twitter before he could take them off. That was the only funny thing about the flight.

It was a little plane, which as a nervous flyer is never a nice thing to experience, and I was tense the whole flight, apart from when we flew over the Stadium of Light which was a cool thing to see. I got especially frightened when we came in to land as we were blown about in the winds and had to cope with the bumpiest landing in the history of flight. At that moment I had a few choice words for the pilot which I shared loudly with the rest of the plane! Apologies for that! I wish we could play all our games at home.

Saturday 17th December
Newcastle United 0 Swansea City 0

Today was another difficult hurdle to get over as the match was designated the official memorial match for Speedo, because of his long association with Newcastle. It still hurts when I think about him but, as we all know, we have no other option but to move on and just respect his memory as best we can. I had a chat with my agent this week about the day and he made a suggestion about my boots and how I could pay my own little personal tribute with them. We decided that I'd get a new pair with 'RIP Gary Speed' stitched onto them, so he contacted Nike and they sorted it out straight away.

After the game, I'll get them cleaned, sign them and auction them off for charity. It's only a small thing, but I just feel I'm paying my own little tribute to him and I hope he'd have approved.

In the ref's room, Lee Mason explained how the tribute would pan out and then I went back and told the team. The main thing was that we'd have less time to get out than normal, which is no big deal to any of us. In the tunnel, I spoke to Speedo's son, Ed, who was with Alan Shearer, so we shook hands too. Ed is a great lad who I've come to know over the last year or so as he never missed a game that his dad was involved with.

The minute's silence was pretty tough today because I thought about Speedo a lot, which just reminded me yet again what a great loss he is always going to be. When everyone started chanting and singing, the hairs on the back of my neck stood up, and I was trying everything I could not to let the emotion get to me, which was tough. What was even tougher though was seeing Speedo's dad, Roger, on the pitch because, like his sons, I've had the pleasure of meeting him on a few occasions now and he seems such a great guy. As I watched him walking off with Shearer and his grandsons, I just couldn't help thinking that the whole episode is just one big waste. I found it hard to switch back on after all that, but told myself just to be as professional as possible and then the Gaffer's words about our 3–0 loss two seasons ago came into my mind. I remembered that we didn't start right that day, and I certainly wasn't going to allow that to happen again.

My eagerness to start well cost me a foul against Demba Ba after two minutes. I wanted to start strong, just so he knew he wouldn't be having it his own way. But in fairness he just got there before me, so it was a foul. Caulks and I spoke before the game about getting properly involved today as both Ba and Best will be the biggest and most powerful pairing we've come up against this year, so if we weren't positive and aggressive we'd be in for a long afternoon. Following my foul, the battle started for real and, while it's important to not get dragged into it too much, I think I can speak for Caulks when I say the opening twenty minutes, when the four of us were battling for a bit of supremacy, was good fun.

Not long after we gave away a silly free kick which led to both Coloccini and Ba being free at the far post with a chance, and I had a little go at Jazz about that as he could have done more to block Coloccini out. I told him to make sure that he boxed him totally out on corners and free kicks for the rest of the match to make sure he wouldn't get another free run like that. Then, five minutes after that, Ba really should have scored after a good move from them which saw Best chest the ball on for him and he shot against the post. I was impressed with Ba. He's clearly a match winner on his own.

Ba taught Caulks a little bit of a lesson about when to try and get involved and when to sit off. Then Gutiérrez had a shot that caused Michel to go nuts with Jazz and Caulks for allowing him the room to shoot. The only other moment of note for me involved a paper plane. I'd never experienced anything like it. The ball had gone dead in front of the massively high stand where our fans were – about a mile in the sky – and as I turned round to jog out alongside Best, I just heard a 'fizz' past my ear, and this huge paper plane speared into the turf between Best and me. I laughed out loud when I realised what it was, and felt like applauding the person who did it because it must have flown 60 yards, and I've always struggled to fly one five feet. An odd moment.

The Gaffer was really pleased with how we'd done in the first half, but had recognised that it was probably going to be decided by who was going to stand up best to the physical side of today's challenge, so he introduced Kemy to give us more in that department. I was chuffed that we'd kept it 0–0 and told the defence and midfield how vital it was that we put everything on the line in the second half to keep a clean sheet. If we managed that, I really felt we'd get a chance at some point to nick it. To those of us who'd played in that last game, psychologically it was massive for us to have defended so well and kept them out, but we all knew it was going to be even harder in the second half.

They stepped it up after the break and, after dominating the first half in terms of chances, Caulks and me were right back amongst it from the off. I actually love the adrenalin rush of being in the middle of it, organising things and flinging myself into blocks and challenges.

Midway through the half, our particular challenge changed when Best had to go off to be replaced by Ameobi. Best had gone down awkwardly and it looked like he'd popped his collarbone, so I went over and had a quick word of commiseration with him because he's a good lad, and I was sorry to see him have to leave injured like that. I was also sorry to see his replacement. Ameobi is a little more direct than Best, and I didn't need him coming on after seventy minutes when I was starting to blow and he was bouncing along as fresh as a daisy – especially away from home.

Fortunately though he didn't really have that much of an impact on the game in any way and, while we still didn't really offer a hell of a lot in terms of a goal threat ourselves, we also dealt with them pretty well, ensuring there were no dramas and seeing out the game with a clean sheet. You know I love one of those! At the end I went straight across to Leon and Kemy and told them well done. They were both excellent in the second half, and when your two central men defend as well as they did today, I can't tell you how much easier it makes things it for me and Caulks. It was important we held on today to build on the Fulham game last week, and try to look at this as the start of a mini run. This is only our third point on the road, and picking one up at places like this could well be critical as the season pans out. I was also pleased today that I hardly gave the flight any mind tonight, though I did have a thought for our fans, faced with such a long trip home. They were magnificent today from the first minute, and it's really pleasing that we were able to give them something to make the trip home a little easier.

Played 16 Won 4 Drawn 6 Lost 6 Points 18 League Position – 12th
(22 more points needed for 40)

Sunday 18th December

The Gaffer had us in for a recovery session this morning which involved massage, twenty minutes on the bike, a few weights and then exercises in the swimming pool. It was normal stuff for a Sunday morning when we have a midweek game to follow the Saturday.

Tuesday 20th December

Morning training today was uneventful, made only slightly different by the fact that straight after it we were on the coach and up here to Liverpool for tomorrow night's game against Everton. We're staying in the same Hilton Hotel that we used for the Liverpool game last month. The only real difference is my room mate. Nathan is injured so isn't here, which means a new roomie for the trip who is one of my best mates at the club, Fede. We became good mates during his first stint here and often have dinner together with our wives as they get on really well too, so it's nice to have friendships like that at the club. However, I've never roomed with Fede before and I have heard some tales that he's a shocking snorer. I guess I'll find out about that in a couple of hours time.

After dinner tonight, a few of the lads and staff stayed behind to watch the Blackburn–Bolton game. Bolton won in the end 2–1 and, as usual, that meant that Steve Kean got loads of abuse from the fans. We were all really hoping for a draw tonight, because while we still aren't thinking that we're in a relegation battle or anything, the fact is that at the moment both of them are below us in the table and the best result for us would have been for both of them to have dropped the two points. We just don't want any of the teams below to gain three points on us.

The Gaffer announced the team earlier and it's the same as Newcastle which means that Jazz has kept his place over Àngel. I'm pleased for Jazz. He's a great lad and has the perfect approach for any young professional. He works very hard every day and always takes training seriously. He's one of those players who is keen to learn, is bright and always looking to improve. Not all young players possess that attitude, so when you see it in someone like Jazz, you can only be pleased for him when he gets his chance to play in the first team. I think he's done brilliantly since he's come into the side and more than deserves this opportunity.

The Gaffer's decision to go with Jazz instead of Àngel means that I'm the OAP at the back with Jazz (20), Caulks (19) and Tayls (22). I know Monks and Àngel have played regularly, but to have defended so well as a unit in our first ever season in the Premier League, I think people sometimes forget how inexperienced the lads are. They've all done a fantastic job and deserve some of the plaudits that are often only reserved for the attacking players in a team.

Wednesday 21st December

Everton 1 (Osman 60) Swansea City 0

I was very impressed with Goodison Park when I walked out. The stands either side of the pitch are very high and give the impression of towering over you and as good as lots of the modern stadiums are, Goodison just gave me the feeling of exactly what a 'proper' ground should look like. The pitch was fantastic too, which is really important for us and the way we like to play.

We started OK, but sometimes whatever you try as a team it can be taken out of your hands by the officials. After just four or five minutes there was a blatant foul on Joey, which the ref, Kevin Friend, didn't give. They broke down the right and went close. I was furious. Not just because the ref had not given the free kick – even though I had a go at him about it – but because an error by him could have had such a negative consequence on us. I know that they're human, and I know that it's almost an impossible task, but when you're out there on a football field, at any given moment every single one of you – including the ref – is looking at the ball. So when a challenge comes in that is obviously a foul, and you look to the ref and see him waving play on, you just can't help but get angry and ask yourself, 'What on earth was he looking at not to see that?' It's the most frustrating part of being a footballer.

A couple of minutes later, Scotty was fouled and this time the ref gave the free kick. As usual I went up and, as usual, I went and stood about a yard or two offside. A few people have asked why I do this and, quite simply, it's because Ruud van Nistelrooy used to do it! The benefit of doing it is that their defender isn't going to come that deep with me because he wants to keep his line, and because I'm out of reach, he can't get his arms around me to stop me from moving or making a run. Obviously, I've got to time my run back on side to coincide with the free kick, but I haven't misjudged that yet. Van Nistelrooy scored quite a few from doing this.

I'm still waiting.

Just before half-time there was an incident that saw the end of Tayls' work for the night. Michel made a great instinctive save which I thought was going in. As it came back out they had another shot which Tayls and me both threw ourselves at. I got the block in, which sent the ball wide for a corner, but it came off my arm, leading to massive appeals from them. Unfortunately for Tayls I landed on him, injuring his knee. When I throw myself in to make a block, all I concern myself with is the ball.

All my weight in that forward motion went through me, into my studs and into his knee. It wasn't nice seeing him leave the field, knowing that it was as a result of me, but it was an accident and there was nothing that could be done about it.

Two minutes later, I went in the book. Handball. Again, I just don't know how referees come to these decisions, and I got the feeling that maybe he was just evening up the one that hit my arm when Tayls got injured. With handball you never get consistency from one ref in the same game, let alone different refs week after week. The laws on handball are pretty clear. They state that for a free kick to be given, the handball must be deliberate, and deliberate is defined as 'hand to ball' not 'ball to hand'. When I blocked in the area, there is no way on earth that I could control my arms. In blocking, I throw myself at the ball, and to do that I have to use my arms to propel myself forward and also to balance myself. Dependent on the split second that the ball is struck, my arms might be down around my chest or above my head. The last thing on my, or any defender's mind at that split second is moving my hands towards the ball. The one he booked me for was even more frustrating. I was closer to their striker than I had been in the box, and footage of it could have been used in an instructional video to show referees that 'this is a case of when a ball is drilled at a player, so close, that there is no way he could move his arms, therefore it has to be accidental handball'. Instead, he books me.

We were a pretty tired dressing room at half-time. Everton had played really well and the first half had been a bit of a shift for us, and it seemed that we only got out of our half once or twice. I was quite vocal to the lads because I thought that as a team we were accepting the fact that we were in the middle of a tough away match at a big club and that our mentality was that maybe we could hold out for 0–0, much as we had in the second half at Newcastle. I was uncomfortable with that approach so early in a match and told the lads that we could get so much more out of this game than just hanging on for forty-five minutes for a point. I said that we really should stamp our authority on the game in the second half and boss the game more. The Gaffer made one change, Kemy on for Gows. He said that Gows had been excellent but he just felt that we needed a little more physicality to the midfield to deal with Fellaini.

As the second half progressed, Drenthe was trying to influence the game more, but Jazz was brilliant against him and gave him nothing. Just on the hour there was a breakdown in communication between Jazz and Scott and Drenthe nipped in and won a corner. I wasn't happy with that and let people know as it's the type of thing that can be avoided. As is often the case with these things, a small issue like that becomes a big one, and that indeed proved the case as they scored from the corner. With our zonal marking we all know our job exactly and where to stand in our zone. Unfortunately for Caulks, he was the nearest man that the ball went to, but it wasn't really in his zone or in Danny's in front of him. The result was that Leon Osman got in front of him, won the header and scored. Sometimes, you just have to hold your hand up and accept it, but Caulks wasn't happy about it.

I had a bit of a scare with twenty minutes to go when Saha turned and got the wrong side of me and I brought him down. The moment I heard the whistle I feared the worst and just turned away from the ref and walked back hoping I wasn't going to hear another whistle, as that would have meant that I'd have been off due to my earlier yellow. I heard nothing and must admit that I got away with one but I knew that if I did anything else in the game I'd be off.

Fortunately about five minutes later Saha was hooked by David Moyes. He'd been reasonably quiet, but there were flashes of real quality which told me that any half chance that might fall to him would be finished in an instant.

We did everything we could to try to make something happen from then on, but to no avail. They protected their lead and in the last ten minutes started to time waste quite a bit and were taking big chunks off the clock. I didn't think that the ref was doing anything about it. It started to make my blood boil and when Tim Howard started to make a real meal of a goal kick I went over and confronted the ref about it. As I did, Fellaini decided to get involved, so I quickly told him that it might be a good idea for him to be quiet for a moment. Or words to that effect. When the final whistle came I was just completely knackered. I just sank to my haunches for about a minute and didn't even have the energy to get up and go and shake anybody's hand.

Fellaini came over and shook my hand, and even though I'd had words with him, he was excellent for them, and was probably the difference between the two sides. He's certainly one of the best players I've faced so far this season and is a real handful and a very strong presence in midfield.

As I left the field the realisation of the defeat, and more significantly, the manner of it started to really build up inside me, and when I got back into the dressing room, for the first time in a long time at the club, I snapped. I felt we could have still got a point out of the game, but for large parts of the game we had just been trying to hang on for ninety minutes in the hope of getting a 0–0. I know we are better than that and I just grew more frustrated as the game went on because I could remember how strong and positive we had been at Man City and Arsenal. All this was flooding through my mind when I got back into the dressing room and I was in a right mood and reacted to the first thing anyone said.

Unfortunately for him, Scotty was nearest to my line of sight and I just exploded at him. I shouldn't have done it – and apologised to him after – because it doesn't really help anyone, but the frustration of the night got to me and I just popped. It's quite rare for me, or anyone really at Swansea City, to react like that. We are always honest with each other and are not afraid to share our opinions but I didn't really need to go off on one in the way that I did. I just worry that continually not getting a win on our travels could ultimately cost us in this league and it is something we are all going to have to work hard at and put right.

If we want to stay in this division, there's no other option. After the game we jumped on the coach and didn't get back to Swansea until 3.30 a.m. A long day. In fact a long two days, and because of the defeat, they feel like two pointless days, as that's exactly how we've returned home.

Played 17 Won 4 Drawn 6 Lost 7 Points 18 League Position – 14th (22 more points needed for 40)

Thursday 22nd December

Players love a moan, and one of the biggest sources of our grumbles are officials in general, and certain referees in particular. Phil Dowd is regarded as just about the best referee out there at the moment. There are a few reasons for saying that. First of all, he knows his stuff – as they all do in fairness. But wherever possible he takes into account actual circumstances going on around him during a match, and doesn't just always strictly apply the letter of the law as most of the others do. As players, we appreciate that it's a hard job, but some referees don't make it any easier by treating us like schoolchildren and not allowing us to engage with them at all. I understand that we can't have it both ways. We've all witnessed the scenes where almost all eleven players surround a referee, abusing him and trying to exert pressure on him. I have to say that hardly ever happens at our club, but when it does happen I know it looks so bad. The trouble is that sometimes that reaction has only occurred, not because players feel the ref has made a mistake, but because throughout a match he has been superior to them, not talking with them and basically treated them like kids. Chris Foy is a ref who seems to approach his refereeing in that manner, meaning it's hard to build a relationship with him. Phil Dowd is completely different though. He is strict, firm and he doesn't get swayed by anyone, but what he also is, is human. He'll speak to you during the match. He'll allow you to speak to him, and he'll also have banter with you when the situation allows. I think if more referees followed Phil's 'human' approach, there'd be fewer issues than you see at the moment because, as I've said, most of those issues come from frustration. The best compliment I can give Phil Dowd is that I'd love him to be our ref every week.

Friday 23rd December

There's still plenty of comment and discussion on the story of the week which was seeing Liverpool taking the field for their warm-up against Wigan, all wearing Luis Suárez T-shirts with the number seven on the back in support of him. Suárez has been found guilty by an independent commission of racially abusing Manchester United's Patrice Evra at Anfield on 15 October. Having seen all the footage of it on Sky, my overriding thoughts are of feeling sorry for Glen Johnson and seeing him warming up while wearing the shirt. Inevitably, the question has been asked of me, what would I have done in the same situation? It's a really tough one. I know that Liverpool have said that they want to see the FA's evidence before commenting on the verdict further, and the T-shirt was a way of showing support to Suárez, but ultimately, as we stand here today, Suárez has been found guilty. Asking Glen Johnson to then wear a T-shirt in support of him put Glen in an impossible position. Personally, I wouldn't have wanted to wear the T-shirt. But, if I was at Liverpool and Kenny Dalglish chucked the shirt at me while he already had one on – well, how could I not wear it? And I'm pretty sure that's how Glen Johnson must have felt. If he had run out on Wednesday without the shirt, you can imagine the headlines in the tabloids the next day and I'm guessing, it would have been the end for him at Liverpool. I just think doing it so publicly undermines everything that we have tried to do in the game in recent years by driving racism out of football. As we currently stand, the FA have found Suárez guilty of making a racist remark and Liverpool have now worn T-shirts in support of the player proven to have made that remark. I just think that sends a mixed message which doesn't actually help anyone involved in this whole sorry saga. I've been a Liverpool fan all my life but the actions of Liverpool concerning this incident have really left a bad taste in my mouth regarding the club I support.

Saturday 24th December

Early start today at 9.30. This is typical of the Gaffer and shows again why all the lads are so loyal towards him. He's so big on the family and brought training forwards so that we could all get away earlier than normal and spend as much time as possible with the family over Christmas. He believes a strong family base is really important in your development as a person.

Straight after training everyone shot off and I went home and picked up Vanessa and a packed car and headed straight up to Birmingham. We're cooking for both our families tomorrow and bought a turkey for twelve people. As usual, the trip up was uneventful – I can do it on autopilot now – until we arrived and Vanessa turned to me and said, 'Ash, I've forgotten the turkey.'

Luckily we managed to rush out and get a smaller one from Sainsbury's which will just have to do now!

It's Christmas tomorrow after all.

Sunday 25th December

Christmas Day! I'm so excited because this is the first Christmas Day off I've had in eight years, because we usually train every Christmas morning. Christmas is always one of those funny times for a footballer because it seems like all your mates and family are out and about partying, drinking and eating whatever they like, but for us, it's important that we are even more professional than ever in terms of what we eat and drink. I'm proud to report that I resisted second helpings today. Dessert wasn't even an option last year as we trained in the morning and then left for London in the afternoon because we had QPR on Boxing Day at seven o'clock, which meant I had hardly spent any time with the family. That's not a great memory, so I was determined to enjoy myself today, which I did. It was Raphael's first Christmas, and who knows, Raphael may be eight or nine before I can spend another full Christmas Day with him.

Monday 26th December

In my mind, the challenge for the QPR game tomorrow is quite simple – it's a game we just have to win, nothing else is acceptable. It is crucially important that you beat the teams around you if you want to avoid being dragged back into a real relegation dogfight and added to the fact that we haven't won for two games now, along with the disappointment of the whole approach to the Everton game, a home win is massively important as it will put a little more daylight between us and them. All the lads in training today felt the same way and we all know that by 7 p.m. tomorrow, we need to be in possession of the three points. No excuses.

I'll be captain again tomorrow and I have to admit it's a role I really enjoy and try to embrace. I've learned off one of the best over the last three years in Monks, so I know what's required. He's been a great captain for the club and always looks after the boys and is really unfortunate not to be in the side regularly, mainly because of the excellent form shown by Caulks. He must be disappointed, but never shows it, and to be honest – and this includes me – we all know he is still the captain anyway. He's still very vocal in the dressing room pre-match and is still in the middle of everything.

Tuesday 27th December

Swansea City 1 (Graham 14) Queens Park Rangers 1 (Mackie 58)

When I went in to the referee's room today I was expecting Keith Curle to be in there, but instead Neil Warnock was there with Joey Barton. I don't know whether this was normal for them or whether because Warnock and Barton are such strong characters, Warnock just likes to try to gain a little advantage before we've even gone out for the warm-up! I'm guessing it wasn't an innocent tactic. The ref also explained about not wasting time to get out on the pitch and said he'll give us a warning buzz at eight minutes to kick-off, and then a final buzz at seven minutes to. If we're not all out and in the tunnel from that point and ready to go, the club get fined, so Pasc is always moving us out when we get that second buzz. Even though we have to get out I'll never leave the door if I'm captain without the whole team, and every week Michel, Scott and Nath are always the late ones and tell me, 'Go on, we'll follow you out,' but I never leave the room without the full XI, we are together from minute one.

The first time Michel had the ball for a goal kick, their striker Heidar Helguson just jogged forward and marked me, so Michel couldn't pass to me. After Michel played the ball up the field, Helguson and I jogged out and I turned to him and said, 'Don't bother doing that all night, it's gonna be really boring for both of us.' He laughed and said, 'I'm sorry, but I'm under orders.' As frustrating as I thought that was, I took it as a compliment.

Apart from a bit of a running argument I was having with referee Lee Probert about everything, the match was pretty cagey up to Danny's goal with not much happening. Danny's goal was the perfect example of the reason that he's at the club and was so sought after during the summer. Like all top strikers he just made the chance out of nothing and finished it well, bending it around the defender and out of the reach of Paddy Kenny and just inside the far post. I was so happy for him because Danny works so hard in every game and doesn't always get the chances that every striker thrives on, but he never hides, always makes good runs and is always available for an out ball, and because he has such a great touch, importantly, he retains possession for us. It's also great for us as a team that we have someone playing up top that can score a goal like that out of nothing. You need that to survive in this league.

You could feel after the goal that it was exactly what the team needed, as we immediately started to play a little more fluently. Personally, I was still having a battle with Helguson. He'd stopped marking me at goal kicks now – it never lasts long – but we were very much in the middle of a physical battle which we were both enjoying. He was enjoying it more than me if I'm honest, because the ref was penalising me far more than him which was frustrating. Lots of what was going on was just the rough and tumble of professional football, and two players just having a bit of a tear-up, but Probert seemed intent on picking us up for every little incident – me, mostly – which was pretty annoying. I can't help but have the feeling sometimes that referees don't truly understand the game and they can spoil what is essentially an honest battle between two committed players taking part in a contact sport. Because of the way he chose to ref it, it meant that I was giving away too many free kicks which ultimately wasn't good for us, as QPR are such a tall team and were clearly looking at set pieces as their best chance of scoring.

During a stoppage in play, Michel came out to tell me to stop giving away so many free kicks. He was right of course and I agreed with him, which meant that I had no option but to call a halt to my battle with Helguson, which was a shame. In another match with another referee, nearly everything we did would have been let go and it's these inconsistencies between referees that annoys us players most.

The match tonight turned just after the second half substitutions, which saw Nathan on for Wayne and Luke on for Àngel. The latter change forced a reshuffle at the back with Kemy having to come in at right back. Almost straight away QPR had a goal kick which Paddy Kenny launched long. Running backwards, Leon got his head to it but only succeeded in looping it over me and Kemy for Mackie to get in between us and score. It was just one of those moments that caught us cold at the wrong time. It was Kemy's first defensive job, only thirty seconds after he'd gone to such a foreign position for him. Mackie was able to exploit that by making his run when he saw where the ball was likely to go. I was slightly out of position as I was still speaking to Joe to find out what the instructions were from the subs that came on in terms of our reshuffled line-up, when Kenny took the goal kick. Throw in the freak way the ball flew off Leon's head and that's how easy it can be to concede a goal when a couple of things go against you. The way we conceded was so unlike us as a back line, and is a rare sloppy goal we've conceded at home. I still had a chance to catch Mackie though but he'd already got the wrong side of me and inside the box so I was very conscious not to touch him and bring him down, as I'm sure I would have got a red. There was another reason why I didn't bring him down. Michel has been in such fantastic form this season that I half-expected him to save it anyway, but to be fair to Mackie he finished very well.

Immediately they picked up their game and their intensity. A couple of minutes after the goal, Jazz was the victim of a pretty nasty late tackle from Joey Barton and I lost it a little and ran towards him, fuming. To be fair to Barton, he just held his hands up and said, 'Yep, that was late, sorry,' and went straight to Jazz to apologise. He was booked, and may have been lucky to escape a red as it was so late, but yellow was probably the right decision.

Kemy then had a great run and shot which emphasised what a shame it was that he had to fill in at right back because he had certainly been having a big influence on the game from midfield, and I felt we missed him when he changed position. After his shot, it seemed we were huffing and puffing but to no avail. Just as I was fearing that it was going to be one of those nights when we might not get another chance, Danny ran into the box chasing a pass and just beat Traoré to the ball who took him down. I was the best part of fifty yards away but even I could see it was a stonewall pen, but the ref and linesman gave nothing. I couldn't believe it! It was such a crucial moment in the match, which in all probability would have seen us winning had it been given and we'd scored. I can't help wonder whether one of the reasons they waved it away, subconsciously, was the Neil Warnock factor. Both those officials would have known in that split second when they had to decide whether to give the penalty or not, that Warnock would milk it for everything he had after the game *if* it was shown subsequently, that they'd got it wrong. Now I'm not saying the officials didn't give the penalty just because it was Warnock, but there's a possibility that the potential fallout they knew they would have received after the game from him is one of the factors they *subconsciously* considered when deciding whether to give the penalty or not at such a crucial point in the match. I have no proof of this, it's just what I have come to believe after so many years in the game of trying to work out why some decisions aren't given. Frankly, it should have been a pen and I struggle to find any other reason as to why they didn't give it.

That was about it for us, and as the final whistle went, I couldn't help but reflect on an opportunity lost and a disappointing game from me personally. I felt that I hadn't played to my usual standard and know I could have done better with the goal. All these things run through your mind as soon as the whistle blows because you know the game's gone. As I was contemplating on my below par display I was grabbed by big Fitz Hall who said, 'Well played, mate.' I was with Fitz at Oldham eleven years ago when I went there on trial when I was just a teenager and he looked after me, taking me shopping and training and stuff like that. He's a good guy and without saying it I think we both felt it was amazing that we'd both come so far in our careers to be shaking hands at the end of a game in the Premier League.

I met Gabbs afterwards to swap shirts in the tunnel and had a chat with him and our agent. After that it was a family Christmas party at the Liberty for everyone, though the edge was taken off it by the result. Points are so hard to come by at this time in the season because the league table has shaped up now and all the teams know which clubs are the ones they need to take points off in order to stay above them, and QPR are definitely one of those that we have to stay above. That's why I'm disappointed that we dropped two points to them today which is so different to how it would have been in the same fixture last season. If we had drawn with them at home back then, I wouldn't have been too worried to be honest, because as a team we knew there would be plenty of other games up ahead of us that we would have taken three points from – home and away. The Premier League is so much stronger than the Championship was, and our away record is poor. I really do feel that every single point is precious, and am scared that not taking full points at home against the teams around us in the division could come back and haunt us. It seems stupid to talk about easy and hard games in this league, but I'm frustrated that today was the last 'easy' game we have at home for a while, and we simply should have made certain of winning it, especially after going ahead. This probably sounds disrespectful to QPR and I don't intend it to be, but when your next run of home fixtures after today is Tottenham Hotspur,

Arsenal and Chelsea, then it's clear that we really needed to take the three points on offer today from QPR.

Played 18 Won 4 Drawn 7 Lost 7 Points 19 League Position – 14th
(21 more points needed for 40)

Friday 30th December

I saw a tweet today from Piers Morgan to Rio saying that Thierry Henry is coming back to Arsenal. I always thought that he was a great footballer and was really disappointed when I heard the news because I've always wanted to play against him, and as it's only going to be a short-term loan, I'll never get the chance because we're still in the Championship.

When I read the tweet I genuinely forgot that we are now in the Premier League – how mad is that? I suppose it just goes to show the speed that all this has happened to us and all the years I've spent in the lower leagues, that some days I genuinely forget where I'm playing football now. I'm glad of that really, because it keeps the excitement of it all going. If I was all blasé and just taking it all in my stride as some players do, I know I wouldn't be enjoying it so much. This way, every day is part of a journey and nearly every fixture is an adventure.

We play Arsenal at the Liberty on 15th January which is during his loan period, and I can promise you this, when that final whistle goes and I have shut him out, I will be within six feet of him and grabbing his shirt! Never again in my life will I get to play against arguably the best striker in Premier League history, so I ain't passing up the opportunity to grab his shirt.

He can hang mine next to Cannavaro's and Maldini's then... ha-ha!

There will be quite a few changes made to the team to face Spurs tomorrow by the Gaffer which may surprise a few people. To me, it's clear that he is looking at the Villa game in a few days time and must feel that is the one that offers him the best opportunity of three points, so he wanted to put out his strongest eleven for that. By making such key changes, he does give the likes of Britts, Danny, Àngel and Caulks the chance of a rest, which would certainly help them towards getting us a win at Villa. It's always going to be a tough choice for the Gaffer at this time of the year, because he has to balance up giving players a rest, as the games come pretty thick and fast around now, against targeting the games that he feels we can win. On current form, Spurs are just about the best team in the country and even with our very best team on the pitch on the back of a week's rest, there's a strong possibility that they would still beat us. That's not defeatist talk, that's just being realistic. Spurs have won four out of their last five away games, beating Blackburn, Fulham, West Brom and Norwich, only drawing a blank at Stoke. That run shows how difficult our task will be, even if we had our first choice line-up. But we are at home and we fear no one at the Liberty and will be looking to take all three points with whatever team we put out.

No doubt some people will criticise the Gaffer's selection, but I like to look at his decision slightly differently. We now have the largest squad since I joined the club in 2008, and by far the highest in quality in terms of the ability of the players contained in that squad. Yes, you could measure one player directly against another player and say he is better, but you are only talking margins here. Take Stephen Dobbie for example. He will play tomorrow, and hasn't started since the opening day at Man City, but in terms of footballing ability, Dobbs possesses as much quality as anyone else in the club. If you look at him as a replacement in midfield for Britts, on face value you could be excused for thinking he won't bring the same qualities to the team as Britts does. But it's not as simple as that. To accommodate Dobbs, Joe will adopt Leon's role more closely and Dobbs will give the team more of an offensive edge by playing in the hole. Time will tell if that works, but Dobbs is the perfect player for that role and I genuinely don't see his inclusion as a weakness.

Jazz will keep his place over Àngel, and Monks replaces Caulker. Luke comes in to play up top, which I'm really pleased to see as he works so hard every day in training but doesn't get too much game time. Along with Dobbs, I don't look at one of those players as being weaker than any of those getting a rest.

For one or two of them it will be difficult as they haven't featured in the first team for a while so may be a little rusty. But in terms of ability and mentality, I have no worries about any one of them whatsoever. Having spoken to them all in training today, every single one of them sees tomorrow as an individual opportunity. Spurs are on such a great run that tomorrow, nobody outside of us expects us to get anything from the game. There's a certain feeling of freedom in a situation like that – nothing to lose. When that's your mentality, shocks can often occur.

Danny's disappointed not to be playing tomorrow, but I think the Gaffer probably sees him as being crucial to getting something in what's certain to be a tight game at Villa Park, and certainly the goal he scored against QPR on Tuesday underlined his importance to us as a team. Danny's a really good player who I played against a few times when I was at Stockport and he was at Carlisle, but I never knew how hard he worked for the team until he came here. He's got the gift of being able to continuously run at a quick pace for the whole game. His energy levels are fantastic. The way the Gaffer wants us to play makes you realise how hard it is to play up front in it, and certain players simply wouldn't be able to do it because you have to be on the move the whole time, often not even getting the ball. Jason Scotland understood it, but he didn't work as hard, but Danny does and as a result he gives us another dimension. He's got goals in him, too. We see that every day in training, and even at the start of the season when he took a few games to get off the mark, no one doubted that he'd come good. The famous one at the time was probably the miss against Arsenal that would have got us the draw, but the point was that he was getting in positions to miss. If he wasn't scoring and he was never in a position to score, it would be a completely different story then, but since he started scoring he's contributed regularly and at important times. To be at a new club in the top division and not score in his first six games must have played on his mind, but since he got off the mark against Stoke he's confirmed that he will consistently score at this level.

His goal against QPR was his sixth in his last eleven starts, and if he carries on that ratio for us for the rest of the season, I can't see that there'll be many English qualified strikers ahead of him in the scoring charts. The QPR goal demonstrates just how important he is to us. Despite the possession that we have in games, the fact is that we are not overrunning teams when we get control. Yes, we manage to outplay teams regularly, but how many games has the opposition goalie been man of the match for pulling off about ten saves? Not often. What Danny brings us and what he showed against QPR is that he can score a goal out of nothing. I feel we let him down sometimes and we don't play it into him quick enough, and I was telling the Gaffer that the other day and he agreed. I know how tough Danny is to deal with defensively, because in training, when the ball's played into him quickly, I find him a real handful, so we should definitely bring him into the game more and utilise his strength and power. One of the best things I like about Danny though, is his mentality. Whatever the Gaffer asks him to do, he does. No argument whatsoever. I've seen players in the past moan and groan about jobs they are given because they can't do them or don't like them, but never Danny. If the Gaffer told him to make dummy runs for ninety minutes and never get the ball, he would, and that mentality is a fantastic attribute to possess and makes Danny exactly what he is, a fantastic team player and a great lad too. He hasn't scored yet against one of the big clubs which is why he'd have loved to have started tomorrow against Spurs but our next home match is Arsenal, and, if selected, I wouldn't bet against him putting one away against them.

Saturday 31st December

Swansea City 1 (Sinclair 84) Tottenham Hotspur 1 (van der Vaart 44)

Not exactly a shock, but what a fantastic performance by everyone today. I think if there'd have been another ten minutes added to the game then we would have seen an upset because we finished so strongly. We all felt that they were wilting and quite happy to get out of the Liberty with a point in the end. That's a nice feeling to have, witnessing a team as good as Tottenham hanging on for a draw against us in such an open and exciting game.

With Monks back as skipper, that meant that I gave up the armband again. People have asked me quite often this year, how does that feel and do I mind giving it up when he plays? The honest answer is not at all. Monks is one of my mates at the club, a true skipper and a great leader of men. I have learned so much from him about how to lead a team which I then put into place when Monks doesn't play. When he does, I'm more than happy to resume my role as back-up to him. In fact, I feel a little freer when Monks is back as I can concentrate solely on my game a little more than when I'm captain.

Walking out today was outstanding. The crowd were right on it from the start and 'Hymns and Arias' was loud and passionate. It's just fantastic to walk out to a reception like that and hear it building and building until the roar at kick-off. It helps that we are playing a big club like Spurs obviously, but fixtures like today's are the ones that we all dreamt about when we were in the Championship and below.

The game started well for me when I hit a sweet, long cross-field ball to Jazz who'd pushed forward on the right wing. I was pleased that we started well because not only is that vitally important when you begin a game against a team like Spurs who are supposed to be superior to you, but also because it shows that we have all learned from the Man Utd game and were not showing Spurs too much respect in the way we did to United. I can't overstate how important the crowd were today in our good start either. They were so loud and intense that being out there on the pitch, I got a very definite feeling that the team and crowd were bouncing off each other.

We were really in their faces from the off, just as the Gaffer had asked, and we got some early corners which also kept the crowd boiling nicely. I had a decent chance with one and got close, but no luck. I've only scored once this year, against Chelsea, and am aware that I need to be more of a threat from corners and set plays to help the team out. I'll be disappointed come the end of the season if I haven't added to that one. I had a pretty tough job today being marked by Younès Kaboul. He's a big lad and very powerful in the air and we had a couple of interesting clashes, but it's all part of the rough and tumble that I love so much.

The Gaffer rammed home to us all week about not allowing them any space. For a period in the first half they did enjoy quite a bit of possession and it could have been dangerous. But the boys in midfield were excellent in closing them down and denying them the space they wanted. We knew that if we gave the likes of Modrić and van der Vaart time, they would kill us. Jazz was perhaps a little too eager in the first half in trying to limit Bale's space and got booked. I went across and told him straight away to be careful, because going down to ten men would have made it very difficult for us.

My main battle today was with Emmanuel Adebayor who is a great striker. Adebayor's a lot taller than me and poses similar problems in the air to those caused by Peter Crouch, but he is a better player with the ball at his feet and quicker. I thought I started quite well against him today in terms of asserting myself.

One thing we didn't want to do tonight was go behind, especially in the way we eventually did, so late in the first half. Assou-Ekotto had a bit of a run at Jazz, turning him, inside and out, before crossing low. The cross itself wasn't going to cause too much trouble, but Joe tried to get in to affect the ball and inadvertently diverted it to van der Vaart, who had been quiet in the half up to then, but scored. The shot hit my elbow as it went in and the ref, Phil Dowd, helpfully pointed out that if it hadn't have gone in, he'd have sent me off for handball!

There was an obvious feeling of frustration in the dressing room at half-time because we'd conceded so late, but there were plenty of positive noises from people too, all confident that we could definitely get something out of the game. Monks and Michel were particularly vocal, both saying that because Tottenham were so open and disorganised that they were certain we would score. They were both convinced that we'd get chances in the second half and that it was vital we took them when they came. It's great when you have players in the team with such belief. It makes a difference.

One change the Gaffer did make was to take Jazz off and replace him with Àngel. I felt for Jazz because, like the rest of us, it was such a big game for him and to be taken off at half-time no doubt looked bad from the outside. But the only reason he was subbed was because of his early booking. With him up against Bale who is such an attacking player, the Gaffer decided that to risk the potential of a mistimed tackle from Jazz resulting in red would not be the wisest of moves, so he removed the ultimate risk of us playing with ten men.

The last thing the Gaffer told us was that he didn't want us coming off at the end as 'heroic losers'. He wanted us to fight to ensure that we got back into the game and to make sure we left the pitch with something. That made a big impact on me.

We started the second half the way we had the first, in their faces and being positive. I decided to be a bit more forceful in my play, too, and tried to carry the ball out more from defence to start attacks and just generally tried to get us on the front foot a bit more. This affects the game because, normally, even though each match is eleven versus eleven, most teams will leave our centre half spare and use an extra man to double mark somebody more dangerous elsewhere on the field. Today, Adebayor was the one up top on his own, leaving either Monks or me spare at times. Teams do this because they assume the centre half will be the worst ball player in the team so don't have to worry too much about us. This means that if I, as the centre half, decide to carry the ball into their midfield, they have a decision to make; either choose to leave me, meaning I'll get as far up the field as possible, gambling that I won't do anything too creative, or send one of their midfield markers to stop me – usually Joe's – which gives me some space to pass in behind them for Joe to run on to and hopefully cause some damage.

Not long after I made a run that nearly came to something with Dobbs, I dropped two good tackles in quick succession on Modrić and Adebayor which the crowd seemed to love. At that point, probably after about seventy to seventy-five minutes, we were so on top and had basically stopped anything coming from them at all. I honestly felt that not only were we going to score, but if we scored soon enough, we'd get a second too. We really were playing that well.

After what seemed like ages in the game we finally got the reward for our excellent second half and all the possession we had and the pressing we'd done. Àngel did some good work down the right and managed to fire a cross in, Danny made an excellent run across the front of Friedel which distracted him, and somehow he spilled the ball right at the feet of Scotty, who side-footed in to send us level.

I genuinely thought we could win it from that point, and as delighted and relieved as I was, I didn't run up and join the lads celebrating, but stayed back with Monks and Michel and just had a quick celebration with them. Almost immediately I started to collect my thoughts and concentrate on the restart. Monks and I agreed we had to keep it tight and simply not allow them any chances, and I passed the word onto Leon. We kept it as tight and despite us forcing until the very end for the winner, it wasn't to be. But importantly, as the Gaffer had instructed us at half-time, we'd definitely left the field with something.

The scenes in the dressing room after the match were great. We had the same pure garage classics that we put on the iPod every week. Not everyone has the same taste in music, so we try and find a beat that gets us up for the game. The music is on before the game when we are getting changed and afterwards too, but only if we win.

Although nothing was said, I got a feeling from the boys who came in to the side that the result was a complete vindication of their selection. Even with the Gaffer's first choice eleven, most judges would have suggested that Spurs would beat us, but to draw with them in a game we dominated so much after the break meant that there was a deep feeling of satisfaction. The Gaffer was delighted and I guess it just proves how good he is at his job. He never felt he was picking a weaker team, just a team picked from what is a very strong and talented squad.

It's just gone midnight so we are now officially in 2012. How did I spend my New Year's Eve? Surely at some big celebrity party with stretch limos and free champagne – I'm a footballer after all! Well, not exactly. We travel up to Birmingham tomorrow (I mean today) for the Villa game, so I've spent the evening watching Harry Potter and writing this diary. It's now 12.10 and time for bed.

This life is just non-stop rock and roll!

Played 19 Won 4 Drawn 8 Lost 7 Points 20 League Position – 14th
(20 more points needed for 40)

CHAPTER SEVEN

January 2012

Sunday 1st January

In for training at Llandarcy this morning at 9.30 before we set out for Birmingham and the Villa game tomorrow. It was a light session for obvious reasons that consisted of a massage, twenty minutes on the exercise bike, some all-round stretching and a quick dip in the pool for a few lengths and some exercises.

There will no doubt be a few changes for tomorrow, but for a couple of us it will still mean playing the two full games. I've spent the day making sure I've taken enough fluids on board, having decent rest periods and also eating the correct foods. It can be a bit dull making sure you eat, drink and rest properly throughout the day, but it's the correct and professional thing to do, and gives me the best chance of performing well tomorrow.

After we arrived and settled in at the hotel in Birmingham – The Marriott on Hagley Road – we had our final team meeting of the day. Tomorrow's team will have seven changes from the Spurs game, which confirms the depth we have in our squad. The only ones to keep their place are me, Michel, Tayls and Nath. The change that will surprise the fans most is the inclusion of Andrea Orlandi. Andrea is a very talented player who I think could be more suited to the Premier League than the Championship, but as he hasn't featured at all in the starting line-up this season, none of the squad were expecting him to start tomorrow and from the look on his face, neither did he.

Looking at the team the Gaffer has picked for tomorrow – Michel, Àngel, Caulks, me, Tayls, Nath, Andrea, Kemy, Leon, Wayne and Danny – apart from Andrea, one with plenty of Premier League experience. Villa have been a bit inconsistent of late, losing their last three home games, albeit to Arsenal, Liverpool and Man Utd, but then going to Stamford Bridge on Saturday and beating them which was a bit of a shock to say the least. They'll have their tails up tomorrow, making our job that little bit harder, but I've got a genuinely good feeling. As a group coming out of that team meeting tonight I could sense that we are all riding the wave created by our performance against Spurs, which means our confidence is up. I haven't got a single negative thought about tomorrow, not one, and I know I'm not alone in thinking that.

Monday 2nd January
Aston Villa 0 Swansea City 2 (Dyer 4, Routledge 47)

Walk this morning, then straight in for the pre-match meeting. The Gaffer told us he has two things that he wants us to achieve in January. First, an away win, second is to beat one of the big boys. The Gaffer often sets mini targets like that and most of the time they work.

It was great getting to walk out onto the Villa Park pitch after all these years. Of all the Midlands grounds this is the one I've been to most to watch games at and, again, it was one of those lovely little moments I've now managed to tick off on my 'to do' list that's based on all those dreams I had as a kid. The first thing that struck me was how big the pitch was, much bigger than I'd expected. All the lads were saying the same, so I don't know if it was some sort of optical illusion but it seemed to be the biggest pitch we've played on this season by far.

There was a funny moment at the toss today with Villa skipper Stiliyan Petrov. I won the toss and because I know which way Villa always like to play in the first half, away from the Holte End so that they can attack it in the second half, I decided to turn them round so that they wouldn't have that advantage, especially if they needed to chase the game second half. As the ref gave the sign to the teams and we all started to swap ends, massive boos started ringing round the ground. Just the response I was after.

In the huddle I said, 'Lads, this is a game we can win, but we need to be patient. We mustn't feel like we need to win it straight away. It doesn't matter if we don't score early, we can win this, even if we have to wait till the ninetieth minute to score.'

We took the lead after four minutes. So much for the influence I have over the team.

We got a bit lucky, to be honest, but that's something you need if you want to win away. The ball was with their left back, Stephen Warnock, who was under no pressure whatsoever when he turned in-field and played a weak pass in the general direction of Richard Dunne. Nathan nicked it before Dunne had a chance to react, shot from the edge of the box and scored. Great finish. I broke my usual habit of staying calm and sprinted up the field to celebrate with him for two reasons. First, he does go into a bit of a sulk when he scores and he sees me standing at the back on my own as if I don't care. Second, I told him this morning when we were having our walk that he would score, so I just wanted to confirm to him that I know everything!

Despite Villa getting stick from their fans after Nath's goal, they came back into the game quickly, reacting well after going behind in that manner. For a good ten minutes we were under siege and they had a flurry of corners, one or two which ended up in a bit of a scramble for us. Since we've been in this league, as a defensive unit we've noticed that this can happen quite often and while in the first few games we did panic a bit and feel that a goal was probably inevitable we've spoken a lot about how to handle these spells now, and also learnt that if we defend them well, they seem to die out as quickly as they arrive.

While we were dealing with that ten or so minutes of pressure I was confident that we wouldn't concede. From what I could hear from the Villa players, they were equally confident that they would score, especially from the corners. They aren't the first team to think that when they see us line up zonally, but on the whole we defend pretty well in our zones. It's not every team's way, but we know what we're doing, are comfortable about it and proved again today that if we stay strong and do what we have to do, then there's no real problem.

The longer the half went on today, the better our football

became. We were playing some really lovely stuff at times and our midfield was creating plenty; much more than usual, actually. I think a lot of credit for that had to go to Andrea. What he was doing really well was providing that key link between the rest of the midfield and Danny, and when we get that right we are a very dangerous side. What Andrea did today was ensure that every time he had the ball his first thought was for Danny and trying to pick out his runs. It gave us a different dimension and we were very dangerous as a result.

Nath deserves a special mention for his first-half performance today. I think it was the best I've ever seen him play. Warnock is a very experienced full back, but I genuinely felt sorry for him today as Nathan skinned him time and again. It was like watching a school match where one team has got a flying winger and all he has to do is knock it one side of the full back, sprint past him on the other, and then pick the ball back up and cross it. Nath must have done that three or four times today and the crowd really began to get on Warnock's back and if ever there was one player who couldn't wait to see half-time it was him.

Unlike theirs no doubt, ours was a positive dressing room and the Gaffer spoke about replicating our first-half performance and just going out there and doing it again. He did say though, how important it was that we scored the next goal. If any chance came, he said we had to take it as 2–0 would be a long way back for them if we could continue the form we had shown in the first half.

Sitting there, I tried to gauge how I was feeling fitness-wise, after the Spurs game, and I didn't feel too bad. During the first five minutes I thought I might struggle because I did feel genuinely knackered, which isn't like me at the start of the game. But as we moved into the game a little more I got my second breath and then I felt fine. It was a good job too, because that coincided with that ten-minute spell they had. I made sure I had plenty to drink at half-time, had a toilet break then, as always, it was on with a clean shirt for the second half and out.

We couldn't have had a better start to the second half as Wayne scored almost straight away. It was his first Premier

League goal and was massively important for us, scoring so soon after the break. I knew that whatever instructions Villa had got from McLeish at half-time would be out the window as a result of Wayne's strike. They had probably been told a few basic things to carry out in the second half; keep things tight for ten or fifteen minutes; stop us playing so freely and try to interrupt our possession more; try to equalise so that they could enter the last fifteen or twenty going for the win. Unfortunately for them Wayne's goal changed all that and instead they found themselves two down, knowing that they were going to have to score three in the second half of a game in which they hadn't created anything up to that point.

After that goal we needed to reinforce that feeling of anxiety onto Villa. Having got the early goal the pressure was off us, which meant that we could set about controlling the game and managing it to an extent where they simply wouldn't be able to get back into it. We did that very well for large chunks of the match. The main clue that we were succeeding on that front was the crowd turning on McLeish. When he subbed Stephen Ireland the ground shook with boos, followed by the 'You don't know what you're doing' chant. They really slaughtered him.

Villa had a flurry of corners, as they'd had in the first half, and because of our zonal defence, Kemy and Àngel had the job of blocking the runs of Ginge and Richard Dunne. The ref had been watching this closely all match and pulled me after the second corner and told me to warn my players about it as he would be forced to give a penalty if he thought it was deliberate. I told him to forget about that because they weren't committing any fouls so how could he give anything? But as soon as he was out of earshot I had a quick word with Àngel and Kemy, just to be careful!

As the half continued we did have to do a bit more defending and really threw ourselves into it with great commitment. Tayls epitomised this with a great defensive header at the back stick when he was flattened by Richard Dunne just after clearing a dangerous cross. He's a big lad is Dunne and it was funny when I went over to check if Tayls was OK as he'd really been clattered and looked like he'd been hit by a train. When I asked him how he was I just couldn't stop myself from laughing at him. I'm not sure he appreciated it!

The game started to peter out for them after that, so much so that their fans started filing out in droves. The response of the Swans fans was superb as they began chanting, 'Is this a fire drill? Is this a fire drill?' We all had a chuckle at that one. Once again our travelling support was superb. Our away fans were as brilliant as always, making noise and really getting behind us! We all really appreciated their effort today.

Not long afterwards and just after Charles N'Zogbia smacked an unbelievable shot that beat Michel hands down, hit the inside of the far post and came straight back out, the ref blew for the end and we'd won our first away game of the season. It was a massive occasion for us. The lads were buzzing in the dressing room and I think we felt that the pressure was off us a bit now, especially as it's the Cup next week which gives us a break from all the questions we get about whether we are going to be able to stay in the league. We made a big statement today coming to one of the Premier League's bigger clubs, who were on the back of a really good away win themselves at Stamford Bridge, and comfortably seeing them off. I think our rivals down below us will certainly take notice of the result and it helps us avoid being dragged into the group containing Wigan, Bolton, Blackburn and Wolves. I think this result will have a big say in the outcome of the season.

Another person who made a big statement today was Andrea. He probably wouldn't be in most fans' starting line-up but I thought he was excellent. He's shown the Gaffer what he's capable of at this level, and I'm sure there'll be nobody happier than the Gaffer himself as he'll feel that he's discovered another option for the team that he can use as the season moves on.

We can look back at the Christmas period with a sense of achievement. After the disappointment of Everton and QPR, to take four points from Spurs and Villa is pleasing. I'm not so sure many experts would have predicted that and I think what we've shown as a group in the last two games is a great resilience about what we are trying to achieve, as for large periods of both games we played really positive, controlled, productive and most importantly, threatening football. The Gaffer has repeatedly said to us that it's the squad that will keep us in this division, not individuals, and he couldn't have a better endorsement of the abilities and strengths of his squad than he's had over the last few days.

Played 20 Won 5 Drawn 8 Lost 7 Points 23 League Position – 11th (17 more points needed for 40)

Thursday 5th January

When I arrived at training this morning the Gaffer pulled me into his office and told me that I will be getting a rest on Saturday for the FA Cup game away at Barnsley. I didn't say it to him, but I must admit my first thought was, 'Finally, I'm getting a rest!'

Seriously though, I love playing matches and I look forward to every one but for me this year it's been pretty intense playing every game and maybe it is a good idea to miss this one. It's not the playing that I'm relieved to be missing out on, it's the away trip, really, and everything that goes with that. I was quite happy when he told me that I wouldn't have to travel and he told me to just take it easy and enjoy the weekend with the family, which is exactly what I intend to do.

Friday 6th January

When I arrived at training this morning, the Gaffer pulled me into his office. Déjà vu. I knew what was coming.

Apparently overnight Spurs had sent an email through reminding the club that the terms of Caulks' loan deal means he's not allowed to play in the FA Cup. After having got my mind in gear for chilling out at home with Vanessa and Raphael over the weekend.

When I went in to see the lads, you can imagine their sympathy when they saw my long face and I told them that I now had to play. They loved it and the banter was flying, especially from

Britts and Tayls. Welcome to life in the dressing room! Even during training the stick kept coming, including plenty from the Gaffer who was also having me off! You've just got to laugh at it all. After training I had to fly back home and get my stuff and tracksuit ready as I didn't bother to pack my bag last night and turned up to training in jeans!

Saturday 7th January
FA Cup – 3rd round
Barnsley 2 (Vaz Tê 29, 65)
Swansea City 4 (Rangel 30, Graham 46, 89, Dyer 54)

We started very confidently today and had loads of possession in the early part of the game. We more or less kept the ball for about the first half hour and at times we were passing it around for fun, but then from a strong Tayls tackle the ball rebounded straight into the path of Vaz Tê, who lashed it from way out and it just flew in! It was totally against the run of play and in fairness I think that Gerhard saw it late. But once again it just showed that no matter how much possession you have, or how much on top you may be in a game, in football a goal can come from nothing and at any time.

Having conceded out of the blue like that it was important that we hit back as soon as possible and we did, with Àngel scoring just a minute later after some really good work by Nath. After that the next quarter of an hour was exactly how the game had been up to the first goal, heaps of possession for us, them lying deep, but frustratingly us not really creating any clear-cut chances.

The Gaffer came in at half-time with a big smile on his face. He told us how much he enjoyed the first half and that he was interested in seeing what was going to happen in the second half and how we were going to react. He said it's easy to play at Anfield or Villa Park but that he'd learn more about us today than seeing us performing in those types of games. I knew exactly what he meant and that he'd be looking to see if we'd maybe be taking the challenge too easy and underestimate them in the second half.

From the sounds the lads were making, especially Monks, I knew that wasn't going to happen.

We couldn't have started the second half better and just a minute in Danny scored a great goal, rolling Jimmy McNulty – a great lad I used to play with at Stockport – using the wind and shooting in from about thirty-five yards. Then, within ten minutes, I was astounded as Nath scored, meaning he'd got two in two. Surely that's never happened before? He is gonna think he is prolific now and I'm going to have to put up with his boring banter.

Once Nath had scored and put us clear, we were completely on top of Barnsley and we began enjoying the game. Playing with complete freedom it seemed like we'd begun to use the game as an opportunity to practise all that we have been working on in training in a competitive match situation. Even I managed to get into the act in terms of attacking by playing a couple of one-twos and ending up in their box, though Danny played it a bit too far for me and the goalie swept it up. Chance gone. Just an empty set of lungs to show for it.

On the hour Orlandi went off after playing well, and his replacement was our new loan signing, Gylfi Sigurdsson. As he ran on I was thinking that I was looking forward to seeing what he would bring to the team and how he'd adapt to our style of play. It was no reflection on Gylfi's introduction but we started getting a little sloppy and took our foot off the gas a little too much. As a direct result of this, Vaz Tê scored a really good second direct from a free kick and I told the lads that was what we deserved for the way we'd been playing.

Even though the goal had brought them back into the game I was confident that we'd see the game through for the win, despite our sloppiness for which we were ultimately punished. We managed to wrap it up at the end thanks to great work from Wayne resulting in a second for Danny. I was pleased for Wayne today. There's not much more you can expect from your winger than him creating goals, and he did it twice today which was great for him. I was also quite impressed with our new boy Gylfi too. I hadn't really seen him play before and I thought he looked pretty good in the half hour that he had and he linked up well with Danny, something that we've missed a bit so far this season.

Despite our slack period in the second half, on a windy day with tricky conditions we played some great stuff against a good Championship team with a very good manager in Keith Hill. The Gaffer was pleased after the game and I think there was a definite feeling from him that we'd gone to a potentially difficult place and done an extremely professional job. I couldn't agree more with that.

Tuesday 10th January

After training today I chilled out and then watched the Arsenal v Leeds FA Cup tie from last night. We are playing Arsenal on Sunday so it made sense for me to watch the game to get a feel for them and see if there's anything I could pick up that might be of benefit come the weekend. The best part for me was the return of Thierry Henry. There's just something about players like him that only the special few have, a presence and aura that seems to make things happen. So what happens? He only goes and scores the winner late in the game in true hero fashion. I couldn't be happier for him – he's one of my most favourite players ever.

Wednesday 11th January

We had a speed session in training this morning which Ryland took. It was on the AstroTurf, which isn't ideal because it hurts the feet, but it's an enjoyable session. It suits some of the lads more than others of course with Scott, Nath and Tayls the quickest, and Monks and Gows, how shall I say… not the quickest! Today it was speed work through cones and poles, where we start at the line and sprint to the first cone when Ryland tells us, twisting through them and then sprinting ten yards to the line when we've come out of them. It's all done to make us sharper and to get us reacting quicker. The first four we did without the ball and the last four we did with the ball.

Tatey and Ferrie both started for the ressies today and I was pleased for both. Ferrie is one of the best players that I've ever played with and has been so unlucky since he first got injured back in 2008 against Birmingham. I just hope he gets the luck that sees him having a successful comeback and has a run in the game without further knocks or injuries. Obviously Tatey's injury was just a little bit different to Ferrie's original, because I don't recall seeing Ferrie in a golf buggy at any point, but despite the cause of it Tatey has worked really hard to get back to hopefully play some part in our debut season in the Premier League. I hope that neither of them have any after-effects following today's run out.

Just finished a meeting here at home tonight with Doey and Duane, the guys from AG Swansea, about Friday's fundraiser for little Hari Kieft. It's going to be a big night I think and it was good to go through everything to make sure it all runs smoothly on the evening.

Friday 13rd January

Unlucky for some.

Normal Friday session today on the AstroTurf, and the Ospreys were training alongside us on the grass. After training there was a bit of fun though. Last week one of the people who put together *Soccer AM* on Sky apparently didn't put in a trick that Nath did against Villa for their 'Showboating' slot. As a result they brought the crew down to the training ground for him to 'Take one for the Team'. What happens here is that they set up this big circular target, which is a bit like an archery target but it's huge, about 10ft high and across. In the middle of the target is a hole and behind it is like a shelf where the victim – the guy from Sky – goes and stands, turns around and puts his backside through the hole and then waits for the pain that will be delivered, hopefully, if someone hits him on the backside with the ball.

Five players were then selected – Nath, obviously, Wayne, Joe, Scott and me and because the Ospreys were training next door they also asked Shane Williams to have a go. The ball was then placed at about eight yards and the idea was to smash it as hard as you could, straight at the ass poking through the hole in the middle. First to go was Shane who just missed with a powerful left foot shot. Next was Nath who missed low and left and he was followed by Joe who really smashed it and made a hell of a noise when it hit the wooden frame, but he narrowly missed too, just to the left of the guy's backside. Then it was me. I was told to grab a ball, walk up to the camera and give my name, then place it and smash it! I wanted to make sure I hit the guy but I wanted to hurt him too! Anyway, I ran up and absolutely leathered it... and I nearly completely missed the whole bloody frame of the target. Power with no precision. Wayne was next and decided to do his own thing. When they told him to go, he just picked the ball up, ran to about a yard away and volleyed it! He still missed, so then decided to punch the guy right in his arse and everyone just cracked up.

Then, just as it looked like this guy was going to get away with not being hit with the ball, up stepped Scotty. Cool as you like he just placed the ball, ambled up to it and absolutely smashed it on the button, right on the guy's backside. There was a pretty decent crowd watching by now, all our lads and the Ospreys and quite a few fans who'd come up to watch us train, and the laughter was ringing around when Scotty caught him.

Hari's charity do at the Manor Park in Clydach was tonight and it was a great success, thankfully. I was so relieved by the turnout and the numbers that supported the event and the amount we raised showed just how generous the public are when there's a good cause to support. I am so grateful to all the people who turned up. All along I wanted it to be a proper event and with all the fantastic auction prizes and the fantastic football freestylers Billy Wingrove and Jeremy Lynch, who put on a great technical show of football brilliance, it was a night that everyone enjoyed. Adrian Davies from Wales, was excellent as usual as our auctioneer. As for little Hari himself, he was ill and didn't feel well all night. He was determined to be there though and he really distinguished himself by being sick on John Hartson. The big man's face was a picture!

Saturday 14th January

Back to training today and it was completely focused on Arsenal. We had a video meeting before training on their possible formations and the team that they might put out. All the lads were under no illusions about the size of the game and all the talk after training was about how massive an occasion it will be for all of us. Despite us all understanding the size of the task that faces us, there was also a very positive feeling that we can actually go out there and achieve something positive from the game. Even though in their last game they beat Leeds in the Cup, their last league game was away at Fulham and they lost, so our view is if Fulham could beat them then there's absolutely no reason why we can't too.

Sunday 15th January

Swansea City 3 (Sinclair 16 Pen, Dyer 56, Graham 70)

Arsenal 2 (van Persie 5, Walcott 69)

Reading some of the press this morning, a few of the experts said that the game would determine just who would be the best passing team, the established pass masters, Arsenal, or us – the new boys. This week the Gaffer has made certain that none of us get sucked into all of that stuff and made sure that we just focused on the game and not the sideshow that comes with matches of this type. He was clear before the game that this was one that we could win and in the huddle we have in the dressing room before we start, there was a definite feeling amongst us that we could do it.

As positive as we'd been in the changing room we experienced the worst possible start when van Persie put them ahead after five minutes. The goal was quite poor from my point of view as we weren't together as a unit and pretty much got pulled apart everywhere. I allowed myself to drift too high up the pitch in an attempt to close down Arshavin, when I really should have just stayed back in my position. I was pretty disappointed about my part in it and even more annoyed that we had conceded so soon.

Thankfully it wasn't too long before we got back in the game. Rambo caught Nath on the foot in the box and the ref gave the penalty straight away. While all that was being sorted out I went across to the Gaffer to ask him what his thoughts were about how we were going about things. He said we needed to keep the ball better and shorten our passes and to understand that we don't always need to look for the long killer ball all the time. I passed that message on to Leon and Joe.

Unsurprisingly Scott scored from the spot, I knew he would. He struck it almost as well as the shot with which he hit the guy from Sky's backside.

It was great to be back in the game so soon and the tempo of the match increased as a result. The game became a bit of a back and forth battle for a period with both teams creating chances and attacking almost at will. They probably had the best chance in this period when I blocked a van Persie shot which then fell to Rambo, but thankfully he didn't take advantage of it.

It was around this time in the match that I was starting to get pretty frustrated with myself and the way that I was playing. I don't know why but as the game was developing I was feeling very anxious for some reason and I sensed that while I was still doing some good things I was also inexplicably doing some silly things. I anticipated a great through ball from Rambo over to our right back area, swept across to pick it up before any of their players could really react and then, for some reason, just played the ball straight to Yossi Benayoun giving away possession! I couldn't believe it.

Caulks had a bit of a bang and had to go off after receiving some treatment. When the ref called him back on, Joe was in possession and played the ball straight to him, but Caulks was obviously just concentrating on getting back into position and didn't see Joe make the pass. The result was that he just ran straight past it! We all screamed at him and thankfully he noticed, and managed to pick it back up before they could nip in. It was so funny to watch despite it being a scary moment.

While we were refuelling with drinks and getting fresh shirts at half-time the Gaffer decided to make a change, with Kemy coming off for Gylfi. Kemy was really disappointed and I had a quick word with him to say well done and for him not to be too down, but at times like that all a player wants to hear is that they are staying on. Apart from his debut against Barnsley I still didn't know much about Gylfi and what to expect but from what the Gaffer says, having worked with him before, he seems pretty confident in his ability. Obviously I've seen him in training but it's only out on the pitch that you really get to see how somebody can really perform.

We continued to more than hold our own in the game and then deservedly went ahead when Joe nicked the ball off Rambo, played a lovely pass in for Nath who finished brilliantly. I was absolutely buzzing for him, especially for the significance of this game. There's been plenty of talk about Nath and England and when it happens people always start by comparing him with Walcott and then asking who's the best out of the pair of them. It really winds me up as they are totally different players, but I guess the comparisons will always continue until Nath finally gets a chance at the top level to show what he's got.

About five minutes after Nath's goal came the introduction of Henry. I was looking over when he shook Arshavin's hand and jogged on and I could sense the buzz going around the ground, even among our own fans. It's not everyday people get to see a guy play who will go down in history as one of the finest to play football in this country. I was excited to see him jogging on too and I was hoping at some point that we'd come into direct contact. He made his way over towards our right back, Àngel, a position from where he'd launched most of his goals in his glory years. Again, it's moments like this that strike such a chord with me and reinforce to me just what a journey I've made and how lucky I am to be in a position to enjoy it.

Just five minutes after Henry's introduction they scored. It had nothing to do with him though, and was more to do with terrible defending by us. I started the chain of events that led to the goal and have to hold up my hand. Van Persie dropped a little deeper into midfield than he had been playing and I made the choice to go with him. Tayls hadn't seen me do that and in

Empty champagne bottles, we celebrated well.

I will never forget the lads I made it to the Prem with.

(courtesy of Dimitris Legakis / Athena Photography & www.swanseacity.net)

Spot the player most relieved to have survived the cable car ride to the top of an Austrian Alp.

(photos: courtesy of Dimitris Legakis / Athena Photography & www.swanseacity.net)

Nath's pull-out bed in Austria.

On top of the world!

A proud moment, leading Swansea out for our first ever Premier League game at the Liberty.

(photos: courtesy of Dimitris Legakis / Athena Photography & www.swanseacity.net)

My first Premier League huddle. "Be aggressive and enjoy it boys!"

Talking tactics with the Gaffer.

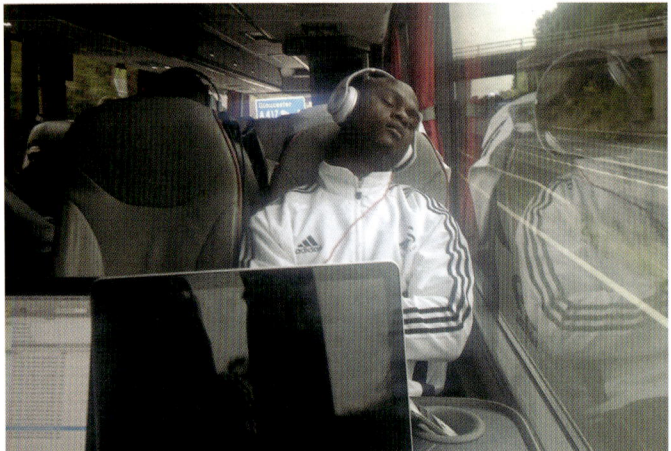

Leroy Lita –
Sleeping Beauty.

Getting the armband from Aaron
Ramsey, always a proud moment.
(courtesy of propaganda-photos.com)

Friday 9 September 2011

13:45	Coach arrive Glamorgan Health Club
14:00	Coach depart Glamorgan Health Club
14:28	Leave Swansea Central for London Paddington
17:30	Arrive London Paddington
18:00	Coach arrive hotel:–
	Melia White House, Albany St., Regents Park, London NW1 3UP
	Tel: (0207) 391 3000
19:00	Staff & Players dinner – The Chester Suite
19:45 -20:45	Physio/Massage – tbc
21:00	Meeting – The Nash Suite

Saturday 10 September 2011

08:30	Breakfast (optional) – The Chester Suite
10:30-11:30	Physio/Massage – tbc
11:45	Walk & stretch – meet in hotel main reception
12:00	Pre-match meal – The Chester Suite
12:50	Team meeting – The Nash Suite
13:10	Depart hotel
13:30	Arrive Arsenal FC., Emirates Stadium, London N5 1BU
	Tel: (0207) 619 5003 Fax: (0207) 704 4001
14:20	Warm-up

Typical away game itinerary.

So close to a historic draw at Wembley.
(courtesy of propaganda-photos.com)

A hard day for the Gaffer – the minute silence for his dad and the Gleision miners.

(courtesy of Dimitris Legakis / Athena Photography & www.swanseacity.net)

Tayls after his clash with Odemwingie at the Liberty.

Being filmed by Sky for *Barclays Premier League World* at our pizza fun day.

Get in! My debut Premier League goal at Stamford Bridge.

(courtesy of Dimitris Legakis / Athena Photography & www.swanseacity.net)

Pointing at my family at Chelsea. Čech's never seen a header like it!

(courtesy of Dimitris Legakis / Athena Photography & www.swanseacity.net)

Proudly receiving my annual cap at the FAW awards dinner in Cardiff.

(courtesy of propaganda-photos.com)

Bumped into Mr Jamie Foxx.

Work on my Grogg has started.
I'm far prettier than that!

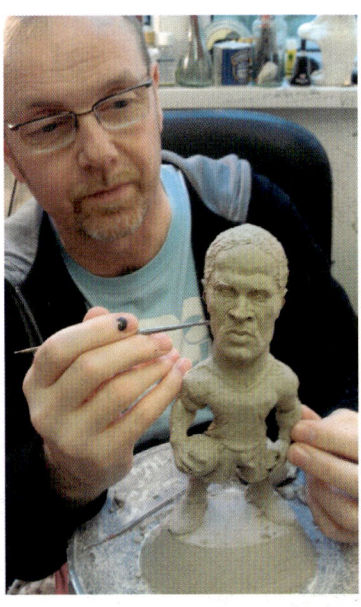

A lonely Bulgaria fan.
(courtesy of propaganda-photos.com)

Training with Wales, always a happy time under our management team of
Raymond Verheijen (left), manager Gary Speed (centre) and Osian Roberts (right).
(courtesy of propaganda-photos.com)

My smile says it all, Suárez down again – after he fouled me!

(photos: courtesy of Dimitris Legakis / Athena Photography & www.swanseacity.net)

Once in a while we get the luxury of a private jet.

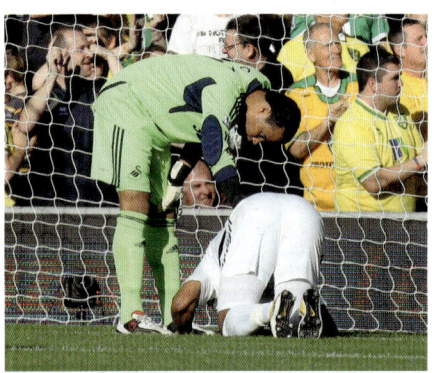

Up against one of the best – Wayne Rooney.

Michel with some advice – "Just count them Ash!"

Fighting back the tears. Just an hour after learning that Gary Speed had died. The match seemed pointless.

Chilling with Raphael at the top of the Rockefeller Centre, NYC.

The boys' Christmas jumpers.

Lee Lucas enjoying my fashion skills.

My boots worn at St James' Park for Gary Speed's memorial game.

Leading the team out at Villa Park.

(courtesy of Dimitris Legakis / Athena Photography & www.swanseacity.net)

HELP AN ORDINARY FAMILY WITH AN EXTRAORDINARY LITTLE BOY
A FUNDRAISING EVENING TO CHANGE A LIFE

Hari's wish
⋆⋆⋆to walk⋆⋆⋆
www.harisfirststeps.co.uk

WillsWorld   and   AG Swansea
www.willsworld.org.uk   www.agswansea.org

Friday 13th January
at
Manor Park Country House
Doors open at 7PM

Special Guests: Ashley Williams, Nathan Dyer,
Billy Wingrove and many more...

Ticket details
£10 Adults
£7.50 Under 16's
(Must be accompanied by an adult)
Guarantee your place at
www.willsworld.org.uk
or pay on the door.

The advertising poster for the WillsWorld Hari Kieft event. His was the real success story of the season.

Nice when the lads get involved with our charity events.

In his 251st Premier League game for Arsenal, a legend leaves the field with my shirt. He could look happier!

(photos: courtesy of Dimitris Legakis / Athena Photography & www.swanseacity.net)

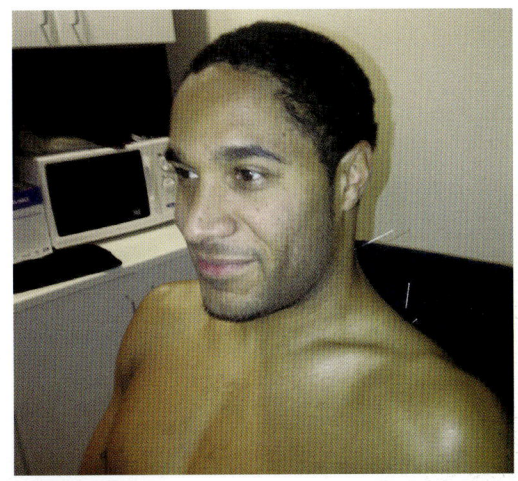

Acupuncture on my neck after the Bolton game.

On the receiving end for once! Being fouled at the Liberty by Chelsea's Romelu Lukaku.

My controversial handball at the Hawthorns.

Personal dinner invite from the Prime Minister.

Speedo's dad and two sons, giving a touching speech in the dressing room.
(courtesy of propaganda-photos.com)

Jordi Gómez strikes again, Nathan can't believe it.
(photos: courtesy of Dimitris Legakis / Athena Photography & www.swanseacity.net)

Beating Balotelli in the air, just before he sits down… again.

Chatting to Nath after his sending off at Wigan.

Enjoying family time at Raphael's first birthday.

One of the perks of living in Swansea – the beach.

Doing the Drake dance with Nath to celebrate his goal.

(courtesy of Dimitris Legakis / Athena Photography & www.swanseacity.net)

Sheep invading my decking, standing very close to the BBQ.

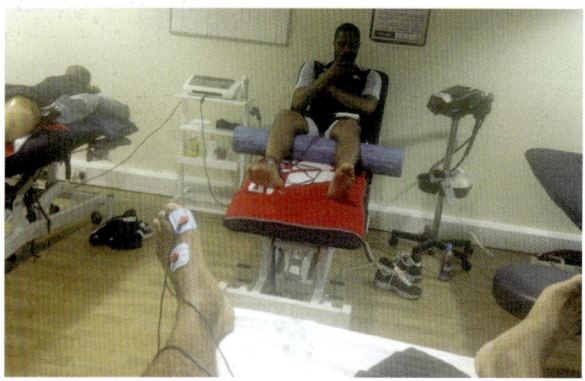

Compex machine on my broken toe after the Man U game at Old Trafford.

Giving Monks plenty of stick for bringing out a book – what type of footballer does that?

Taking the field against Liverpool, with Hari Kieft bravely walking alongside after all his troubles.

An emotional moment as I walk out a proud dad with Raphael in my arms.

(photos: courtesy of Dimitris Legakis / Athena Photography & www.swanseacity.net)

Me and Andy Carroll about to throw down. Thanks Joe, I can handle it.

One of the best arenas I've ever played in. MetLife Stadium, New Jersey.

(photos: courtesy of propaganda-photos.com)

Training at the New York Giants' complex.

Sharing a joke with the Gaffer, Chris Coleman.

fairness probably wouldn't have expected me to, so he left Walcott to go towards the ball, assuming that I'd be there to cover. On seeing all of this in front of him, Caulks had no option but to drop a little deeper and play everyone on side. This basically meant that our backline was all over the place. I shouldn't have gone in with van Persie and Tayls shouldn't have let Walcott run. I'm very disappointed with the goal. We never defend like this so it was really annoying. They'd now scored two, and I felt I could have done more on both. In such a high profile match that was very hard to take.

Still, as angry as I was, we scored straight from the kick-off which was not only hugely satisfying, but showed that as a team we possess great mental strength. It was our new player, Gylfi, doing exactly what the Gaffer wanted, linking midfield with attack. He played a great ball through to Danny who tucked it away with a confident finish. As chuffed as I was with the goal, I used the time at the restart to have a word with Tayls again about their goal. It probably looked like we were arguing, but we weren't. We were just discussing it quickly before the game restarted to make sure it didn't happen again now that we'd got ahead. We have both played non-league with some tough guys and often you will see me and Tayls shout and talk aggressively to each other, but we are just used to doing this and neither of us takes it to heart or anything like that. We just get the point across like men and move on.

About five minutes later I had my first coming together with Henry, and the challenge deflected off me for a corner. There was a little confusion when the corner came in and thankfully the ball fell to Mertesacker rather than Henry who somehow managed the miss the goal from about four yards out. My heart was in my mouth when it fell to him but it just skewed off his boot and went behind.

As we moved to our positions to restart and Michel waited for the ball boy, Henry came and stood next to me so I asked him if I could have his shirt at the end. He smiled and just said, 'Sure.' I was happy with that but, to make sure, I said, 'Thanks. And don't forget.' He just laughed.

Apart from a foot race with Walcott that I managed to win, the final whistle came without any more defensive dramas for us and was a fantastic moment. Beating Arsenal at the Liberty is one of those results that will go down in the history of the club. There was a fantastic reception from the fans and I took a brief moment to soak up the atmosphere. It was amazing to realise that we'd finally beaten a top four team and also done it by playing so well. Once I'd had my moment of reflection I swung round and looked for Thierry, and who was there shaking his hand and asking for *my* shirt, but Caulks! But my new mate Thierry pointed over to me and said, 'He's already asked.' That's experience for you, Caulks lad, and I ended up with the best shirt swap in my collection to date!

As I turned to walk in after acknowledging the fans, who had been absolutely fantastic throughout the game and had created such a fantastic atmosphere, I felt a tugging at my elbow and it was Kemy trying to pinch Henry's jersey off me. I turned round and he was laughing his head off so I slapped him and told him to get his own. He must've taken me literally because by the time we were all back in the dressing room and celebrating the win, in he walked clutching Thierry's spare shirt!

The dressing room was absolutely bouncing by now. Everyone recognised what a fantastic result it was for us and the celebrations certainly reflected that. The Gaffer was over the moon too. As I watched him going round to every player, shaking their hand and congratulating them, I remembered him speaking to us in the meeting we'd had before the Villa game when he'd asked us to achieve two targets – win away from home and beat a top four side. We've ended up doing both in the next two games! It's a pleasure to win these games from a personal point of view, but when we do win the Gaffer is genuinely thrilled for us, not himself. He even managed to take the piss out of me for ending up with Henry's shirt. 'I thought I saw you asking him for it!' he said. Guilty!

My agent was down for the game again, so along with Vanessa, Jazz and Kyle Copp from our under-16s, we all went for some food at the Village Hotel down by the marina. There was plenty of banter and fun flying round, but me being me, as the night was going on, I started to reflect on my own performance and wasn't happy. I knew I hadn't had the best of games and, as chuffed as I was about the win, deep down I knew I hadn't played well and that always bugs me. Football is always about the team, and when you are a professional footballer you always understand the bigger picture.

Played 21 Won 6 Drawn 8 Lost 7 Points 26 League Position – 10th
(14 more points needed for 40)

Monday 16th January

I am my biggest critic, so if I feel that I have underachieved on a personal level, I dwell on it until I get a chance in the next game to put it right. Most players are like this and hate making mistakes. I would rather the team win and I play poorly than to have the game of my career and lose, but it still bothers me.

Tuesday 17th January

Unbelievable reading the papers and watching Sky since the Arsenal game. It's as if the world has finally woken up to Swansea City. Everyone is praising our play, the manner of our victory, how we came from behind and also how we reacted when they equalised and basically out-Arsenaled Arsenal.

Wednesday 18th January

Chris Coleman rang me today to say that he was being announced as the new manager of Wales. He said that as one of the senior players he wanted me to hear the news from him and that he was hoping to pick up from where Speedo had left off. I was grateful that he took the time to contact me, and sensed that it was an awkward phone call for him to make, obviously due to the circumstances behind his appointment. We didn't chat long and he said that he'll contact me again and arrange to meet for a coffee to talk about things in more detail in the next couple of weeks before the next game. I had the feeling that he was really pleased to have the job, but couldn't celebrate the fact due to Speedo's death. It must be very hard for him to deal with a situation like that, especially as he knew Speedo so well, but nobody will hold that against him. Everyone knew that somebody would be appointed at some time and there's no doubt that Chris was a good choice in fairness, having had success in the Premier League with Fulham and being a young manager from the same era as Speedo.

I just hope that, as much as possible, things can stay the same on and off the pitch as they were under Speedo. To change all the staff and playing style now would be such a shame when we are all so comfortable with how it currently is and we have worked so hard to get here.

I do have one question though – and this is nothing to do with anything Chris did or didn't say – but it's over the future of Raymond Verheijen. I know Raymond pretty well and he worked so closely with Speedo at times that the line between manager and assistant manager would often become blurred. There's nothing wrong with that at all, it worked for Speedo to trust and work so closely with his assistant in that way – the results speak for themselves. Chris and Raymond don't know each other so to expect them to pick up that sort of relationship from the word go is unrealistic. From what I've seen about Chris's approach in the past, he's very much a hands-on number one, so I can't see him allowing someone like Raymond to have a role that would overlap his as manager too much, as Speedo was happy to do. And that's fine. If we carry on and do well Chris will deservedly take the plaudits, but if it doesn't go well Chris knows he'll have to face the criticism. That's what football management is about, so I just can't see how they could have the same close relationship as Speedo and Raymond enjoyed. I guess time will tell on that one.

I'm still being asked loads of questions by the media about my reaction to the Arsenal game. I answer them dutifully, but all I really want to do is forget the game and move on. I hate dwelling on a bad game as it reminds me of the mistakes I made during it. We conceded two goals and we never concede two goals, especially two goals where arguably I've been at fault. I want to just remove it from my memory and concentrate positively on what's to come. It's been hard to do that this week though because the Arsenal game is all anyone wants to talk about. Completely understandable, but I'm still annoyed. The Gaffer sensed it today too and pulled me after training to have a word. He basically said that he knew and understood that I was annoyed but told me that at the end of the day we won the game so I couldn't have been that bad. I was grateful for his support and his words did help, but I still can't completely shift the anger I have towards myself about my performance in the game.

Thursday 19th January

Decent training session today, with all the lads still buzzing about the Arsenal game. A good win really does wonders for the confidence and training becomes far more enjoyable as a result. After training I had some media to do over the phone with an interview with Sky Sports radio and then it was over to the tower at Swansea Marina where I had an interview at the restaurant at the top, The Grape and Olive, with Sky's Bianca Westwood for *Soccer Saturday*. On the way home I had a final interview with Ed Berryman for *Match of the Day* magazine.

When I got home I saw that the Gaffer had been doing some interviews too and had gone public on potentially signing a new, longer-term contract with the club. He said he was optimistic about signing a deal. It was good news to hear that.

Because of the impact that the Gaffer has had on the club since he's got here, and especially after the way that we've started in the Premier League and managed to sustain our particular way of playing, nearly everyone I meet asks me about him and what he's like. First and foremost, to me he's just a really nice guy. I might be different to some people, especially those in professional sport, in that I like to be surrounded with people who are first and foremost decent human beings. If you follow sport then you will have heard many times over the years something like, 'Oh yeah, he was quite an unpleasant bloke in real life, but he was a winner and that's all that matters.' Well not to me it doesn't.

I'm not sure I'd like to work for a manager who was some sort of football genius but treated me like a piece of dirt. The Gaffer isn't like that, but it's important to emphasise that the Gaffer isn't weak. Far from it, but you can be a strong and driven person and a nice one at the same time, which is exactly what the Gaffer's like. When he arrived at the club, on his first day he just sat with me on the training field for the best part of an hour, just talking to me about life in general. I'd just got married and we spoke about that and about my mom and dad. He was clearly very proud of his family and emphasized the importance of keeping close to my family. He explained why family and good friends are so important to anyone, but especially to people like us who earn our living in the public eye. His view was that our family keeps us linked to the real world because it's so easy to get lost in the old 'fame and fortune' thing. I agreed completely.

After our chat I remember thinking, 'Well, fair enough, we'll find out in time if he's going to be a good manager, but he's a really decent guy and that's half the battle.' That's still very important to me and obviously he's proved he's far more than just a decent manager. Yet despite all the praise and plaudits he's had personally in recent times, he's still exactly the same guy who sat down with me that afternoon.

I think I can speak for all the lads at the club when I say that if any of us had a problem in our lives – personally or professionally – we could go to the Gaffer and get some help with it. I know I certainly could anyway. He has the ability of making you feel important when you speak to him about stuff as if your views and opinions really count and, also, when the time is right he'll let you in to his world and explain what's going on with him, if that will be of any help to you.

It must be hard being a manager because every week of your life you have to disappoint people by leaving players out of teams, and then you often disappoint those ones picked by taking them off in games for whatever reason. Some players left out or subbed won't agree with the decision and will take it badly, but all I can say is that in my time with him I've never seen anyone fall out with him or hold a grudge towards him. That's rare at a football club and speaks volumes for his character, understanding and the way that he manages us all.

Even his much publicised personal problems, such as losing his own parents so close together quite recently, never dragged him down in his day-to-day work with us and, if anything, inspired me even more because of the dignified way he dealt with those heartaches and appeared so strong and positive throughout. When you witness a person in such a demanding, high profile and stressful job, dealing with such tragedy in such a dignified fashion, well, there's no way that you can't be anything but affected positively by it. He will find the positive in anything. Whether it's been a bad performance or defeat or whether it's something outside of football he has the gift of turning it around so that something constructive can come out of it. He'll often use life lessons that he has learned to develop us as footballers and people. He's big on motivational quotes and if he finds something new and relevant he'll always share it with us.

The Gaffer simply gives you energy. Ten minutes in his company normally means you won't feel better about yourself at any other point during that day. He's just an inspirational person, and anyone who has met him professionally or maybe just bumped into him in and around the place will know what I mean.

On the football front he just gets it. I know his career was ended early so he didn't get the chance to gain his football knowledge playing. He's an empathetic person, meaning he brings the best of both worlds, playing and coaching. He has the knowledge you would expect of a person who played football for years and years, but because he himself *wasn't* playing through those years he also brings an incredible amount of theoretical knowledge that a top footballer might not learn and understand until he was about forty-five. He's managed to provide the perfect blend between practical and theoretical knowledge. I'm not sure there are too many people in the game who can demonstrate that. I think a lot of this knowledge has come from working under the best coaches at Chelsea.

He's a pleasure to work with because his knowledge of

football is so deep but also because he knows how to handle you. My previous manager, Roberto Martínez, generally treated everyone the same, so in my case, even though I'd have played more games than any other outfield player towards the end of the season, he'd still make me train the same as everyone else, which meant no day off for three months! I understand it's my job and that was his approach, but in reality those training sessions weren't adding anything to me at all. If anything there's an argument to say that they were having a negative affect. The Gaffer is different. He looks at players and sees how much they've been involved and tailors their training involvement accordingly. After February/March last season I only took part in full training sessions a couple of times a week, if that. He knew that I looked after myself away from the training ground and the amount of games that I was playing meant that my aerobic fitness levels were high and he recognised that well-managed rest was probably more beneficial to me. He was right. By the end of the season I was as fresh as I'd been at that stage for many years.

He considers people's circumstances, too. While I'm really settled and happy at Swansea City, I keep a house in the Midlands and all my family and Vanessa's live nearby. That means that whenever it's appropriate, if we have a game up that way or generally in the north, he'll often give me an extra day off so we can both see the family. He does this with all of the players. How many times have you heard the phrase about a struggling football manager, 'He's lost the dressing room'? Well, in the Swansea City dressing room, that's about as far away from the truth as it can possibly be.

On the football front and the way he approaches his job, he's so organised it's not true. Absolutely nothing is left to chance and everything is planned for. That attention to detail in itself gives you confidence as a player because you have complete faith in what he is doing as it stems from such an organised base.

I've never come across a coach or manager in the game who is more organised than him. I don't know whether it's what he learned under Mourinho, because his attention to detail is supposed to be legendary, but it's very impressive all the same. Every day in training the Gaffer will turn up with a clipboard and a piece of A4 paper with four pitches drawn on it to represent the training pitches at the club. On that piece of paper he'll have marked down all the players with all their numbers and what is expected of them in that session on each pitch – it's all spot on. That will change every day and none of the info is wasted as he then files them all away so that he can refer to them in future to see what he's done with which group of players previously.

He never drops this focus he has or the level of detail and even when he was going through such a tough time with his dad he would turn up exactly the same, giving 100 per cent. He's the first member of staff through the door every day and last one to leave. We knew what he was going through yet he was still being so thorough and professional about it, so there was no way that we were going to be anything but 100 per cent professional ourselves as a result. Often it's the unsaid things that impress you most in life: actions not words.

It's not just what he brings to the club in his day-to-day work that is of benefit to Swansea City as a business either. His reputation throughout the game is so high that I know for a fact that he has attracted players to this club who were uncertain about coming here and were offered better money and longer deals elsewhere. Yet because it was him they came. Scott Sinclair might have had the pick of several clubs before he came, and the likes of Wayne Routledge and Danny Graham put Swansea before other clubs just because of the Gaffer. You can't really put a price on that sort of influence, and I'm sure if the time ever comes he will probably be just as persuasive when players are being chased by other clubs to leave. He's certainly created an environment where leaving him and what he has put in place at the club would make a very tough decision for anyone considering leaving.

In fairness, I'm sure the Gaffer would be the first to admit that Swansea City has been a perfect fit for him, too. He was able to pick up the foundations laid by Roberto and Paolo, tweak it, improve it and then managed to take us over the line when the other managers hadn't been able. That's life sometimes. 'Right place, right time' is definitely an accurate cliché and in sport it is even more crucial.

Friday 20th January

Before training started this morning we all said goodbye to Butts (Tom Butler) and Beats (Craig Beattie) who are both leaving the club. They are two great lads who I like a lot and it was really sad to see them go, but in particular I'll really miss Butts. He has been unlucky with injuries but was a really top player when I arrived at the club. When you have a run of injuries that keep you out for long periods, and at the same time the club gets sustained success, what often happens is the team gets away from you a bit. Not only are you battling to get your fitness back, but you are also battling to get into a team that is playing at a higher level than the one you left. Sadly for him, nothing stands still in football, and the emergence of the likes of Nath, Scott and Weezy meant that Butts was always facing an uphill struggle. But the best thing about him is that throughout it all, since he's been fit again, he's turned up for training every day and not only has he given 100 per cent in every session, he's also remained the life and soul of the squad. He's popular with everyone at the club, and most of that is down to his unique sense of humour, which is so wrong it's right! He's not necessarily the most politically correct of guys, but he's such a funny guy who sometimes goes over the top but no one is offended and he gets away with it because he's just Butts. He's hilarious and I can guarantee that not one person at the club would have a bad word to say about him. There was a time, I have to say, when Andrea Orlandi wouldn't have held that view. Well, you probably wouldn't if a future team mate shot you in the leg with a kids' air rifle as you turned up for your first day's training – a Tom Butler story that has gone down as legend at the club.

There's talk that he might be looking to find a club in Australia.

He'd fit in well out there, but whatever he chooses I hope he finds a club and has a really good end to his career. He's one of the good guys and deserves that.

Saturday 21st January
Sunderland 2 (Sessègnon 14, Gardner 85) Swansea City 0

The pitch was terrible today. It was the first thing that we noticed when we had a quick stroll on it before the warm-up. It's not the first time this season we've had a bad surface and obviously, for our passing game, the better the quality of the pitch, the better chance we have of playing to our maximum. Still, just because the pitch isn't the best doesn't mean that we worry about it or go into the match negatively. It's just a case of assessing it and then getting on with it. We are used to turning up at certain pitches now to find the pitch is all dug up!

After the warm-up, we went back into the dressing room as normal, but none of us expected what greeted us when the linesman came in to call us out to the tunnel. He came in, large as life and started to make jokes about our small team, and in particular had a pop at Leon, Joe and Nath. He was only small himself, and as he launched into his routine, the jaws of the lads began to drop. His act didn't last long though, as you can imagine what he was saying went down like a lead balloon just five minutes before walking out for a Premier League match, so Leon and Joe shut him up pretty sharpish. As he walked out, the lads were still shaking their heads in disbelief. It's one thing having a joke in the camp, but an outsider can't just walk in and start taking the piss out of us. That wouldn't be accepted in anybody's workplace. He got told sharpish to 'be quiet mate before we get stuck into you!'

We started the game really well today and got straight into our passing rhythm, until the game was halted due to a bad injury for Nicklas Bendtner after Rangel caught him in the face. I have to admit my first reaction was that he was making a meal of it, but he had to go off and took his time too, so it must have been serious. It looked like he had damaged his eye as far as I could see and it's never good to see a fellow pro leaving the field with an injury as potentially serious as that.

After about quarter of an hour we had an excellent chance to get ahead which fell to Scott after a great passing move which saw Nath play a top ball across the goal, only for Scott to blaze it over. As I watched the move develop and saw Scott move into position to take Nath's pass, I was certain he was going to score, so it was so frustrating to see him put it over because when you get a chance as good as that away from home so early in the game you just have to put it away. Have to.

I've learned in my years in the game that right after your team has spurned the opportunity to score there's often a double whammy as the opposition make you pay for it straight away. That's exactly what happened today as they came straight down the pitch and Sessègnon scored. It was so frustrating.

I'm sure Martin O'Neill will say it was a great goal, and to the neutral it was. But from my perspective we were just undone by a simple one-two in our right back position which isn't good enough for the mind-set that we should have been in for a tough game away from home. Ironically, if Wickham hadn't had such a heavy touch, the move might have come to nothing, but as it was it went straight to Sessègnon who delivered a great finish that gave Michel no chance. Going behind after fourteen minutes was not part of the plan.

Just a minute after the goal I was in some serious pain. Caulks and me both covered round for the same through ball and collided. My instant reaction was that I was in trouble, and as we are both big lads the collision wasn't pretty. My forearm went into his stomach and his knee collided with mine. My knee was killing but I could move it OK after a few seconds, and by the time the doctor came and had a look at my knee it was getting a little easier. He had a quick look and told me what I knew, in that it was nothing serious and that I'd be able to run it off. The physio also said that Caulks was OK too, which was a relief as you don't want to lose any defender just after you've lost an early goal away from home.

Still, the game started again quick enough, but even then

there was plenty of controversy. I never knew this before today, but apparently when two players clash like me and Caulks did, and both are injured at the same time, neither has to go off in the way that every other player who gets injured during a game has to. This was a huge bonus for us as obviously the game would have restarted without us having a centre back on the pitch, so when I realised what the ref was saying I must admit I was laughing inside, but managed to hide my joy. Good job, too. The Sunderland fans, players and management went nuts when they realised that we weren't being asked to leave.

We remained comfortable for the rest of the half, keeping the ball with ease, but I wasn't too happy with the treatment that Nath had put up with from Kieran Richardson throughout the half. As captain, as we walked off at half-time I tried to speak to the ref, Chris Foy, about it. Every time that the ball was played in to Nath, Richardson was marking him so close and so tight that he was pushing him off the ball. It was ridiculous, and in my eyes was a foul every time. Yet time and time again, the ref was either missing it or ignoring it. The longer that nothing happened from the ref, the longer Richardson carried on. I'd mentioned it to the ref during the game, but he just ignored me, so as we were walking off I went up to him again and pointed to the places on the pitch where it had happened and asked him to please have a look at it in the second half. Sadly, he gave no real response and left me feeling really frustrated. As captain, I have a right to do this, so I don't know why he thought it was OK to ignore me. It is disrespectful and annoys me even more, because refs often say in their meeting that we should talk to them during the game, but whenever we do, this is the reaction we get. It just doesn't make any sense to me.

In the changing room everyone was pretty upbeat about how we'd done and were very positive about the second half too. Monks was pretty vocal, telling us to continue what we were doing and, pretty much as I thought, that we just had to create more clear-cut chances on goal than we had done. Then the Gaffer came in and told us all 'well done' and how important it was that we kept getting Gylfi on the ball in behind their midfield line where he was causing them problems. All in all everyone was certain that there was no way that this game was beyond us at 1–0 down, and we left the dressing room certain that we had enough quality to turn it around.

After a decent start to the half the game turned a bit moody, with little niggles here and there, until on the hour something happened out on the left by the halfway line that seemed to involve Joe. I didn't see it, but it all kicked off and everyone seemed to be having a pop at him. Naturally, even if Joe's temper caused it, you still aren't going to let the opposition give your team mate any abuse. As I got there to calm it all down Seb Larsson had a pop at me and really wound me up by being extra busy and trying to get Joe into trouble. Larsson annoyed me for the bulk of the game and even though I'd gone in with the intention of calming things down, it wound me up that he was trying to do the exact opposite. He was shouting towards the ref, 'He's grabbed him round the throat. He's grabbed him round the throat,' and I knew that hadn't happened so I said to him, 'Stop lying or I'm going to grab you round the throat.' But he just kept on and then turned to go towards the linesman shouting out the same thing, so I grabbed him, which he didn't like, we had a little tussle and that seemed to stop things. Tayls was also annoyed with Larsson, so let him know that if there was a 50-50 coming up, he'd 'rattle' him. I smiled because that boy can tackle!

People like Larsson annoy me, though. They hang around until there's an incident and then they just can't wait to get in the middle of it and stir it up and cause trouble. These days there's no place for violence and fighting on the pitch and that's right and proper. But, if there was, Larsson would be the last one in the middle of it so I get annoyed when people like him try and stir it all up, knowing that nothing bad is going to happen to them. To be fair it appears Joe had done something because he was looking at the ref quite nervously, as he was the ref who sent him off at Blackburn, so he was desperate not to have given him an excuse to do it to him again. Thankfully, despite Larsson's best attempts, it all blew over and we just got on with it.

Once we were back playing there was another moment when

I started to lose a bit more faith in the ref. I went up for a header in our box and I had the most blatant ever shove in the back by Wickham, and to my horror, the ref – who was looking straight at me – waved play on! I couldn't believe it. I was so angry that my head just went and in case I did or said something stupid to him all I could think of doing was to just walk away from him. Trouble was, Michel took the kick quickly and as I was walking towards the touchline desperately trying to keep my temper, I heard somebody shout and when I looked round the game was going on! That's the trouble sometimes. Some of the decisions made by officials baffle you so much they just drive you to distraction.

It wasn't the last thing he missed either. Larsson was again at the centre of it with a terrible two-footed tackle on Scott that would have been absolutely horrible if he'd connected. Credit to Scott, he didn't make a meal of it and just got on, but Tayls, who was still boiling from Larsson's behaviour earlier, nearly lost his mind he was so angry about it. And yet the ref gave nothing. We'd been told that two-footed challenges, whether they connected or not, were straight reds and he gave nothing. He followed this up straight away by ignoring a blatant deflection from a shot by Joe, and gave a goal kick when it was clearly a corner. The trouble with this sequence of events is that we as a group of players feel that the referee is now affecting the game in a very negative way for us, which can only lead to one thing – frustration and anger. None of us mind when the difficult decisions go against us because it's a difficult job and that's life sometimes, but missing those clear ones in the way that he did just wasn't good enough I'm afraid.

The Gaffer made a change in midfield with just over ten minutes to go by bringing Josh on for Leon and going to a diamond in midfield, hoping that Josh's creative qualities would have got us back into the game. But it wasn't to be. It was nothing to do with Josh or the change, but we gave away possession in the middle of the pitch really cheaply, they countered from it straight away and scored. The classic goal out of nothing which was such a poor goal to give away in terms of the way we lost possession so easily. If we had hung on to the ball at that point, not only wouldn't we have conceded, but I really felt confident that we would push on and get an equaliser. We had 69 per cent possession today – away from home – which is almost unheard of, yet lost 2–0, largely down to our own indiscipline in two moments. To be honest though, with all that possession we still didn't create enough clear chances. We have to learn to be more clinical at certain moments of the game and make our possession count.

I felt for Danny today because for all that possession I think there was a period of about twenty minutes where he didn't really touch the ball. He works so hard, always on the move and making himself available, that something must be wrong somewhere if he doesn't touch the ball for so long. I think we have to try and mix things up a bit more and instead of trying to go around the back all the time, we sometimes need to think more direct and shoot a bit more. For all our 69 per cent possession, we had just four shots on target. I just don't think that's good enough. When Dobbie played, you could sometimes be frustrated because he gave you the impression that he would shoot from everywhere, but I think I'd rather we tried that than almost not shoot at all. I know the Gaffer feels the same way because his benchmark is to have ten shots on target each game, but we just didn't do that today.

The frustration isn't eased when I look at today's results either. If you are going to lose, you really hope that all the teams around you have a bad day too. But Bolton, Villa, QPR and Fulham all won and Blackburn drew away. A string of results like that turns a bad day into a very bad day. The positivity of the result against Arsenal will count for nothing if we lose games like we have today. Last week 40 points seemed just a matter of time. This week it seems as far away as ever.

Played 22 Won 6 Drawn 8 Lost 8 Points 26 League Position – 13th
(14 more points needed for 40)

Tuesday 24th January

Back in work today after spending Sunday chilling out with my mate Titus and our families, before heading down to Birmingham in the evening. Yesterday I had another restful day, before then completing the journey back to Swansea last night. As soon as I walked in this morning the Gaffer said to me, 'Do you want to give Harry Redknapp a call to see if he'll let Caulks play against Bolton on Saturday so you can have the weekend off?'

I laughed and knew what he was getting at. So I started preparing to play because there was no way that Redknapp is going to allow Caulks to turn out in a Cup match.

Wednesday 25th January

Because I'm more than likely playing on Saturday when most of the other lads are going to get a break, the Gaffer let me off outdoor training, so it was just massage, bike and gym for me. I didn't complain.

It was Fede Bessone's birthday today, so this evening me and my family, Michel and his family all went to Fede's for a meal cooked by his wife. Lovely evening just chilling and watching El Clasico in the Copa Del Rey and Liverpool in the Carling Cup semi against Man City. Speaking as a fan, I was delighted to see Liverpool going to Wembley tonight by drawing 2–2. Speaking as a mate of Bellars', I was thrilled to see what an impact he had on the match, especially as it was against the manager who sold him, Roberto Mancini. He was everywhere tonight, influencing the game from the start with his speed and quality, but to score the equaliser, which was effectively the winner, was a fantastic bonus for him. Bellars has never played at Wembley which is why I'm happy for him and I'm glad he's finally going to get there.

Thursday 26th January

On the way to training today, Sky Sports radio rang me for an interview, and then it was the same as yesterday, no outdoor training. The Gaffer's just trying to save my legs a little at this stage of the season as he knows that I don't lose my fitness if I have a few days off the intensive stuff. Throughout the season, it's all about managing ourselves and our bodies and the Gaffer is really excellent at doing that.

When I was watching *Frozen Planet* on the BBC tonight I got thinking about the number of points that are going to be required for survival in the Prem. We never set any points targets inside the dressing room, but the general rule is 40 points will see you safe. I don't know how many points we will eventually need, so the only thing we can do is literally take every game as it comes and try to win that and if we do that then I'm sure we will be OK.

As we stand after the Sunderland game, we have 26 points from 22 games. As positive as that is, I've become aware recently that clubs down the bottom have had some wins. Bolton have just beaten Liverpool, Blackburn's last two results have been a draw and a win, Wolves seem to have a good win now and again, and it's only Wigan who are dropping off a little. Because of this, it might even be more than 40 points to stay up which is definitely going to be a tough challenge. Based on our home form there would be no danger as we still hardly concede and look far more threatening with our possession. But it's away from home where ultimately our survival will be won or lost, I think. Coming up after the FA Cup we have Chelsea at home followed by West Brom away. I don't care how we do it, but we have to be looking at four points from those two games. I believe we can beat Chelsea, such is the confidence we have in each other at home. Then, if we do get a positive result against them, why on earth would we think that we can't get a result at The Hawthorns?

The Gaffer has been quite clear since the Sunderland defeat that we shouldn't be in that mind-set of looking down at the table because you just get yourself into a sort of always-looking-behind-you mentality which brings with it potentially an edge of desperation and pressure. He believes that we should be asking ourselves the question, 'How high up the table can we finish?' That's a completely different mind-set. Because we had a bad result at Sunderland the first thing myself and most of the lads did was to look at what teams around us did. If they won, it makes the defeat seem even worse. Then you look at a team like Norwich and see them winning and you start to feel a bit fed up as there's no reason why we shouldn't be doing as well them, if not better. It can really get into your mind if you are not careful, which is why I welcome the Gaffer's approach of thinking about how high we can finish. At the moment we are in the company of the likes of Everton, Aston Villa and Fulham. If we remain surrounded by them at the end of the season, history shows us that we'll be in the top ten because that's where they always seem to end up.

As you can imagine, I missed quite a bit of *Frozen Planet* thinking about all that.

Friday 27th January

In training this morning the Gaffer focused on team shape for Bolton tomorrow. The team will be completely different tomorrow, with the Gaffer bringing in most of the fringe players. As I've known all week, Caulks can't play, so no day off for me! In truth though I don't mind. Of course there are times when you are envious of some players getting a breather, but if someone told me that I'd have to play in every single game until the day I retire I would be happy with that.

I had some great news today about a future Wales fixture. We will be playing Mexico in a friendly at the end of May in New York's MetLife Stadium, home of the American Football teams, the New York Giants and New York Jets. I'm buzzing about that news and couldn't be happier. I love New York and can't believe I'm actually going to play a game of football there for Wales. Sometimes I can't believe this is all happening to me, a bloke who just nine years ago was working in a petrol station, filling up cars belonging to the likes of Juan Pablo Àngel of Aston Villa.

Madness.

Saturday 28th January
FA Cup –4th round
Bolton 2 (Pratley 45, Eagles 56) Swansea City 1 (Moore 43)

What a rubbish start to today I had.

At about 11 o'clock I stretched up while sitting down and my neck popped. It just clicked and I couldn't turn left anymore. What a nightmare.

I went to the medical room to see the physio, Rich Buchanan, to have treatment straight away which involved intensive massage, heat treatment and stretching which was proper painful as he had to force my neck left, the very way it didn't want to be forced! I had treatment for an hour straight, and apart from it being one of the more painful hours of my life, it showed zero improvement. I missed out on the pre-match stroll, and instead went to lunch looking like a robot with a Compex muscle stimulator machine in my pocket and wires coming out of it stuck to my neck. From my sympathetic team mates I had plenty of stick because I couldn't turn to my left at all, with most of them calling me from that side, trying to make me turn!

After lunch it was another half hour of treatment which didn't really seem to help at all. Then it was shovelling down the pain killers and just an acceptance that I would have no option but to get on with it, so it was just off to the ground.

We didn't start too well today to be honest, a little shaky, and not straight into the flowing way we have come to expect at the start of games. In terms of the defensive unit, with Gerhard the goalie, Monks and Fede all coming in, it was also quite tough to just jump in and play 'the Swansea way' across the back when you haven't had many minutes recently. As for me, well, I was in a world of pain, so that didn't exactly help towards a cohesive defensive unit either.

As the half developed, we were definitely off it and Bolton began to dominate a little, which was more down to our poor play rather than anything special from them. While that's not ideal obviously, at least you get the feeling that it can be easily turned around. They also had a run of corners during this period, which was absolutely great for my neck as I think every one landed on me!

Wayne then managed to score, but it was ruled offside. I couldn't tell if it was or wasn't from where I was, but we could really have done with that goal standing as going in front away from home, especially when we weren't playing particularly well, would have been a massive bonus. The game continued for the rest of the half much as it started, with them on top and us really struggling for any fluidity in our play. Just before half-time Luke showed everyone exactly what levels of brilliance he is capable of by taking a ball played into him, turning, pushing it past Wheater, using his pace and strength to get by, and then producing a really cool finish. The whole thing was world class. Timing-wise it was just what we needed and I knew that we would be able to build on that in the second half.

But that never happened. Just on half-time the ball was played up to Leets and Boyata nicked it off him. In his frustration and enthusiasm to get it back, Leets gave away a free kick. All of us knew how crucial it was to defend the free kick, but the ball played in came beyond the defensive line and Prats of all people nipped in and scored and not for the first time this season we'd conceded right at the worst possible time. At times like this you just get that sinking feeling as soon as the free kick is given. You know you can defend it and it's just before half-time but then you also know that sod's law means they will score.

That's exactly what the Gaffer thought, too, because I have never seen him as angry as he was today. To say his language was colourful is an understatement, and the odd tea cup was spilled. His anger was mainly directed at our inability to manage the game during the first half, and the general lack of purpose and control we had demonstrated. He made a point of praising Luke and Fede for their contributions but he gave the rest of us a real pasting. Nobody likes to have that, and it's not the Gaffer's usual style. As far as I'm concerned, we are all big boys now with roles and responsibilities to carry out. If we don't? Well, then I think the Gaffer has every right to tear into us.

We knew exactly what was required in the second half and

began well enough and it looked like we were starting to take a bit more control of the game and beginning to get the purpose back in our game that was lacking in the first half. But then – as often happens when you are chasing a game – disaster struck. Martin Petrov put in a shot for Gerhard to deal with, but unfortunately he spilled it when he really should have held it and Chris Eagles nipped in to score. It was a very frustrating moment but none of us were angry with Gerhard as we all know how tough it is to come in and play in a high intensity match like this when you haven't played, especially for a keeper.

After that, unsurprisingly they came into the game more, especially Prats. He got in for a couple of headers, one which hit the bar, and he also anticipated a back pass from Jazz which fortunately came to nothing. He hasn't enjoyed the best of starts to his time at Bolton and, as much as I wished he'd have had his good game against someone else, you could see that his workrate was still as high as ever and, as he'd often done for us in a Swansea City shirt, he'd made sure that that workrate led to chances for his team.

Just after the hour the Gaffer made his changes, taking off Leets and Wayne for Danny and Nath and, despite starting to push a bit more, as the time went on there was just a feeling among us that the game was slipping away.

I had a final half chance at a corner, but it was on the wrong side of my neck and, as I craned it to get in some power and direction, a volt of pain shot through it which was enough to make me misdirect it and that was that really. In the end it must have seemed that we went out of the Cup with a bit of a whimper. That's a difficult thing to admit and an extremely disappointing way to end our run in the Cup this year.

Not much was said after the game today, even by the Gaffer who'd already made his point at half-time and left us stew a bit after the game. We were a pretty sombre bunch as we made our way to Manchester airport for the flight home. We've had plenty of good days this season, but today wasn't one of them, and we only have ourselves to blame.

Sunday 29th January

We've got Chelsea on Tuesday the Gaffer had us in for training when normally we'd have the day off. Because my neck is still in spasm, for me it was just treatment on it, then back home for a kip. After that it was back over to the Liberty for more treatment on my neck from physiotherapist Kate Rees. Feels a little easier tonight now thanks to all the treatment it's had today.

Monday 30th January

Because it's an evening kick-off tomorrow we didn't have to go into training until 5.30 p.m., and Stuart Pearce was the Gaffer's guest who sat in on the pre-training meeting and then watched us train too. He didn't mix with us really and just took a watching brief, but had a chat with Britts, because they were both together at West Ham, and Josh and Caulks because they've been with him with England's under-21s. The Gaffer said that he expects Torres to play for Chelsea tomorrow. The last goal he scored in the Prem was against us. It was also the last game that I scored in too. Nice to know I've got the same scoring ratio as Fernando Torres.

Saw on *Sky Sports News* tonight the outcome of Gary Speed's inquest. Even though I've spoken at length of his tragic passing, when it came on the news, it was still a jolt to hear them talking about it so matter of factly, almost as if I was hearing the news for the first time again. Just hearing them talking about him again just instantly made me feel so sad about it on so many different levels; obviously on a family level for his boys, his wife and his mom and dad; then there's the football level and the impact it might have on the future direction of Wales after such a run of recent success under him; then of course on a personal level, as I thought so much of him as a bloke, and still have to remind myself that he's actually no longer with us.

I couldn't help thinking that I wished it wasn't being reported, and that it could all have just been done in private for Speedo's family and nobody else as if it just wasn't any of our business. But then, having said that, as I was sitting there watching it human nature took over and I became just like anybody else I guess; intrigued to hear what was coming out and just trying to make some sense out of what was being said. Having heard them say that they can't be certain that he intended to kill himself is probably the worst thing of all. If that is the case then it's even more of a tragedy than if he had meant to do it. If there was a note explaining what it was all about and that he was ending his life because of X, Y or Z, then as horrible as that still would be, at least the intent of Speedo would have been known and his reasons for it, bringing some closure to his family. Now, to think that the coroner is suggesting that Speedo might just have been making some sort of point and actually may have fallen asleep, never intending to kill himself, is almost too much to bear.

Speedo was a great man with a loving family and loads of friends and I just hope that after today everyone moves on, including the media. We should remember Speedo for the great man that he was, and just allow his family, especially his boys, to rebuild their lives in peace and in privacy.

Tuesday 31st January

Swansea City 1 (Sinclair 39) Chelsea 1 (Taylor og 90)

There was a very positive buzz in the dressing room as we got ready after the warm-up today. Saturday wasn't mentioned and there was a real feeling that we were going to get something from another top four team. It was really cold in the warm-up, so in the dressing room all the lads – the forwards, I mean – were getting into the Under Armour skins. I stuck with short sleeves, as that's part of the rules from the centre half union... and definitely no gloves either!

As we thought, new signing Cahill was on the bench and Torres was up front on his own. It's no secret that Torres has been a shadow of the player we saw in his time with Liverpool and, from a professional point of view, it was up to me and Caulks to ensure that any confidence issues he might have been suffering from were magnified by our treatment of him. That basically means that the pair of us went out to bully him physically from the start. I don't mean that we had a plan to deliberately injure him, but we thought that if we got into him and dominated him, then we'd have a chance to keep his confidence levels low. Professional football is not a picnic and most of the time only the strongest in body and mind survive. That's just the way it is.

After Joe had set the tone by getting in a tough early challenge on Meireles, and then kicking the ball into him for good measure, a break led to three chances for Danny, Gylfi and Joe, from which we frustratingly didn't score. I then had my first real pop at referee Andre Marriner. He ignored a foul on Danny by Luiz which led to Sturridge getting in a shot which went through my legs. It should never have been allowed to get that far due to the earlier foul, so I gave the ref both barrels to liven him up. After that I wanted to see how consistent he was going to be, so I put some big challenges into Torres and he only gave one foul, so I guess that was fair enough as we were being quite physical and rough with him.

For periods in the first half, Chelsea got possession of the ball and put us under some decent pressure. We knew this would happen at points during the game, and we have got used to it now when we play the top teams. The trick is to not let it rattle you, keep calm and understand that these periods will pass. During this period, as well as concentrating on defending, I continued to organise the troops throughout and keep everybody on their toes. The best part of all of this was hearing the frustration of Chelsea's players as they failed to break us down and seeing the look on their faces when they began to realise that we weren't going to be the pushovers that maybe they thought we would have been.

Once we got hold of the ball again, we managed to win a corner just before half-time and Scott reacted to the second ball and scored with a looping finish. Due to his connections with Chelsea he tried not to celebrate, but I'd told him before the game to celebrate if he did score. It's not like he had played in their first team for the last ten years and if you score a goal, in my eyes, you celebrate that goal anyway. So I picked him up and everyone was buzzing and celebrated with him. I'm not sure he was happy that I picked him up, as he tried to not even smile – but that made it a more amusing moment for the rest of us.

Just before half-time I had to have more words with the ref as Malouda got frustrated and caught Leon quite late with a challenge that could have been a nasty one. I basically asked him to make sure he protected our players against anything late like that. He said, 'Yeah, I've got it covered,' and walked away. Predictable response, I guess.

The Gaffer was pleased with what we'd done in the first half and there was a collective feeling in the dressing room that we had managed to outplay some of the best players in the world for long periods and that gave us confidence. He encouraged us to remain brave with our passing, but warned us that they would probably come at us stronger during the second half. Before we went out I had a quick word with Nath about Ashley Cole. He'd been booked just before half-time and I told Nath that he'd either be subbed or sent off, because Nath had been frustrating him so much.

In the early part of the second half we continued to be strong with everything we did with them and more than matched them all about the field. As positive as we still wanted to be, it's only natural that when you are in the lead – especially against a top team – that eventually you will fall back deeper, no matter how much you keep encouraging the lads to attack. I think it's almost a subconscious feeling of knowing that you are ahead in the game, so maybe you don't need to take that extra risk to get forward, and before you know it you get pegged back more than you really would like to be.

After about an hour Chelsea made their first change, taking off the pretty ineffectual Romeu and bringing on Michael Essien, who I've always rated very highly whenever I've seen him on the box. Almost immediately he began to have a big effect on the game, not only being very good on the ball but also by breaking up lots of our attempts to get a bit further forward. As the game went on his influence grew; I started to get concerned. It was clear that we weren't going to get as much of the ball as we usually do at home, so we all had to work really hard to influence the game without the ball, and to ensure that all their possession came to nothing. As a result of that, the nearer we got to full-time, the more convinced I was that we would just hang on to the win. I was concerned about one thing, the way the ref seemed to be letting Chelsea get away with continuous fouls against the likes of Nathan and Danny, and throughout the second half I was constantly on to him to make sure he gave the lads protection.

I don't think the ref needed any persuasion from me five minutes from the end though, to deal with a wild challenge by Ashley Cole on Nath. You could see it coming a mile off. Nath's got such quick and nimble feet that full backs get really frustrated and either lash out or make a rash challenge, and because Cole had already received a yellow for his first-half lunge, then the ref had no option but to show him red when he did it again. But even after Cole's red, or maybe because of it, Chelsea continued to foul Nath and then Luiz really clattered him which got me pissed, so I let him have it. I also made sure the ref – and any other Chelsea players in earshot – knew that carrying on like that was unacceptable. Daniel Sturridge, who seemed like a good guy during the game, came over to me and told me to chill out because it was near the end of the game and there was no need to get into trouble with the ref. I said, 'Cool, but I'm not going to stand by and watch him (pointing to Luiz) clattering Nath without saying something.' Sturridge just nodded.

Chelsea continued to press and just when we thought we were going to hold out and get our second win over a top four side in a month, they equalised in a way that was almost too hard to take. It was deep into injury time and Bosingwa made one last, almost desperate, run to the corner of our box. He turned Luke twice, who'd come on as sub for Scott about a quarter of an hour earlier, and hit a hopeful cross. Unbelievably it hit Tayls, wrong footing Michel, before going in. I just stood there stunned. I couldn't believe it. After all the work we'd all put in against a top side, to get so close to victory and then have it snatched away from you in such a cruel way was a tough one to take. I looked around at the lads, like Joe and Leon, who had worked tirelessly in midfield in the second half when we had so little ball, and the disappointment in their eyes was painful.

Within seconds the final whistle blew. We had come so close to beating another top four club in a result that would have done so much for our season and our search for 40 points, but it wasn't to be. There was nothing to say to the lads as we walked off, and the dressing room was a little subdued.

On a personal note I was voted Man of the Match by the sponsors, and while I'll roll out the cliché of preferring to swap that for a win it's always nice to get recognised in this way and am grateful to whoever chose me.

I've had a little time to reflect on the result now, and being disappointed to just draw with Chelsea is a measure of how far we have all come in a relatively short time. Rather than look at the two points dropped, it's far better to focus on the point gained in, let's be honest, a game most neutrals would have thought we would have lost.

Still, onwards and upwards, that's 27 points now. Four wins and a draw and we're safe. Roll on West Brom.

Played 23 Won 6 Drawn 9 Lost 8 Points 27 League Position – 13th (13 more points needed for 40)

CHAPTER EIGHT

February 2012

Wednesday 1st February

A day off today and not a lot to report, apart from some bad news I received tonight that Ferrie has been injured at the reserves game against Arsenal down at Parc y Scarlets in Llanelli. The news is a bit sketchy on him at the moment, but all I can hope is that it's not another bad one. He's worked so hard to get back to fitness and to get injured so soon again on the comeback trail could prove to be too much for him to take. My fingers are crossed that it isn't a really bad one. The thought that his career might have ended on a freezing cold rugby pitch in a reserve game is not something such a great player like him deserves.

Thursday 2nd February

I saw Swansea City fan Nic Grey off from the training ground this morning on his walk to the Hawthorns in time for Saturday's game to raise money for our Hari Kieft fund. When he told me what he was thinking of doing, I was impressed, as I've travelled the route so many times that I know exactly how far it is. I expected that like most fundraisers that he would have some support like a car or van going with him to look after him when he needed a break, but I found out that he's doing it all on his own, just him and his back pack – I couldn't believe it! The weather is really rubbish with snow forecast everywhere, so what Nic's doing is incredible and as I watched him walk off, I was full of admiration for what he's attempting. It never ceases to amaze me the lengths that some people go just to help others.

Friday 3rd February

I had a quick glance at the papers this morning and both the Gaffer and John Hartson have had quite nice things to say about me and how I've performed at the top level so far this season. There are times when you can read lots of criticism as a player, so it makes a nice change to read stuff like that which suggests that I'm doing my job properly. That's all I've ever tried to do.

The weather was horrible in training when I went in and I suppose one bonus with the AstroTurf, even though it plays havoc with your joints, is that the surface is pretty consistent no matter what the weather. Usual stuff today, the day before a match, light, sharp and fun and then finished off with some set pieces.

After training, it was a case of sorting out all my gear and then on board the coach to Birmingham, which is one of the shortest trips we do at about three and a half hours. Once we'd settled in at the hotel, the Gaffer called for a 9 p.m. meeting to discuss the Baggies and he emphasised that they were the team that provided us with our first win in the Premier League, so what a perfect opportunity to deliver our first double of the season. He also told us that if we get ahead in the game tomorrow, as he expected us to do, we had to manage the game better than we had in the last two. He told us we needed to be tighter in possession and less naïve about time, not time wasting as such, but not rushing to get the game restarted if we're ahead. He warned us to be most organised and aware in the first fifteen minutes, the ten minutes before and after half-time and the last ten of the match. If we managed those periods more sensibly and professionally, it would help us protect the game more in the event that we had something to hold onto. It was an important message that the boys understood. It was a positive meeting and I left with the feeling that all the lads believed we can get something tomorrow.

We know it will be a tough game and he pointed out that any team that Roy Hodgson puts out will be very well organised, disciplined and have a very solid game plan that they will not veer from. I think if we approach things in the right frame of mind tomorrow from the very start, then we have every chance of returning to Swansea with all three points.

Saturday 4th February
West Bromwich Albion 1 (Fortune 54)
Swansea City 2 (Sigurdsson 55, Graham 59)

I don't think I've ever been as cold on a football pitch as I've been today. I hate the cold and today it was arctic in West Bromwich, and by the time we arrived at the ground the snow was so thick I was worried whether the game would go ahead.

The snow of course also had a big effect on charity walker Nic Grey. The bad weather meant that he had to change his route and had to walk an extra 25 miles to avoid the Brecon Beacons because there was a risk he wouldn't have got over them. Over the last couple of days I've been texting him to see how he was doing, as he's been walking over snow covered Welsh hills, alone. He must be mad, but all for a good cause! What started out as a great adventure had become quite a dangerous escapade and I must admit I started to get worried for him when I understood just how bad the conditions were becoming. I'm delighted to say he made it safely and I was pleased to see him at the ground when I got off the coach and was able to drop him a couple of tickets. It was the very least I could do. He's raised so much money, probably the biggest single sum of all our fundraisers and I'm always amazed by the generosity of people when it comes to the charitable work I get involved with.

When I got inside the ground I dumped my stuff and had my usual stroll straight out onto the pitch to check it out before going back in and getting ready for the warm-up. Usually, most of the lads come out too, but not today. Not one of them came out to have a look. They were all clearly lacking the Nic Grey spirit, and they all looked at me as if I was crazy when I got back in the dressing room shivering. Still, at least the bitter cold wasn't a surprise for me when we all piled out for the warm-up.

I think it was a bit of a surprise for West Brom's Jerome

Thomas though. When we got out there and started doing our stretches and stuff, I looked over to West Brom and there he was, running round in a coat! And when I say coat, it was a big coat, one of those big sub's coats that players wear when they are on the bench trying to keep warm. I'd already seen the team-sheets in the referee's room and I knew he was playing so I couldn't help but laugh at how funny he looked, preparing for the game like that, hardly buzzing in anticipation.

We started well today and had far more possession than I thought they'd allow us if I'm honest. I thought they would press us far more than they did, making it difficult for us to get into a rhythm and play, but instead they just dropped in, gave us the ball and tried to stay solid. It was classic Italian tactics really, which is no surprise for a Roy Hodgson team I guess.

There was a little moment of controversy midway through the first half that I was at the centre of, which was unintentional for once, and also involved their centre back, Gareth McAuley. It was when he and I challenged for a header while I was defending a corner and straight after we went up he was screaming for handball. I, of course, remained silent and tried to look as innocent and unconcerned as possible which is quite hard to do when you know that the ball has just smashed you square on the hand, and the referee's whistle which you are expecting to hear straight away never comes. So yes, Gareth, as you quite rightly shouted, the ball hit my hand. But – and here's the grey area that makes the referee's job a nightmare – I genuinely never intended to handle the ball.

What happened was that he got ahead of me and I knew that he was going to head it, and I realised quite quickly that I was struggling. Because I knew that I wasn't going to get to the ball before him I then decided to put my arm in front of him and try to get him off balance. Instead, at that instant when I threw my arm across him, the ball arrived, smashed straight onto my fist and flew away as far as it would have if Michel had come and punched it. From any player's point of view, it was definitely handball, but I can honestly say that in no way did I intend to punch the ball – I didn't even see it. The punch just happened as a consequence of me deciding to throw my arm up to put him off to prevent him having a free header. If you follow the laws of the game to the letter then it's not handball because there's no intent. But to accept that, you've got to take my word for it. But, to be fair, I would have been pissed if I was a West Brom player, and I can fully understand their anger out on the pitch at the time.

When the ball smashed into my hand, my hands were frozen stiff and, because I hadn't made a proper fist, when the ball hit my knuckles it just sort of cracked them. The pain was instant and agonising, but of course the one thing I couldn't do was react to it. In fact, because all the West Brom players were running round and screaming, I couldn't even risk glancing down and looking at my hand, even though the pain was so bad that I did wonder if I'd broken a knuckle or something, but that was more to do with the cold.

After the bulk of the half going our way, certainly in terms of possession and from not allowing them any real chances to worry Michel, they had a flurry of corners later in the half which put us under a bit of pressure. Gylfi headed one clear off the line and it was a period that we all just dug in and did everything we could do to keep them out. I made sure that everyone in front and around me were concentrating on defending and dealt with the pressure. It's normally a case of a word here and a shout there, anything really to make sure we all remain completely focused on what we are doing. In the middle of all of this, and to spice it up a little, I had a bit of a clash with Odemwingie on the edge of our box after the ball was cleared up field, which carried on all the way back up to the halfway line. As usual, it was nothing, just a bit of shoulder barging and we went forehead to forehead at one point. Not much was said and we both just got on with it as soon as the ball came back towards us.

When we got back in the dressing room at half-time I'd never seen a team of footballers looking so cold. Everyone was freezing and desperate to get warm. The staff had laid on loads of warm towels for us and we all changed kit, so as we warmed up it wasn't long before we forgot about the cold and got to discussing what had happened in the first half and how we could improve for the next one. The most important thing for the Gaffer was that we'd reached half-time without conceding and for us to remember what a positive that is away from home. He also told us to remember that West Brom had a far better away record than home, so to make the most of the growing doubt that they will have in their minds about that and remain positive. He said that the three points were there for the taking – if we remained brave enough with our passing.

By the time we came out for the second half there was loads more snow on the pitch and, bizarrely, it was all at the end that we were defending. The annoying thing about snow is that it clogs the sole of your boot in between the studs, making your boots very slippery, which as a defender is absolutely the last thing you want.

We again felt comfortable in our possession and control as the half was developing, and just as I thought that we could begin to step things up a little, they scored from a very sloppy goal. It came from a corner, and while we made contact with the first ball, all we managed to do was to flick it to the far post. As Leon and I turned to close down Fortune, he miss-hit it but it still went in at the far bottom corner. This is what can sometimes happen when you mark zonally at corners as we do. Players can become unmarked for the second ball, which puts pressure on us to make sure that we close down and are aggressive with our blocks. I felt a mixture of anger and a feeling of being hard done by because we just didn't deserve to be behind and knew we'd have to score again soon to get something out of the game.

I just didn't expect us to score as soon as we did.

Gylfi scored it and, credit to him, he got into the box to get on the end of Tayls' cross. Runs like that from deep are exactly what you want to see from your attacking midfielder. Apart from his excellent run, what pleased me most was the character the boys showed by getting back into the game so quickly. It's so disappointing to concede a goal in the Premier League, especially in a tight game away from home that you believe you are edging, but to score a goal so quickly on the back of the disappointment of conceding spoke volumes for the character in our side.

Within five minutes we got another that proved to be the winner which really summed up exactly what we are all about as a team and the vision that the Gaffer sees regarding our style of football. It was a move that almost all the lads had a hand in, finished off with a classic striker's movement by Danny to get across the centre half and then provide a great finish. If you want a blueprint of what we are trying to achieve as a team that goal was it. It was a pleasure to watch it developing in front of me, and the best thing about it was that it gave us something to defend for the last half hour, and I like nothing more than the responsibility of doing that.

It nearly all went to pieces soon enough though.

After a scramble the ball flew under Caulks and dropped to Odemwingie who had found some space and was wide open at the back stick. My heart stopped as he had so much time to take a touch and slot it home and rob us of our victory. But for some reason he took it first time and blazed it over. Caulks and I looked at each other and both had the same stunned look on our faces as we knew we'd got away with it.

For the last period of the game it was just a case of keeping Leon and the back four close and tight, with him just in front of me and Caulks and ensuring we managed the game correctly which we did by shouting and talking a lot more. There was just one final moment of concern before we could claim the three points and if my heart stopped when Odemwingie had his earlier chance, it nearly exploded when I nearly gifted them the equaliser with seconds to go.

I won a good header and cleared. They then won the header back which was going to land on the edge of the box. As I've done hundreds of times, I just moved forward to clear it and eat up vital seconds. Instead, for some reason as I swung my leg towards it the ball just slipped off my boot! It was one of those horrible, slow-motion moments where all I could do was watch, holding my head as Fortune ran in one-on-one with Michel in the six-yard box. I was already rehearsing all my apologies to the lads and the Gaffer, especially as the Gaffer had made such a point last night of managing the last period of the game if we found ourselves ahead! Luckily as Fortune shot the ball it hit Michel's heel which was enough to deflect it onto the post and then out. I was so relieved. Maybe it was payback for Chelsea's late deflected goal last week.

More or less straight afterwards the final whistle went and I made straight for Scott to congratulate him for digging in, sticking with it and defending well in a match in which he had hardly seen the ball and in conditions that were about as bad as they can be for a player of his ability. I wanted to make a point of congratulating him publicly today as he'd done fantastically well and really helped the team in seeing the game out for a win.

We were a very cold but happy bunch as we trouped off after saluting the fans who were magnificent today – even as loud as they were at Villa Park I reckon. We were all looking forward to the hot showers and warm towels to get some blood moving through us again, but guess what? No heating in the showers. We were so cold that they still felt lukewarm and, as you can imagine, after running round in the freezing cold for two hours the boys weren't happy to have to jump into a cold shower. But the win was all that mattered and the knowledge that we'd done our first double in the Prem was a fantastic bonus for us.

Played 24 Won 7 Drawn 9 Lost 8 Points 30 League Position – 10th
(10 more points needed for 40)

Sunday 5th February

I watched the *Match of the Day* re-run this morning. Roy Hodgson wasn't best pleased about my 'handball'.

Gylfi played well yesterday, scoring one and making one. He's been a great addition to the squad and has provided us with something that we were probably lacking a bit, making that link between our midfield and attack. When we get that right we know that we will fear nobody. The more Gylfi plays for the team the better he's going to get as obviously the way that we play and the system that we use will be different to anything most players coming from the outside will have experienced before. Obviously Gylfi coming in means that someone has had to move out and unfortunately for him, that player has been Mark Gower. It's a shame but that's just the way it is sometimes. I'm sure Gows feels a little hard done by because he'd done nothing wrong and was probably playing as well as at any time in his career. It's another reminder for all of us not to get too far ahead of ourselves and to just take one game at a time.

Monday 6th February

We got the details for our trip to Tenerife today. It will be great to get away and everyone's looking forward to it. The flight duration and the time difference in Dubai made it a second choice. As much as we'd all have loved the Gaffer to have picked Dubai for probably a whole host of selfish reasons, from a footballing perspective it is the right decision. Tenerife has a purpose-built sports complex and even though Man City practically own the Middle East they still went there. I've never had a mid-season break away in the sun before, but know plenty of players who have and all say it's been a great benefit to them. It can get a bit of a grind at this time of year, and with the fixture list giving us two weeks off, and the fact that I've played every game, it's something I definitely need.

Interested to read West Brom's centre half Gareth McAuley in the press today moaning about my potential handball on Saturday. He reckons that when he went to the ref, Jonathan Moss, he was given three different reasons why he didn't give it. First was that it was a poor header. Second was that he (Moss) didn't see the handball and, third, he said it was too close to me to do anything.

I love referees.

Tuesday 7th February

I had a quick chat with the Gaffer today about the win on Saturday and it was nice to reflect on our first double this season, especially away from home in such tough conditions. We talked about the various reasons for our victory. Obviously Gylfi scoring so quickly after going behind was key, but for him the main reason was our defensive display throughout the team, and one person summed that up best for us, Scott Sinclair. Scotty's a confidence player who gives the impression on the field that he's full of it, but in reality he probably doesn't believe in himself enough and actually lacks a bit of confidence. Sometimes I wish I could sit him down and make him understand how much he terrifies defenders when he's at full tilt running at them, then cutting in and shooting. I'd hate to play against him doing that every week. He's another one of our squad who has every attribute to be a top player in this division, and I wish he could see that for himself. Sometimes he might struggle a bit if things go wrong during a game, his miss-kick with the open goal against Man United for example. So when I spot that I try and gee him up and get positive with him, but ultimately his confidence is going to come down to him and how he deals with things. I sometimes feel guilty during games because as much as I want to boost him, I sometimes end up giving him a roasting because he's not carried out his defensive duties 100 per cent. There's a theory that attacking wingers shouldn't have defensive duties and should just play to their strengths. That may be a luxury you can get away with in the really top sides but at Swansea, with the way we play when we haven't got the ball, everyone has to defend from the very front, all the way to the back to ensure we either get it back quickly, or defend our goal. That includes our striker and wingers as well. On the whole they do a great job, way more than other teams' attacking players, but when they don't it's my job to gently remind them.

The Gaffer's told me that Scott re-watches and analyses his games more than anyone else in the squad. I always have a look back at the DVDs to see how I've done, but the Gaffer said Scott's quite obsessive about this and I think that's a great strength and shows he really cares about his career. We forget sometimes that he's only just turned 23 so we can't expect the finished article for a while yet. But when he is I've absolutely no doubt that he'll be one of the best wingers in the division.

But I'm still gonna be shouting, mate, if you don't tackle back against Norwich on Saturday.

Wednesday 8th February

We are predominantly using the AstroTurf pitch at present and still sharing it with the Ospreys, which isn't ideal for lots of reasons. Today it meant that we had to start our training at 9 a.m. and not 10 a.m. because they'd booked it for earlier than they normally do. It's not a huge issue, and compared to where I've trained earlier in my career it's far better, but the club has got to address our training facilities sooner rather than later because it will make such a massive difference to us when they do.

Thursday 9th February

Fabio Capello quit yesterday as England manager and Harry Redknapp is the clear favourite to take the job, meaning the Gaffer is now being linked with becoming the next Spurs manager. He'd never discuss a rumour like that with us, but the speculation isn't surprising. If he continues guiding us in the manner that he is, it's only going to be a matter of time before one of the big clubs comes calling. In the longer term the opportunity to manage one of the top six of Arsenal, Tottenham, Chelsea, Liverpool and the Manchester clubs will probably only come along once in a lifetime, and at present the betting money would be on there being a vacancy at Tottenham due to the link with Redknapp and England. If Redknapp were to go to England tomorrow I couldn't see the Gaffer leaving in the middle of a season, but if he was offered it at the end of the season, then who knows?

Friday 10th February

Tomorrow's game is massive for us, and if we beat Norwich we'll move above them in the table. We've both done really well in our debut seasons but the fact that we've not been above them at any point this season is something that will give us an extra spur.

Grant Holt gave us a little bit of a backhanded compliment on Twitter a couple of days ago. When asked what he thought of Swansea, he tweeted, 'good team nice ground shame there welsh' [*sic*]. He'll probably get a lot of stick tomorrow, but regardless of his tweet I'm expecting a big, physical battle as they will choose from any combination of Holt, Simeon Jackson or Steve Morison. We are expecting that they will go long at every opportunity and play lots of balls down the channels for their front men to chase and generally bully their way to a win.

Josh played in the first team in training today as Joe's got a bit of a hamstring, so he'll play instead of Joe. Joey's become such an influential player that we'll miss him of course, but Josh is a very talented player. Also Gows comes back into the squad for the first time since the Spurs game on New Year's Eve, and I'm really chuffed for him. Gows is a great lad and I like him a lot, so it will be great to have him in the dressing room again. Gows is a proper footballer who has all the old values and is all about the team. He's the heart and soul of everything and the Gaffer absolutely loves him and understands the values that he brings to us as a group. There's never a dull moment with him either and he's always looking to banter someone, so it'll be a bit livelier in the dressing room tomorrow.

Gows more or less played every game in our promotion season last year, but if he's found it hard not playing so much this year, he's kept it to himself, encouraged the lads and been completely prepared when called upon. He's equally strong with either foot, and there are very few English players in the game these days that have that. As I've said, Josh will play and I'm sure he'll do well, but Gows gives the Gaffer a great option on the bench, and I for one am happy to see him there.

Saturday 11th February

Swansea City 2 (Graham 23 & 87)
Norwich City 3 (Holt 47 & 63, Pilkington 51)

Norwich started the match with a high pressing game against us which we expected. I came up against Holt almost straight away and came out on top in the early exchanges where I won a couple of headers, but even though we seemed to start OK, after about twenty minutes I sensed there was something wrong with us. I didn't like our attitude as a team. We seemed off the pace and weren't winning the second balls and generally we just weren't being physical enough.

After about twenty-odd minutes, Danny finished off a great move to put us one up, which I was hoping would settle us down a bit and deliver the control that we'd been lacking to that point. But Norwich wouldn't allow us to settle and start to build on the goal, and then there was a clash between Holt and Àngel that really wound Àngel up and left him holding his face. I jogged over to try and calm things down to hear Holt saying he'd done nothing and that Àngel was making a meal of it, but Àngel was insistent he'd been caught with an elbow. I didn't see it so can't really comment but, whatever happened, Àngel was pretty hot about it.

At half-time, even though we were one up, I still wasn't completely happy and the Gaffer was interested in the way that Norwich were deploying the full press against us, especially from goal kicks. It's the first time this season we've come up against a team who have gone man-for-man against us from goal kicks. This means Ward pressed up against Gylfi, leaving Danny one v one with Martin. This was a risk for them and a couple of times we nearly got in by hitting Danny and him winning the header. Most of the chat in the dressing room was about this and how we should try to exploit it more. One of the things I enjoy most about football, and especially in the Prem, are the new challenges all the time and the testing thing of trying to figure them out.

We really needed a positive start after the break to shake off the first-half lethargy, but we didn't get it. Norwich won a free kick – from a clear dive – but what followed was a complete farce! The free kick came in, I won the header and everyone thought that it was going out for a corner but Ward kept it in and then hooked the ball back. Holt and I challenged for it, he won it, but headed it straight into my head which took it past Michel for the goal. Michel said if it hadn't hit my head he'd have saved it. Just another incident to add to my long list of massively frustrating football moments.

Within five minutes we conceded again after we lost the ball high up the pitch. They broke down our right which meant we all got dragged over and then Pilkington decided to shoot. When he did it deflected off Tayls straight past Michel. I couldn't believe it. We now were 2–1 down after conceding twice in six minutes, but more worryingly we weren't playing well. As I walked into position waiting for the restart, my feeling was that the game was far too important just to throw it away like this and we had to get back in it quickly. We were a little more positive for the next ten minutes, but it was clear we were nowhere near our best for some reason and then Holt put the game beyond us, scoring as he did from a counter attack.

The Gaffer made a change almost straight away with Gows coming on for Josh and when he ran on Gows passed me a piece of paper from the Gaffer with the change in formation on it along with the words, 'KEEP GOING'. It was typical of the Gaffer. He'd sensed that I was frustrated at half-time, and he knew that the events in the second half would hardly have helped that. Personally his message was just what I needed to concentrate my mind again and continue to drive the team on.

We finally started to get amongst Norwich a bit, and probably should have had a pen when Wayne crossed into the box and the ball appeared to hit the arm of the defender. Then, chasing the game meant we lost our shape and we nearly paid for it when Naughton hit a great strike that Michel had to deal with. Losing your shape is never a good thing, especially when you play as technically as we do. Michel's clearance led to a corner for us which in turn led to another wrestling match with Holt, and this time I managed to get in front of him and he pulled me down. Penalty. Danny scored it.

We threw everything at them after that and were really unlucky not to score again. Danny had a great chance just after the penalty which he dragged wide and then Caulks got up and headed powerfully at a corner. The ball went straight at Ruddy who saved it, but a foot either side and he wouldn't have sniffed it.

We just left it too late to start playing and the ref soon blew for full-time. I was angry and frustrated at the final whistle, not just about dropping points at home, but more about how we played, especially the way that we didn't stand up to the physical approach that Norwich brought with them, you can always be outplayed by another team but outbattled? There's no excuse for that.

Played 25 Won 7 Drawn 9 Lost 9 Points 30 League Position – 11th
(10 more points needed for 40)

Sunday 12th February

We arrived in Tenerife today, probably the perfect thing to do to get yesterday out of the system.

This trip is all about getting a mental break from the usual day-to-day goings-on, to get the sun on our backs and it is definitely a perk of this job that we all appreciate. It isn't a pampering session as such as we still have to train, in nice bright conditions I might add, but after that, our schedule is very relaxed and we have free time to enjoy as we see fit.

We met at 11 a.m. at the training ground before setting out for Bristol. Every member of the playing staff is out here apart from the first year pros. The banter started flying almost straight away and it was clear that even just the trip out here today has gone a long way to turning around our mood from yesterday. We had lunch at the airport before boarding a Ryanair flight which was an experience in itself. Those of you who have never flown Ryanair before need to do it at least once in your life!

The hotel is fantastic and after dinner the Gaffer got us in for a quick meeting to give us some minor rules, but above all he told us to enjoy ourselves and relax.

Monday 13th February

After breakfast today it was off to a local complex for training. We are still on second day recovery so it was a light session that consisted of jogging, stretching and a little bit of ball work. It was really nice having a session with the sun on your back. It made such a change from cold Llandarcy!

After the session it was back to the hotel for a shower and

lunch and then we were told to have a siesta in the afternoon. Now these are the type of rules I like!

After dinner we had a quiz where all the staff and players took part. There were three rounds – music, sport and general knowledge – and, very suspiciously, the staff won. My group came second, Monks' team was third and Tatey's last. No surprise there.

They have to buy dinner for everybody tomorrow!

Tuesday 14th February

Very tough training session this morning at the training complex. Plenty of physical work in the session, which combined with the heat meant it was exactly like a pre-season session. And there's me thinking we were out here for a nice rest.

Again we were sent to bed this afternoon for our siesta, but Nath and I couldn't sleep, and even if we could have, with Caulks and Danny coming in to see us and our neighbours – Tayls and Wayne – hopping over the balcony every two minutes for a chat, we were never likely to get much shuteye anyway.

Highlight of the day was undoubtedly the evening meal paid for by Tatey and his losing team mates. The lads were right up for making the most out of the quiz-losers' misfortune by going somewhere pretty plush. We ended up going to a Japanese restaurant owned by the Gaffer's mate and Sky TV pundit, Chris Kamara.

Wednesday 15th February

To follow on from our free night last night we had the morning off, which meant, predictably, that none of the lads made it down for breakfast. There were plenty of sore heads among the lads, but Nath and I weren't too bad to be fair!

We all turned up for lunch with a few lads looking the worse for wear and feeling a little sorry for themselves. Most of the conversation was reliving the antics of the night before and there was plenty of funny stories flying around.

After lunch we had a choice between golf and jet skis. I'd

never been on a jet ski before so picked that, and about ten of us decided to go out on the water. Luke and Nath found it hilarious that I drove round on my jet ski at a sensible pace; none of this speeding rubbish and showing off! Pleased to report that nobody fell off and I absolutely loved it. I will definitely be doing that again.

The rest of the lads played golf and Monks won. Gows lost as usual. No point in him competing anymore.

After last night's late one, tonight most of the lads were knackered and went to bed early. I didn't do much, just chilled with Nath and Luke and watched the Arsenal v AC Milan game in our room.

Thursday 16th February

Up early for breakfast this morning before another training session at the complex. Now I'm a bit of an early riser, but when I got up and went out on the balcony, for the fourth day running our German keeper Gerhard was already up and out on his sun lounger and getting the rays in. I'm not saying anything about the stereotype about the Germans and their towels, but Gerhard hasn't missed a moment to get on that sunbed, and his roomie, Dobbs, hasn't had a look in. I don't understand why though. Gerhard looked like a bottle of milk when he arrived and still looked like one lying there this morning. I'm sure he must be using factor 150.

Our final day in the sun sadly. Training this morning was sharp and we all got a good sweat on.

Then it was back to the hotel for lunch, and a trip to the airport well in advance of our 4 p.m. flight on Monarch to Bristol. We had to get there early as they don't allocate seats, so there were plenty of grumbles from the lads about that. There's nothing worse than a flight sitting next to an annoying person. Luckily I got next to Tayls and could chill watching my *Transformers* DVD.

After landing it was a coach trip back to the training ground, where we picked up our cars and I was back home by 10.30. It's been a long day but a great week, especially as we lost the last game and a few of us were sulking afterwards. The timing was perfect as now we are all close again and ready to attack the next part of the season and really give it a go. When you are living with each other twenty-four hours a day like we have been, you grow closer to your team mates and the banter is constant and just flies round. It's been an important few days.

Friday 17th February

Because we have no game this weekend I knew that the Gaffer would put on a tough session this morning for the last one of the week. And I wasn't wrong. However to my surprise it didn't involve me!

We did our usual warm-ups and stretches and then the Gaffer pointed to the lads like me, Leon, Joe, Nath who have played in most of the games so far, and said for us to have a light session with Ryland. He then pointed to the lads who have been sub quite a bit and not played often, like Luke, Leroy and Dobbs, and got them all onto the full-size pitch and put them through a thirty-minute each way, eleven-a-side game. All of us on the side line couldn't help but have a sly smile to each other.

To be honest I wouldn't have minded playing in it but, like everything in life, when you feel like you have just got away with something it's like a little victory. And that victory is made all the sweeter when you then see the look on the faces of some of the boys who can't believe you've got away with something and they haven't. Priceless.

Tuesday 21st February

I had a text off our press officer at the club this morning to say that there was a letter for me at the Liberty from 10 Downing Street. Interesting. Can't be the knighthood yet surely!

Raphael didn't sleep well last night, and as all parents know the sleep deprivation part of bringing kids up can hardly be described as fun. No training today thankfully, but still spent most of the day moping round like a zombie. Hope he sleeps tonight.

Thursday 23rd February

This morning's session was all about starting to prepare for the Stoke game and the tactics we'll be using. We all know what they are about, how direct they are and how they try to exploit any weakness with as much physicality that they can get away with, so it's a matter of small adjustments and altering a few things in our normal game.

I picked up that letter from Number 10 today, and to my surprise it was a personal invitation from David Cameron to attend a St David's Day celebration next week. I have absolutely no idea why I have been sent the invite, but I'm very grateful and it's a nice piece of memorabilia to keep. Unfortunately, it's on the 29th – the day before St David's Day – which is also the same night as the Gary Speed memorial match for Wales against Costa Rica and I'm not missing that game for anything. It's a shame though, as it would have been very interesting to visit No. 10!

Friday 24th February

One person who won't be at the Wales game next week is Speedo's assistant, Raymond, who's gone public today about how he feels he's been treated by the Welsh FA and has announced his resignation from his role with the team. I haven't spoken to Raymond for a little while, so apart from the paper talk and a couple of his tweets, I didn't know where he stood on the issue, or what was likely to happen to him in the future. It's clear now that he won't be involved with us again, and from my point of view I have to say it's a shame he's not sticking around as he was so important to what Speedo was doing with us. But for his own reasons he's chosen to walk away and I guess whatever's behind this it will remain the business of him and the Welsh FA. I always got on well with Raymond and, despite being a little in the dark about him at first, really began to respect his knowledge of the game and the way that it is played. He completely immersed himself in the theory of football, was an excellent communicator and he really managed to get his views across in the many team meetings we had. A typical Dutchman, he didn't lack in confidence, but I grew to like him and I'm sorry he's chosen to leave in this way.

Saturday 25th February

More work on Stoke this morning, particularly set plays and defending crosses. The session was tough, and just in case we didn't already know it, we are now under no illusions just how tough a physical battle it will be tomorrow. We beat them pretty comfortably at the Liberty back in October, but they are a completely different proposition at home, and we all know that.

Sunday 26th February

Stoke City 2 (Upson 24, Crouch 39) Swansea City 0

Breakfast as normal this morning, apart from one thing. Mr Nathan Dyer made it down too. After explaining to him what the jugs of orange juice and bowls of cereal were for, we sat down and enjoyed breakfast!

When we all got back together for lunch and to go through our usual pre-match stuff, we noticed Michel was missing. One of the physios came in and announced that he'd been ill all through the night with some sort of bug and definitely wouldn't be playing. Obviously, I was worried for Michel personally and wanted him to get better as soon as. But, selfishly, I was more gutted and frustrated that we'd be without him today. He's been sensational for us this season, and Stoke City away is not the fixture that you want to experience a key loss to your defensive unit. My thoughts then turned to Gerhard. If you had to pick a fixture *not* to make your Premier League debut in as a keeper, I'm guessing most goalies would say, 'Stoke City, away.' I didn't give it too much thought, Gerhard is a very capable goalkeeper with plenty of experience and importantly a good mentality and I knew he'd fit into our defensive unit with no real issues.

When we arrived at the ground I took my usual look at the

pitch and – surprise, surprise – it hadn't seen a Flymo for a while. The groundsman actually looked a little embarrassed as we kicked at the grass with our feet, clearly not thrilled by what we were being asked to play on. Swansea City is a team that likes to play football on the ground, Stoke City isn't. That's not me making some snobby opinion, that's just me stating a fact. I have no problem whatsoever with how Stoke City play. I actually admire them for sticking to their principles in exactly the same way as we have stuck to ours. The difference is they can affect our game by messing with an external factor – the pitch. Anyway, it's up to us to deal with it now. It's not a new idea anyway. It often happened in the Championship and we now try to take it as a compliment.

In the huddle I was short and sharp with what I had to say. I told the boys that this was going to be a real physical test for us, and so we'd see where we were with that. I also said that we would need eleven men to win the game today, so we'd all have to stick to our jobs to get the win. The boys gave a very positive response which was good to hear.

Very early on the ball found its way to Scott, who had a great chance but missed. It was a really good opening and I must admit that my mind flashed straight back to Sunderland and I hoped we wouldn't end up ruing his miss as much as we had up there. Not long afterwards we had to deal with our first long throw by Ryan Shotton, who has a decent throw but not as good as Rory Delap who wasn't playing. We set up exactly as we'd been told to in training, me and Tayls on Crouch with Caulks in the space to attack everything from a free area. We dealt with it OK, but it was certainly a sign of things to come in terms of the battle.

In fact it only took another minute or so for Walters to begin throwing his weight around as he kicked Joe and I had a full go at the linesman for not flagging for it. This was followed by Crouch heading Tayls' head, which to be fair was an accident and more to do with the great leap by Tayls. It was a decent bang but Tayls just got on with it. This clash was quickly followed by another two or three fouls, so at the next break in play I spoke to Howard Webb to ask for some protection for our players. He told me he'd protect us if he saw them as fouls. He is another ref who I respect. He lets you speak to him and will explain his decisions if needs be.

Midway through the half Caulks demonstrated his confidence and how much he's developed as a player by getting out of a tight spot in the right back area by playing a few one-twos and attacking up the pitch. Both of us should do this more often as it's such a surprise to them. Teams don't always know how to deal with it, so rigid are their defensive set-ups. However, when we do we need to know that Britts is there as cover, which he was today.

Five minutes later Stoke took the lead with a Matt Upson header which was a terrible goal for us to concede. It's all very well saying that they're good from set pieces, but we defended it awfully. Àngel wasn't strong enough when blocking and Caulks will know that he should have done more when the ball arrived in his space, because a free header six yards out isn't good enough.

At the restart there was some more pushing and shoving between Joey and – shock – Walters. I got involved this time and calmed it down and told Joe not to bother getting involved with him as that's their game not ours. Then, when play began again it was clear that they had already decided to slow the game down and waste time and were taking forever with dead balls. After one long throw by Shotton that took ages I again had to go and have words with the ref and tell him it wasn't on that they were starting this so early. Fortunately he seemed to agree and said he was looking at it.

A couple of minutes later we were punished by Shotton's next throw as Crouch scored from close-in to double their lead. Unsurprisingly, I was angry. We knew we'd be up against this all day and between me, Caulks and Gerhard we should have done better. From my point of view it was pretty difficult because I had Crouch attacking the ball from behind me. For a central defender, having a much taller man behind you is as bad as it gets really, but it's no excuse. Two-nil down to two set pieces, it was so frustrating. It's not as if we didn't know what was coming.

It just wasn't good enough from us. As they celebrated, a horrible thought went through my mind about the number of times I'd seen top teams come here and go behind and then get the life squeezed out of them by Stoke and not get back in it. We still had half the game to go and I wasn't handing it in just yet, but knew that we'd really given ourselves a mountain to climb.

In the dressing room Monks and Tatey, who were subs today, spoke to us about the goals and explained from their perspective where we'd gone wrong and what we needed to do to stop it in the second half. I agreed with them. The Gaffer as usual stayed completely positive and urged us to get something back early and promised the game would change instantly if we did. As usual we were up on possession stats, and he said they'd get very anxious if we got back in it quickly.

We started well enough and showed good intent and aggression. I got involved with Whitehead and then had a wrestling match at an attacking corner with Upson who had been assigned to me so marked me all day. I was impressed with him. He's had some stick from people over the years but he didn't leave me for a second at corners today and did his job well.

Because we'd failed to do what the Gaffer said and not got the goal, Stoke did what Stoke do and got their men behind the ball, stayed organised and committed and ground out the win. Fair play to them. It's what they do and shows yet again that success in football can be achieved with completely different philosophies. We huffed and puffed a bit as time began to run out but unlike Norwich last time out, when I thought until the last minute we'd get something to save us, I never had that feeling at all today. Really, we finished with a bit of a whimper offensively which was probably the most disappointing aspect of our play.

After the game the coach took us back to the services on the M4 where the Welsh lads had left their cars, and then it was straight down to the St David's Hotel in Cardiff to meet up with the Welsh squad for our memorial game for Speedo against Costa Rica on Wednesday. As I got into the car and drove off, I did so with a heavy feeling of regret about today, and regret is not a good feeling to be associated with as a footballer, especially as their win today has seen them leapfrog us in the table. It's Wigan away next, and if we don't want to get sucked into what's going on beneath us, we're going to need a better performance against them, and a win.

Played 26 Won 7 Drawn 9 Lost 10 Points 30 League Position – 14th
(10 more points needed for 40)

Monday 27th February

After breakfast this morning we had a meeting with all the staff and players that was taken by Osian Roberts. It was an extremely sombre and emotional gathering and must've been particularly hard for Osian as he was so close to Speedo, having been given his chance to work at such a high level of football by him. The main purpose of this morning's meeting was to address the situation with Speedo's passing, confirm what was expected of us this week and also look forward to the future. Osian was such a close friend of Speedo's and he was clearly upset at having to address the squad and I really felt for him. He spoke well, and I will always remember and respect him for that. After Osian's speech we then had a short video of some of the highlights of Speedo's career as a player and a manager which was so inspiring to watch but as you can imagine left a lot of us quite choked. Since Speedo passed, time has moved on for the rest of us and despite thinking of him regularly I have to be completely honest and say that he hasn't been at the forefront of my mind to the extent that he was back in November when it all happened. I found the whole meeting quite moving and also upsetting. But having said that, I really think the meeting was needed in order that we could all try and close the chapter a little bit more in our minds.

After the meeting Chris Coleman came up to me and said that he wanted to speak to me in private. I could tell he had something delicate to tell me and he started by saying that, as it had been under Speedo, I was going to be his vice captain and that any time that Aaron couldn't play I would be his captain.

Once Chris had explained that he then went on to tell me that because Bellars was so close to Speedo he thought it would be a nice gesture to let him captain the team and take us out on Wednesday as Aaron wasn't playing and would I be alright with that.

Easy decision.

I agreed 100 per cent with his suggestion. I thought it was the right thing to do, so Chris said he would have to speak to Bellars first to make sure he was happy with the idea too, which it turned out he was.

NB: In life, I refer to Chris Coleman as the Gaffer, but because Brendan is also the Gaffer, I thought it might get a bit confusing. So for that reason only, he is mentioned in this diary as Chris.

Tuesday 28th February

Well, last day of prep for tomorrow's game and I have to say that it's been the weirdest atmosphere that I have ever experienced in the lead up to a game.

We are all professionals and it is the ultimate achievement to win a game of football for your country, but you can only do that by adopting a certain attitude – a professional one. You have to be focused on the game – and your jobs within that game. This game is completely different. The circumstances of it mean that you'd have to be a robot not to have been affected emotionally by what we've already experienced this week and, no doubt, what we will experience tomorrow night, meaning it has been completely impossible to immerse ourselves into the game as we normally would. Every conversation has involved Speedo and everything on TV has been about him too, and quite rightly so. He was our manager, so it's still tough to deal with playing for Wales without him at the forefront. I've never experienced anything like this before in my whole career.

Thrown in on top of all this has been the fact that we've had a new manager in charge of us which would be uncomfortable for everyone at the best of times. In what has been an extremely difficult situation for him, I think Chris Coleman has handled everything brilliantly. He has taken the pressure off us where he could in terms of talking to the press about how this match is all about Speedo and not him or the players and he has taken very much a back seat role in the camp, allowing Osian to take the lead. The lads have respected him for that. There have been glimpses at times that he is a pretty uncompromising character and he's certainly given us the impression that he won't be a walkover. I get the very strong feeling that when we next meet up after this game in the summer he's going to be quite strict.

Interesting times ahead.

Wednesday 29th February
Wales 0 Costa Rica 1 (Campbell 7)

When we went down to breakfast this morning, we were immediately reminded that this was going to be a far from normal day. We watched as the likes of Alan Shearer, Steve Harper – close mates of Speedo's from his time at Newcastle – and various other characters from the football world turn up at our hotel to pay their respects to Speedo and his family at the game. There's almost been an air of attending a funeral about the place and I'm sure for those of you that have been to a funeral, the last thing you would have wanted to do straight after it would be to play a football match. It's been a tough day and I don't think I'm the only player in a frame of mind not particularly suited to playing a game of football.

When we arrived at the ground I did my best to snap myself out of it and tried to prepare myself in the dressing room in exactly the same manner as any other game I've played for Wales. But of course the events we experienced meant that was never going to happen. Once we were changed Speedo's dad, Roger, came and spoke to us all in the changing room. It was really tough to watch and listen to this extremely decent and honourable man, heartbroken by the loss of his son, but we were all grateful that he had taken the time to come and speak to us and that his words were so touching and emotional. He is a very brave man who has the respect of us all. Writing this now, as a dad myself, I can't even begin to think about what Roger has been going through recently and what was going through his mind as he spoke to us.

After he'd gone, we had no option but to try to switch back on to the game and Osian reminded us that we were going to be in for a tough game because Costa Rica are a decent team and play a different style to European teams, which would make things difficult for us. One final emotional moment to deal with prior to the game was the moment that we were led out by Speedo's two lads, a perfect tribute to their dad, who I know was so proud of them. Ed and Tom were unbelievably strong and held it together brilliantly. They were an absolute credit to their father – as they always have been. Out on the pitch, first there was the minute's applause followed by possibly the most emotional rendition of our anthem that I've ever been involved in and all the time the fans held up cards that spelt out, 'Gary'. Bellars was understandably very emotional standing as he was between Ed and Tom.

Soon Howard Webb blew his whistle and the game began. Maybe understandably, it wasn't the best of games for the neutral.

It was a very slow start by us and I actually got the feeling that they were expecting us to take the game to them, which meant that it was a bit of a stalemate in the opening five minutes or so. Then, just as we started to be a bit more assertive, we conceded a really poor goal. Defensively we all got pulled out of position because nobody stayed with Campbell who made a good run off the ball and finished well. The goal was greeted with complete silence in the stadium. It was such an anticlimax and not the start we wanted. I love to keep a clean sheet so when I lose that so early in the game the feeling is one of bitter disappointment, but it's happened to me heaps of times now so I just have to get on with it.

After about twenty minutes I went up for a challenge with Ruiz and we clashed heads. He rolled around a bit and had some stick from the crowd for making a meal of it, but I have to say I don't think he did... this time. It was a decent clash to be fair and as I had the momentum, it must've hurt him a lot more than it hurt me! From then on, I wanted to encourage the team, so I started some of my shouting and screaming, trying to get the lads around me a bit more active and for them to realise how important it was for us to get a grip of the game. It was the most aggressive mood I'd been in since we joined up on Sunday.

The match turned into a bit of a chess game after that, with some nice possession play from us, but nothing that you'd say really threatened them. Just before half-time we had a couple of corners and should have equalised from one of them. First Steve Morison had a great header which hit the bar and as it was going goalwards I had another little tear up with their lad at the back, who'd been wrestling me every time I'd gone forward. Howard Webb spotted it this time, shouted across to me and said, 'Just keep it calm, Willo!' I really enjoy having Howard as a ref. I've got a good relationship with him. He understands players really well and as he was our ref on Sunday that didn't harm matters either!

The second chance at a corner fell to me. As soon as it went over I realised instantly what a good chance it had been and that I should have done better with it. The ball dropped to me so quickly, that I was on the turn and it was a half-volley. I should've scored but I'm a centre half… what did you expect? Seriously though, I was absolutely gutted because it would have been a great time to score for so many reasons, not least of which it was right on half-time.

Just as Chris Coleman had told the press leading up to the game, he took a back seat and let Osian take the half-time team talk. Osian felt we needed to move the ball quicker and with better spacing all over the pitch. He emphasised that we needed to work on everything that had served us well over the last few games for Wales that we hadn't shown in the first half and for us to remember everything that we had worked so hard on under Speedo and to put it right. He was right of course but I think that because of all the unique attention surrounding the game we didn't start it as we usually would and once you do that as a team it's very hard to get into it later on. The start is the most important part of the game.

In the second half they got their first corner quite soon after the start, and the way we dealt with it was a departure from the way we generally deal with them at Swansea. At Wales we always man-mark from corners, which is not a problem for me at all. I haven't really got a preference on which way to mark, either man for man or zonally. I'm happy to follow whatever instructions I am given. I was told before the game who I'd be getting at corners – Miller – and I just did everything in my power to make it difficult for him to get the ball. When the ball came in I just tried to be as physical as I could and tried not to let him get a run at me. Pretty standard stuff really, but vitally important you don't lose concentration and just do you job properly.

Apart from a clash with Cunningham when he really clattered Adam Matthews, that was pretty much it for me in the game, and I was subbed in the 71st minute. Fans often want to know if it is planned, especially in friendlies, but it wasn't tonight. I was slightly surprised to see my number but I was fine with it. I'm hardly ever subbed so I never get a rest in games, so actually I appreciated the gesture with it being midweek and in between our two Prem games.

We couldn't get the game back, and after the usual handshakes at the end it was back in to the dressing room where there was one final moment that will live long in the memory. Speedo's son Ed came in and asked if it was OK to speak to us all. It was an incredible thing to witness such a young lad, obviously hurting over the loss of his father, but speaking so positively and confident about everything. It was actually pretty hard to take, but in a good way if you know what I mean. I'm not going to say what was said because I think it's private between him and the squad, but to have the confidence to speak to a team of professional footballers like that and not be nervous was a brilliant effort by him and left a big impression on us all. I was really proud of him and when he started to speak to us I just prayed that he'd get through it all OK. I needn't have worried. Once he'd finished, he then walked around the whole dressing room and shook everyone's hand and thanked us. There was nothing we could say really, so we all just thanked him too. It was quite a surreal moment. His father would have been immensely proud of him.

Once that was done and we all started to get changed, Osian and Chris spoke about the game and the playing side of things, but sensibly there was nothing too heavy and not too much detail. From my point of view the game as an occasion was very similar to the Villa game at home on the day that Speedo died. There was something bigger going on than just a game of football tonight and quite rightly the game itself came a distant second to it.

We now have to look forward and, for Wales, that means World Cup qualification. The man who made us believe in that possibility is no longer with us, but me and every other single player in the squad, will do everything in our power to make his dream a reality. If we can it will be one small way for us to repay his son for the bravery he showed in our dressing room tonight.

CHAPTER NINE

March 2012

Friday 2nd March

We'll be doing something a bit different defensively at Wigan tomorrow by marking man for man at corners for the first time this season, instead of zonally as usual. The reason for this is the goals that we conceded at Stoke last week. Wigan are a big side too, and the Gaffer had a chat with Tony Pulis after the game and he said that Wigan are very strong in the air from set pieces, so for one week only it's going to be man for man. It's no problem as I've done it plenty of times and did it for Wales on Wednesday, so I know what I have to do but it's a harder task for midfielders and strikers if they are defending on corners to stay with their man. The Gaffer said that I'll be having Alcaraz and Caulks will have Caldwell, so it's just a question of concentrating, not giving him any space and stopping him get a run on. It should all work out… hopefully.

I always try to remember who players are marking on set pieces just so I know who to shout at, but more importantly, to tell any subs that come on what they're supposed to be doing.

Saturday 3rd March

Wigan 0 Swansea City 2 (Sigurdsson 45, 54)

With it being Wigan today the usual talk in the press has been about us meeting up again with Roberto Martínez. People are always interested in whether any ex-players get to speak to their previous managers before a game and what they think of him. Well, I didn't see or speak to him at all before the game and to be brutally honest with you none of us who were at the club under him were even the slightest bit concerned about him when we were chatting about the game ahead. It's not something any of us obsesses about. It was big news at the time when he left, obviously, but as I've mentioned before in this book the only real certainty about football is that at some point we all move on. When Roberto decided he was going, as far as us players were concerned it was a case of good luck to him, because in reality, from that moment on, he really didn't figure that big in our lives any more. We all just moved on. You get used to that in football. I didn't have a close relationship with him outside of football, so haven't kept in contact with Roberto, but I do sometimes get the odd text off different ex-managers of mine.

One thing I noticed quite early today was how the Swansea fans drowned out Wigan's. I know they're having a poor season and fans can be fickle at times like this, but I was quite surprised by the number of empty seats, bearing in mind we never see a spare one at the Liberty now we are in the Prem. I've been to the DW to watch a few games in the past when Titus played here, and they'd never made that much noise so I knew our fans would out-sing them and that actually became clear in the warm-up. A lot of times this season it has felt like we are the home team and I can't overstate how important it is for us to know we have such fantastic support behind us. There's nothing worse as a player than going to someone else's patch and feeling like you're on your own, so I hope fans don't underestimate how much their support means. We do hear it and we do appreciate it.

Midway through the half there was a freak incident involving Tayls. Somehow, he managed to cut his finger on Di Santo's boot and there was a lot of blood. It had sliced a gash into his finger and was a really bad cut that was definitely going to need stitches. Trouble was, I didn't know that at the time. I could tell that he had done something by the way that he was shaking his hand as he was running back into position. I just shouted across to him to forget about it and just concentrate on the game. I thought it was pretty odd that he was making such a deal out of it and actually he even seemed to be panicking a bit, but I couldn't see the amount of blood that was pouring out, so had no sympathy with him at all. About ten minutes later, Joe gave a free kick away at the edge of the box, and I heard Tayls still going on about losing blood, and I just looked across at him and told him to man up forget about his bloody hand!

We went 1–0 up courtesy of Gylfi, and his goal was a contender for goal of the season so far. We had a bit of possession between me, Tayls and Scott, then we nearly lost it but Tayls – sliced finger and all – slid in to win it back and then Leon flicked to Caulks who ran forward with it quickly, before clipping a lovely ball to Gylfi. Once Gylfi had got it out of his feet with his first touch, he just curled it up and over Al-Habsi with his second, a truly magnificent piece of football. It illustrated exactly what I've moaned a bit about this season regarding us needing to shoot a bit more from distance when the opportunity presents itself. In the two months or so that Gylfi has been with us, he's shown everyone what an important skill it is and, more importantly, how good he is at it. I'd have him shooting even more if it was up to me. It's just rewards for him too as he always stays behind after training with Scott and practices his shooting from distance after we've all finished.

When we got in at half-time, Tayls disappeared into the shower room with the doc, still complaining about his finger and again I wondered what he was going on about, but soon forgot about him as I was just concentrating on getting some fluids down me and getting my stuff sorted for the second half. When the Gaffer started giving his team talk, right on cue came these screams from the shower room courtesy of Tayls, and the noise he was making sounded like he was dying from behind the wall! At one point, the Gaffer had to stop talking and with a smile popped his head round the wall and asked, 'Is he OK?' and was shaking his head and laughing at what he'd seen. We all laughed at the look on the Gaffer's face, and of course the continued wailing from Tayls. When I went in to see him after the Gaffer had finished speaking I could see how bad the gash in his finger was. It was clear that he'd lost a lot of blood and he said that when I'd been having a go at him he was already feeling faint because of it. In fairness, he stayed out there twenty minutes after cutting it and the last thing he'd have needed for the rest of the half was my

Brummie accent shouting at him! Respect to my tough north Walian friend.

I had a bit of a clash with the ref, Andre Marriner, in the tunnel as we left the dressing room, or rather didn't, for the second half. Even though I've made light of Tayls' hand injury, when the ref's buzzer went, he was still being treated by the doc and wasn't ready, so I told the lads to ignore the buzzer as we weren't going out without him. Next thing, there was a knock on the dressing room door from the ref, so I went and told him about Tayls and that we weren't ready. He was having none of it and told me that we must get out there and start without him. There was no way on earth I was going to allow that to happen, and I told him, so there was a bit of a stand-off as I was insistent that we would not be leaving the dressing room without Tayls. Fortunately, as we were mid-discussion, Tayls shouted that he was done. I must admit I did wonder whether the ref might get proper stroppy and possibly even book me – even though I was polite, but firm, in my stance. I did know that the situation had really annoyed him though and I hoped that it wouldn't be something that he'd carry over into the second half. Referees are human after all. But at the same time I've always been told you never leave without your whole team behind you.

Before the restart, I went over and had a quick word with Tayls because he hadn't really had a rest at half-time or a chance to collect his thoughts due to the doc working on his finger. I told him that it was vital that he got straight back on it as he was going to be up against Moses who'd come on as sub. Probably not the news he wanted to hear at that exact moment!

A couple of minutes in, they showed us that it was not going to be a stroll to three points for us as there was a crazy ten seconds in our box where anything could have happened. It began with my decision not to give away a needless corner. I tried to clear the ball but only succeeded in smashing it into Tayls' chest (at least it missed his hand!). The ball dropped to one of them who tried an overhead kick that hit Leon on the head and could have gone anywhere. I was pretty relieved when it was over and that they hadn't scored as a goal then would have completely changed the match. Once again it was no surprise to see Britts in the right place at the right time as he just has this incredible knack of covering our mistakes.

Within ten minutes we got the goal that was to seal our win, and once again it was thanks to a fantastic strike from Gylfi but he'd never have scored if he'd heard the conversation Caulks had with me. We were lined up at the far stick, waiting for Gylfi to sort out the ball, when it became clear from the way he was standing that he was going to shoot. Caulks was fuming when he realised and he started going on to me that Gylfi should put it out to the back stick for him to score and that he never crosses, and stuff like that. Then the ref blew and Gylfi ran up and put it straight in the top corner – fantastic finish! At the split second it flew in Caulks looked straight at me and just cracked up – the sheepish look on his face said it all. It was a really funny moment.

What wasn't so funny was the ref's decision to send off Nath for a high challenge on Jordi Gómez, which brought back bad memories of the home game. It was never a red card. It was an absolutely terrible decision and as soon as I got to the ref that's exactly what I told him, but he ignored me completely. A bit of a melee developed, as the lads weren't happy with the meal that Gómez had made of it, but I just got hold of Nath, who was absolutely distraught and wouldn't leave, and walked him away from it so that he wouldn't get into any more trouble. As we walked away I told him not to worry and that we'd still win the game. In a funny way, once it had all calmed down I realised that the incident would make my job a little easier for the rest of the game as I shouted to all of the lads that we all needed to do it for Nath now. The response from each player told me everything I needed to know. We certainly wouldn't lose the game from a lack of motivation.

I was pretty angry at Gómez for his part in it because he knew that it was hardly even a foul from Nath. Both players had their feet high because of the bounce of the ball, and he knew that if he could just nick it, the only possible outcome would be Nath's foot hitting his, which would give him the ammunition to just scream as loud as he could to let the ref think that he was hurt and then roll around on the floor to emphasise the fact, exactly as he'd done to me at the Liberty. Every single one of us know exactly what he's doing, yet all around the world referees still fall for this type of stuff. In fairness to him, I have to say that it's not cheating, more gamesmanship, and if referees were stronger and just stood over him and told him to get up then it would soon stop. When they actually send off someone like Nath for such a pathetic amount of contact then all they are doing is giving the likes of Gómez a licence to do exactly the same to somebody else week in, week out.

The immediate fallout from Nath's dismissal however was that the Gaffer took Gylfi off and brought Tatey on. Apart from the circumstances I couldn't have been more pleased for Tatey, as he has worked so hard to get here. By that I don't just mean his recovery from his broken leg in the freak golf buggy incident but, more importantly, his journey from the bottom division like the rest of us. He captained us in the Man City game and was as gutted as the rest of us to have been on the wrong end of such as bad scoreline but unlike us, due to his injury, he'd never had the chance to put that right personally. When he originally had the accident there was a time when he thought he'd miss the rest of the season completely, which would have been a complete tragedy for him, so when he made it back on I was delighted to see him out there.

With the game now ten men against eleven, especially protecting a lead, our mentality changed. The match altered, as well, as we were absolutely cruising before the sending off, but when we saw what Gómez had done to Nath the anger levels clearly rose. It also had an affect on them too. They now saw a way back into the game that had been previously denied to them, so they got a little feisty as they were doing anything to get that goal to get them back in it. With that as the backdrop, it's inevitable that there are going to be flash points. And one duly arrived just about ten minutes after Nath had gone.

It happened when Caulks got injured after trying to prevent the ball going for the corner. He was actually off the pitch, but realising that we had a corner to defend he rolled straight back on. It was clever thinking by him, but I also have to say a bit naughty, especially from Wigan's point of view. Anyway, Wigan's players now realised that the game would have to be stopped for Caulks to get treatment, so a couple of their players rushed over, stood over him and started to abuse him. That in itself was interesting as not one of them had said a single word to him when he was stood up, and towering over them, but waited until he was lying down, unable to do anything. Obviously there was no way that I was going to let that happen, so I got there and started pushing them off him at which point everyone jumped in and got involved and it all kicked off. I ended up head to head with Diamé and trying to balance out not giving an inch against not doing enough to get sent off.

Anyway, as me and Diamé were at it, the linesman got involved and got us apart and I knew then I was in trouble as they can be notoriously busy and you never really know which way they are going to go. I was pretty nervous as he spoke to the ref and realised that I'd done exactly what I hadn't wanted to and that was to give him the opportunity to make a negative decision against me, especially after our dressing room door disagreement. As he called me over I feared the worst especially as Diamé and I had gone head to head, so was relieved when I saw the yellow.

Not a hell of a lot more happened in the game after that. We defended superbly from Danny up front all the way back to Michel, and I can't really remember them having a single clear-cut chance all the time that we were down to ten men. The Gaffer was delighted as we walked off and as I shook hands with him he grabbed me and said, 'That was great defending, I knew you'd keep a clean sheet today; I could see it in your eyes!' He was right too. I know most people see clean sheets as a reward for goalkeepers, they get an award for them at the end of the season after all, but as far as I'm concerned that goal is mine also, and the Gaffer knows that every game I take to the field the one thing I desire above everything else is to keep that goal intact. It's a bit of an obsession for me, and it really hurts when we concede so the Gaffer knew how much today meant to me.

The dressing room was absolutely bouncing; one of the best

atmospheres we've had in there all season, with plenty of music on – Scott's iPod – and loads of banter flying round. Everyone was on a massive high as we all understood the importance of the result, and it was a definite release of the tension that we'd all displayed when we'd arrived at the ground. At one stage the Gaffer was taking the mickey out of Scott by saying it was the first time he'd ever seen him defend and head balls out at the back stick! I'm not sure what anyone outside the dressing room would have made of it, but there were plenty of screams too as the lads got into Tayls about the noises he was making at half-time and were mimicking him. It was a great half an hour being in there and one of the fantastic rewards for being a footballer and winning a game.

Of course, there was one person not buzzing and not involved in all the madness, and that was Nath who was just sitting there quietly. Most of the boys went over to speak to him and told him to keep his chin up, but that was easy for us to say as none of us are looking at a three-game ban and losing our place in the side. All courtesy of Jordi Gómez. One day he is going to be on the end of a really bad tackle and scream for real and I bet he stops his antics after that!

Played 27 Won 8 Drawn 9 Lost 10 Points 33 League Position – 14th
(7 more points needed for 40)

Sunday 4th March

Really nice to reflect on such an important win yesterday. Taking three points off Wigan to keep them bottom is a massive result for us. No disrespect to them but we knew coming into the league that in terms of survival Wigan would definitely be one of the clubs we'd need to finish above. As a result of yesterday I'm feeling much more confident about survival, especially as we're now 13 points ahead of Wigan and Bolton, and 11 ahead of Blackburn, Wolves and QPR. Our win has even put us above Villa and I'm not sure many would have had us above them at this stage of the season. The most important thing is that survival is very much in our own hands now, as apart from Villa and Wigan, we have all the other teams to come. Positive results from those games will guarantee survival, no matter what we do against the likes of Man City, Tottenham, Man Utd and Liverpool. It's as simple as that really.

Tuesday 6th March

Hari is having his life-saving operation in St Louis today and it's also my father-in-law's birthday, so I see that as a good omen. It's crazy to think that all the hard work everyone did at the beginning of the year has achieved something as amazing as giving someone the gift of walking.

Wednesday 7th March

After training today I had an interview with Leon Mann on a Swansea beach for *Football Focus*. It was absolutely freezing doing the interview, but I hope I came across well. It should be aired the day of Fulham game.

Thursday 8th March

It's World Kidney Day today and I was asked to visit the renal unit at Morriston Hospital. I met all the people going through their treatment and I really enjoyed hearing all their stories and trying my best to cheer them up. One older guy was a massive Swans fan and had his shirt on and scarf at hand. He was an absolute character and kept the nurses on their toes. It was amazing to see this guy so enthusiastic and bubbly when he was going through his treatment and in pain. It gave me a lift for the rest of the day. With these types of visit I always think if it can brighten just one person's day, then it is worthwhile me coming down.

Friday 9th March

Training on the AstroTurf this morning as we start looking forward to the Man City game. We all realise how difficult the game is going to be, but at home we fear no one. We believe we can beat anyone in the league especially after the performances against Arsenal, Spurs and Chelsea.

Saturday 10th March

I started to feel ill today. My stomach got worse as the day went on. I felt sick, had a fever and then the diarrhoea started. Now anyone who has had diarrhoea knows how bad it can be and I'm not talking a loose stool, I mean proper diarrhoea! We are playing Man City tomorrow and this is the last thing I need. The thing about diarrhoea is it makes you dehydrated, so you know as a footballer you need to drink as much as possible to counteract this, but when you feel sick as I've been and water makes it worse, it's been a problem. All I can hope for is a good night's sleep and that I wake up feeling much better.

Sunday 11th March

Swansea City 1 (Moore 83) Manchester City 0

Happiness is a dry fart.

Sorry to start match day with such a crude statement, but it pretty much summed up where I was before kick-off. I was visiting the toilet constantly through the night and felt awful when I got up this morning, so was just praying that I wouldn't get caught short at any stage. I got hardly any sleep last night at all, with maybe twenty trips to the toilet. I felt totally weak and dehydrated on the way to the ground, but just tried to put that out of my mind and once I had made the decision to play I told myself not to use the illness as an excuse.

Before the game I took anti-diarrhoea tablets and as I gulped them down I just hoped they would last for at least ninety minutes! Sprinting for a ball with Mario Balotelli, wearing white shorts in front of 20,000 people, is not exactly the place that I'd have wanted the magic powers of the tablets to wear off.

Before the game the Gaffer focused on one big difference between today and our first game. We are now an established Premier League team with 27 games under our belt and a win against Arsenal, so why would we fear Manchester City? As a group we are extremely confident at the minute and we honestly don't care who we play against, we genuinely feel we can win.

I took the usual trip to the referee's room with Pasc and the team-sheet for our briefing with the ref, and Kolo Touré came in and was the nicest man in the world, head and shoulders nicer than any other captain I've met this year. Then it was out onto the pitch to get the job done. I thought it was important I got the right message to the lads in the huddle today, so I went down the aggressive route. I told the lads that if we could beat Man City we had the chance to make a massive statement to everyone who has doubted us in this league, and that the result of the match was in our hands not theirs. I finished by saying that we must show them no respect and get right after them from the very first moment.

The lads must have taken me at my word today, because just five minutes in we won a penalty after Joe Hart brought down Wayne. An early goal like this would have done wonders for us because so often this season we've not had the early goal that our play has deserved. Just before Scott took it, I said to Tayls that he didn't look confident, and I'd never seen that in Scott before at a spot kick, as he usually takes control of the situation. I think Joe Hart got into him quite a bit which was the main problem. Hart was just continually shouting at Scott, 'I know which way you are going,' and he obviously did because he pulled off the save. I was gutted when it didn't go in, but our attitude and commitment since the start had been so good that I didn't think it was going to cost us, and instead of dwelling on Scott's miss, I still really felt super confident that we would get the win, though maybe we'd now need to grind it out more than we'd have needed to if we'd got the early goal. When I got the chance I had a word with Scott but he seemed confident still so I wasn't worried.

As the half developed so did my battle with Balotelli, and I have to say that he's an odd lad. He's clearly a very talented footballer, and he's a big, strong lad – bigger than me anyway – and I couldn't understand why he didn't put himself about more instead of just going to ground at the slightest contact. It first happened after about twenty minutes or so, when I followed him to the halfway line. The ball was played up to him, I got a foot in and he went down like a sack of shit! It was actually comical, so

I just looked down at him, laughed and told him to get up. But that moment certainly set the tone for our 'battle'.

Soon afterwards Balotelli again showed his lack of appetite for the battle when he just sat down in the middle of a challenge! We went up for a header and I made a point of just trying to be as aggressive and extra physical with him as I could be, within the laws of course, and see what happened. From my experience there aren't many strikers that like to be that physical these days, and many of them can be bullied off their game. Me and Caulks definitely identified Balotelli as one of those and that was our basic plan today. Anytime that there was contact with him it was to be as physical as the referee would allow us to be.

For the next minute or so all I could hear was him moaning in Italian about the last challenge which he obviously thought was too heavy. The more he moaned the more I knew our defensive plan was working. Then, the next thing he did saw me burst out laughing. He picked the ball up on the halfway line, turned and shot! I couldn't believe it! I laughed at him straight away but then, to my horror, I realised it was a decent hit and it had a chance! For a split second it looked like it would go in, which would have wiped the smile off my face, but thankfully it went wide so I could carry on being smug about it... ha-ha.

Talking about it at half-time to Gows and Monks, they said that they did the same thing, burst out laughing on the bench when he tried it, but then had that horrible 'uh-oh' feeling when it looked like it could be heading in, before it went wide and they could be all smug again... which is pretty easy for those two at the best of times.

A couple of minutes after Mario's optimistic attempt we had a brief break in play and I tried to get in a huge lungful of air. I was starting to blow and was doing everything I could to keep my breath. That's why I was so pleased we'd done such a number on Balotelli so early, because he'd gone so far into his moaning shell that he wasn't really causing Caulks and I any problems. The last thing I would have wanted to deal with as I was struggling to get to half-time was a busy striker who knew I was struggling. Because of the fluid I lost on the loo last night, combined with having not eaten a great deal in the last forty-eight hours, I never really got my second wind and struggled through the rest of the match. It wasn't a good feeling to have.

Mind you, if I was feeling bad it was nothing compared to Gareth Barry, judging by the look on his face when Mancini hooked him on thirty-seven minutes. It's not nice to get dragged off at half-time, we all take that as a bit of an insult. It's not a nice feeling, but to be hooked during the first half, in front of everyone, well, I just looked at Caulks and said, 'Wow.' I thought it was really ruthless from Mancini and it was clear that he didn't care about any embarrassment that he might have caused Barry because he didn't say anything to him or even shake his hand! Still, for us it was great news. It was a very public statement by Mancini basically saying, 'We can't cope with them.' That's pretty much the message I passed on to the boys, and despite my bowels not being particularly overjoyed at the thought of chasing after Agüero, who'd come on for Barry, I was right up for it. I had a score to settle with Agüero also, with him having a field day up at their place.

We didn't have much longer to go till half-time but that was still enough for Balotelli to continue with his antics. Joe won the ball cleanly off him but he stayed down, moaned and then waited until he could have words with the ref. When he started I made sure that the ref saw it from our side too, so I jogged over and said, 'Don't listen to him, you're the ref not him, and if it was up to him every challenge would be a foul.'

They then had their best spell of the match and had a run of three consecutive corners, which really got the adrenalin flowing. I know fans are on the edge of their seats at this point, praying that we don't concede, but from my point of view it's when I feel most alive and most central defenders I know relish these moments. Not for a single second do I feel negative about it and wish for the whistle to blow, instead I focus on organising everyone and winning any ball that comes my way. I never stress or worry at these moments as the defence are very experienced at dealing with them. As long as everyone does their job, there isn't an issue.

Back in the dressing room we absorbed the knowledge that we had completely dominated the league leaders for forty-five minutes and we knew, especially after the Barry substitution, that Mancini would be ripping into them. The Gaffer told us that we'd been outstanding in the first half but the first ten minutes of the second half was probably going to be the most important period of the match. They would look to get a foothold in the game, which made it all the more important for us to get straight back into our rhythm and control the tempo of the match again. As I got some fluids into me and listened to the Gaffer, I realised that we had just totally dominated Man City in a first half for a second time in a season, but were obviously looking for a completely different second-half result compared to the first occasion.

At half-time I decided that because I was now really experiencing the effects of my illness I wasn't going to go up for any corners in the second half. That meant that instead of needlessly running up and down the field, especially when a corner breaks down and you have to sprint back, I would just stay where I was. For the rest of the match I wanted to limit my workload as much as I could, and concentrated on doing my job. I knew that at some point City would turn up the intensity and have a spell where they would be on top, so I needed to make sure that I'd be right physically to deal with that.

On the hour I had my first real challenge of the half with Balotelli and, as in the first half, he again went down very easily. I decided to have words with him so I told him to man up, get on with the game and stop looking for fouls. He didn't say a word back to me, and that lack of reaction from him told me everything I needed to know in terms of where we were with our personal battle today. In our team, as we aren't the most physical or aggressive of teams, someone has to adopt the role of the team's enforcer, because every team has at least one. I know I'm going to get some stick for referring to myself in this way, but sometimes that's the case. Despite how placid and laid-back I am off the field, I enjoy what I do on the field in terms of standing up to opponents. I don't see my time as a footballer as being one where I'm going out of my way to make friends with my opponents. It's just not that important to me and I don't care what opposition players think of me. The bottom line is that I'm going to do whatever I need to do during the ninety minutes to win the game for my team, my club and to do it the best that I can so that ultimately I can be well rewarded for it, allowing me to provide for my family. Six or seven years ago I had nothing and that feeling drives me on more than anything else.

As we got into that last important ten minutes, I had that frustrating feeling that despite our dominance, the goal wasn't going to come. I've experienced that quite a bit this season. Sometimes that's been because we've either not been clinical enough when the chance has come our way or we simply haven't found enough ways to work their keeper when we've been in control, and that appeared to be the story again today. But just as I was beginning to think that settling for a point against the league leaders wouldn't be a bad option, up popped Luke to deliver all three. I was buzzing for Luke that he scored it and despite feeling completely knackered, I wasn't going to miss celebrating the goal with Luke and it was great to see him mobbed by the lads. To score what turned out to be the winner against Man City was just a brilliant moment for him.

As we left the huddle nearly all the lads had something positive to say and it was a great feeling that we now had the opportunity of seeing out the game with something to hold on to and realising that we were so close to getting a massive win, arguably the biggest in the club's history.

But it wouldn't be us if there wasn't another twist! They attacked and threw a cross in and, as soon as I saw it was coming in, I just jumped as high as I physically could to try and clear it, but instead ended up getting clattered by Michel. I fell awkwardly and the pain in my ankle was nothing compared to the pain of seeing the ball go into the goal and hearing everyone behind in the away end cheer and celebrate. I couldn't believe it. I was gutted and the mixture of pain from my clash with Michel and the feeling of seeing them score was gutting. But then I saw Mancini pointing and cursing so I knew something was up and turned round to see the lineswoman on the far side with her flag up. What a welcome sight! It was actually a déjà vu moment, from when her flag went up at Anfield when Kuyt had 'scored'. As Michel picked up the ball and dawdled over taking the free kick I turned away, clenched my fists and smiled as I knew that they weren't going to get another chance. League leaders beaten, job done. No better feeling.

When the final whistle blew, the atmosphere was fantastic as it was all game and peaked at that moment. I turned to Caulks and we just hugged and we were quickly joined by Michel who was ecstatic too. I was so glad that we'd all seen it through, won, and buried the ghost of that last half an hour in Manchester. When I walked off their pitch in August they were all whooping and hollering after putting four past us, but today the only whooping and hollering was from us, because apart from Joe Hart the Manchester City lads walked straight off the pitch and Hart's was the only hand I remember shaking from them. I know Joe from nights out and events in general over the years. He is a great lad and has always made a point of congratulating me on my career whenever he can. He's a tough competitor as he showed today by sledging Scott, but he's not big time at all and he went round the whole team to say well done, which is a great credit to him. I also think he's one of the best goalkeepers around.

In the dressing room the Gaffer called us all together and told us that the result would be remembered forever at the club, such was the significance of beating the league leaders so comfortably and he told us he was exceptionally proud of us and that we should all be proud of ourselves. I've no idea what he said after that, because the Imodium tablets must've worn off and I had to run to the toilet. As I sat there I was so relieved it wasn't a Cup match, as I definitely wouldn't have made it through extra time.

Played 28 Won 9 Drawn 9 Lost 10 Points 36 League Position – 11th
(4 more points needed for 40)

Monday 12th March

The whole Williams household was ill throughout the night so we didn't get much sleep so I got up early with Raff to watch cartoons.

Had plenty of congratulatory texts following yesterday and having had time to let it sink in, it was a fantastic achievement and the Gaffer was right; it's one of the greatest results in the club's history and to be a part of that is really humbling. Behind the victory though is something that shows how determined this squad is. A few weeks ago now our training pitch was dug up and to think we are in the top flight and trying to compete against some of the best players in the world and have had to train on AstroTurf, and only when the rugby boys aren't training on it, is not good enough really. I think it's a credit to the lads that we just get on with it without moaning but then again maybe we should moan just to try and get our facilities and equipment up to speed with everyone else we have to compete with on the pitch. By beating Man City we have proved we have the players and we have one of the best managers in the Prem, but when I saw Man City's training ground last week looking so amazing, with them travelling around on golf carts, it's clear we don't have the facilities. Obviously we don't expect those facilities here, especially not the golf buggies as Tatey wouldn't be allowed to drive, but we deserve more than we have at the moment I think, just to make it more of a level playing field, if you'll excuse the pun. We have heard that we are going to move to our own facility at Fairwood but whether that will be next season, I doubt it. I just hope the Chairman realises how important it is to our future success.

I felt a bit better today so popped into Wind Street with my agent, Tayls and Jazz and had a Nandos. It was proper comfort food and as I'd not eaten properly since last Thursday I was just relieved to keep it all down.

Wednesday 14th March

Went to open the new offices of Save Britain Money in the Enterprise Park today which was enjoyable. All the staff were dressed in Swans shirts and The Wave radio station was there too. It was an official cutting of the ribbon do which was fun and then I spent time afterwards signing autographs.

After that, I went down to meet the lads from Street Football Wales of which I'm a patron. It's a great initiative and really portrays people who are homeless in such a positive light. I like the fact that in a football match nobody judges you about anything apart from whether you can play or not. They're a great bunch, both the organisers and the players, and I hope this initiative goes from strength to strength.

Thursday 15th March

I finally got verified on Twitter today, so now a nice blue tick appears next to my name!

Saturday 17th March

Fulham 0 Swansea City 3 (Sigurdsson 36, 66, Allen 77)

Well, the run is over, and I am GUTTED.

I just can't believe it. I knew it would happen one day but I always kind of thought it would be through an injury or perhaps a suspension. To have to lose my record of 169 consecutive games for Swansea as an outfield player – one that I am very proud of – to a bloody virus of all things, is hard to take.

It started yesterday after the train journey up from Swansea. I wasn't feeling 100 per cent as the journey developed and almost as soon as I got to my hotel room I was sick. Then the shits began, and I was non-stop on the toilet every five minutes and just lost so much fluid – from either end – that I felt horrendous. I couldn't drink, and eating was out of the question too as everything that passed my lips came straight back up. I knew I was struggling and also knew it was way worse than what I had before the Man City game. Whether that was just the start of this one, I don't know. All I do know is that what I experienced yesterday and today was the worst I've ever felt in my life.

The sickness and diarrhoea just wouldn't stop, and finally I started to get dizzy and could only see clearly if I shut one eye. I went to see Kate the physio and she could tell instantly how much I was struggling and told me to lie down straight away. As I lay down, I started to cramp up everywhere, in my neck, my fingers, feet, hamstrings, quads – everywhere – it was a nightmare. I found a comfortable position to lie, sort of on my back with my arms across my stomach, and any movement I made I'd cramp up, so I just tried to stay as still as possible.

It was about that time that the Gaffer got back from a supporters' club event in London with Chris Coleman and was told that I'd been ill, so he came up to Kate's room to see what state I was in. I looked up at him, one eye closed, completely still and groaning. He asked Kate how I'd been – she gave him the gory details – then he turned to Kate and said, 'I think he'll be able to play won't he?' As much as I knew if I had a chance the Gaffer would play me, just as we have done many times before, this was different. But instead of saying no, I said, 'Yes, Gaffer, I just need to get some water down me and a good night's sleep and I'll be ready.' Kate just looked at us like we were crazy!

Anyway, I must have got about an hour's sleep max – and that was interrupted constantly – and every time I had to go to the toilet to be sick I'd just start to cramp up again. It was no surprise that by this morning I was still feeling absolutely awful. Normally I'd be in with Nathan and that would have been a complete nightmare for him, but he's still out of the squad because of his sending off at Wigan, so at least I didn't have to worry about that as I was in a room on my own.

By then I'd also reached that stage where I was still retching, but there was nothing at all in me to bring up, which was the worst feeling of all. I'd realised in the middle of the night that I wasn't going to be able to play, but I felt so ill that it hardly registered with me that my run was going to come to an end – that shows how bad I was feeling. At about 6 a.m. I sent a text to Kate to tell her and let the Gaffer know that I'd pulled out, and then I texted Vanessa. Luckily she was in London staying with a friend before the game, so I just waited for her to get up and put her phone on and then get over to the hotel, pick me up and take me home.

By the time she travelled across London to Chiswick, where we were staying, I was in seeing the doctor. When Vanessa saw me she couldn't believe how bad I looked. She said afterwards that if there'd been more people in the room she'd have walked straight past me. The skin around my face had lost all its fluid and looked really sunken and drawn with a yellow tinge to it, especially around my eyes, and my hands and feet were all shrivelled up and looked as if I'd spent twenty-four hours in the bath. My wrists and ankle bones were sticking out, as were my ribs, I thought I looked like a refugee that you'd see on the news! It was crazy how much weight I'd lost in such a small space of time. The doctor said it was the worst case of chronic fluid loss he'd ever seen and was considering putting me on a drip. He explained that because the human body is predominantly made up of water and that I'd lost so much and hadn't replaced any, the instant weight loss and change in my appearance was the only thing that *could* happen. He said that left untreated, diarrhoea is a killer, especially in the young and old so it was vital that I got fluids into me quickly.

The first thing he said he had to do was stop me being sick any more, so he gave me an injection in my backside to sort that out. It was one of the worst pains I've ever felt and I was a bit aggressive towards the doc as he gave me no warning. Sorry for that, doc. Nice way to start a Saturday morning! After that I said I was going home, but the doc said that was out of the question and that I had to stay at the hotel. I started to refuse but he was clear that if I wasn't going to stay there the only other option was hospital. He told me that if I didn't stop being sick and take some fluids on he'd have to put me on the drip. But if I started to keep the water down, that would be OK. When it came to match time he went off to the game with the rest of the staff, having told Vanessa that if I continued to be sick she'd have to take me to hospital. He warned me that if I didn't go to hospital, the next stage would be hallucinations and then seizures due to the lack of fluid. I must admit I didn't really fancy that so agreed to stay in my room.

So there we stayed, and fortunately the sickness injection worked and I was able to get some fluids into me as the time passed. It was really difficult because I couldn't hold Raff or have him too close, but he just wanted to snuggle me and he couldn't understand why I wouldn't touch him. I felt bad because we were stuck in this hotel room with a couple of toys and not much for him to do. By about quarter to three, Vanessa and Raff were fast asleep so I grabbed my laptop and searched for a website which shows live games, found a stream that was showing the Swans and watched the game. It was a weird experience to say the least as I can't ever remember watching a Swans game live before as I've always been playing! I was trying to keep still on the bed because as I was watching I was continuing to cramp up, but then Gylfi scored and I went nuts, woke Vanessa, frightened Raphael and went into spasm, but I was absolutely buzzing for the lads and got more excited as the game went on. It wasn't long before it began to dawn on me that I was watching the performance of the season from the boys... and they were doing it without me!

Of course a little bit of me was disappointed that I wasn't involved – and slightly concerned that they'd never played that well with me in the side, ha-ha – but in reality I was chuffed to bits and so proud of the way the boys played. It was unquestionably our best away performance of the season and despite flying into cramp now and again I really enjoyed watching the game on the laptop. I was a fan for the afternoon and I loved every second of it. Ironically, the *Football Focus* programme with my interview with Leon Mann was shown today on BBC1 and was explaining my stats about my consecutive run of games and how I never miss one through injury or illness. I'm trying not to think that this has jinxed me!

After the game I had a nice text off the Gaffer who said that he'd told the lads how much my run had meant to me and that he'd told them to go out there and win the game for me, which they had. That was a really nice gesture that I appreciated.

I hadn't been sick for a while and had managed to keep the fluids down so I decided after the match finished that it was best to go back to Birmingham as it was only an hour and a half away, so I left the hotel with tablets for just about everything from the doc. When I got home, my dad came around and he couldn't believe how much weight I'd lost, and was shocked that I was struggling to even walk that well too.

It turns out I've got the norovirus which the doc thinks has been in and around Swansea apparently. It's the worst I've ever felt in my life. I just hope I'll be all right for the Everton game.

Played 29 Won 10 Drawn 9 Lost 10 Points 39 League Position – 8th (1 more point needed for 40)

Sunday 18th March

Despite feeling absolutely awful all day and lying down doing nothing, the news I woke up to today about Fabrice Muamba certainly left me counting my blessings. As I write, he's fighting for his life in a London hospital after collapsing on the pitch last night at White Hart Lane, playing for Bolton. I can't begin to think what his family are going through at the moment, but just hope and pray he can pull through this and recover. It's too early to think about the future yet, but all I hope is that he can stabilise in hospital and then have a swift recovery.

Monday 19th March

Not playing on Saturday and just watching as a fan allowed me to appreciate a masterclass taking place before my very eyes by arguably the most valuable player that we have in terms of the way that we play our football, Leon Britton. He's simply the best player I've ever played with. No matter how much people think they know football, the only way you can ever appreciate Britts is by playing behind him like I do. He's an absolute dream. Monks, Caulks and I were talking about him the other day and he cuts our workload down by at least 50 per cent, doing what he does in front of us. It's incredible how many times this season I've seen a move developing, spotted the run of the striker and where the ball is going to go, and just as I set off to deal with it Britts gets in there, somehow comes out with the ball and sets us up going forward instead. I've never played with a player who possesses the awareness that Britts does. Though I'm used to him now I am still sometimes amazed out on the field when Leon pops up, dispossesses someone, then just plays a perfect ball into space for Joe or Gylfi that they can just stroll on to and start something creative for us. People who criticise Leon, and amazingly there are a few, point to his limitations – he's small, he never scores, doesn't play long balls, but every single one of those are actually his strengths. His size means that he's got absolutely perfect balance and his quick feet see him prosper in the tightest of situations. He never scores, but that's because it's not his job. His job is to break down our opposition's play and get us playing. If he went looking for goals he would open out such a hole in front of us that our defence would suffer. People who criticise him for lying deep simply don't have an understanding of the way we play and the role he has in that, which he carries out magnificently. And as for the long balls, well, when I was a kid I was told the sign of a good player is one who never gives the ball away. When I last looked, Leon was second only to Xavi in Europe in passing accuracy, up around 93 per cent. How anyone can criticise anyone for that needs a reality check. His biggest strength is probably that he has embraced his so-called limitations, and delivers everything he does within his own framework to almost 100 per cent perfection. Against Fulham on Saturday he was as close to perfection as a centre midfielder as you can be and, despite how ill I was feeling, watching him actually made me feel a little better. As we got into the game and I could see how well we were starting to play, and Leon's part in that, it was great to enjoy it from the point of view of just being his mate rather than his team mate and I was chuffed to see him have such a fantastic game.

Tuesday 20th March

Travelled back down to Swansea today. Feeling a little bit better but still rough. Feel very hungry and want to eat all sorts of crazy foods. I lost so many nutrients that I just need to replace everything and I'm still struggling to drink much fluid at any one time but I know that's vital, so I'm trying to drink as much water as possible.

Wednesday 21st March

Had another day off today and it was much of the same, eating and resting. My energy is coming back more and more each day. I'm looking much more like my old self now and also putting some more weight back on, so I'm hoping to be fit for Saturday.

Thursday 22nd March

Trained today for the first time since I was ill on Friday as the Gaffer didn't want me in until I felt right, and that was today. I only did part of the session and got through it, but only just. I just hope that I start to recover soon because I was way off in training today and know I'm struggling for Saturday.

Spoke to the people from Disney after training who want me to take part in a soccer camp in Florida in the summer with Bellars, Paul Robinson and a couple of other players. Sounds really exciting and took my mind off feeling so shite.

Another thing that helped me in that regard was what was waiting for me when I arrived at training; about six boxes from Nike with different bits and pieces in them such as boots, trainers, clothes and luggage. I felt like a kid at Christmas again ripping into all those boxes. Some players take this kind of thing for granted but it wasn't so long ago that I would struggle to afford to buy Nike boots for myself playing non-league, so I really appreciate things like this.

Friday 23rd March

I was still mulling over whether I was going to be fit enough to play tomorrow, but my mind was made up after a quick chat with the Gaffer at training. He asked me how I felt and I said that I thought I was OK but was a little unsure and certainly didn't want to let the lads down by making the wrong decision. The Gaffer agreed, but then said, 'Look, if you are telling me that you're fit, then you will play. You are the third best centre half in the Premier League this season in my eyes, and if you're fit you play. It's as simple as that, Ash.'

It was at that moment I decided I was fit and knew I would play.

Saturday 24th March
Swansea City 0 Everton 2 (Baines 59, Jelavić 76)

I knew within five minutes today that I shouldn't have been on the pitch.

Despite feeling fine in the warm-up and wanting to play and making what I thought was the right decision, the intensity of the game just got the better of me and I was struggling pretty much straight away. My fitness was poor, I felt very weak as if my strength had just faded away, my balance wasn't there and, the worst thing of all, my coordination was shot to bits. It was like I had just returned to pre-season training and instead of being eased back into things gently, I'd been thrown straight into a competitive match. I started to struggle and it felt as if I'd forgotten how to play football.

Before that all began though, and frankly putting into context any apprehension I was feeling over the after effects of my illness, we as a squad paid our tributes to Fabrice Muamba and sent our own public message of support. The idea of the tribute was simple; we were to wear T-shirts bearing a 'get well soon' message on them, and wear them throughout the warm-up, before peeling them off and handing them to a fan in the ground. A really nice idea. But unfortunately, and I know all about the old saying 'it's the thought that counts', there wasn't a hell of a lot of thought that went into the T-shirts that were handed to us in the dressing room. I just watched *Match of the Day* tonight and there were some really tasteful T-shirts that players wore, some with a big smiling face of Fabrice on it, others with a heartfelt message just below the club's crest – tasteful. Ours just said, 'GET WELL SOON FAB'. The size of these T-shirts was awful and neither Leon, Scott, Nath, Wayne or me for that matter, are XXXL, but that was the size we were all given. What was meant to be a really heartfelt gesture turned into a farce in the dressing room when Leon disappeared putting his on. What a joke. I'm not taking anything away from the sentiment of the message – which was heartfelt from us all – but, honestly, it was drowning me, so God knows how the other lads were getting on with theirs. Still, all of the lads are genuinely wishing Fabrice well, and just hope and pray for good news in the coming days and weeks.

I met Phil Neville in the ref's room today to hand over the team-sheets. I'd never met him before and we had a quick chat and he seemed a really nice bloke. That's one of the differences for me I guess, this season, is that it has seen me meeting with players like him before games, and realise that I've been watching him on the telly since I was a teenager. It all adds up to make this such a special season for me, better than anything I've ever experienced before.

Out on the pitch, before my energy levels had started to drain away completely I'd had a couple of clashes in the first couple of minutes where both Cahill and Jelavić just threw themselves down looking for the free kick. I didn't say anything to Cahill when he did it, as it was so comical, but when Jelavić did it almost straight after I gave him some because I wasn't going to let them think they could start that stuff today and get away with it.

To be fair to Jelavić though, I was quite impressed with him overall and couldn't see why he wanted to get involved with the play acting because he could certainly look after himself. I had a little battle with him in the left back position about quarter of an hour in and he was all high elbows, very awkward and physical. He plays tough and I have to say, as someone who uses that as part of my game, I always appreciate and respect a striker who throws it back at you. Pretty much throughout the half we had a bit of a battle, but by then my batteries were starting to run seriously low and that was not really what I needed today.

It appeared that it wasn't just me who was struggling either. As a team we weren't getting anything like the success we would normally expect at home in terms of our passing accuracy and possession. After about twenty minutes, Leon came over and said that Cahill was just sticking with him off the ball all the time and was just not letting him play. We've seen this before and it can be really frustrating for Leon because in most games he is at the absolute heart of things, pulling all the strings and running the show. When Cahill sits on him like he did today, then obviously he won't touch the ball as much as he would like and we suffer a bit as a team as a result. What usually happens in cases like this though, is that it places a bigger emphasis on me and Caulks in terms of bringing the ball out of defence and actually getting beyond Leon. The trouble today was that Jelavić was working so hard to close the two of us down it was really difficult to get things started and, because my fitness had gone, I wasn't particularly looking to carry the ball forward anyway. All these things were having a negative impact on us.

Still, we did manage to force a corner which is always potentially an important moment in a game. That is as long as the opposition haven't worked out what you are doing, of course. The plan from this corner was to work the ball to Joey for a shot. Obviously, we know the signals and runs that trigger the move to get the ball to Joe, and as soon as we all did our movements, we quickly realised that Everton had got themselves into the exact position to prevent Joe from shooting. As soon as it happened Phil Jagielka turned to me and asked with a smirk, 'Was that for the Allen shot?' I had to laugh and just said, 'Maybe!' and he laughed back and said, 'Yeah, thought so!'

There's not much to say about the rest of the half apart from the fact that they were beginning to frustrate us by strangling the life out of us. They set up so well to restrict us in the midfield, with Osman, Gibson and Pienaar either breaking up everything we tried to start or just keeping the ball away from Leon and Joe. Then, when we did go a little more direct, Jagielka was stopping absolutely everything we threw at them. He was having one of those games when everything seemed to be going straight to him and it gave the impression that he was stopping us on his own.

There was one little flashpoint just on half-time when Joe was booked after clattering Neville. Anyone who knows Joe knows that he has a short fuse – little man syndrome I think, Joe? – and I had a feeling he'd boil over at some point because Neville niggled him throughout the half and finally had a little pull and a go at him which saw Joe losing his head and giving the ref the easy option of showing him yellow. I'd never change Joe at all, and this bit of dog he's got in him has elevated him above the many 'bigger' players that he has come up against this year, but as he jogged back into position I just told him to keep his head and not to do anything stupid as we needed him on the pitch. I emphasised that he was totally outplaying Neville, so to just keep it cool. We could not have coped with losing him to a red today.

There was no big depression in the dressing room at half-time, the message from the Gaffer was to keep doing the same things and continue to pass through them, no matter how much they pressed us. We knew he was right, of course, and no matter how difficult they made it for us we were all completed committed to the Gaffer's beliefs. Personally, I was knackered during the break and I knew it was vital that I got as much fluid on board and that I tried to eat something. I managed to get a banana down me and a protein bar too, and then just took what was left of the break to rest up as much as I could. I don't know whether it was because I felt so drained, but as I sat there and tried to recover I just had a feeling that everyone else looked a bit knackered too. If they were, I thought we were certainly going to have our work cut out after the break as Everton would have been delighted with the success of their plan and would certainly be right up for the second half.

When we got back out there, the banana and protein bar didn't seem to have the desired effect on me because almost straight away I laboured over a clearance and it got blocked by Pienaar which led to a chance for Jelavić. I was furious. It didn't lead to anything but I know how crap and sloppy it would have looked to everyone. That sort of lazy clearance is not something I would do normally, and in fact if one of the other lads had defended like that I'd have given them an absolute rocket. But I think it was just a symptom of me being mentally tired, which was a direct result of my physical tiredness. As the half went on I just got more tired, both mentally and physically. This was a game I wasn't enjoying at all.

Just before the hour I gave away a free kick that was to become the pivotal moment of the match. Baines got a good run on and we clashed on the edge of the box, with the ref giving it straight away. I don't know about this one. If I'm honest there was no way I was going to let him get past me, so maybe that's what the referee saw, but if you watch it again and slow it all down, the contact was him running into an area occupied by me. What am I supposed to do? Disappear? Or just step aside to allow him to pass? If I'd changed my direction and hauled him down, then fair enough. No complaints. But when I just maintained my position it was frustrating to hear the ref's whistle, but predictable enough these days I suppose.

And then, of course, he goes and scores.

I'm still so angry about that while writing this that I don't want to say anything more about it, apart from it being a great strike. Grudgingly.

The Gaffer gave it another ten minutes or so of us huffing and puffing and then he made a triple substitution to try to rescue something from the game. The instruction that the subs brought on from him was to be really positive and go for the equaliser. That may sound simplistic, but it was important we threw everything at them because I'd prefer to lose 0–2 at home after having given it a go than stick at 0–1 having been cautious. The main risk of that all-out gung-ho approach is that the shape of the side goes, which is pretty much exactly what then happened.

A couple of minutes after the substitutions, Everton broke. Jelavić had a fantastic opportunity and, fortunately, drilled it wide. Normally I would have found some way to have got a block in, but by this point I was totally gone, mentally and physically, and even though all I really wanted was to drive the team on and try to spark some sort of positive response, I was physically incapable of doing it. It was so frustrating.

If Jelavić's free shot had been a warning, then it wasn't really heeded because just a couple of minutes later he scored the goal that killed us. Fellaini, who has probably been the toughest opponent I've faced and one of the players of the season for me, got the turn on me which I should have dealt with it better. He then crossed to give Jelavić a tap in. As I went over to my position for the restart I felt as tired as I had ever felt during a game, and for the first time in my professional career I felt like just walking off there and then, and I don't say that easily. This awfully negative frame of mind I'd got into meant that I just couldn't see us coming back from two behind. I tried to see positivity in the lads around me but I think it's fair to say that the belief had gone.

The game dragged on for the last twenty-odd minutes before the ref put us out of our misery, but if I'm being completely honest it totally passed me by and our defeat was deserved. We will have to move on from this game quickly and just write it off as a very bad day at the office. That was the feeling of everyone in the dressing room afterwards and it was one of the quietest atmospheres we've had in there all year. Personally, I know I struggled today and it's not good enough to say it was because I've been ill. Once I declared myself fit I had a duty to my team mates to perform to the best of my ability and I fell short of that. And I'm not happy about it at all.

Played 30 Won 10 Drawn 9 Lost 11 Points 39 League Position – 10th
(1 more points needed for 40)

Monday 26th March

Fantastic news today from America that Hari Kieft's operation has been a success and he's walked thirty unaided steps already. I'm made up about that and just hope that everything is going to turn out for him as we all hope now and those thirty steps are going to lead to many, many more.

Thursday 29th March

Every day this week training has been a struggle as I've recovered from both the Everton game and the virus. It's been like a pre-season in the middle of the year. This week hasn't been pleasant at all. I've tried to do as much gym work as possible to build back some of the muscle and power I feel I've lost.

Friday 30th March

Trained on the AstroTurf again this morning and starting to feel a bit stronger. This week has been a tough but good one and I've been glad to be out there getting a sweat on and working hard.

Saturday 31st March

Back up in London again today by train, and it brought back horrible memories of the Fulham trip. I know it's just a psychological thing but I couldn't even bring myself to eat the food that was prepared for us, and I think I actually started to make myself feel sick and I'm never like that because I love my food. The club's got a top chef called Michael Knight, who's also the Wales chef. His food is superb but I could hardly look at it today. I hope this is only going to be a temporary feeling because I felt really ill again on the train, but I know I'm healthy now so it's obviously a mind thing. Just wish I could finally put it all behind me.

Seeing that it's Spurs tomorrow it means that Monks will come back in as obviously Caulks can't play as Spurs are his parent club. As brilliant as Caulks has been this season, I'm delighted to be back alongside Monks as he has helped me loads in my career, and to go along with that he's such a nice guy too. He's taught me so much about defending that I couldn't have wished to have had a better teacher when I joined the club in 2008. Funnily enough, we were talking the other day about the bloke who's managed to pretty much keep him out of the side this season, Caulks, and how I've actually being trying to help him in many of the same ways that Monks helped me when I arrived. The best way to describe Monks is that he's a proper defender. Even though the way our careers have panned out has meant that I've played lots more games than him now, when we line up tomorrow I'll still feel that he is the senior out of the two of us, even now after I've played 170+ games for the Swans. What Monks brings to the team and squad though, is so much more than his playing ability, as considerable as that is. He is an outstanding captain both on and off the field, and assumes the responsibility for everything to ensure that the rest of us only have one thing to worry about – our performance. He gets everything sorted – tickets and issues with the management or staff. He has the respect of everyone at the club from the chairman down to the tea lady. He's a credit to his profession. He's underrated as a player too, especially at this level. I'm not going to say anything other than Caulks has been sensational this season, but will we be weaker tomorrow with Monks back in the side? No, not at all. Monks may not have the strength and speed of Caulks, but he makes up for all of that with his positional play and reading of the game. In that, he's second to none, and if we'd not had Caulks this year I have no doubts whatsoever that with Monks in the side we'd be in exactly the same position that we are now.

CHAPTER TEN

April 2012

Sunday 1st April
Tottenham Hotspur 3 (van der Vaart 19, Adebayor 73, 86)
Swansea City 1 (Sigurdsson 59)

I felt loads better today even though I still wasn't completely back to 100 per cent. The improvement in me is the result of a good week's training where I really put it in. The main focus for me was to work hard, which I did; really hitting the gym both before and after regular training and doing plenty of weights. Importantly I also managed to match the commitment in my training with my commitment in my eating! I've really eaten like a king this week, as I knew I had to scoff and drink as much as possible to continue to put some weight back on after such a rapid loss from the Fulham trip. The hope was that all the food and drink intake would give me back all the energy that was missing against Everton. I was back to my usual weight this morning, meaning that I went into the game feeling much stronger. That fact alone gave me a great boost to my confidence.

In the huddle I think Monks' view is never use the 'F' word once where 25 times will do. I remember when I first joined the club, and Monks was skipper, at least half the team that Roberto Martínez brought in were foreign, and they could speak hardly any English, and there was this mad ginger bloke foaming at the mouth and just effing and blinding at them before they'd even had a touch of the ball. They didn't understand a word he was saying – though they probably got the gist to be fair – while the rest of us English speakers just looked at their faces and had to suppress the laughter. It was hilarious. As time developed and the lads like Andrea, Jordi and Gorka Pintado got used to

Monks' tirades, they still hardly understood a word that he said. So instead of trying to make out the message he was attempting to get across, they would all challenge each other to count the number of 'Fs' he used. It was so funny, and when he rattled them off in good order again this afternoon, it did take me back to those early days at the club. By the way, there were nineteen today.

My Wales team mate Gareth Bale was lively for the first time after ten minutes today, and his run and cross brought out the best in me, and hopefully showed Adebayor that I wasn't going to let him have things his own way today. As usual from Balo, his final ball in was real quality, and I had a split second to decide what I was going to do with the ball arcing towards Adebayor. In a situation like this anticipation is everything, and these are the moments that are affected most if you are not 100 per cent on top of your game. It's a split second decision. If I'd hesitated then Adebayor would have got ahead of me, and players of his class and talent only need one such chance during a game to score. So it was vital that I got across in front of him before the ball reached him. I was buzzing that I got to it before him, not just because an effort like this will prevent a goal, or because it'll lay a little marker down in Adebayor's mind, but because it proved to me that I was a bit sharper than maybe I thought I was before the start.

Five minutes later we should have got a penalty. Tayls made a great run into the box, before being pulled back – twice – by Gallas. Instead of going down Tayls did the decent thing, by staying up on his feet, and tried to get his cross in. Predictably in moments like this, his cross came to nothing. As I watched him get into the box, and the angle that he took, I was thinking just one thing – penalty. It had to happen and when Gallas grabbed him, I was screaming to myself, 'Go down!' but Tayls, being the honest lad that he is, didn't. We had a chat about it afterwards and I told him that it's all well and good staying up and being honest, and fair play to him for that, but had he gone down, it wouldn't have been a dive. Gallas had his arms on his neck and shoulder, meaning it was a foul and also meaning that he had every right to go down. There's a line between that and blatant diving. I hate players who dive when there has been no contact made, or those who deliberately run into you in the box, instigate the contact themselves with your leg, and throw themselves down, because that's straightforward cheating. But if you have been tugged back like Tayls was then, if you are in the box and have no real chance of scoring or setting someone else up, go down! The stakes in football, especially in the Premier League, are just so high now that you'd be stupid not to make the most of every opportunity that presents itself to you, no matter what form that opportunity takes. I want to make it clear that I'm not advocating diving in saying that, I just feel sometimes, as a team, we are naïve about little things like that.

Before long they launched another attack through Balo, who got past Àngel, causing Monks to go to him, and completely stretched us across the back four. I still managed to get a touch on the cross when it came in, but it wasn't a great one because I was stretching so much and I didn't get enough power on it to clear our lines completely. I only managed to touch it out of the box and away from any immediate danger. The next split second seemed to turn into slow motion though. Even though the ball ran straight into the path of van der Vaart I still had the chance to block it, but the problem was that as I tried to get up I paid for my earlier stretch by not having a strong enough base to get back up properly, and slipped as van der Vaart curled it just above my head and into the corner of the net. Personally, throughout my career, if ever I've been involved in conceding some goals in the previous game, I try even harder than normal in the next and hope to not concede a goal where I am to blame. It's a personal thing to me but the team benefit too. I was so angry to be associated with a goal like this, especially after last week.

My mood wasn't helped by the ref, Andre Marriner, a little later after Scott Parker absolutely clattered Danny in a challenge. It wasn't just the challenge that annoyed me, but the fact that he had let go a series of what I thought were fouls. I didn't think that he'd given us much during the match at all, so I decided to let him know what was on my mind as I was fuming at the lack of protection he was giving us. What was funny was that Monks was straight in too, as normal and had a go at him for exactly the same reason. We're like a double act when we play together; all over the refs. In hindsight I guess I do feel a little sorry for the ref as pretty much for the whole ninety minutes all he hears is me and Monks whinging at him, shouting 'Andre, Andre, Andre.' Anyway, I went a little far this time, because at the next stop in play he called me and Monks over and gave me a warning. He told me to calm down and told Monks to get control of me. Fair enough I suppose, but I wouldn't have been so angry if he'd have protected our players more. Monks is so different to me in that he initially gets as angry as I do, but has the ability to calm down pretty quickly, whereas I stay cooking for a while longer. This is where Monks is such a good player alongside me, he knows me inside out, knows that I respect him and will listen to him, so he just told me to chill out a bit as we walked away. That's all I needed really and began to focus on the game again.

At half-time the Gaffer felt that we were dwelling on the ball for too long in midfield, especially Joe and Britts, and that we needed to get the ball forward much more quickly, as he could see that Gylfi had acres of space in behind their midfield. He explained that this was one game where we needed to move the ball quickly because Parker is so active in their midfield, managing to close everybody down so soon. The only way to defeat someone as potentially destructive as Parker is to play quickly around him and frustrate him by not letting him get a challenge in. If we manage that, the way he plays will only lead to one thing – fouls. The Gaffer's talk emphasised that if we could replicate the speed of passing we'd shown in the home game, then we'd control the tempo again and we would definitely score.

We started the second half exactly as the Gaffer said and we nearly got an immediate reward. Gylfi had a fantastic shot from distance, but it was matched by Brad Friedel's save. It was sensational, one of the best I've ever seen. I wouldn't swap Michel for anyone but to see a keeper make a save like Friedel did, and also just witnessing his all-round play, as desperate as I was for us to score I genuinely appreciated the excellence of his save.

Luckily it wasn't too long before we finally got past Friedel. The ball was played into Wayne and he showed fantastic strength to hold off Ekotto, chested it down to Gylfi who had the ball at a difficult angle but managed to drive it into the ground, then up and beyond Friedel. It was a clever piece of skill from Gylfi and a great strike.

As we went back for the restart and Monks was shouting to us to stay on it, I really felt that we would go on and score another one. There was no doubt whatsoever that we had them on the ropes. The only worry in the back of my mind was that with the attacking players that Spurs have it makes them an incredibly dangerous side who can win a match by scoring out of nothing. The challenge for the next half hour as far as I saw it was to ensure we prevented that from happening.

We got to about twenty-odd minutes to go when they had a corner and took the lead. To say it was disappointing was an understatement because the goal looked poor from a defensive perspective. In reality there was very little we could do about it. Van der Vaart took an inswinging corner aimed at Adebayor, who was standing in between me and Monks which in itself is not normally a problem for us. The only difference today was that Adebayor is 6ft 5ins, which unfortunately does pose a problem. To be fair, it was a great ball that was swung in very high and Adebayor just got in a great leap and powered it in. When a guy who is so much taller than us gets in a good leap, unless you've managed to tip him off balance slightly there's not a hell of a lot you can do as a defender. As disappointing as it was to concede what in effect was such a simple goal, sometimes you just have to hold your hands up and accept it as one of those things. There isn't much you can do when a quality ball is played into the box, that's why it's so important to stop the cross.

The killer blow in the game for us came with about five minutes left when Adebayor got his second, another header, and put the game beyond us. Similar to his first goal from the corner, I'm sure to the neutral this was another goal where we can try and pick holes in it and blame someone, but to be honest from my perspective I'd have to just say that it was another good goal from them. It was created by Aaron Lennon, who was fed the ball, pushed it past Tayls, who is a quick player as well, got to it first and then stood it up at the back stick where his 6ft 5in striker was waiting to nod it home. There's nothing more to say about it really. It can be that simple when you have players of that quality. There was very little Monks could do with Lennon's ball in because as a centre half the worst ball in the game for you is one to the back stick where you have to back track and try to get elevation against someone who is attacking it and running on to the ball. That was exactly the position Monks found himself in against Adebayor. Even though we continued to press and didn't give up, we knew that being two goals behind them at home with just five or six minutes left meant it was going to be an impossible task, which it proved.

There was still enough time for a lovely touch from the Gaffer involving Gows. He knows that certain fixtures will mean more to some players than others, and he knew how important it would be for Gows to play at White Hart Lane as he'd spent so long there as a younger player without actually playing a first team game for them. So he brought him on with a minute to go and a funny moment happened as soon Gows ran on to the pitch. I thought that there was no point him finally making an appearance at his favourite football ground if he didn't get at least one touch of the ball, so I wanted to get the ball to him as soon as I could. Trouble was, he didn't look up to see me so I just drilled it towards him without realising that he wasn't ready in the slightest, meaning that the ball just bounced off him, went straight to Spurs who went straight on the counter attack with Gows sprinting after, and won a corner! He jogged over to me as we were setting up to defend and said, 'Thanks for that, mate,' and I just said, 'Sorry, pal,' and we both burst out laughing. It was just one of those moments. The Gaffer had seen it though because when he was talking about the game in the dressing room later, he turned to Gows and me laughing and said, 'Gows said thanks for that pass, Ash.'

There was a big contrast in the dressing room after this game compared to the Everton one. After that we were all very down as we felt like we hadn't really performed, but today, we knew we had competed really well against them and caused them plenty of problems, and if it hadn't been for Friedel's excellence, we'd have scored two goals, which might have changed the final outcome of the match.

Played 31 Won 10 Drawn 9 Lost 12 Points 39 League Position – 11th
(1 more point needed for 40)

Monday 2nd April

I forgot to mention yesterday a funny story about Gows that happened in the dressing room before we got changed. He's a big character, a typical cockney always looking for the humour in anything. Oh, and he can moan for England too, but a story came out about him yesterday that just cracked us all up. For some reason, Gows doesn't get his own boots from his agent like most of us do, so has to buy them himself. Anyway, it turns out that he had a chat recently to Josh about it, and Josh being the decent lad that he is, said that he'd get a pair from his sponsors, Nike, and give them to Gows, as they share the same size feet. Because Gows knew that we'd hammer him for pestering a kid to get some freebies, he tried to keep it a bit quiet. The schoolboy error he made was not telling Josh to keep it quiet too. When Gows was in the toilet, someone innocently brought up the topic of boots and Josh naively mentioned that he'd got a pair for Gows. As you can imagine that went down a storm with us all asking Josh what he did that for and trying to find out if Gows really did beg for a pair. We couldn't wait for him to emerge from the loo so that we could unload a bucket-load of abuse onto him for scrounging a pair of boots. Then the story got even better. It turns out that when Josh asked Nike for the spare pair, he forgot to tell them that they weren't for him, so when he handed the brand new bad boys over, Gows' delighted face soon changed to one of horror when he saw that they had 'McEachran' stitched in on both sides! We all absolutely howled when Josh told us that, as we could all imagine the look on Gows' face when he saw Josh's name on them, realising that he'd never be able to wear them because of the stick we'd be giving him. Gows is not known as a cockney wide-boy for nothing. Not only did he still take the boots off Josh, he thought he'd get away without us finding out whose boots they were by blacking out 'McEachran' with a marker pen. Unbelievable! We were in tears laughing and couldn't wait for him to come out of the toilet. When he emerged we thought that a subtle bit of stick would be the best approach, so as he walked back in we all just gave him a little round of applause. His face was a picture and was so confused because he had no idea at all why we were doing it. The look of confusion soon turned to horror and embarrassment when someone told him what we now knew. We all cracked up and even the Gaffer got involved in the banter too!

Sky Sports put me, Vanessa and Raphael up in a hotel today, the same one as that horrible Fulham trip, bizarrely, to take part in a football phone-in programme called *Premier League World* which was hosted by Andy Townsend and Craig Burley. It goes out live everywhere in the world apart from the UK and was great fun. Andy Townsend was a top man and really good at his job. As soon as the cameras went on he became professional and I was very impressed with him. I was there to talk about the games over the weekend and took calls from everywhere. I even had one from the Lebanon. I enjoyed the day and must admit it's something I'd love to do more of, and might even consider doing it once I've finished playing.

Tuesday 3rd April

Had a good chat with Tayls today about the Spurs game, where we covered a few specifics of how we linked up and how we can improve things. He's always looking to find ways to become better at his job and is really a great lad, a good player and someone who I think could go to the very top. He's come so far in such a short space of time, so for him to have performed to such a high level this season is incredible when you think that just two years ago Dean Saunders wasn't even picking him in the Wrexham side in the Conference. The only time this remarkable rise caught up with Tayls was probably for a little spell in mid-season this year when the season's exertions took their toll on him and that dip in fitness and energy affected his form. That's understandable though, when you look at his record and realise the most he's ever played in a season is 30 league games, and that was in his first season last year. You can only build up your playing strength over the years, and with such a long season in his legs this year I reckon he'll be stronger next year and then you'll see him improve even more. In terms of ability he's a proper player, and a proper left back too. He's one of the quickest in the team and the way he looks to play, linking up with Scott, getting forward and always offering himself by overlapping all the time, I'd say he's already in the top half dozen left backs in the division. The art of being an out-and-out full back has been lost in recent years, but Tayls is a bit of a throwback in that regard. In terms of his development he needs to understand just how dangerous he is in getting forward and running at defenders in the box. I mentioned on Sunday how he should really have gone down when Gallas was all over him in the box, and I stick by that, but whether he stays on his feet or not he should do more of those direct runs into the area, rather than offer himself outside Scott all the time to get a cross in. If he consistently gives himself an option of running more directly into the danger area, he'll not just add another dimension to us as a team but also to himself as a player, because really, he's got everything else. He's lightning quick, has great awareness, and boy does he love a tackle. I've seen quite a few wingers this season have their feathers ruffled by him and then disappear for a while. That's a great bonus to have in any team.

Thursday 5th April

The Gaffer told us today that he'd be changing things tomorrow against Newcastle by leaving out Danny and Scott, and going with Luke and Nath. It was no biggie to hear that. He's changed the team before and there's not one of us in the squad who thinks that we are too big not to play. It's part and parcel of a long season and I'm sure he's just trying to use the squad a bit more, especially as we have another game coming up on Wednesday at QPR.

Friday 6th April
Swansea City 0 Newcastle United 2 (Cissé 5 & 69)

How on earth we lost this game I'll never know. With almost 70 per cent possession, we didn't score and somehow managed to concede two. I don't think I've ever been so frustrated after a football match.

We got off to the worst possible start conceding after just four minutes after Tayls cleared the ball into the middle of the park. It wasn't one of his best clearances and it didn't get very far up the pitch, and this started the chain of events. Because Tayls had moved out of position to make the clearance, it had meant that I'd gone across to his left back position, and as soon as I saw Tayls clearance fall straight to Gutiérrez, I knew I might be in trouble. Gutiérrez played the ball straight to Cabaye, who played a great ball on to Cissé. Effectively, Caulks was left on his own at that point because the quality of Cabaye's ball meant that I just didn't have enough time to get back to my central position and Tayls didn't cover the middle. Even though he had more or less a free shot, I still thought Michel would save it as he always does but it wasn't to be. I was so annoyed because I realised that I was involved in conceding a simple goal again, even though I couldn't really affect it. I was also annoyed because, critically, we were down early at home against a team who were set up ultra-defensively in the first place, which meant that they had just been delivered their dream start.

Still, following this very irritating setback we quickly got on the ball and in no time started to control the game. Apart from a little clash out on the touchline where I bundled Cissé into the advertising boards as I wanted the ball back quickly, and another header with Ba that I won, I had very little to do. Joe,

Leon and Gylfi had loads of possession but Newcastle were just lying deep and doing everything they could to ensure that they didn't allow us to have any direct efforts on target. It was as if they were happy for us to have the ball, and weren't interested in going on the offensive for one minute. That's the trouble you get into by conceding the early goal because it meant that they had something to hold on to.

The Gaffer was clear at half-time that we needed to produce more chances for all the possession we had. I'm sure if you're a fan reading this now who was at the game, that's exactly what you would have been saying at half-time too. They hardly had a kick in the first half but had one chance and scored, whereas it felt like we had all the possession and hardly any chances. As a defender this can be so frustrating because you feel a little helpless as you can see what's happening in front of you, i.e. we are not being direct enough, but apart from shouting and giving instructions there's not a hell of a lot you can do while standing back and watching it from the halfway line. Still, there was no despondency in the dressing room, just the frustration of not making the most out of what we had and the Gaffer was very confident that if we just managed to be a little more clever with the ball then our chances would come.

It nearly came for me too after about five minutes in the second half. We'd won a corner and the ball played into me was absolutely perfect. It was one of those ones where you know from the moment that it's in the air that it is heading straight for you. Now I know that when you watch us out there at moments like that, you are probably thinking that I'm a cold-hearted professional with ice in my veins and that I'm just going to professionally get my head on it and hit the target. No. When a ball comes in like that, I still feel exactly as I did as a 13-year-old kid on the local pitch. Inside I'm thinking 'It's coming to me, it's coming to me… I'm gonna score!' The day I lose this genuine, almost childlike joy for the game, I guess, will be the day that I walk away from it.

Their second goal absolutely killed us, coming as it did after total possession and control by us. Caulks and I had got swapped when we were defending and hadn't managed to swap back, which meant that I was on the right and marking Cissé instead of Caulks. Cabaye had the ball and I could tell that Cissé wanted to run inside me, so I covered that and forced him to change the direction of his run to the outside of me. I probably over-covered, leaving a bit too much room on the outside, but I wasn't overly worried about that because I'd always rather him be wide of the goal than receive the ball centrally. I actually wasn't too bothered if the ball was played to him, as I knew I'd have enough time to turn and cover and probably get the block in, as from his body shape the only thing he'd be able to do would be drill it back across at Michel's near post. No real danger. What came next was almost too ridiculous to believe. Cissé continued his move as I'd thought, wide towards our right of the box, and Cabaye played an excellent through ball, at pace, straight into his stride. Instead of hitting it left-footed, he started to shift his feet and looked like he was going to try and bend it completely against the natural trajectory of the ball – ridiculous. All of a sudden, by him doing that he made it an easy block for me so I just slid in, expecting to feel the ball cannon off some part of my body. Instead, the ball looped gently over me and Michel, and just dropped in under the bar. I just looked straight at Cissé in disbelief. I have no idea if he meant it, but Michel was convinced he didn't and he was looking straight at him through it all. But I have to say, having now seen it on TV, it looks spectacular. Only he will know if he meant it, but speaking as a defender I have no doubt that it was a massive fluke. Probably.

After that we saw out the rest of the game pretty much as we had done throughout, with almost total possession, stringing together loads of passes and with them sitting really deep, allowing us to play in front of them but succeeding in preventing us from getting in behind. All I can remember in that last twenty minutes was us with the ball and not getting a chance. I was totally frustrated by the end of it, especially when I reflected on the fact that for the total lack of possession and attacking intent they had two goals to show for their two shots. The Gaffer said pretty much the same as he'd said at half-time, that in games like that where we have so much of the ball we need to penetrate more with our possession. He also said that's what 10 million quid will get you, referring to Cissé. Having seen him close-up twice today I have to agree with that.

After the game my agent, his wife and kids, along with my brother-in-law, wife and baby, and Vanessa and Raphael and I all went down to the Village Hotel in Swansea Marina straight from the stadium for a bite to eat, and who was there having a post-match drink, but today's match officials! It was slightly embarrassing to think that less than an hour before I had been effing and blinding at them, but they were great and we had a good chat, so I think they understand. It was good to talk to them and maybe this sort of thing needs to happen more so that we can break down some of the barriers that no doubt exist between players and some officials. Howard Webb said that he'd never been involved in such a strange game before, with one team having so much possession and losing, and I laughed and told him I hadn't either! It was the first time I'd had a real chat with him, and he seemed like a top guy... for a ref. Ha-ha.

Played 32 Won 10 Drawn 9 Lost 13 Points 39 League Position – 14th
(1 more point needed for 40)

Sunday 8th April

The Gaffer pulled Caulks and me in after training for a meeting. He doesn't want us trying to go forward too much any more, especially in the QPR game on Wednesday. He just pointed out that first and foremost we have to be behind the ball and not in front of it, because if a move breaks down and one of us is upfield, then even if Leon has dropped back we're still going to be exposed defensively. It's fair enough, I suppose, even though I like to get forward, but maybe QPR away is not the game to do it.

Tuesday 10th April

Travelled down to London to stay in the same hotel again as we did before the Fulham game. Bought back some very bad memories and did make me feel a bit uneasy.

Wednesday 11th April
Queens Park Rangers 3 (Barton 45, Mackie 55, Buzsaky 67)
Swansea City 0

I have just tweeted this to our travelling fans:

> Can only apologise for those of you that paid good money to come
> and watch that garbage performance tonight! #SafeTripBack :(

I'm fully aware of the costs of travelling to away games, especially a midweek one like this where, additionally many will be travelling straight back and going into work in the morning on the back of just a couple of hours' kip. So I can only apologise for that shambles of a performance tonight. It was the first real bad game we've had this season, possibly with Norwich perhaps, and on the back of Newcastle they've had nothing to cheer about all week and I felt responsible to them for that.

This was our fourth defeat on the spin. That's no points out of a possible twelve. It's simply not good enough, especially as the defeats have come against teams who, with the possible exception of Spurs, we should be looking to beat. To get nothing at all from those four games is not acceptable. It's all the more bizarre to think that we have only scored once in those four games, which came on the back of our destruction of Fulham.

I never spotted this shocking performance coming at all. Before the game I was so focused on my job and what was at stake that it was a joke. Monks and I are usually quite relaxed before a game, but he could tell that I was in a completely different place today focus-wise and he came over to me in the dressing room and said he was loving where my head was at today, 'all serious and angry'! He was right too. I just wanted to get into a dark frame of mind where I was completely and utterly ready for a battle.

Once I'd changed I went into see the ref, and it was Lee Probert who was the fourth official last Friday against Newcastle. When he started the meeting he asked me, 'Are you gonna be calmer today?' and I replied, 'Probably not.' He just laughed. QPR's captain tonight was Joey Barton, and he was coming across to everyone as though butter wouldn't melt again. It was very amusing, because I think we all know with him that it's only going to be a matter of time.

In the dressing room there was some apprehension, but it was a good apprehension if you know what I mean. We all knew how important the game was and, despite the four defeats, if I'm being deadly honest we all feel that we are safe now. But that isn't the target. It never was. The Gaffer has made it plain from day one in this division that he wants us to finish as high as we can. If we do that, relegation or a relegation battle simply won't appear on our agenda. I think the reason for the apprehension tonight is that QPR are in a relegation battle, and as such you never know what you are going to get. The league table never lies, especially after thirty-odd games, so the facts before the game suggested that QPR were not a very good side. The flip side of that though, is that they would potentially be scrapping for their lives, so we knew that in all probability it was going to be a tough night.

The game began well enough for us really, and there were no real clues as to what was going to follow later, especially when we had a couple of chances that, had we taken them, would certainly have changed later events. The first fell to Scott from a corner where he missed his kick following a scramble when it seemed certain we were going to score. Then, just a minute later, I had a good chance to score from a corner myself. I had Clint Hill on me and unsurprisingly, he was marking me tight the whole time, especially at the exact moment I was about to head the ball, by pushing and pulling every part of me. Still, it was a decent chance and I certainly need to step up and score some more goals from these opportunities. One goal so far this season is not good enough and is disappointing.

On the half hour I had my first clash with Zamora. He's a decent target man with good quality to his game, but I didn't leave this game remembering much about his quality because for the length of time he was on all he seemed to do was moan. He moaned after that first clash, and from that moment on he moaned at the ref constantly. The trouble with that is that at some point, no matter who you are, the ref will eventually give you a free kick, and that could be the moment in the match that turns things in their favour. As the match went on, and his moaning continued almost after every challenge, I just found him more and more annoying.

The rest of the half passed without much incident from my point of view. There was a big appeal from them for handball after the ball hit Caulks' hand and then bounced on to my elbow. It was just one of those things where it just hits you and, fortunately, the ref agreed. I was just relieved at the time because you can never second guess the way a ref will look at it. It was quite late in the half and the last thing we wanted to do was concede to them that late in the half.

But then we conceded in the 45th minute anyway.

Quite simply it was one of the worst goals we have conceded this season, mainly because it came from us having possession. If they score through some sweeping move when they've had the ball it's still like a knife through the heart, but for us to lose possession and gift them a goal is just the most annoying way to concede. I played a ball out to Tayls, and he must've taken his eye off it because it went under foot. Because of that, he then fouled Zamora when he didn't need to, giving them a dangerous free kick. Unsurprisingly, it was an excellent ball whipped in by Taarabt, that went over me and Zamora, but dipped straight towards the onrushing Onura. In fairness it was a good header out from Àngel under big pressure, and while it wasn't the longest of headers towards the edge of the box, it fell between Wayne and Gylfi, so we should have had no problem at all in dealing with it. Instead, the boys just didn't respond quickly enough and Barton nipped in and rifled it home. It was typical of us lately. A soft goal. As usual I was furious, mainly because we made a catalogue of errors of our own making which gifted them a goal at the most important moment of the half. As Barton ran away screaming his delight to his fans – that really cheered me up! – my anger turned to an almost instant depression when the realisation hit me that we'd conceded and that there was no time for us to respond. Whoever it was who first said that the stroke of half-time is the worst time to concede a goal knew exactly what he was talking about.

As usual I was first into the dressing room and I was so angry with what I'd just witnessed that as soon as I entered the room I volleyed a bottle of water, which hit the roof, burst and went everywhere. As the lads trooped in, nearly everyone was fuming and the rest just sat down in silence.

Then the Gaffer came in.

He was absolutely furious! It was the worst I've ever seen him, barring Bolton in the Cup. He was absolutely boiling. Straight away he whipped Wayne and Tayls off, shouted across to Tatey to tell him to go on, telling him to 'Get the ball, pass it simple, and defend like a man!' He raged at us for a while and ended by saying, 'You all need to grow a set and start playing properly!' As I say, he doesn't lose it often but when he does it has far more impact and, as with the Bolton game, we all knew he was 100 per cent correct.

The feeling as we left the dressing room was that we needed to score the next goal in the match to turn things around and if we were to get anything out of this game, we simply had to score next.

After ten minutes of the second half, Mackie scored QPR's second goal.

Again, the reason for the goal was quite simple. We didn't defend as if our lives depended on it. I was to blame initially, getting too tight to my man and slipping, allowing him to move the ball on to Mackie – I'll hold my hand up for that, as I should have done better. But Mackie still had his work cut out as we had a great opportunity to block his shot. I have to be brutally honest, and say that Àngel's attempt to block it just wasn't good enough. He was really close to Mackie, and all he needed to do was spread his body, make a challenge, and I'm absolutely certain that had he done that he'd have got something on the ball. Instead he didn't attack the ball at all, just turned his back and kind of jumped out of the way of it. As defenders we have got to keep that ball out of the goal at all costs. That is the only way you can look at it. Making blocks is something I pride myself on and see as absolutely integral to my game, and all of that is down to something the Gaffer said to me about it last season. In order to bring a bit of simple psychology into it, he said that we should imagine that our kids or loved ones are on the goal line and that the opposition are trying to smash them with the ball, so we should do everything to stop them. I know it's simple, and maybe to some of you unrealistic to look at it that way but that's exactly what I think of now when I'm in that position. I just think of Raphael standing there about to be smashed over the line by the ball, so there is no way that I'm going to allow that ball to hit him. It works for me.

It was from that point on that we really stunk the place up. The goal really knocked the fight out of us. I'm happy to take the plaudits when we do well, but it's a team game and I was the captain of the team on a night when we completely lost our belief and fight so I include myself in this completely. From that second goal we delivered the worst display of a Swansea City team this season.

Ten minutes later they scored a third with a decent strike, and that was us done. Game over with more than twenty minutes to go. Embarrassing.

The last twenty of the match was as horrible a period I've had in a Swans shirt as I can remember. We just weren't in it in any offensive way you'd care to mention, and if I'm honest all I cared about was making sure we didn't concede another. What was even harder to take was the way that their players put the strut on and trotted around like they were world-beaters, and watching and hearing them doing that did not make for a pleasant twenty minutes. QPR seems to be another bogey ground for us.

The final whistle was a relief and not a lot was said afterwards by anyone. It was a very quiet dressing room and coach trip home. I think we all felt embarrassed about tonight and just wanted to get home back to our families and the comfort of our homes.

Apart from the embarrassment I felt for our fans there was one thing nagging away at the back of my mind about the dismal run we are now on, and it goes back to that Fulham game. That win took us to 39 points, and while we have genuinely not looked at the season as a battle for survival, there is absolutely no way that any team in this division is going to be relegated on 39 points this year. Because of the way teams at the bottom will continue to take points off each other, the fixtures will not allow it. Therefore I'm wondering whether the fact that we are 'safe' has now become a problem for us. I would be gutted if 39 points is all we end with this season – even if we are safe. We need to look at Blackburn at home next week and all realise that we need to end this shocking run there and then.

All I can say is sincere apologies to all of you that were at Loftus Road today.

Played 33 Won 10 Drawn 9 Lost 14 Points 39 League Position – 14th
(1 more point needed for 40)

Thursday 12th April

At training today we had a meeting with the 'power group'. The Gaffer introduced this last season, and uses it at a time when we are struggling or if something needs to be discussed. When he feels it's right, he calls a meeting with the senior boys. It's the usual suspects and there's about eight of us. We all have a say and then he asks us to go and lead the rest of the meeting, and it's at that point we get everything off our chests. The good thing is we haven't had to have many of these meetings this season, but it was needed today. We call it the 'power group' to wind up the other lads who aren't part of it! Anyway it was a good meeting today and we discussed a lot of things from training to match day. We all gave our opinions on how we think we need to get back to winning ways, and it certainly cleared the air.

Friday 13th April

We had our usual Friday morning meeting before training today where we watched some footage of Blackburn's recent performances and then went out to train. Everyone had a very serious head on today which told me one thing for certain: We will win tomorrow.

Saturday 14th April

Swansea City 3 (Sigurdsson 37, Dyer 43, Dann og 63) Blackburn Rovers 0

When all seems to be going wrong around you, as has been the case since the Fulham game with our string of defeats, you can always trust the footballer to think of things logically. The one thing he falls back on in times like this is good old-fashioned superstition. When we go through a tough period like we have done we all have a think about changing little things we wear or routines we follow, because we believe it will result in an upturn in our fortune. So today I changed my boots and went back to a pair of old faithfuls from the Championship last year to bring me – and the team – some luck.

There was a fantastic atmosphere in the dressing room today. I think it would have been easy to get wrapped up in this run of defeats and really allow it to erode the confidence we have felt as a squad throughout the year. But in reality, the clear-the-air meetings we've had this week, allied to the fact that we are completely certain that our future is still in our hands, meant that the feeling before the game was almost that of a start of season game – full of optimism, compared to one with fear that we've probably had in recent weeks.

We started confidently enough before the ref and lino came together to somehow decide that Tayls had committed a foul. Even by my standards it was early to have a full go at them, but I just couldn't see how on earth they had made that decision. This was quickly followed by a slight contact with Yakubu in the box which saw him go down like Mario Balotelli. I quickly told him to get up and reminded him that I was aware how strong he is, so told him not to go down that easy again. His smile suggested that he knew he was trying it on.

A little bit later there were handbags between me and David Dunn. Now Dunn has a big mouth, and after we clashed he took exception to it so had a pop at me, which I responded to straight away. As we jogged back he was still carrying on, so I carried on giving it back to him, at which point the ref had heard enough and came over to speak to us. I understood why he got involved, but the fact was that I hadn't committed a foul. It was just that Dunn didn't like it and when he started to dish out the abuse, I gave him exactly the same back, so if there was a guilty party in this it certainly wasn't me. When the ref started to speak to me I pointed to Dunn and simply said, 'You'd better tell him.' Schoolyard stuff really.

It wasn't too long into the game when we took the lead with another great goal from Gylfi, who bent it round Paul Robinson from the edge of the box after getting the ball from Joe. For a split second, I thought – hoped – he was going to dink over to me at the far post as I'd managed to lose Lowe, but as I was thinking that he just bent it into the top corner. For once we'd got the first goal as a reward for our dominance in possession, and when I jumped on the top of the celebratory huddle I could really sense the release of pressure from the boys as I think we all felt that we would now go on and win the game.

Just a couple of minutes later we sealed things, thanks to Nath who finished off a great team move. Dann made an error which Scott pounced on, he played it to Danny, who unselfishly rolled it to Nath for him to finish. Mind you, as far as I'm concerned it was the biggest slice of all time by Nath that somehow beat Robinson, but he said that he meant it when we went in at half-time! We weren't having any of that, so battered him for it – always got to keep these flair players grounded!

At the break the Gaffer was delighted with the performance, and wanted us to up our endeavours in the second half and really make a statement. I was a little more direct with what I said. I saw no reason why we couldn't score a real hatful against them. I could tell after we scored our second that they didn't fancy it at all, and I could see no reason why we couldn't run away with it, so I told everybody to be totally ruthless in the second half. That's one of my criticisms of us this year. When we have been right on top of teams and, importantly, in front, we never really turn it up on them and finish them off.

Despite my call for ruthlessness we only added one in the second half, so the rout I was hoping for didn't occur. The goal itself was all about Scott, who made a fantastic run and crossed for Gylfi who claimed it. But he actually played it into the post and it rebounded back to Dann and went in off him. It was great play by Scott, who showed yet again that he has the ability to do this sort of thing, and he does it so effortlessly. I wonder sometimes whether Scott knows how hard it is for a defender to defend against runs like the one he made today, because from a defender's point of view he can be almost unplayable.

The rest of the game just passed without incident, especially for me. Bearing in mind that Blackburn had to win the game to have any chance of staying in the division, they didn't show the level of fight that I'd hope we'd demonstrate if we ever found ourselves in the same situation.

They got a little ragged in terms of their shape towards the end, which meant that Nath had much more room behind than he is usually allowed and that in turn meant that I could try my long diagonal ball to him more often, so I had four or five hits towards him. I love playing that ball as it gives me plenty of confidence when it comes off, and I always get a nice round of applause from the fans too, and there's nothing not to like about that!

We decided to have a huddle at the end to show our unity and I've read tonight that some people are saying we did it because we think we are now safe, but that wasn't the case at all. It was just a very public sign of us celebrating together because after the four defeats, we've had a bit of stick from the very same people who were praising us in February and March. As a group we have said all season that the only people we can really trust are the people in our dressing room as, sadly, there are plenty of people out there who are looking to pull you down at the earliest opportunity they get.

Back in the dressing room everyone was really up, and it was a great feeling knowing that we'd grasped a real opportunity that was offered us and won what was potentially a tough game convincingly. I'm just relived that our horrible run is over, and with it, we've broken the 40-point barrier. Even though we haven't discussed it at all as a squad, what that means now is that barring some bizarre mathematical turn of events in terms of goals scored and conceded, we should all be playing Premier League football at the Liberty Stadium next season.

I put it all down to my lucky boots.

Played 34 Won 11 Drawn 9 Lost 14 Points 42 League Position – 12th
(Still not mathematically safe – 1 more point required – 43)

Tuesday 17th April

Good feeling in training today, reflecting on a great performance and result on Saturday. Now we're looking forward to potentially guaranteeing our safety against Bolton on Saturday. Even though we still won't count any chickens, I can just sense the Blackburn win has lifted any pressure the lads may have been feeling about our remaining games because there's a huge difference between 39 points and 42, and you've got to go back to West Ham in 2003 for some one to take the drop on 42 points.

After his goal on Saturday, Nath was bouncing which was great to see. Nath's one of my best mates in the team and as my roomie has had to put up with me and my moans all season long. He started the season on fire, bringing his form from the Championship straight into the Prem from the first whistle and, take my word for it, that's a very hard thing to do. After a few weeks this year the Gaffer gave him a really good compliment that we gave him heaps of stick for. In a team meeting he pointed at Nath and said, 'You are the best defensive winger in the league.' We all paused for a minute and then burst out laughing and slaughtered him because I don't think there's a winger born who wants to be known for his defending, so we all thought that was really funny. As usual the Gaffer was spot on. I lose my temper with players who don't assume their defensive responsibilities but with Nath – even though he suffers the odd lapse – I know that he fully gets his role in the team when we haven't got the ball, and that awareness has been crucial to our defensive success this season. Obviously, going forward is where Nath really wants to catch the eye, and he usually does. I can think of two performances that stand out this season, one away and one home. The away game was at Villa where he tortured Stephen Warnock, but at home against Chelsea and Ashley Cole was the other game that stuck in my mind. Nath got about him from the start and made his life a misery. I honestly knew after ten minutes that Cole was going to be sent off because he was getting angrier and angrier every time that Nath went by him. In the end the inevitable happened and he got his second yellow. But what happened next also showed another of Nath's strengths. When the game was restarted and Luiz absolutely clattered him just as he, Cole and Meireles had been doing all night, as usual Nath didn't make a meal of it, he just got up after treatment and got back on with it. His temperament is superb.

Like all of us Nath knows that he needs to improve, and he knows in which area that is. It's his end product. Over the season we've talked about it loads of times, but it's in his goal scoring and his crossing that he needs to improve. If he can do that he'll be an England player, I have no doubt whatsoever about that, because he's got everything else that's required. People always bracket him with Theo Walcott and despite being completely different players, I can understand that. In terms of improving his end product, there's a risk that he doesn't make too big a deal about it. There have been a few times this season when he's got himself in a good position through some fantastically relaxed and natural play, and then as I'm watching him, just praying that he'll whip an instinctive cross in, I can see him tense up and start to worry about what he's about to do. He'll delay it and then when he finally delivers, he balloons it and gets angry and frustrated, which obviously can become a negative thing for him. It's not as if he's not aware of this, and I know he's doing everything to improve so I'm sure he'll continue to develop and will get there in the end. I love having Nath in the side though, because he gives us that bit of an X-factor as he demonstrated against Warnock and Cole. More importantly, from my point of view he makes our job so much easier. So congrats, mate, for being officially the best defensive winger in the league!

Wednesday 18th April

I spoke to the Gaffer today and asked him if it was OK that I'm doing this diary and that I'm looking to get it published at the end of the season. He said it was fine but that I need to remember that I'm still playing so to be careful. I asked him not to say anything to the lads yet until it's all sorted, in case I don't get a publisher... but mainly because the lads will slaughter me!

Friday 20th April

Straight after training yesterday I jumped in the car and shot up to Birmingham to watch Drake in concert at the NEC. I planned it down to the last detail and we were going to head straight back down to Swansea after the concert so that I could be up nice and fresh for training today. We went to get on the M5 and it was totally closed. All the times I've been up and down that motorway and I've never known it to be closed before. Typical. The only option was to get back to my house in Birmingham, set the alarm for 5.30 a.m., and head back down this morning, which I did. I'm now writing this on the coach going back up the M5 for tomorrow's game. One thing I won't miss when I finish playing is the motorway.

Saturday 21st April

Bolton Wanderers 1 (Eagles 14) **Swansea City 1** (Sinclair 6)

As we've done countless times this season we started well today, but for a change we got the early goal as a reward. I played a ball out to Scott who'd held his position nice and wide out on the wing, in a much a better position for him to attack his full back. We did a lot of work like this last season and had some real success from it and even though I know that defenders are generally better in the Premier League, I know that this is something that would succeed if we were able to do it more. Today it resulted in a great finish from Scotty and I was really pleased for him. As I celebrated with Michel I could just see the confidence oozing from Scott. Michel and I had a laugh while the rest of the lads were celebrating and Mich asked me why he didn't do that every week. In fairness, if he did he'd probably be playing for Real Madrid and not us!

It was just what I always want though, a great goal as a reward for our excellent start. I had a really good feeling that we'd get a positive result after Scott's goal. We were very close to being safe but they were right in the heart of the relegation battle, so the longer we stayed ahead the more chance the pressure would get to them and hopefully the crowd would turn against them too.

Around this time I'd started to enter into a real battle with Kevin Davies, who I'd met in the ref's room earlier and who was a really decent bloke. We'd already had fouls given for and against us by Phil Dowd, and Davies proved what I already knew in that he's certainly an awkward customer who really uses his arms in almost every challenge. Because he carries them so high I had to protect myself so that I didn't get caught with an elbow. It didn't bother me though, and I must admit for some bizarre reason I really love battles like that. After one particular tussle after the goal the ref ran by and asked if we were both happy and we both replied, 'Yep!' and said nothing else. That's what you want, really, a referee with empathy for the game and the battles that form part of a competitive match. I love that approach to refereeing and it's why Dowd is one of the very best.

I was really disappointed when they scored because it wasn't a great goal for us from a defensive point of view. We'd had a warning a bit earlier when Àngel got caught a little upfield and they'd played a ball in behind him that Caulks had managed to get across and cover. No matter how good a piece of defending that was by Caulks, the reality is if it keeps happening there's going to be a time when he won't be able to get across, and that's when they're going to hurt us. That's what I told Àngel at the time, and for the goal it was a similar thing really. Petrov got in behind Àngel and crossed a great ball for Eagles to run onto. Eagles was playing in a position in around Davies and not exactly up front, so he was difficult to mark. Looking at myself in this, I should have checked over my shoulder to see if there were any runners coming into the box and I didn't. I failed to react to Eagles and I was pretty disappointed with that. But the main reason for the goal was the source, and it was far too easy for Petrov to get his cross in down our right side.

Despite the goal I had no doubts at all that we were going to outplay Bolton the longer the game went on, despite them having a period after the goal when they got their tails up and had more of the game. During periods like this it's even more important that we commit to our passing game, and to ensure that it works effectively, everyone has to make themselves available to their team mate in possession of the ball to give them options. I had to remind Gylfi of this halfway through the half after I tried to pass the ball in to him, but because he was already turning his back on me before it got to him, their centre back was able to just jump in and nick it. When our team is pressing like this, because he's our extra midfielder, it is so important for Gylfi to come and receive the ball in small, tight areas. Michel noticed it too and told me to tell him that, 'He needs to come and get it.'

About five minutes later I was in the book for a bit of a stupid challenge, and whichever way I looked at it a booking was fair enough. I initially thought I could win the ball but in the end I was way off. When you give away a stupid free kick like that, all you are thinking is, 'Please don't score from this now' as it would all be down to me and my lack of judgement if they did. As the ref came across to book me, I said to him, 'Aw come on, that's my first foul.' He stopped dead, reached to his back pocket and said in his microphone to the other officials, 'Right, that's it. He's off for dissent!' I absolutely shat myself and said, 'WHAT?' Then he just started laughing and said, 'That got you, didn't it?' and then booked me! I couldn't believe it! That had never happened to me before with a ref, and I just got back into position in shock, and then started to laugh. It's so much better when we have human beings reffing us that don't treat us like naughty boys. More referees like Phil Dowd and respect levels between officials and players would rise instantly.

A little later Caulks was cleaned out by Michel when a cross came in and needed some treatment. I took the opportunity to have a word with Gylfi to make sure he understood that when they press us when we've got the ball, he's our spare man so he must come and get the ball straight off Michel from goal kicks or kick outs. He agreed so it was no big drama. It is just important to remind the lads of their jobs from time to time. I also had a bit of a laugh with Davies and the ref because Davies and I were talking when Dowd came across, and we both said to him – seriously – to just let us have a scrap and don't blow for any more free kicks! He just laughed and said, 'You two are crazy. I've got to blow if it's a foul, which is all the time the way you two are going on!' We just laughed and said, 'You haven't, just let it roll!' He just shook his head, laughed and walked off, and Davies just smiled and said, 'Back to it, then!'

Even though they had come into it quite well after their goal, and they'd had a decent spell up to the break, the Gaffer was completely calm about things when he spoke to us at half-time. His message was simple and clear; we just had to keep doing what we'd been doing but just turn it up that little bit and he felt that we could win comfortably. To be honest that's exactly what we all felt anyway. There was no anxiety at all in the dressing room and there was a quiet confidence about us that left me in no doubt that the game was pretty much ours for the taking.

To be fair to Bolton though, they were certainly still up for the fight after the break, and Ream and I had a couple of tussles at the first two corners. I kept beating him to the ball but then he would just literally push me out of the way. It was ridiculous really, so I tried to tell the ref that every time I tried to head it, he would just push me with both hands out of the way. I don't call that being physical, like the battle Davies and I had been having. It was just that he was getting beat and then doing anything he could to get himself out of the mess he was in. I never normally moan to refs about challenges, but what he was doing was ridiculous.

Five minutes later we should definitely have scored when Scott had a great chance to set up Gylfi, but chose to try a back heel instead. Caulks was fuming when the chance went, but I thought that Scott couldn't have seen Gylfi otherwise he surely would have passed because Gylf just had a tap in. Whatever the reason I knew that we couldn't afford to waste chances like that. Clear-cut chances don't come along that often in the Prem and we have seen in other games this season that when we have missed good chances the other team has come down our end and punished us. Rather than getting all down about the chance going begging, I was more concerned with just trying to get the defence focused again so if they did get down our end we didn't compound the miss by letting them score.

Apart from a great effort by Danny that hit the bar, we'd had our best chance and for the rest of the game it was just about shutting them out. They knew that a point wasn't ideal for them in their situation, so they really ramped things up and it got a little hectic at the back in the closing stages. Still, despite some busy defending there wasn't really a moment where I thought they might score. As you'll know by now there's nothing I like more than backs-to-the-wall defending, when I can get really stuck in and get into organising the back four, so I was happy throughout that, especially as we walked away without them adding to their score.

The whistle went and after the handshakes I felt a little flat at just getting a point. I think we were the better side by quite a distance today, and if we'd got a second I think we'd have won comfortably. The Gaffer had a different take on it though. Even though he agreed that it was another game in which we'd performed really well and probably hadn't got what we deserved, he also said a point and a draw away from home in the Prem was precious, so we shouldn't forget that.

I caught up with Sam Ricketts in the tunnel afterwards and swapped shirts with him. He's one of my mates in the game, especially when we are away on Wales camp. We've had similar careers really, with me coming from Hednesford and him coming from Telford, so naturally we have something in common. When I first got into the Wales camp he looked after me, having played for Swansea before and we've been mates ever since. He's a good guy and it's one of the bonuses of getting into the Prem now, being able to follow in his footsteps and actually be on the pitch against him and compete on equal terms. Because of the similarity of our backgrounds I think it means a little more to us than perhaps those players in the Prem who've never really had any setbacks in their careers. As a result I felt quite proud being able to swap my shirt with him after all these years. A nice moment to end the day.

Played 35 Won 11 Drawn 10 Lost 14 Points 43 League Position – 11th
(Still not mathematically safe – but bizarre things need to happen!)

Sunday 22nd April

Lovely day today. It was Raphael's first birthday party which we had at our house in Birmingham. It was his birthday yesterday, but obviously we couldn't do anything then, so we had all the family and friends round today. I can't believe he's one already, the year has really flown. He had a fantastic day and everyone enjoyed themselves. It was one of those family days that was great from start to finish and it was lovely to just chill out and focus on him for a change.

Tuesday 24th April

The Gaffer had us try something different in training today, and set us up to work on a 3–4–3 formation. I don't think he intends using it any time soon, but just wants us to have another string to our bow if we want to change things at any point in the future. He included Andrea in the formation on the left side, so that's why I know that it's just something he's thinking of for the future because Andrea's not in the team at the moment, and hasn't been for ages, so today must have been just an experiment.

Wednesday 25th April

We worked on 3–4–3 formation again today. The Gaffer said he wants to try something new as we are safe now but he also wants to win the game. This is maybe a plan B for when things aren't going to plan and we need to play a bit further forward and higher up the pitch. We went through a lot of scenarios in the game, like where we should be at certain situations. It's a lot more work for everyone apart from maybe the front players and I'm not sure if it will work for us but it will sure be interesting anyway.

Thursday 26th April

Àngel slipped down the stairs at home last night and is injured. I don't think he will be able to play this weekend and obviously that has slightly messed up what we worked on yesterday as he was going to play in an advanced right wing role. Nath went into his position today and is used to playing there so it will not be a problem, but I was quite looking forward to seeing how Àngel would have fitted in there.

Friday 27th April

The Gaffer confirmed this morning that all our work this week was going to be put into practice tomorrow because he's going with the 3–4–3 tomorrow. We had a meeting about it, which also featured a lot about Dorus and how he'd affect things for them, and it was just a question of trusting what we'd done in training this week and committing to it. We've worked really hard on it on Wednesday and Thursday, by playing 11 v 11 during training, and the main casualty is Tayls who won't be involved, meaning Andrea is playing after all.

I've been working on this diary since July last year and didn't want to tell anyone at the club until it was all done and dusted and then just tell the lads when Dave (Brayley) has sorted out the publisher and stuff. But in the dressing room today, Monks just made a casual announcement that he's got a book coming out tomorrow! I couldn't believe it! There was only one thing I could do. I just gave him heaps of stick! It was so funny, I just laid into him saying I couldn't believe he'd written a book and did he think he was all big time now and stuff like that, and actually was hammering him for about ten minutes. Then the door opened, and in walked the Gaffer. He got involved in it straight away, and I thought, 'Please don't say anything about mine yet Gaffer!' Anyway the first thing he said was, 'I can't believe you lot, all bringing out your books and diaries, what's going on here?' I just stood there, laughing inside thinking, 'This is it. I'm going to get the biggest shower of abuse any Swans player has ever had.' But not one player picked up on it! I'd just spent ten minutes hammering Monks, the Gaffer comes in and makes a statement which clearly means someone else has written something, and not one of the lads picked up on it – how thick is our team?

I just had a giggle to myself, went and sat back down and let the Gaffer change the subject. I really can't wait until the boys finally find out, especially Monks, because they are going to hammer me. Should be fun!

Saturday 28th April

Swansea City 4 (Orlandi 1, Allen 4, Dyer 15, Graham 31)

Wolverhampton Wanderers 4 (Fletcher 28, Jarvis 33, 69, Edwards 54)

All season long I've thought someone was due a smashing by us. I knew it would come and today it did but, frustratingly, it only lasted for about twenty-five minutes. That was still long enough for us to get three goals up. I knew this would come at home too, as our defensive record at the Liberty is as good as almost anyone in the league. I pride myself on the lack of goals we concede at home, and I pride myself on my defending, full stop. I am much happier with a 1–0 win than a 3–2 victory. For goalscorers it's all about the goals. For me it's all about the clean sheets.

But today? Well, let's put it this way, when the final whistle went I got myself off the pitch as quick as I could after shaking some hands and clapping the fans, simply because I felt embarrassed. Even though we drew, and the result in itself wasn't the end of the world, to me it didn't feel like a draw. It felt like a 5–0 defeat, and that's a pretty horrible feeling to have.

I don't think many of the players are keen on 3–4–3 because we all know it's quite a tough formation to play in, because you have to do lots of other jobs that you don't normally have to worry about. The formation really takes you out of your comfort zone, but having said that I think that it's always good to try something new in terms of formation, just to understand and learn if we are capable of delivering it at some point in the future. I try not to get too hung up on tactics like so many 'experts' seem to do out there. We all know how to play the game, and whatever formation you choose to run with, ultimately it's still just a game of football. I think a lot of people lose sight of that sometimes.

There was also a little focus in the media about Dorus and his return to the club and how maybe he'd made the wrong choice by joining Wolves in the summer. Only he would know that of course, but today was just Dorus' second game in the Premier League, so on the face of it it's been a pretty disappointing time for him. But I'm sure that all Dorus really cared about today was performing well, and maybe even keeping a clean sheet. Sadly for him, that hope lasted all of twenty-four seconds.

It was a fantastic move by the lads, typical of many we have done this year without adding the finishing touch. Today that was supplied by Andrea, who was making his first start since his injury at Villa. He actually felt a knock that he'd had on his calf in the warm-up, but understandably he didn't want to miss out having not played for so long and so declared himself fit. I doubt he thought his decision would have paid off so spectacularly though. He was involved in the build-up and then fed Scotty who in turn played a lovely ball in for Andrea to flick it over the despairing Dorus. As you can imagine the crowd went nuts, as we all did, which was understandable because as I've banged on about week after week all the lads know how important it is for us to get a lead early. That said, I don't think any of us really dreamt it would ever be this early. It was a fantastic feeling scoring so soon, and I've certainly never played in a game where my team has scored so quickly.

Within fifteen minutes we'd not just built on that start, but used the confidence to deliver something special, because – almost unbelievably – we were 3–0 up. Joe scored after four minutes with a deflection that must have had Dorus wanting to scream. It really was turning into one of those days for him. Then about ten minutes later Nath scored, which meant just one thing – our dance. Obviously, goal celebrations are one of those things that have grown over the years, and most players have a little plan that they will have spoken about to do when the goal comes along. When Nath scored today he looked towards me straight away, so I sprinted up to him and we carried out our plan. It was from a Drake video called HYFR and he does this dance at the start of the video when he is a little kid. Nath and me always laugh about the dance and said a while ago we'd do it if we score. As his goal had taken us 3–0 up in a quarter of an hour, I didn't think there was ever a better time to do it.

After our dancing interlude I jogged back to my place, probably feeling as good about my football as I had since before the start of my illness in the Man City game, back in early March. As I waited for the ref to restart I couldn't help but think that the game was now over in terms of winning, and it was just going to be a matter of how many we were going to score. It was not just because we were playing so well and attacking so freely. It was also based on the fact that we just never concede at home, so to concede three was unthinkable! From the buzz that was coming out from the stands, I think the whole stadium was thinking the same too.

To be fair to Wolves though, they didn't just roll over. Instead they actually started to get a foothold in the game, and I had to make a couple of blocks in quick succession. One was a full-blooded shot which hit me full in the back; a real stinger that took me straight back to the type of thing that would happen when I was a kid in the cold and would see me fighting back the tears because it hurt so much. The other was a better block – on Doyle – that I felt was one of my best blocks of the season as it was a certain goal otherwise. What these two moments showed me was that there was a definite swing in the game. They had clearly decided that they were probably going to lose, so were throwing caution to the wind. A period like that was always going to happen but even at 3–0 you don't want it to happen, and you still want to keep a clean sheet. The reality though, was that we were getting sloppy and not doing all the boring, basic things that we normally do so well. And as a result we began letting them back into the game.

As I feared, from some more sloppy play they got a toehold in the game with a very good header from Fletcher. At the very moment the goal was scored – heading a far post cross back the way it came, looping over Michel and dropping into the net – I honestly didn't think there was much more I could have done. As a defender you never want the striker to get to the front post and score in front of you. So in a position like this where I was a bit stranded, I dropped in front of him to cover that side. If he manages to score from way back there, it's a matter of saying 'well done'. Michel was fuming with me for letting him have his free header and I was saying to him that even if I had been closer to him, I couldn't have done anything about it as he had headed it at his highest point, and it was a great finish. But as I reflect on it now, it's all very well telling Michel that there was nothing that I could have done, but if I want to be a top Premier League defender, frankly that attitude isn't good enough. I should have demanded more of myself and I should have made much more of an effort to have got close to him.

Within five minutes we had restored our advantage with a goal from Danny. We had now scored four goals in thirty minutes, something we'd have killed for before kick-off. But I wasn't overly happy with the way things were going. Instead of celebrating, I had a long chat with Michel about the goal, and then Monks came across and agreed that he wasn't happy about his part in it himself, allowing the cross to come in as he did. Even though we'd scored four, it was clear that defensively things weren't going as planned, so we just agreed to get back on it and make sure we didn't allow them any more freedom to get any crosses into the box and to just defend better.

Defend better. Yeah, right.

Just two minutes later they scored again. I was probably the angriest that I had been on a football pitch during the entire season, and I've had a few moments. By now I could see that we weren't coping with our new system at all, so that was annoying enough. Then as they built the move and I could see what was happening, I was getting angrier because of the room we were giving Jarvis and the easy way that we allowed him into a position to shoot, almost unchallenged. Still, despite that, I did manage to get back onto the goal line and cover Michel who had been beaten with the shot, but then for reasons I still have no clue about I missed an easy clearance, falling backwards, and the ball went in off my shin. I still can't understand how I missed it, because I would clear a ball like that 99 times out of a 100. When I realised what had happened I nearly snapped. It doesn't occur often, but I do have a decent temper and when I blow, anything can happen. Luckily the ball was next to me, so I just slung it away as hard as I could, but in reality I was so angry I could have punched anyone or anything. Fortunately for Fletcher, who seems like a good guy, my anger had peaked when I threw the ball away, and he just said, 'Unlucky, mate.' I just stood there, eyes on stalks, saying nothing, staring at him, and he just looked at me like I was a psycho. To be fair, at that moment I was, but my anger was laced with embarrassment, both for me personally in the complete hash I'd made of the clearance, but also in the way that we were throwing the game away. As I walked back to await the restart, my mind was all over the place and just wanted to get in for half-time so that we could sort this mess out. The fact that we had scored four goals and were still leading by two meant absolutely nothing to me.

For the last ten minutes of the half the Gaffer abandoned the experiment as he could see that it just wasn't working, and brought Andrea back into left back. He was struggling with his calf, but at least we had a back four again. After one more run by Jarvis, which I defended poorly, my head was all over the place with anger and frustration and I just needed to get back into the dressing room.

When we got in there, the atmosphere was one of complete frustration that we had got 3–0 up and let them back in. There was no feeling of triumph whatsoever about our four goals, instead we were all gutted and the room was as flat as if we'd conceded four and not scored them. I knew as we sat there and listened to the Gaffer with his new instructions that we were going to find it hard to be as effective as we'd been in that first thirty, because you can't just switch it on and off like that.

Also, Wolves were now a very dangerous team because having scored the two they were playing with complete freedom and knew how we'd be feeling. As they were already down, they had absolutely nothing to lose and no doubt would want to use the second half to finally give their fans something decent to cheer about.

Just a couple of minutes in we had a corner where I clashed with my marker, Spearman. I think anyone who came into contact with me from then on was going to have it from me. I tried to score to somehow lessen the embarrassment of my horrific goal line howler, and as he was wrestling with me I had a full go at him to get his hands off as I was so desperate to make something positive happen. But the only thing that did happen so quickly afterwards was that they scored again from a quick free kick. 4–3. Unbelievable. Our back line and midfield were all over the place and to be staring at a scoreline that showed us conceding three goals absolutely served us right, such was the shambolic way we were playing.

For the next ten to fifteen minutes it was the game from hell. We were gone mentally. We all played with the fear of knowing we had scored four goals at home but could now maybe find ourselves walking away with nothing. It was a horrible feeling and, as I've said, it meant that Wolves were transformed into a team who believed anything was now possible, and belief is key in pro sport.

At that point they had plenty and we had none.

Then with about twenty minutes to go our greatest fears were realised when they equalised. It was now 4–4 after we'd been 4–1 up. At home! Again, from our point of view, it was shambolic. I slipped at the start of it, which in the final analysis was the difference between getting back to block Edwards' shot, and missing it. I should have won the first header, then Leon got in the way of Monks who could have stopped it, but this only compounded loads more positional errors that in the end cost us the goal. As I was getting up off the turf I could see the Wolves players celebrating with their fans and my main concern was realising that there was now a very big chance that we were going to lose a game in which we had scored four at home. Completely ridiculous and actually unthinkable.

Fortunately that final indignity was spared us. But it so could have happened as they still managed to outplay and outpass us, which was an embarrassment in itself. After a break by Joe was stopped on the edge of their box, they broke and put together a quick passing move which saw Knightly blazing high and wide. I went nuts at Joe, but it wasn't aimed at him particularly, it was just the whole situation that we'd been at the mercy of a wild shot from actually losing this game. It really didn't bear thinking about.

As you can imagine, the final whistle was such a relief and I just wanted to get out of the place as soon as possible. It was then I heard the boos. I have to make it clear that I've never liked it when fans boo their team, I have never booed anyone I was watching. They rang out at the Liberty today and that was disappointing. Tonight people have been tweeting me saying that it was aimed at the ref, but I'm not having that as I'm sure it was for us. I got really friendly with the block button on Twitter this evening. Sometimes I really do think that fans believe that because we get paid so well, and have the nice cars and other things, we don't care about games and results like today. But what they forget is that this is not a hobby for us. It's our livelihood. It's our job. I don't know what those fans who booed think of their own livelihoods and jobs, but I take a massive pride in mine, and I will not allow anyone to ever question my care and professionalism towards the club I represent. I hope you've realised by now having read this far that there's no bigger critic of myself than me, and it may come as a surprise to some people but that's the same for the vast majority of players I've ever played with, and especially the lads who are part of the Swansea City squad of 2011/12. Therefore to have to hear boos ringing out – which is the ultimate insult after such a fantastic season – was just the icing on the cake of a pretty awful day.

The ironic thing of course, was that the booing began at the very moment that we were mathematically safe from relegation and had guaranteed the club another season in the Premier

League. The last time we had experienced a moment that guaranteed us a season in the Premier League had been the final whistle at Wembley.

I don't recall many boos ringing out then.

Played 36 Won 11 Drawn 11 Lost 14 Points 44 League Position – 12th (Survived)

Monday 30th April

My anger and embarrassment about Saturday has dissolved slightly. As awful as it was to chuck away such a dominant position in the game, in what should have been a celebratory performance for everyone, the realisation has now dawned that it is 100 per cent certain that we're going to be playing Premier League football next season. It should feel a bit better than it does I think, but the fallout from the game and the boos still leave a little taste in the mouth that I'm not too happy about. Nonetheless, it's such a magnificent achievement by the lads to have secured our status with two games to go. Looking back at Saturday, one of the reasons for our success is one of the few players to emerge from Saturday's game with any credit, little Joey Allen.

By a long distance Joe is the best young player that I've ever played with, and as the season has progressed so has he. He's developed so quickly and effortlessly that it's easy to forget that he was just 21 when the season started, and to play more or less every game in the Premier League in the most intense area on the pitch, centre midfield, is just incredible. The signs were there in pre-season. There was something different about Joe from the off this season, it was as if he wanted to make a statement this year and he wanted to dictate and control games. He was no longer content to just be a part of games and he's really taken his play up a notch so far this year. It's been more obvious to me than maybe anyone else this year, because he's come and got the ball off me far more this season than last year, and not only has he improved in that area, he's far more assertive when he's on the ball. It's as if he wants to make a statement every time he's got the ball, though never recklessly. He has shown great maturity by just giving it short if the opening isn't there. He's pretty much been sensational in midfield with Leon. They compliment each other so much.

What I love about Joe though, is his aggression. He reminds me so much of me when I was young. You don't see that so much any more in many youngsters coming through these days, but Joe's got it in buckets. But again, to underline his development, he's learnt to control it more, and even though he did get a red card this year, at Blackburn, he's mostly managed to channel his aggression in the right way. I think we are kindred spirits in a way and get on really well, and I've spoken lots with Joe about how I used to be and how you just have to change and use the red mist in a positive way whenever possible. The only thing he needs to add is goals. It's not as if he can't finish. His side foot against Wolves in the first game showed that he can finish and, OK, the goal on the weekend was a deflection, but if you don't shoot you don't score and I think he needs to add that to his game now he's cemented himself as a top player in a Premier League team.

This season, like he did on Saturday, Joey dominated centre midfielders who have been playing that position for years and years. Nobody knows what the future holds, but if Joe hasn't attracted the interest of a proper top four club in this country in the next couple of seasons I'll be absolutely stunned, but as long as he stays with the Swans we'll know we have a genuinely gifted player and, longer term for Wales, I can see him being first choice for years and a future captain of his country. It's been a pleasure this season to see him blossom so much.

CHAPTER ELEVEN

May 2012

Tuesday 1st May

Just thinking this evening how good this year's Premier League is. We are all fans and it's been so entertaining at the top and bottom of the league. I don't know who is going to win the league but it's definitely going to go down to the wire. I'm so glad to have played in this year's league. With Man City beating Man United last night it means the league is wide open. I for one can't wait to see what's going to happen and it's amazing to think we are potentially going to have a say in the outcome as we go to Old Trafford on Sunday.

Wednesday 2nd May

Had a top secret photoshoot after training today with Adidas at the Liberty Stadium. There was a bit of a panic about the boys tweeting pics of next year's kit and apparel before the launch, so we weren't allowed to have our phones in the shoot. Me, Danny, Nath, Joe, Tayls and a few others had to do all sorts of shots on front of the green screen, pretending that we had scored or we were angry on the pitch and so on. It was a bit of a laugh and everyone had fun with it. The new kit looks really nice and it's the first time I've seen a group of lads happy with the following season's kit. As we are a moaning lot that's normally what we do, but the lads were buzzing as this one is similar to Real Madrid's kit.

Thursday 3rd May

While I was at training this morning a load of sheep had found their way onto my decking – and I mean about twenty sheep. My dogs were having a seizure inside trying to get to them. Anyone who's on Twitter will know that in my old house I used to get wild horses in my garden. Now I've got sheep at my new one. Growing up where I did, this is very bizarre to me as we had no wildlife around us. Just one of the joys of living in Wales I suppose. Very strange though, sharing your garden with random wild animals.

Monks and me were interviewed after training by Bianca Westwood for Sky Sports and decided to hammer Gows and tell the world about the nappies he wears during training to try to sweat off the excess fat on his backside. I think Bianca wanted us to reveal some deep, considered opinions about our successful season, but when you put Monks and I together, the last thing you are going to get is sense. I also took the opportunity to try to convince the world that my header against Čech was our goal of the season. In my eyes it was anyway. Čech never moved!

Friday 4th May

I heard today that the guys at The World of Groggs up at Pontypridd have started work on my Grogg. I can't wait to see what they come up with. I hope they make me look beautiful, ha-ha!

Saturday 5th May

We paid Man United the right amount of respect this week. We've talked a lot about the fact that they will be going all out to win. Having lost to City they will be trying to score a lot of goals because winning the Prem could come down to goal difference. All week we've worked on not letting their midfield players, especially Scholes and Carrick, get the ball off the back four and then have enough time to spray passes all over the place. They definitely have the quality to drop a 60-yard ball at someone's feet, especially Scholes. What we've worked on is making sure that Gylfi and Joe get up to them and stop them turning without any pressure on them.

Whatever happens though, we all know that we are safe now

and we feel that we have earned the right to just enjoy these last two games, starting at Old Trafford tomorrow. We never wanted to enter these two games needing something from them to stay up, so as players, staff and fans, I think all of us should just come together over the next two games and really enjoy and celebrate our success.

Sunday 6th May

Manchester United 2 (Scholes 28, Young 41) **Swansea City 0**

Because of the importance of the title race on our match we all wanted to know what was going on with City up at Newcastle. As it would have a definite effect on how United would approach the game with us, we watched the Newcastle v City game on the bus to Old Trafford and then carried on watching it in the changing room. We didn't see a single United player around, so we knew that they were watching it too, and with the score at 0–0, it meant that United were still very much in this title race. When we got the knock on the dressing room door for Pasc and I to leave and go to the captain's meeting, City scored. When we got in there you could have cut the atmosphere with a knife, because Mike Phelan and Patrice Evra were absolutely fuming. It wasn't the most pleasant of captain's meetings that Pasc and I have had this season, and we couldn't wait to get out of there.

If Evra's mood was bad in the ref's room, I made it worse at the toss. The Gaffer had suggested that if I won the toss, I should spin them around and not let them play the way they normally like to in the first half. When the coin came down the right way that's exactly what I did, and judging by the look on Evra's face he didn't really appreciate my decision!

The game almost turned into a personal disaster for me after just five minutes. I went quite high up the pitch to challenge Hernández because I just wanted to get tight to him and let him know I was about, but my foot stubbed the back of his heel hard and I felt pain in my left big toe instantly, which just got worse and worse all game. It was a clumsy challenge from me, and one that I would regret, as I've since found out that my toe was broken in it. It could have been much worse and forced me off, and I would have hated my season to have ended in a whimper there and then.

Even though my toe was really starting to trouble me, and they had a ten-minute spell when they were on top, I must admit I was really loving my defensive duties in this early period. I cut a lot of crosses out with some headers and performing well like that gives you confidence when you are really under pressure. It somehow makes you feel bigger on the pitch because you believe you are managing to comfortably deal with everything they can throw at you.

Around twenty minutes in there were a string of free kicks given by the ref and it was important that we kept our discipline in defending them. To remind the lads I was calling out, 'Don't go early' and 'Be brave'. The commands are aimed at all the guys in the defensive line because the whole aim for us has to be to keep the defensive line as high as possible so that Michel has more space to come and catch it when the ball comes in. It's all about understanding our roles and carrying out our plans with discipline. My screams and shouts are just designed to remind the lads that.

When it eventually came, their goal was one that we could have prevented, but once Tayls gambled on winning it outside the box, and didn't, we were always struggling. Tayls' decision meant that Joe had to cut out Valencia after he'd beaten Tayls, which then meant Carrick was free as Joe had left him. Once the ball went back to Carrick, all I could do was just hope that he wouldn't strike it so well that no-one could block it. But he did and it went straight to Scholes who flicked it past Michel to score. As usual when we concede, my annoyance levels shot through the roof, so I just turned around and walked back to my mark simmering nicely.

Even though Hernández had a great chance with a header, we certainly didn't experience the onslaught that everyone probably thought was going to come after the goal. They were on top and needed a hatful if they were going to threaten Man City after they'd beaten Newcastle, but I was still very confident that we'd go in at half-time without conceding another. Sadly I was proved wrong.

The second goal when it came was also very annoying. Scott gave possession away twice after first Tayls and then Joe had cleared balls up to him, and seeing those mistakes result in a goal left me furious again. It was in my nature to have a full go at Scott, but at the back of my mind I could see that he knew he'd made a big mistake, so I just left it. The reaction of Young after the goal made me laugh – or would have done, if I hadn't been so angry. He ran past me into the net, scooped the ball up and ran with it back to the halfway line without celebrating. It was clearly a statement for the fans saying, 'We're not done with two, and we are gonna get a hatful here.' It was a joke really, because despite them having a lot of possession both goals had come from poor defending by us rather than sustained brilliance from them. In fact, I was actually thinking that if we could score we'd be right back in it for the second half. Despite what Young was trying to convince his fans with, I could tell that not all was well with United as Rooney had given Jones a couple of roastings for wasting crosses, and I think the general feeling with them was that despite their two goals, we were not a team that was going to fold and concede the four or five they needed at least to put some pressure on City.

As usual when the ref blew the whistle for half-time, I ran straight up the tunnel before anyone else. This time my urgency was more to do with the terrible pain I was having with my toe. I got my boot off straight away to have some treatment on it and took some pain killers.

The Gaffer was quite pleased considering the goals came from two individual mistakes. He knew that, other than that, we'd soaked up their pressure pretty well, and they hadn't really caused us any problems. His main message was that we needed to break better and keep the ball. He was spot on about that and I said that I thought that we should be keeping the ball better, both with better clearances from us at the back into better areas but also with players like Nath, Gylfi and Scott needing to do better for us when they were dribbling the ball out from midfield, and protecting the ball first and foremost. We have to understand that we don't always need to look to score from our possession and play the killer ball only to lose it.

We started the second half confidently and got our passing going, which is crucial to us as it frustrates the other team so much. We had a corner after about five minutes but it broke down, allowing them their first real trip into our territory since we'd come back out. In fairness to Nath, he chased Young down perfectly and actually managed to nick the ball away from him for a corner. Both Michel and I made a big fuss of Nath for this as it's so important to us. The guys at the back love it when our attacking players get back and do a job on defence. You will always see us congratulate them for it. It was another good piece of work by the best defensive winger in the league!

As the half went on and they didn't look like adding to their first-half goals, I knew we were getting under their skin when Rooney fouled Leon and was probably lucky not to get yellow. I felt Rooney was getting frustrated with the limited chances he had coming his way. I could just feel it simmering with him, so when he fouled Leon with that wild challenge it wasn't a surprise.

Tayls made us all laugh soon afterwards when he got into a great position to hook the ball away for a throw, but instead totally miskicked out for a corner. We were under the cosh a little bit at the time, and his face was a picture when he realised what he'd done, so to have a laugh about it released some of the pressure he was feeling. Tayls must have agreed as he had a bit of a snigger too as we were lining up to defend it.

Just after the corner was cleared the ball came back down the left-back channel, but Scott got himself between Valencia and the ball and took the hefty challenge from Valencia. The ref gave the foul and I made a point of going across and telling Scott well done. As with Nath earlier, but probably even more so with Scott, I felt the need to say well done because Scott is on my side, and usually he hears me onto him all the time to defend, so when he does it as well as he did to Valencia I want to be the first to congratulate.

Not long afterwards Rooney finally popped and was booked for a foul on Leon. The way Leon defended and read the play was brilliant, and I think that had frustrated Rooney more than anything else. That was pretty much the end for Rooney, and five minutes later he was off, being replaced by Berbatov. Caulks and me had a decent chat when the change was made, and we were just making certain that we both understood how important it was that we stayed on it and didn't slack just because Rooney had gone off.

Apart from a little five minutes when they had a flurry of corners and I was in my element organising the lads, trying to get my head to anything near me and chucking the odd block in, United didn't really have any more clear-cut chances in the game. Even though we didn't really threaten them either, it was a fantastic defensive achievement for us to draw the second half 0–0 at Old Trafford when they were looking to score a hatful to stay in the title race.

There was one final, painful, and amusing moment for me though. Because they had failed to score in that second half Rio must have started getting excited and thought he was a 21-year-old again, because he made a crazy run out of defence, playing a one-two as he approached the edge of our box. As soon as I saw him play it I started to cover because the last thing I wanted was for him to score as I'd never live it down. As I cleared it we clashed and I hurt my knee, I knew he'd got hurt too and when I looked over I saw him holding his hip and not moving. He had some treatment, but not long after he got subbed and I must admit I thought the worst and was gutted for him. Chatting to him afterwards though, he was OK.

The whistle soon came and, to be honest, I had run myself into a bit of a standstill. My toe was pretty bad at this point and my knee also hurt after the clash with Rio, but more than that I was just knackered. It's been a long, hard season and today was also very hot, so as I stood there feeling tired I was pretty relieved that our final away game was done and dusted. I enjoyed the feeling of knowing that there is just ninety minutes left in the season before we get our break.

I spoke to the physios after the game about my toe and they were of the opinion that it was broken, so they told me to have two days off, keep weight of it, take anti-inflammatory tablets and have it strapped tight to the next one. As I left Old Trafford I had a last look round and couldn't help but feel a little satisfied about things. Nine short months ago we left the blue half of Manchester on the back end of a 4–0 scoreline. Today we were walking away after another defeat, this time by two. It wasn't ideal to be leaving the city after conceding six goals there, but the most important thing is that we'll be back here next year, and across at the Etihad too. Despite the pain in my toe and my knee, that thought made me feel as satisfied as I had been in a long while.

Played 37 Won 11 Drawn 11 Lost 15 Points 44 League Position – 12th (Safe)

Monday 7th May

Everyone has been tweeting me over the weekend, laughing about the bad language I'd used in the game on Saturday that had been picked up on *Match of the Day*. Everyone was having a laugh about it but it's just one of those heat of the moment things, and when you are in the game and the adrenalin is flowing that's how most footballers talk. We don't do it off the pitch, or maybe some do, but it was interesting for people to hear how intense things can be when in the game.

Talking of intense, that just about describes the pain I've been having in my injured toe. I hardly slept last night as the pain was shocking. I took some pain killers but they didn't seem to work that well and it just throbbed and got worse as the night went on. It was such a simple way of injuring it and for such an innocent knock the pain has been ridiculous. I've been told today not to train this week and to keep my weight off it and there's a big doubt that I'm going to be able to play next weekend. But missing Liverpool at home in our last game of our first season in the Premier League? That's not going to happen.

Wednesday 9th May

Jonathan Wilsher came up with the idea today for Hari Kieft to walk out with me at the front of the squad against Liverpool on the weekend. My son Raphael is a mascot too and will also walk out with me. He thinks it will be a lovely way to end the Hari story with everyone involved. A lot of fans and the public have been great in trying to raise money to help this little boy be able to walk, and I think it's nice that we all will be able to celebrate seeing him walk out onto the pitch. I get a lot of credit for it but I'm just the front for everyone's hard work. I just hope he agrees and wants to walk out with me. It will be a special moment in my career to walk out with two special boys this weekend.

Thursday 10th May

Player of the Year night tonight at the Liberty, and with just the one game to go against Liverpool on Sunday I have to admit it was the first time this year that I've really allowed myself to relax and reflect on what we've all managed to achieve.

There was a nice moment for me when I was given the club's Ambassador Award, which recognised my work away from the club with the things I get involved with through WillsWorld. As brilliant as my life is, and as fortunate as I am to earn good money and receive recognition, what would be the point of all that if I did nothing to help others less fortunate? I owe that outlook to my mom and dad for the way they brought me up, and also to Vanessa who is the most level-headed person I know. She is the real strength behind WillsWorld. In reality I was collecting the award for the three of them, and was delighted and proud to do so.

But the night did have one big winner with Michael Vorm scooping the Supporters' Player of the Year, Players' Player of the Year and Away Player of the Year.

I can't think of a more deserving winner in all my years in the game. He's easily the best goalie I've ever worked with, and without doubt the best in the Prem this year for me, and I include Joe Hart in that who I rate incredibly highly. I think what gives

Michel the edge over all the other keepers I've played with is his speed and agility. He's been incredible in so many games this season, but if you want to see how good he is, just come and have a look at him in the five-a-sides in training. It's ridiculous! His speed and reactions are amazing, and the saves he makes are so incredible the boys just end up laughing. It gets to the stage that if you are picked on his side in the five-a-sides you know you are going to win. It's unheard of for keepers to keep clean sheets in five-a-sides, but it's become commonplace for Michel. Even when we have shooting sessions he's almost impossible to beat. Loads of times someone like Danny would rifle a shot that looked like it was going in, then Michel would somehow manage to get a hand on it to block it, only to see the ball spin out to Danny to side foot home the follow up, but for Michel to then save that one too! How on earth he's the number three keeper in Holland I'll never know. After a couple of weeks in training his nickname became 'Super Cat'. I know people have always likened keepers to cats, but, honestly, when he started plucking saves out of everywhere in training, and getting so high to tip them over the bar and stuff, we'd all just stand there and say, 'Jeez, did you see that? He looks like a cat!' Someone came up with the 'Super Cat' tag because he always seems to get up so quickly. It's almost as if he always lands on his feet. He's got a sixth sense for goalkeeping, a real feel for it, and has been incredible for us. But maybe his biggest strength is his temperament. He's as passionate as they come, very vocal on the pitch and in the dressing room, but always in control. Lots of keepers are quite highly strung but not Michel. He's super cool and laid back in everything he does on and off the pitch, and gives people like me so much confidence having him behind us. He's only had one howler really this year, and that was the goal against Arsenal, but he just held his hand up and got on with it, no dramas whatsoever. I can see him becoming one of the game's great modern keepers in the next couple of years. And above everything else he's a really popular lad in the dressing room; liked by everyone. No wonder he walked away with a hatful of awards last night!

Every single one of them completely deserved.

Friday 11th May

There was a whisper in training today that Àngel might be able to qualify on residency grounds for Wales. That's got me thinking and is a really interesting one. Whatever the outcome of that may be, on a playing basis I'd love to have him in the squad, and he'd be a real bonus to Wales' quest to reach the World Cup. He's been easily one of the best attacking right backs in the Prem this year, and for me I'd put him up there with the likes of Kyle Walker with no hesitation. He possibly wouldn't be first in the list of defensive full backs, but it's his positivity that sets him apart. He starts so many moves for us that it's not true. He's high on our list of assists this season, but if you look at the number of moves he's involved in that lead to a goal, I don't think we have a player more involved in our goal-scoring moves than him. Even though his attacking is a strength, I've seldom seen a winger get the better of him, and in terms of heading, he's excellent in the air and pretty much beats every winger he comes up against. Occasionally he can get caught out of position, but that's often down to how much he gives us offensively. He is often way upfield when the oppo begin a break.

He's been integral to the club now for the past five years and completely understands the philosophy of the club and also exactly what the Gaffer wants from him. He's great on the ball, very comfortable and is an amazing athlete, regularly topping our running stats for ground covered during a game. He's like a Rolls Royce in that regard. One thing that I see that maybe the fan does not is the timing of his runs. He pops up sometimes taking the ball in his stride with such simplicity that it looks effortless, but I'm aware where he should have been before the ball being played, so to see him picking the ball up in attacking areas so often shows me that he has an uncanny knack of making the right run at exactly the right time, and that is a very difficult skill to perfect. Like all of us defenders Àngel is a bit unsung at times and I'm sure, like Scott and Tayls, he's probably fed up of me moaning and nagging him about letting crosses come in and the like. But I have to say that his strengths far outweigh any weaknesses he may have, and I'm always happy to see his name on the team-sheet. And I'd be more than happy to see him appear on a Wales team-sheet in time too.

Pob lwc with that, Àngel.

Saturday 12th May

I heard today that I will be doing some coaching at Walt Disney World, Florida in the off season. I go there with my family every year, so to be doing something I love there will be amazing. Craig Bellamy did it last year and passed on my details. They do a soccer camp at the Wide World of Sports complex, which is one of the best sports complexes in the world. Kids from all over come and play and you just help the coaches deliver the session. With me having my own soccer camp, this fits in great for me.

Sunday 13th May

Swansea City 1 (Graham 86) Liverpool 0

The main story for me going into today has been my toe. Or should I say my very painful toe. I haven't had an X-ray because there is only one game left, so there's no point really. Having examined it closely, both physios agreed that it's definitely broken. The only treatment I've had this week is a course of anti-inflammatory tablets, Ibuprofen cream, lots of ice and the Compex machine that I used on my neck at Bolton. The toe prevented me from taking part in any training, one of life's unexpected bonuses I suppose, but I have been doing plenty of gym work instead, and have been under orders to stay off my toe until today. I had some Emla cream to smear on it before we went out which is usually used for tattoos and minor surgery. It's an anaesthetic cream, and when applied all over the toe it numbs it totally, which allowed me to play.

There was a great atmosphere around the place when we went out for the warm-up today, largely to do with the Gaffer's request for everyone to get Elvis-ed up, which took an unexpected turn in the dressing room. The Gaffer was just about to finish his dressing room huddle with him in the middle when he said, 'And boys, we've got to do it for Elvis.' With that, in walked Kevin Johns in full Elvis suit, sunglasses and guitar and singing 'Viva Las Vegas'. Stunned doesn't quite cover it!

There was a truly fantastic moment for me before the game when I walked out onto the pitch. It was one of the most amazing moments of my life, both from the perspective of being a parent and also since I've decided to get involved in charity work.

The project we got involved in this season with Hari Kieft has been one of the most rewarding of my life. I know that I get the headlines for it, but truthfully there were several other people who could just as easily have walked out on that pitch holding Hari's hand. Hari's story was first brought to my attention by the guys at AG Swansea, Doey and Duane, two outstanding young men who don't get nearly as much credit as they deserve, so I am delighted to mention them here, along with my wife, Vanessa, who is involved in WillsWorld with me. When I walked out with Hari today, I genuinely felt like I was representing all of those people who have helped Hari to walk. There was a slight concern about how Hari would cope with walking on the grass, because he is still very much at the start of his journey to walk, even though he has confounded all the experts by the speed with which he's progressed. Despite our concerns he did incredibly well. The people of Swansea should also congratulate themselves, because so many of them have helped raise or donate money to give the gift of walking to this little boy. It was a very special moment walking out with him, and I'd like to use this diary to publicly thank you all. The referee, Mark Halsey, was perfect today when he realised what was happening and the reasons behind it. He actually held Hari during the handshakes in the centre circle and, before we walked out, told me to take as much time as I needed. He didn't care about kicking off on time or anything else, and told me that sometimes there are more important things in life than just sticking to someone's schedule. His attitude to the game and to life in general is brilliant. He's a very positive person, and I'm very grateful for his kindness today.

The second element of walking out was, of course, taking the field with my own son in my arms, as captain of my club in a Premier League game against Liverpool. It was simply the best feeling ever. I can't really put it into words how good it felt doing that with him, but anyone who is a dad will understand the feelings I experienced I'm sure. It was indescribable. I knew, however, that after all the pleasantries I had to switch on and approach the game in the right manner. I was quite brief in the huddle and just said, 'Gents, well done this season. We have done great, but there's one more to go, so let's make a statement and finish the season off right.' I didn't feel the need to say anything else, and having looked at them all I just knew that we'd win today. To me the result was never in doubt.

Even if I'd had any doubts they would have been dispelled by our start, because I'm not sure Liverpool had a touch in the first three minutes. It was a great start, which didn't surprise me in the least. It wasn't the first time we'd started a game so fantastically positive at home this season, and when it happens it feels magnificent. I guess if there was one moment that demonstrated just how confident all the boys were today, it was early on when the 'Super Cat', Michel, took the ball in his six-yard box, drew Carroll, dummied him, and nonchalantly passed the opposite way to Caulks. He's such a cool customer that it's a pleasure to play in front of him, and I haven't seen him flustered all season.

I think it was halfway through the half before they threatened us today, when Shelvey had a shot from distance. I could see how it was shaping up so just instinctively dropped a little deeper quite quickly to give me more time to deal with his shot if it came. When it did, he hit it straight at my head so I just held everything firm and headed it back. Those ones can sometimes hurt a bit if you time it wrong but, as the Gaffer's put in my mind, I'm never going to move out the way of it, just in case Raphael is on the line!

Even though we didn't create many clear chances, as we often don't, as the game developed so did our control over it. Not for the first time this season this control took the form of bringing out the frustration in the opposition. With about ten minutes to go until half-time Carroll took a shot from the edge of the box that went wide, with Suárez screaming at him to be played in. When it went out, Suárez just turned and gave Carroll some stick, which he ignored. I'm not surprised to see Carroll reacting like that because Suárez just seems to give his whole team stick throughout the game, so I'm sure they are used to it by now, and ignoring him is probably the best policy.

The only other moment of note in a half that was really comfortable for us was the WWE wrestling show between Carroll and I on the stroke of half-time. I must admit I'd already had a few nibbles at him leading up to this flashpoint, so when I followed him up to the halfway line and took him down with a kick, I kind of knew that it was going to provoke a reaction. And it did. He jumped straight back up and went for me. The main problem was that little Joey jumped straight in to separate us, which knocked us both off balance and swung us round as we were grappling. This balance shift meant that Carroll kind of ended up doing a suplex wrestling move on me as he was going down! It was obviously a key flashpoint moment in the half and there were players everywhere coming in and getting involved and it looked like it could have all kicked off for a moment. But, to be perfectly honest, it didn't really bother me in the slightest. As I've mentioned before, the truth of it is I'm not trying to make friends with anyone from the opposition when I'm out on the field, I just want to do the best for me and my team and if people don't like that, or don't like reading about it here for that matter, well, I can't really apologise for that. It broke up quickly enough, but I could tell from his eyes that his head had gone, so that was really good for us. Once it was over I just looked at him and laughed. As I did I heard the Gaffer shouting out from the sidelines, 'Well done Ash!' I think that's one of the things that the Gaffer likes about me is that I don't have a problem getting in someone's face. Anyway, we both got yellows and I could tell from the buzz in the crowd that everyone enjoyed it, so at least it gave the fans some entertainment!

As soon as the lads made it in to the dressing room after me the stick began to flow. They were all laughing and Wayne and Luke were giving me stick, generally mocking me. It was just like being back in school! As soon as the Gaffer came in though, the very first thing he said was, 'Well done Ash. You don't ever let anyone disrespect you, ever, in your life. Well done!' I smirked back at Wayne and Luke... ha-ha! Once we'd all settled back down and got our drinks into us, he came back in and told us he was very pleased with the way we played throughout the first half when we were on the ball. He was really happy with the way that we moved it so well and created some decent chances. He also pointed out how successful our pressing was off the ball and that we hadn't given them any time to settle or to get into any rhythm. He just wanted us to pick all of that straight back up, and he was certain that if we did we'd go on and win.

A few minutes into the second half I had my first clash with my mate from the first game earlier in the season, Suárez. Having played against him twice now I just have to say that I don't like the bloke. They won a corner, and I appealed to the ref to say that it had come off him last. He said something to me with a bit of a snarl, so I just told him to shut his mouth or I'd shut it for him. I must admit I was waiting for him to start and so let him have it, but I didn't care. I don't like the superior manner he brings on the field with him. Basically I have no time for the guy at all!

About five minutes later my other adversary, Carroll, almost scored with a pretty impressive overhead kick. I was annoyed with myself as I thought I should have dealt with the long throw better, and I would have been absolutely fuming if he'd scored. But a great save from Michel prevented that. He's so good that sometimes it's actually a shock when he doesn't make the save.

Despite them coming back into the game neither side had any clear openings, but we were still desperately trying to move forward and had two great moves in quick succession, where first Àngel and then Tayls overlapped and got into fantastic positions to put in dangerous crosses. Àngel put his too long and straight over the keeper and bar, and then Tayls did exactly the same with his a minute later! Obviously neither player intended to do this, but it's so disappointing when it happens. I have to say that this season I think it's happened too much and the result is that there is often no end product to a really good move. Caulks in particular fumes with this, and did again today when Àngel put the first one over. His feeling is that when the same happens to us, and we have to defend a move like that, it feels like the opposition hardly ever lets us off by putting their cross behind. They always seem to make us work. When Tayls then did exactly what Àngel had done, Caulks just looked at me and couldn't even bring himself to speak he was so frustrated. I just laughed at him.

But as if to prove us both wrong, near the end Àngel made yet another great run down the right flank and this time found the perfect cross to Danny, who had made a deeper run, and he just swept it in past Doni. It was a fantastic finish, and well-deserved for all the running Danny did again today. Seeing the ball beat Doni was an unbelievable feeling as I knew that it meant that we were going to win. There hadn't really been a moment in the previous eighty-five minutes when I thought that they would score, so they certainly weren't going to in the last five. And as you now know, they didn't. Our final game in such a brilliant season had seen us beating my boyhood team and football royalty, Liverpool, at home. Absolutely fantastic.

My relief at hearing the final whistle was felt on many levels; relief that we'd beaten Liverpool; relief that the season was over and that we'd ended it on such a spectacular high. Above all I was relieved that I could take off my boots and get some flip-flops on as my toe was absolutely murdering me! The cream I'd put on wore off after about half an hour and might have contributed to my bad temper when it all kicked off with Carroll! We reapplied the cream at half-time, and that gave me some relief again, but with about a quarter of an hour to go it all kicked in again, so by the end it was really painful once more. I just kept making sure that nobody got too close to it in case someone stood on it. I didn't want to end such a fantastic season in tears in front of everyone!

In the handshakes at the end I had a nice long chat with Bellars about the Wales trip to New York that's coming up. While we were talking, Carroll came up and made a point of shaking hands with me, and we wished each other all the best for a good summer. It's funny when you go up against someone like him, because you know the perception people have of him in terms of the rough stuff that he has in his locker. But all you can do is stand up for yourself, give as good as you get and just see where that ends you up. Today, I think where it ended up was that we both now have a mutual respect for the other, that possibly wasn't there before the game, which is good to know.

After the handshakes and my chat with Bellars, I couldn't wait to get into the dressing room to take the pressure off my toe, and it was a pleasure to throw my flip-flops on, even though it just continued to throb and ache. I didn't really care though, because we had a lap of honour to do, and I was able to do it with Raphael – his second appearance on the pitch in two hours! The parade around the pitch was great and there was a great buzz with the lads during it and I think it was as if we all started to realise what a special season it has been. Also, because Danny had scored so late today, we were all still buzzing from that, as were the crowd judging by the ovation they all gave as we circled the pitch. To be out there and witness the applause was fantastic, but truthfully it was just as special for us as players to be able to thank the fans for their incredible support this season. They have been great for us, something I have made no secret of all year. At the start of the season the Gaffer asked us all to make the Liberty a fortress, as he knew before a ball was kicked that the key to our survival was winning our home games. To do that we had to turn the Liberty into a venue that would be so daunting for the opposition that they would just lose heart. We certainly achieved that on a number of occasions when we'd ensure they went minutes without even touching the ball, but another reason for the despair some teams must have experienced was the noise made by our fans. When you think of the teams that visited the Liberty this season, Liverpool, Arsenal, Spurs and the Manchester clubs, I can't really remember one occasion where I've thought, 'Fair dos, their fans are loud.' It's not an exaggeration to say that the Swansea faithful have completely drowned out every support that has come to the Liberty, so the fans deserve as much credit for turning the stadium into a fortress as us. None of the lads in our squad take our fans for granted, and a highlight for us – among many away games – was probably our 3,000-odd fans drowning out 72,000 or more Man United fans even when we were 2–0 down. God knows what they'd have done if we'd won!

Just reflecting on that parade, and also today's result, I think these fantastic fans have witnessed a season that will – and should – go down in history as one of the greatest in the long history of the Swans. When you think of the money thrown at so many teams in the Premier League, and the budgets that some of them operate within, then our achievement of ending our debut season in the Prem in 11th position, and only missing 10th on goals scored, is one that shouldn't be underestimated. Even today, Liverpool's starting line-up cost £120 million, set against ours of around £7.5 million. With figures as stark as that, then maybe we can understand why, at the start of the season, almost every pundit with an opinion said we'd go straight back down. I even remember one saying that we'd threaten Derby's record of 11 points as the fewest ever achieved in a Premier League season. It's so nice to be able to prove people like that wrong, but more importantly prove ourselves right.

Speaking personally and honestly, I simply feel privileged to have been a part of this season and also blessed to have captained this great team so many times. We have had so much great press this season, and have changed so many opinions about us as players and as a team that it has made the way the season has turned out even more special. Apart from the likes of Wayne, Luke, Leets and Scotty – and Monks who played there in about 1973 – none of us had any Premier League experience, so despite whatever personal confidence we entered the season with, it was still a big step into the unknown for the bulk of us. When I look at how players like Leon, Joe, Tayls and Nath have not just performed, but regularly outperformed, so many seasoned Premier League players, week in week out, having probably been regarded as lower division players by most people, I can't begin to tell you how fantastic it has been to be a part of that. It might take a few years for people to look back and realise just how good the players in our squad have been this season, but when they do they will see what a fantastic group they have been.

On top of everything we have achieved personally has been the fact that we have played our game in a manner that has begun to alter people's views about how football can be played in the Premier League, especially for a club looking to survive. I think our biggest achievement has been to make people realise that you can play attractive, passing and possession football in this country – especially as a smaller club – and win games. Clearly that has been the vision of the Gaffer, and he has given us the tools to go out on the field and carry it out. As I looked around the dressing room after the win today as we were getting ready to go back out for the parade, and remembered how brave they have all been this season in playing football in the manner that the Gaffer has urged us to, I appreciated just how hard the lads have worked to deliver the Gaffer's instructions, and it left me with a massive feeling of pride.

Personally, and unsurprisingly I guess, this has been the favourite season of my career since I joined Stockport from non-league back in 2003, and the Prem has certainly allowed me to experience some great games and great grounds every week. Playing in the top division has always been my dream, and being able to call myself a Premier League player is just a fantastic feeling that I still sometimes can't really come to terms with. I also love the impact that this season has had on the people of Swansea, and that fills me with great pride. When I take the dogs out for a walk I now see young kids playing football in Swans shirts in the park instead of Man United and Chelsea shirts as it always used to be. What used to be even worse was seeing the kids playing with a rugby ball, but that doesn't happen so much now either! The impact the club has had on the city and the community has been massive and shouldn't be taken for granted by those who sometimes criticise football and footballers. The bulk of us actually do know how important our success benefits Swansea and, if we didn't, the Gaffer continuously reminds us that we are representing the city and not just the club.

The beauty of all this from my point of view is that we have achieved all of this with no real stars or big names with big egos. The undoubted star of our show is the team, and that is absolutely central to the Gaffer's footballing philosophy. Everybody has played their part in our success, especially the guys who haven't played as much as some of us but have given their all in training every day to help prepare the first team for the Saturday.

I think people will look back on this year as one of the best ever, and every single member of the Swansea City squad should be extremely proud of that.

I know I am.

Played 38 Won 12 Drawn 11 Lost 15 Points 47 League Position – 11th (Another year in the Prem!)

Monday 14th May

Nice to wake up this morning knowing that not only have we finished completely safe in 11th position of the Premier League, probably nine places higher than where the critics placed us last August, but also that we beat the mighty Liverpool in our final game. Obviously the Liverpool games were the first two I looked at when the fixtures came out, and I'd be lying if I didn't say that I hoped that we wouldn't be needing a win from the final game to stay in the division. But the comfortable way in which we dealt with them yesterday, maybe that wouldn't have been a problem after all. Still for all the joy of yesterday's result, there is a tinge of sadness because it may well prove to be the last ever time I line up alongside the freak that is Steven Caulker in a professional football match.

I liked Caulks from the start as a bloke, and was impressed with him on the field from our first game together in pre-season. He's an absolute athlete, who is so fit that it's actually scary. When he first got here he'd had some sort of operation not long before, but he just pitched up and won the bleep test. It was very impressive and so is his physique! He is absolutely ripped and is probably the best shape of any footballer I've ever seen. He's around 6ft 4ins, does his time in the gym and, really, I can't think of a single centre forward in world football who if he went up against Caulks would make me think, 'Oops, I think Caulks might struggle today.' To coin a cliché, his strength is his strength.

Because of the success we've had as a team this year, it's easy to overlook how it happens or perhaps take it for granted. I found it hard when I first came in, but that was at a lower division and I was in my early twenties. Caulks walked in here aged nineteen and in the Premier League. He looked like he'd been playing this system all his life. The Gaffer sees his two central defenders almost like quarterbacks. The instruction he gives us is that at any point during the game we have to assume the responsibility of starting our possession, and deciding what we are going to do with it. We have to decide whether to play it wide to our full backs, look to play Leon, Joe or Gylfi in, or – if the opposition aren't pressing – dribble forward to their half and then decide to carry the ball deeper still if we're not challenged. It took me a long time to get my head around the responsibility of these extra duties, yet Caulks has taken to it like a duck to water. To illustrate the difference, the stats [courtesy of eplindex.com] speak for themselves. Take Jamie Carragher and Daniel Agger on Sunday, compared to me and Caulks. Carragher attempted 31 passes and Agger 32. Caulks almost matched that on his own, attempting 59, while I chipped in with 82. Now I know our critics will say that lots of those are short passes made across the back four and to the keeper, but what they fail to understand is the responsibility that comes with trying to complete 80-odd passes, often needing to pick the right pass under pressure. Someone like Ryan Shawcross, for example, will often attempt less than 20 passes a game, so what that means is that he can just concentrate on his defending for the bulk of the game and nothing else. Caulks can't do that. He's had to understand that his role is crucial to the team offensively as well as defensively, and with every game he's improved in that area. To see one so young assume such responsibility has been impressive. As much as I love playing with Monks, I've loved the responsibility of having Caulks alongside this year as I've been able to talk to him throughout, on and off the field, trying to help him develop in much the same way that Monks did with me. Above all else, he's a defender and some of the times he's won the ball this year, when he's had no right to but has used his speed and athleticism to get there have been incredible. The only real problem he has is that he's not our player!

I know the Gaffer wants him back next year, but frankly I'll be amazed if we do. If I was Harry Redknapp I'd tie him down to a long deal right now, and put him straight in as my cornerstone centre half for the next five years, just as he's done with Ledley King. I genuinely believe that if Caulks progresses over the next couple of years as I expect him to, he'll be England's first choice centre half for years.

Tuesday 15th May

Two years ago today my good friend and team mate Besian Idrizaj died. Such a sad loss and it is still hard to comprehend that he isn't here. I got on really well with him and he was such a talent. I took a lot of time out of today to think about him.

Wednesday 16th May

Wow! Just found out that Dalglish has been sacked by Liverpool! That can't be down to us beating them surely? The most worrying part of this news though is that the Gaffer has been put in with the favourites to succeed him, along with Roberto. Interesting. I'm sure the next week or so is going to be full of rumour and speculation. I really hope Roberto gets it, mainly because that'll mean the Gaffer is staying with us.

Thursday 17th May

Somebody told me today on Twitter that I finished with the most passes and most blocks by a defender in the Prem this season. I'm over the moon with this, especially in my first season. What I like about it the most is that it shows both sides of my game. I can play on the ball but I don't forget that my job is to defend and block shots. Well wouldn't you if you thought the opposition was trying to hit your loved one with the ball?

Friday 18th May

Saw today on the internet that the Gaffer has turned down the chance to go to Liverpool. As relieved as I am about that, I am a little surprised. He's never said anything specific to me about leaving the club, quite the opposite in fact. He's made no secret of the fact that he's the happiest he's ever been professionally and personally. He loves his job at Swansea and he loves the area too, and he's a big reason why the likes of Wayne and Danny came to the club, because he painted such a positive picture of not just the club but Swansea as a place to live. However one thing the Gaffer has always told us is to have ambition and always make the best of ourselves, and even though he's never said it, I'm pretty sure that goes for him too. Once one of the big clubs came calling, I was certain that he'd at least go and listen to what they had to say, so I'm quite surprised that he's stopped it all in its tracks today. I'm also relieved too, because after such a fantastic season the last thing I wanted was to have to start back next pre-season with a new manager. The upheaval a new manager brings is not great for players, and under the Gaffer I think we all felt that the days of change were going to be gone for a while yet. Hopefully him rejecting Liverpool will mean that he's going nowhere, so I'm relieved at that.

Monday 21st May

The car came to pick me up from home in Birmingham this morning at 6 a.m. – proper early start – for the first leg on our trip to New York to play Mexico for Wales next weekend. Dave Edwards from Wolves was already in the car, and we were driven to the Hilton Hotel in Cobham, Surrey, where after all the hellos, we had training at 3 p.m. at Chelsea's training ground. As you'd expect, it was a very nice complex but we didn't get to see too much of it because we just used one room for pre-activation before going out, and then it was straight out onto the pitch for training. It was quite a relaxed session, where we just did some passing drills and then small sided games. Some players haven't done anything for nearly three weeks and some only finished last night so it was a tough one to judge. My toe felt fine so I did the whole session, but I've got a feeling I'm going to regret it tomorrow.

Tuesday 22nd May

We flew from London Heathrow this morning, Virgin Atlantic first class. It was a lovely day in London and the sun was blazing when we took off. We flew in our suits but as soon as we took off all the lads slid into the Virgin PJs and then changed back into our suits before landing. It was a perfect flight, and we went straight through immigration at JFK. Our waiting coach took us straight through Manhattan to our hotel in New Jersey, across the river, called the W Hoboken. It's a lovely hotel, really modern and we were all relieved when we arrived that we wouldn't have to stay in a crap hotel for a week. The weather here though – what a joke this is. We landed to overcast grey skies and when we speak to people back in the UK, they've had great weather like when we left. Can't believe this, who would have thought? No training today because of the flight, so we just have to make sure we are hydrated and do a lot of stretching. A few of us went for a little walk around the hotel to try and get our bearings. After that, it was dinner and off to bed, but trying not to get to sleep too early so we can get on US time asap.

Wednesday 23rd May

Woke up at 6.30 a.m. this morning which wasn't great, but I suppose it is 11.30 a.m. back home, so not too bad. When I got down to breakfast I heard that some boys have been up since 4.30 a.m! Apart from us bantering with them, they need to sort it out by tomorrow really as we are here for a week and have training and a tough game at the end of it, so we've got to avoid jet lag. We need everyone at their best physically in this game which is already difficult enough with some players' seasons having finished three weeks ago.

Had a coffee in the hotel bar with Bellars this afternoon and Juan Pablo Àngel was there. His team, Chivas, are playing against

New York Red Bulls tonight and they were staying in the same hotel as us. We had a chat about the MLS, talking about the good and bad things about playing in the US, as I think it interests most players at some point in their careers. The funny thing is I was sitting there thinking the last time I saw him had been when I was about seventeen years old and working in a petrol station when he was at Aston Villa. I used to serve him his fuel all the time. Funny how life goes sometimes I suppose. Oh, and he didn't remember me!

I went to the Yankee Stadium tonight in the Bronx to watch the Yankees play. I had never been to a baseball game before and what an experience it was. We had the choice between free time in New York, watching the Red Bulls game or going to the baseball. As I have been to NY before I chose baseball, as most of us did, and it turned out to be one of the best sporting events I have ever been to. Such a great atmosphere. Everyone had a good time and the boys loved it, getting into the spirit by wearing the hats and pretending we knew what was going on. We were constantly on the big screen and they kept announcing that Craig Bellamy and the Welsh football team were in the house. It was a good night all in all, then back to the hotel afterwards to get some much needed sleep for training tomorrow.

Thursday 24th May

I didn't do much training today as my toe is giving me some real problems, especially when I wear my football boots. We are training at the NY Giants training complex and it is by far the best facility I have ever worked in. We haven't even seen half of it yet but it has everything here you could possibly want. We wanted to come and watch the Giants train before us, but we were told we weren't allowed to. When I think back to our facilities at Llandarcy compared to this, I have to laugh to myself.

Friday 25th May

Same again for me at training today and it's frustrating as I want to be out there participating. I can do some of the training, but after a bit the pain is too much and I have to stop. Finally the sun has found us and we are all happy to train with it on our backs. We are training next to the MetLife Arena where we are going to play on Sunday. It looks huge, on the same kind of scale as Wembley and they tell us it goes down into the ground also, so it's going to be even bigger when we get in there. We have a few young lads with us like Jazz Richards and it is great experience for these guys to be here on the other side of the Atlantic and seeing new things and playing in these facilities. After training we came back to the hotel, where it was more coffee outside and people watching. I think I could do this all day in America because there are so many characters everywhere you look. Jermaine Easter is such a funny guy and has had us all in stitches. The amount of times we have tears rolling down our faces watching these Americans is unreal.

Saturday 26th May

We trained on the pitch in the stadium today, but it was completely empty. It's an enormous venue and I can't wait to get out there for real tomorrow in front of the fans and in a live atmosphere. It should be something really special. The pitch is terrible as they have recently just laid down grass. If you pull it up you can see the AstroTurf underneath. The medical staff here found some more of that magical Emla cream so I could train pain-free. Vanessa flew in to NY today with the little man and my dad for the game. They are staying in Manhattan but as soon as they dropped off their stuff in the hotel they came to see me over in Hoboken. It was great to see them after I have been away for a week. The funny thing was Vanessa and my dad were knackered and slightly delirious which was amusing me a lot and Raff was full of life, loving the hotel room and going crazy. Some more of the boys' families arrived for the game today. I was glad to see my family arrive safely and, after a while together, they went back to their hotel for me to get a good night's sleep for the game tomorrow.

Sunday 27th May

Mexico 2 (de Nigris 43, 89) Wales 0

Well, I know the result wasn't the one we were looking for, and neither probably was the performance, but in terms of experiences in this incredible season for me, it probably couldn't have finished in a better way. Quite simply, the MetLife stadium here in New Jersey is by far the best arena I have ever played in. Now that wouldn't have been such a strong statement for me to make a year ago, but in the last twelve months I've played at the Etihad, the Emirates, Wembley, Stamford Bridge, Anfield, White Hart Lane and Old Trafford, grounds I'd never played in before, but the MetLife – on every level – was just something completely different. It is an absolutely unbelievable stadium, massive in scale but also spotless from top to bottom.

All the lads were completely relaxed on the coach on the journey in. We'd had a great week and as it was our last game of a very long season, while we wanted the win we kind of felt the pressure was off as we were just ninety minutes away from ending our seasons, so that was a nice feeling to have. On entering the ground there were loads of police everywhere with sniffer dogs that had to sniff all around the team coach on the outside before we were allowed off and into the ground. I managed to speak to Vanessa on the phone when they were outside the ground waiting for tickets. Vanessa said that since they'd arrived, the atmosphere outside the stadium had been crazy with loads of Mexican fans. She said it was more like a festival than a football match; there were stalls and music all around. I love that atmosphere and hoped that the sounds outside would be transferred inside when we took to the pitch.

When we came here to train on the pitch yesterday, we didn't go into the changing room, just straight onto the pitch. Today we saw them for the first time and they literally took my breath away. We were given the changing room of the NY Jets, so everything was painted green. I have never been in such a huge dressing room in my life. When I say you could have had a five-a-side pitch in there I'm not exaggerating. In addition to the massive changing area, there were four shower areas along with extra warm-up areas and massive TV screens everywhere you looked. I have to give it to the Americans, they really know how to build a complex. Added to the massive scale of the rooms, all over the walls were loads of Jets art to look at. It was simply a top quality changing room. There is also a changing room for the NY Giants which is where Mexico got changed, and there's also an away changing room in addition to the two main ones. It was a fantastic environment to prepare for a match, and I must admit as I started to get myself sorted I felt really privileged to be in there.

As soon as we went out for the warm-up, I knew that Mexico were going to have one hell of an advantage over us, as it was so, so hot. It was one of the hottest temperatures I've ever taken the field in. I always wear studs to play a game, but when I tried to warm-up in them, it was clear straight away that I was going to struggle wearing them as the pitch was just too firm underfoot. I changed to my moulds quickly enough during the warm-up, and they felt more comfortable straight away. We needed loads of water around in the warm-up because of the heat, and we all took every opportunity to refuel, otherwise we'd have really struggled once the game began.

When the game started we were forced to change things almost straight away as we'd practised all week on them playing one up front, which is what they always do. However they started with two up top, in de Nigris and dos Santos, so we had to do a bit of work in a short space of time to sort things out. As Gunts isn't a centre half we were still trying to bed in as a partnership anyway, so this change wasn't ideal. One of the things we'd worked on was me covering his channel, so that he knew that he'd always have back-up there, but that went out the window when they began with two up top because I had my own man. This meant I wouldn't be able to cover Gunts as I'd have wanted to. He's a great lad, Gunts, one of my mates in the squad who's also a very good player that I rate highly. He is naturally gifted, quick and can run all day too.

As you know, I like to make my mark on my opposing striker

as soon as possible, just for him to know that he's going to have an uncomfortable afternoon. But it took me over ten minutes before I had the opportunity to let dos Santos know that I was around. We challenged for the ball and clashed slightly, then I had a little hack out at him, which was a little silly really, and the result was giving them a free kick in a dangerous area.

The line I called for the defence to hold for the free kick was OK, but then we dropped way too early, giving them a free header from a cross whipped in at pace, which, luckily for us, hit me in my face and shoulder on the way to goal. Mind you, as soon as it hit me I panicked because I thought that it could have deflected in. The last thing I wanted to do in such a magnificent stadium was score an own goal, so I was relieved when that didn't happen.

As the half progressed it was clear that Mexico were enjoying decent possession but, more worryingly, we were getting penned in much more and were resorting to trying to hit them on the break. We knew before the game that they would have a lot of the play in periods during the game as we were playing away from home and when all's said and done, they are one of the world's top twenty teams. The heat was also starting to have an effect on most of us, making it much harder to get around the pitch. Mind you, one player it didn't seem to be affecting was Joe. He had a great half, broke up lots of attacks and kept possession for us really well. He's been outstanding for club and country all year and to see him continuing to play to such high standards in those conditions was very impressive.

Apart from a couple of chances, I really felt confident that we were going to get to half-time all square, but once again this year that wasn't to be. Firstly I think that Hal Robson-Kanu could have made it harder for dos Santos as I felt he skipped past him too easily, allowing him to get a cross in. And we all know how I feel about that. There wasn't much that Gunts or Browny could have done about it really, and credit to de Nigris for his header. It was a terrible time for us to concede and if we could have gone in 0–0 at the halfway mark I think that would have been a good forty-five from us.

I was very vocal in the changing room, more than usual in fact because I felt that although we were all tired and it was ridiculously hot we were going a bit soft mentally towards the end of the half and that was where the goal came from. I know that we all like to think that for a footballer everything in the garden is always rosy, but, frankly, a professional dressing room is not the place for shrinking violets when things don't go well. I've been on the back of many a tongue lashing when I was younger, and sometimes it just has to be done and people just have to front up to their responsibilities.

The Gaffer made a tactical change to get Joey playing defensive midfield on his own in the Britts position, with Rambo and Dave in front.

There was no let-up in the heat when we went back out but we started the half well enough and seemed like we were keeping the ball better until Rambo gave it away about five minutes in. However Browny made another good save after they'd broken into the box. Browny was having one of those games where even if we did make a mistake, he'd pull something out to save us. He did it again a couple of minutes later when he pulled off a top save from a point-blank header by dos Santos. I was really pleased for him, and delighted that he played so well today, really taking his chance well. He was definitely one of our best players.

Adam Matthews had a knock on the hour, which saw him going off, and as he was having treatment, Rambo, Browny, Bellars and me had a chat about what we needed to do in the last half hour. Obviously, when you play the largely passing game that we do with Wales, there's always the opportunity to go direct instead and start playing it long up-field for Steve. That was an option for us and I said we needed to make our minds up what we wanted do at this point, especially from goal kicks. On the occasions that we'd hit Steve up to that point, there was a feeling that it was coming straight back, and Bellars agreed, saying that they were pretty strong in the air so he didn't really see that there was going to be much benefit in going long.

With twenty-odd minutes to go the substitutions started to be made, and one to go was dos Santos. I'd been very impressed with him. He was a constant threat, very tricky, and made plenty of good runs. I was pleased to see him leave the field goalless, and also hoped that the guy who came on would make less runs because I was getting knackered! One of the subs we made saw Jazz coming on for his debut. I was absolutely buzzing for him, and it was a great reward for his excellent performances for the Swans in the Prem this season. I just had a quick word with him and told him to stay solid and keep it simple on the ball, which he did.

The heat was starting to take its toll on lots of us at this point, and as disappointing as it was, I don't think it was a massive surprise when they scored. They could have scored a couple of minutes before they did, when they had a shot that Browny pushed round the post after I'd dropped back on the line. My legs were so heavy at this point that I was chuffed Browny got a hand on it as I was thinking about the Wolves nightmare again and didn't want to have to hack one away on the line and risk shinning one in again. The goal, when it came, was a bit scruffy. They played a ball in behind us and de Nigris managed to get ahead and just redirected with his chest past Browny. It was one of those when I guess you could argue that someone should have got ahead of him, but if that had happened it would probably have been an own goal anyway. The ball in killed us really, and when he put it where he did we were always going to be in trouble.

When the final whistle came I just stood still for about a minute because I was absolutely knackered. I think everything just caught up with me at that moment, the exertions of the match, the heat, the effects of a long season – everything. When we got back inside the Gaffer congratulated us and said we'd done well in what was a tough game in very tough conditions. He said it had been a great opportunity for him to get to know us and for us to learn about him, and that he was pleased that we'd matched them for forty-three minutes in each half. He pointed out that we could have done a bit better when we broke and could have made better decisions to get some more chances, and I agree with him on that. He congratulated all of us on our individual seasons with our clubs, and also thanked us for working so hard during the week and said we all now deserved a break. He got no argument from me about that.

After the game my family came to the team hotel and we had some food and chilled out for a while. I was also due to catch up with the Gaffer (Brendan), who had come out to watch the game with his wife, but my phone's been broken so we haven't been able to contact each other, which is a shame. I was hoping to speak to him about the Liverpool stuff and hopefully hear him tell me that he's not going anywhere. Anyway, it was great catching up with my dad, Vanessa and of course my little lad Raphael and, after we said our goodbyes, I had a well-earned drink with the lads. It would have been rude not to!

Monday 28th May

Well, that's the end of my diary. Eleven months, 47 games of football, Premier League survival and the worst ever case of diarrhoea known to man! I hope you've enjoyed reading it as much as I've enjoyed putting it together. I've tried to be as open and honest as I can be, and hope I've given you a flavour of what it's like to be a footballer, trying his best to survive and prosper in the best football league in the world. I've got about six weeks off now to recharge the batteries, get away from football, and then roll up in July to start it all again in our second season in the Prem. Already people are tipping us to go back down again, and are throwing 'Second Season Syndrome' at us, but I can't be doing with all of that. We have a talented squad, all the better now for our season in the top flight. We have a solid club structure to take us forward, and a chairman who will I'm sure be looking to give some cash to the Gaffer to strengthen us further for next year. Above all, we have the Gaffer. Nobody will be working harder than him to ensure that come July we'll hit the ground running and be in a position to emulate the successes of this season. As much as we've all achieved collectively this season, the real credit for it all goes to him. Thanks for reading, good luck.

Ashley Williams. Premier League footballer (thankfully).
New York.

Wednesday 30th May

Well, I thought the above entry was going to be the end of my diary, but sadly it's not. I was completely genuine when I wrote that last entry, but the events of the last forty-eight hours have thrown everything upside down. The Gaffer has joined Liverpool.

He rang me today to confirm what I already knew from looking at the internet, that he was off to Liverpool. It's not uncommon for a manager to ring you like this. Paulo did it when he left. But I was much closer to Brendan than I was to Paulo, so it meant quite a bit to me that he took the time to call. He thanked me for everything I'd done for him, said I'd always worked hard for him, that it had been a pleasure working with me and for me to make sure that I keep things going forwards next year. The call went by in a bit of a haze to be honest, because listening to him speak made it all too real that he's now actually gone and that we are going to have to start again without him.

I am genuinely pleased for him, because if the move to Liverpool is what he thought was best for him at this time of his life, then that's fine. There's only one certainty in football, and that's that we all move on. But I must admit that, selfishly, I'm gutted because I've just lost the best manager I've ever had.

Again, probably selfishly, I can't help feeling that we're back to square one at Swansea now and I've got that feeling of apprehension. I've been here before. I felt this way after Roberto and then again after Paulo. To be fair, after Paulo, Brendan came in and it proved to be the most enjoyable two years of my life as a footballer. I've learnt so much from him but, importantly, not just about football but about life as well. The lines in football are so strongly drawn, that I'd never call Brendan a mate. But within the parameters of a football club he was as close as you could get to that. And now we are going to have to start again. And I have to tell you now, as talented as our chairman is in spotting managers who buy into the club's philosophy and move us forward, he certainly isn't going to find another one like Brendan.

When a manager leaves, most players think about self preservation. 'What is this going to mean for me?' I don't know if a fan knows how much of an impact a manager has on a player's life. Brendan knew exactly how best to treat us, which was like human beings, but without us once ever taking liberties. He looked at our personal circumstances and managed us accordingly, which for me meant him allowing me to spend decent time with my and Vanessa's families in Birmingham. His man management was exceptional.

Roberto for example, didn't really look at things the same way as Brendan, and while I never had a problem with that, as I know I get well rewarded for what I do, my life outside of football was non-existent under Roberto. Just as with any job you care to mention, the stresses and strains of the negative side of it often have the biggest depressing impact on those closest to you, in my case Vanessa and my mom and dad. Under Brendan I think it's easy for me to say that not only has it been the best time in my career, it has been the most enjoyable for them, too, because he always understood the family's needs, and always welcomed them as an extended part of the club. There are far more managers out there unlike Brendan than like him, so as I sit here writing this, the odds are that my life is going to change quite dramatically when I finally get back to Swansea in July. Normally I don't look at things as better or worse, I just focus on them being different. But whoever the chairman brings in to replace Brendan, I just can't see things getting better on or off the field.

In terms of what Brendan actually did for me as a player, it's hard to know where to begin because he developed me in every area, probably as much off the field as on. One of the biggest things he developed in me was how I presented myself as a professional person, understanding the responsibilities I had to the club. As I've mentioned before, he made sure that I lived my life properly and made sure I always put my family above anything else. I think he just made me realise that if I was professional about everything I did then, really, the football would take care of itself. In terms of the football, the main thing he always said to me was to understand that my role was as a second centre half, next to a taller centre half like Caulks.

He was clear that in the modern game you couldn't go with two huge centre halves anymore. You needed a smaller one like me to bring a different dimension to the centre of defence, because after all what's the point of having two big centre halves if you're playing against two smaller, quick centre forwards, which is what you often get in today's game. The target he gave me every game was to be as near to 100 per cent pass completion as I could be, which would have been almost unheard of just four or five seasons ago. Off the ball, I needed to be super aggressive. Since Brendan arrived and instilled that into me, especially this season when he handed me the added responsibility of captaincy, I have gone onto the field with absolute clarity in my mind about what me role is in the team. And when it's laid out so simply to you like that, it somehow seems easier to deliver exactly what Brendan wanted. He always supported you when it worked, as can be seen in his comments after my tussle with Andy Carroll in the last game. He was absolutely delighted in the dressing room afterwards, because seeing me standing up to Carroll was exactly what he had in mind from me. I've been lucky to get some plaudits this season which have been lovely of course, but if you have a look at the way I used to perform under Paulo, more laid back and less intense, and compare that to the way I performed this year, then any plaudits I did have were down to Brendan because of the way he changed me as a player. I've always looked at myself honestly and under Paulo I was a good player, but didn't really have what was needed to succeed in the Premier League. Brendan gave me that extra 10 or 20 per cent which meant that when the Premier League came along I didn't look out of place and, as I say, that improvement was testament to him. Thinking of it all now, I'm just happy that I had the chance to work with him.

It's funny because when I started this diary I had absolutely no idea what the future would hold, either with Swansea City or Wales. Even though we were all confident with the Swans, we didn't really know what to expect and I remember reading reports at the time that ranged from us staying up comfortably because of our style of play, which is obviously what happened, to getting less than ten points and going back down with the lowest points total ever. Similarly with Wales, after we'd got beat by England at the Millennium, the pressure was on Gary Speed and the future probably looked a little bleak internationally. But look what happened. Wales is now at its highest position in world football for donkey's years, and the Swans beat Arsenal, Liverpool and the eventual champions Man City in a season which won us headlines all around the world for our brand of football. I wonder what odds you'd have got for that at the start of the season? One thing's for certain, they wouldn't have been as big as the odds of betting that neither Speedo and Brendan would be in their posts by the season's end. It just goes to show that in football, as in Brendan's case, and in life, as in Speedo's case, nothing can ever be predicted. There is only one certainty in life, and that is uncertainty.

But despite the loss, for differing reasons, of both Speedo and Brendan, I don't think I've ever been more optimistic about my footballing future. With Wales, we all feel that we can have a real run at qualification for the World Cup in Brazil. Speedo has put in place such great foundations that we all feel we can finally break this hoodoo and qualify. Chris Coleman has come in and is clearly going to be his own man. He's a strong and determined fella, but he's a football man first and foremost who is committed to carrying on in Speedo's style, and I can't think of anyone better to have come in to carry us forward. He impressed me greatly with the way he came in and handled himself at such a difficult time for us all. Do you believe in omens? The only time Wales have qualified for a World Cup was 1958. The venue? Brazil. Surely that reason alone will mean that this is the one that we will finally qualify for and give the great Welsh public the first chance in a lifetime of cheering on our nation on the highest possible stage. I cannot wait for the chance to make it happen.

For the Swans, the situation is less clear, but I still feel enormously optimistic. Yes, the second season will be hard, and I'm not certain that those of you who have not been lucky enough to play football under Brendan will ever really realise what we have lost. He is simply the finest manager I have ever come across. But we all still remain as players, and as long as the board appoints someone who understands what we are all about as a club, and someone who builds on what Brendan did and does not try and dismantle it, I honestly feel we can thrive in the division. In Michel, Joe and Leon, we have three players who would grace and improve any team in the division, and I include Manchester City and United in that. If we didn't have them, and wanted to sign them, they would probably cost Swansea about 40 million quid. But we do have them, and when you add in the likes of Danny, Scotty, Nath and Tayls, we have a core of players that are the envy of nearly every club in the division.

Me? I couldn't be happier. I'm going away to recharge the batteries with Vanessa and Raphael in the summer, return refreshed with only one thing on my mind – future success and achievement with Swansea City and Wales. I simply can't wait for 2012–13 Premier League season to start.

Who knows, I might even write another diary.

Thanks for reading.

Also from Y Lolfa:

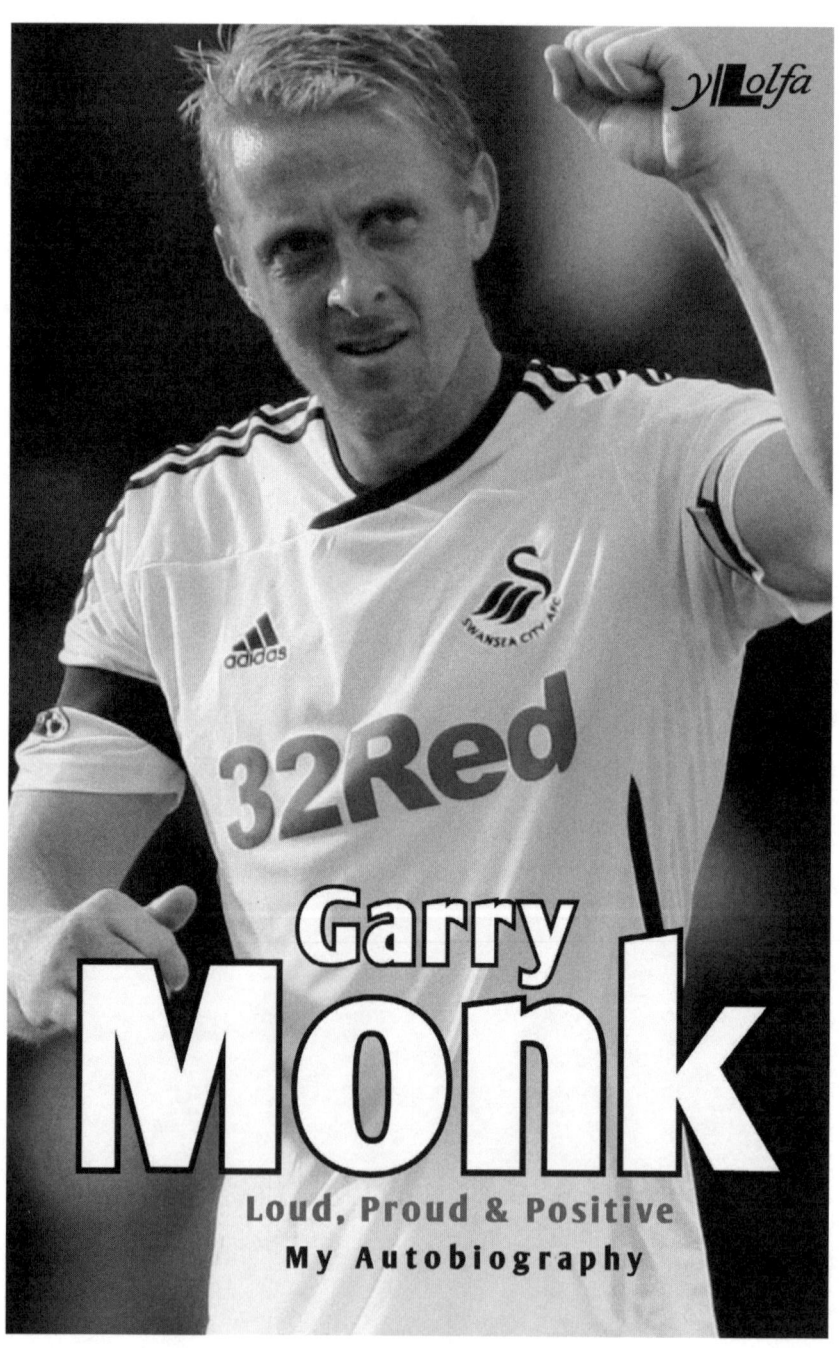

£9.95

1912 – 2012

Proud to be a

Swan

The History of Swansea City AFC

Geraint H. Jenkins

y Lolfa

Hardback £14.95

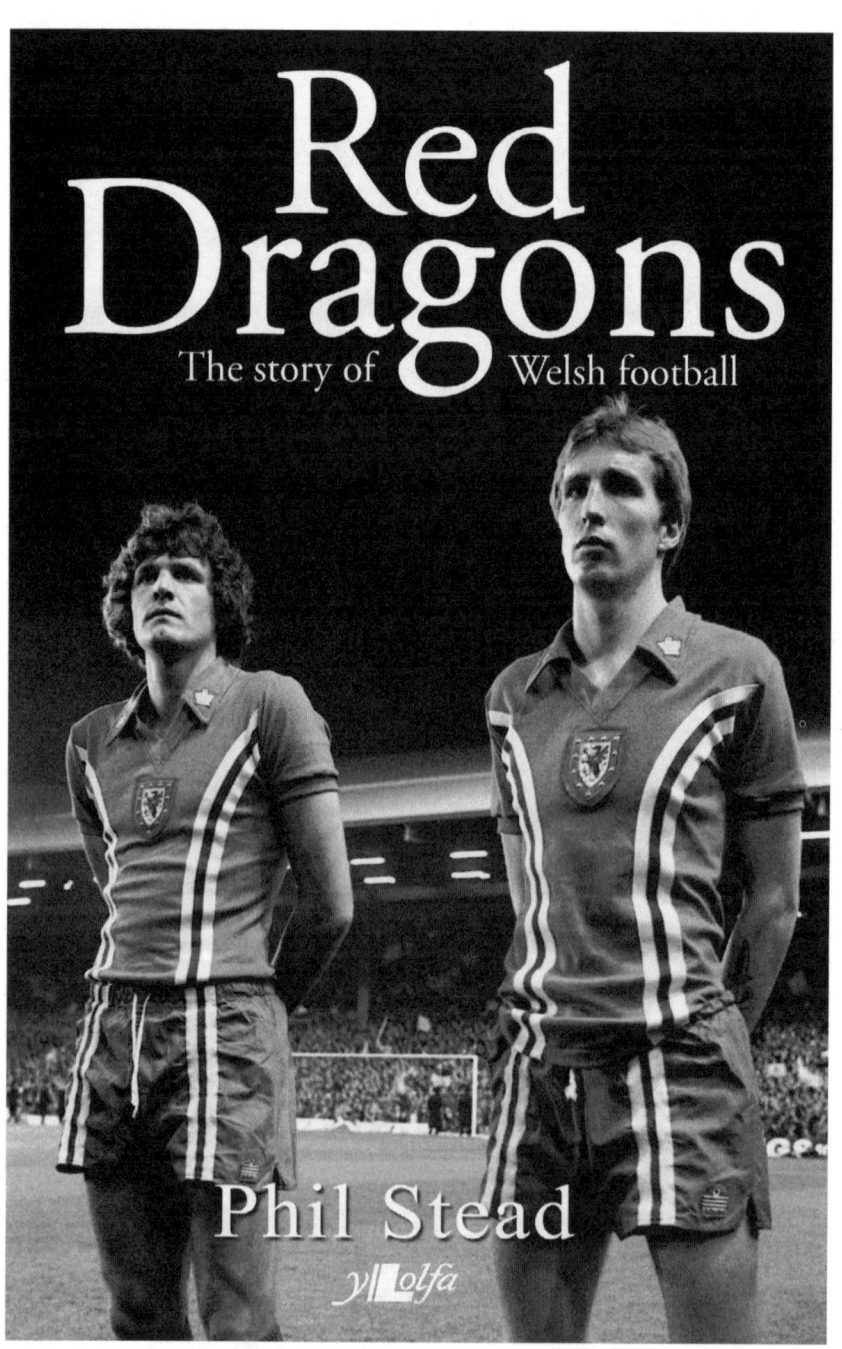

Red Dragons

The story of Welsh football

Phil Stead

y Lolfa

£14.95
Hardback £24.95

"This must-read book tells the story of the Swans' rise to the Premiership in a vivid way. It will bring back wonderful memories for the Jack Army."

Garry Monk

The SWANS GO UP!

Geraint H. Jenkins

y Lolfa

£4.95

Ashley Williams: My Premier League Diary is just one of a whole range of publications from Y Lolfa. For a full list of books currently in print, send now for your free copy of our new full-colour catalogue. Or simply surf into our website

www.ylolfa.com

for secure on-line ordering.

TALYBONT CEREDIGION CYMRU SY24 5HE
e-mail ylolfa@ylolfa.com
website www.ylolfa.com
phone (01970) 832 304
fax 832 782